PENGUIN (penguin logo) CLASSICS

THE PENGUIN FREUD GENERAL EDITOR:
ADAM PHILLIPS

THE "WOLFMAN"
AND OTHER CASES

SIGMUND FREUD was born in 1856 in Moravia; between the ages of four and eighty-two his home was Vienna: in 1938 Hitler's invasion of Austria forced him to seek asylum in London, where he died in the following year. His career began with several years of brilliant work on the anatomy and physiology of the nervous system. He was almost thirty when, after a period of study under Charcot in Paris, his interests first turned to psychology; and after ten years of clinical work in Vienna (at first in collaboration with Breuer, an older colleague) he invented what was to become psychoanalysis. This began simply as a method of treating neurotic patients through talking, but it quickly grew into an accumulation of knowledge about the workings of the mind in general. Freud was thus able to demonstrate the development of the sexual instinct in childhood and largely on the basis of an examination of dreams, arrived at this fundamentally discovery of the unconscious forces that influence our everyday thoughts and actions. Freud's life was uneventful, but his ideas have shaped not only many specialist disciplines, but also the whole intellectual climate of the twentieth century.

LOUISE ADEY HUISH was formerly Mongomery Fellow in German at Lincoln College, Oxford. She has translated a variety of philosophical, psychoanalytical and literary texts. Her specialism is Austrian literature and she is the editor of three volumes in the bicentenary edition of the works of Johann Nestroy.

DAME GILLIAN BEER is King Edward VII Professor of English Literature at the University of Cambridge. Her publications include *Darwin's Plots: Evolutionary Narrative in Darwin, George Eliot and Nineteenth-century Fiction* (second edition, 2000), *Open Fields: Science in Cultural Encounter* (1996) and *Virginia Woolf: The Common Ground* (1996). She has edited Virginia Woolf's *Between the Acts* and Jane Austen's *Persuasion* for Penguin. She is at present working on a study of island narratives.

ADAM PHILLIPS was formerly Principal Child Psychotherapist at Charing Cross Hospital in London. He is the author of several books on psychoanalysis including *On Kissing, Tickling and Being Bored, Darwin's Worms, Promises, Promises* and *Houdini's Box.*

SIGMUND FREUD

The "Wolfman"
and Other Cases

Translated by LOUISE ADEY HUISH
with an Introduction by GILLIAN BEER

PENGUIN BOOKS

PENGUIN BOOKS

Published by the Penguin Group
Penguin Group (USA) Inc., 375 Hudson Street, New York, New York 10014, U.S.A.
Penguin Group (Canada), 90 Eglinton Avenue East, Suite 700, Toronto, Ontario,
Canada M4P 2Y3 (a division of Pearson Penguin Canada Inc.)
Penguin Books Ltd, 80 Strand, London WC2R 0RL, England
Penguin Ireland, 25 St Stephen's Green, Dublin 2, Ireland
(a division of Penguin Books Ltd)
Penguin Group (Australia), 250 Camberwell Road, Camberwell, Victoria 3124,
Australia (a division of Pearson Australia Group Pty Ltd)
Penguin Books India Pvt Ltd, 11 Community Centre, Panchsheel Park,
New Delhi – 110 017, India
Penguin Group (NZ), 67 Apollo Drive, Rosedale, North Shore 0745,
Auckland, New Zealand (a division of Pearson New Zealand Ltd)
Penguin Books (South Africa) (Pty) Ltd, 24 Sturdee Avenue, Rosebank,
Johannesburg 2196, South Africa

Penguin Books Ltd, Registered Offices: 80 Strand, London WC2R 0RL, England

"Analyse der Phobie eines fünfjährigen Knaben" first published 1909 in
Jahrbuch für psychoanalytische und psychopathologische Forschungen 1(1); "Nachschrift zur
Analyse des kleinen Hans" first published 1922 in *Internationale Zeitschrift für Psychoanalyse* 8(3)
"Bemerkungen über einen Fall von Zwangsneurose" first published 1909 in
Jahrbuch für psychoanalytische und psychopathologische Forschungen 1 (2)
"Aus der Geschichte einer infantilen Neurose" first published 1918 in Freud,
Sammlung kleiner Schriften zue Neurosenlehre (Vienna, 1906–22), 4
"Einige Charaktertypen aus der psychoanalytischen Arbeit" first published 1916 in
Berlin Goethe Society, *Das Land Goethes, 1914–1916* (Stuttgart, Deutsche Verlagsanstalt)
English translation published in Penguin Books (U.K.) 2002
This edition published 2003

Sigmund Freud's German texts collected in *Gesammelte Werke (1940-52)*
copyright © Imago Publishing Co., Ltd, London, 1940, 1941, 1946, 1947
Translation and editorial matter copyright © Louise Adey Huish, 2002
Introduction copyright © Gillian Beer, 2002
All rights reserved

LIBRARY OF CONGRESS CATALOGING IN PUBLICATION DATA
Freud, Sigmund, 1856–1939.
[Selections. English. 2003]
The "wolfman" and other cases / Sigmund Freud ; translated by
Louise Adey Huish, with an introduction by Gillian Beer.
p.   cm.
Includes bibliographical references.
ISBN 978-0-14-243745-2
1. Psychoanalysis—Case studies.   2. Neuroses—Case studies.
I. Huish, Louise Adey.   II. Title.
RC509.8.F745213 2003
616.89'17—dc21   2003043300

Set in Adobe New Caledonia

146122990

Contents

Contents

Introduction

> There is often a great deal more of the past in the future than there was in the past itself at the time . . . one learns little by little that a thing is not over because it is not happening with noise and shape or outward sign. (Anne Thackeray Ritchie, *Chapters from Some Memoirs*, 1894)

Ritchie's modest formulation is suggestive, particularly published as it was at just the period (around 1895) that Freud realized that buried memories are active in present disquiets and that this insight can have therapeutic significance. Ritchie perceives that the surplus of meaning – and the potential for meaning – carried in any moment is realizable only in the future and that the past persists, implicit in every present moment though not happening 'with noise and shape or outward sign'. Silent, unformed, distorted in its representation, the thing 'that is not over' remains. Like Freud, Ritchie was fascinated by the individuality of peoples' lives and by their symptomatic behaviours; unlike him, she did not theorize out from the example to a system. Her several volumes of memoirs are content with fragments, what she calls her 'witches' caldron' of the great. Her biographical accounts are partial, fugitive, evocative, and often very funny. As a child she watched the procession of adult grandeur to her father's house. Like little Hans she was sceptical of the truth-claims of the adult world. Freud, though, believed in the possibility of completing the story, ironing out the ellipses in behaviour, and mining the foreign and embedded minerals in the striations of the past. His heroic confidence that totality can be achieved in the re-creation of a person's experience *for that same person* is at the core of his achievement. Yet it is achieved through a method that acknowledges that there is always more than one story being told and that interpretation must always include more than one voice. In his case histories Freud shows himself listening, delaying, overlaying meanings one on another while the person who is his subject tells and withdraws, shares and refuses to share glimpses of the past, of which 'there is now a great deal more . . . in the future'. The spaciousness of Freud's narrative method – as well as the claustrophobia often produced in the reader wrestling with these contested accounts – gives a grandeur of scale to these histories of ordinary lives.

It may seem odd to start with so little regarded a figure as Ritchie to set alongside Freud at the beginning of an introduction to some of the case histories. However, the setting of Freud and Ritchie momentarily side by side does serve to remind us of how animated and widespread in the latter part of the nineteenth-century was the discussion of personhood, of reflex actions and of the 'hidden self: self in the depths' (as Eneas Sweetland Dallas called it in *The Gay Science*, 1866). Moreover, Freud acknowledged how valuable had been his reading of fiction writers such as George Eliot in coming to assess his own experience. George Eliot, in particular, with her refined mixture of homily and empathy in her investigation of inner experience offered an expansive reading for Freud to ruminate on. The techniques of production in nineteenth-century fiction, particularly serialization, also help to shape Freud's account of his working method, and perhaps the method itself with its series of encounters. In serialization may be found the same suspension of the action at a point of uncertainty, the revision of meaning in the next instalment, the use of repetition and of nicknames and catch-phrases to sustain narrative continuity, that the reader meets in Freud's case histories. And Freud was remarkably free in his assimilation of fictional examples to the activities of his patients and his own interpretative processes. Not only was this true of such major and underpinning articulations as the Oedipus complex but throughout his work are scattered examples indicating the degree to which literature, and its characters, lay flush with everyday encounter for him.

This is not to say that a person's surface 'character' – the amalgam of presence, behaviour and opinions by which others judge – was Freud's preoccupation. He specifically denied as much in the opening sentence of his essay concerned with those who suffer collapse in the face of success ('Some Character Types Encountered in Psychoanalytic Work'), where his principal examples are from characters in two plays: Shakespeare's Macbeth and Lady Macbeth, and Rebekka West from Ibsen's *Rosmersholm*. The essay opens:

When the physician undertakes the psychoanalytic treatment of someone suffering from a nervous disorder, there is no sense in which his interest is engaged first and foremost by his patient's character. He is far more interested in the meaning of his symptoms. (p. 323)

However, Freud continues at the end of that same paragraph, 'he observes that his investigation is threatened by resistances with which the patient counters his efforts and may attribute such resistances to his patient's character. Character now has the first claim on his interest.'

Freud views the outward manifestations of character as a coherent self-representation that must be questioned, or as a carapace that shields a pulpier inner being. Character both resists and provides a pathway to hidden story. In his analysis of *Macbeth* Freud vacillates between viewing Macbeth and Lady Macbeth as actual persons displaying certain neurotic symptoms and as the creatures of a playwright of great insight who has split one person into an endoubled figuration. That is to say, after a long discussion in thoroughly historical terms of the theme of childlessness in the play, Freud ends his discussion by following the German critic Ludwig Jekels in considering Macbeth and Lady Macbeth as aspects of a single being, providing a new explanation for the transfer of guilt and remorse from the one to the other. He shifts levels between character analysis and dramaturgy with no sign of intellectual unease.

In all his responses to literary works, Freud is aware of the needful obscurity or indirection with which motive is there presented and understood. At the same time he is quite robust in casting off the occluded surface when he wishes. So, on the one hand he comments on *Macbeth:*

I think we must abandon the possibility of penetrating the triple layer of obscurity into which the poor state of preservation of the text, the unknown intentions of the poet and the mysterious meaning of the saga have settled. (p. 336)

But toward the end of the essay he disturbs the boundary between a universal sense of guilt and the actual play of *Oedipus* in the phrase 'the two great criminal intentions'. In the play the *intentionlessness* of Oedipus is crucial to the tragedy: Oedipus simply does not know that he is killing his father and marrying his mother. The situation is different, it seems, in the Oedipus complex:

The results of analytic work regularly lead us to the conclusion that this obscure sense of guilt is derived from the Oedipus complex and is a reaction to those two great criminal intentions, killing the father and engaging in sexual intercourse with the mother. (p. 347)

Intentions may be symbolic and fictive but none the less powerful for that. Freud's appropriation of literary figures and texts demonstrates how freely he can dispose the materials of the psyche and how strongly he can bring to bear the imagined within the realm of the everyday.

The realm of the everyday was hazardous for Freud as he wrote up his case histories: in the social and intellectual world of early twentieth-century Vienna it was only too likely that gossips would recognize the persons described. How could he avoid this and yet give a true account of the case? He had to balance a thorough account of the individual and his symptoms (in the cases collected in this volume the three individuals are all male) with pseudonyms and changed circumstances that would avoid identity being unlocked. Moreover, he was wary of what he calls in the preamble to 'The "Ratman"' 'the irksome attentions of a city that focuses quite particularly on my activities as a physician' (p. 125). This importunate fascination with his practice Freud reads, probably quite correctly, as threatening. It may be significant that all Freud's case histories – of which there are really very few written up publicly over a long professional life – occur in the earlier part of his career. But his alarm concerning privacy found a particularly revealing solution in 'the paradoxical state of affairs whereby one may far more readily divulge to the public a patient's most intimate secrets ... than the most harmless and banal features that distinguish his personality' (p. 126). The personality is immediately recognizable; the secret life is entirely concealed and its expression is distorted before it reaches the surface of appearance. The extraordinary distance between day-to-day social encounter and the fullness of revelation from within allowed Freud to be both circumspect and thorough. It also served to reinforce the justice of his account, which itself relied on demonstrating how much that cannot be guessed is held beneath the surface of personality.

Of the three cases being considered here, that of Little Hans probably caused the least trouble about secrecy, since children's rights to privacy are ordinarily disregarded, both then and now. As it happens, this is also the case with the greatest surface brio since the young boy Hans persistently asks questions that will not conform to adult categories. Moreover, when – as frequently occurs – he is lied to by his parents he shows himself to be no fool, continuing to inquire in the face of their false stories and denials. This intrepid five-year-old child suffers from agonizing terrors; these are what have brought him to the attention of Freud. But there is a sense in which he is not so much a patient as an offering to Freud from his father, who was an early acolyte. The text is distributed here not as dialogue only but as a several-tiered set of relationships. Hans asks questions and converses with his parents. His father interprets his conversation in Freudian style and sometimes presses on Hans an interpretation way beyond the scope of his inquiries, interpretation that may forestall Hans's search or even sharpen his anxiety. The mother's individual conversations with the child are reported to the father and glossed by him before they are handed on to Freud.

The father offers a coherent written record of the family conversations to Freud in instalments, who comments, sometimes with approval but sometimes with a warning against over-intervention. A father–son relationship of mentor and pupil is generated between Freud and the father – a relationship that also activates anxieties within the marriage, which then bear back on the unhappy Hans. Or the happy Hans: since the child displays remarkable resilience, despite the dread of horses that is his main symptom of anxiety. Freud met the child face to face once only.

The account of Hans's conversation begins when he is not yet quite three years old and the first exchange is between Hans and his mother about whether both male and female have 'widdlers'. In the very next paragraph he is three and a half and his mother is threatening him that if he touches his penis she will call the doctor to cut it off:

'What will you do then when you need to widdle?'
Hans: 'I'll use my botty.' (p. 5)

The child's insouciance is set against the mother's zealousness. Her threat here, and the parents' insistence that a stork is coming to bring the baby at the time of the birth of his little sister, both demonstrate how historically and culturally conditioned are adult truths and lies. When the baby is born and Hans sees, taken aback, the bloody bedpan, his father observes:

Everything he says shows that he connects the unusual circumstances with the arrival of the stork. He is on tenterhooks, looks askance at everything, and *there is no doubt that the first stirrings of doubt about the stork are gaining a foothold.* (p. 6)

Paradoxically, as the emphasis shows, the father feels pleasure at the child's resistance to the false tales being fed him, even while propriety demands that the parents continue to enforce this account in the face of the groans and blood that the child has encountered. Hans is interested by the manifest function of his penis – to allow him to pass water – and intrigued that neither his mother nor sister have much to show and yet succeed in passing water perfectly. He uses the 'widdler' at first to create the categories of organic and inorganic: creatures widdle, machines don't (but he wonders about the engine being drained of water at the station). So his interest in the penises of giraffes and horses is mainly at this stage to do with their size, commensurate with such big animals, and he begins to be concerned because of the very small size – the invisibility – of both his sister's and his mother's widdlers.

From the outset for Hans epistemological and sexual investigations are inseparable, and he is struggling in a world where he is required to accept information as true that he senses to be false (and known by his parents to be false). His trust for his parents, and his passionate attachment to his mother, are therefore stained with the possibility that he is being comprehensively deceived. In his extensive footnotes to this first chapter Freud acknowledges, with a little condescension in the humour, that Hans in his attempts to make sense of the animate and inanimate world by the marker of the widdler is behaving 'no worse than a philosopher of the Wundt school' – who insists on consciousness as such a marker (note 5, p. 15). And as Freud remarks in section II Hans also has the inner confidence to tease his father:

Hans's audacity in recounting his fantasy and the countless fantastic lies woven into it are far from nonsensical: it is all intended to enable him to take revenge on his father, whose attempts to mislead him with the stork fairy-tale have filled him with fury. (p. 105)

That confidence alternates with anxiety. The parents use a kind of teasing that pitches over abruptly into threat. The mother threatens to leave him and not come home any more '(He had probably been naughty, and she threatened to go away and leave him)' (p. 34). The father, in a throwaway remark, records:

There is an imperial guard who stands at the entrance to Schönbrunn, and I once told Hans that he arrests naughty children. (p. 31)

The child comes to grief. He begins to display a fear of horses so hampering that he cannot venture into the street. He dreads being bitten by a horse and he is terrified by a horse that collapses. And since horses, carts and carriages were at that period the principal means of transport in Vienna's streets the boy is in a parlous dilemma. Strikingly, the father immediately begins to interpret the problem in a sentence singed by jealousy thus: 'Sexual over-excitement caused by his mother's caresses is no doubt at the root of the problem' (p. 17). Although Freud accepts this motivation in general (a sudden increase in affection for his mother) he points out that 'Anxiety, then, corresponds to repressed longing, but it is not entirely the same thing as the longing: the repression also stands for something' (p. 20). Unlike the father who rushes to judgement, Freud uses delay to open out the significations of the child's words and actions: 'I do not share the view, much-favoured at present, that what children say is entirely arbitrary and unreliable. Nothing is arbitrary when it comes to the psyche' (p. 85). Moreover, he comments in a style poised between lawyer and novelist on the role of the mother who has persistently urged the child not to touch his penis, telling him 'That's dirty'. The husband blames her, as Freud puts it, 'not without some semblance of justice' for her 'all too frequent willingness to take the child into her bed' (a bed seemingly intermittently shared with her husband, though described by him as 'her bed'), but Freud asserts that 'we could equally well reproach her with having precipitated his feelings of repression by her energetic rejection of his attempts at seduction ("That's dirty")' (p. 12). He ends the paragraph with the vatic comment:

But she plays the part Fate intended for her, and hers is a difficult role.

Suddenly, the reader is moved from the realm of social negotiation and custom to an enforced naturalized *generalized* role for the mother. She cannot help but act it out, a tragic figure fixed as a point on the Oedipal triangle.

The father, understandably, presents the dialogues between himself and Hans as the fulcrum of meaning although, as Freud points out, the father quite frequently intervenes too fast to hear the full meaning of what Hans is telling him. So, some of Hans's fantasies must wait for *further-father* Freud to elucidate. In the background we can just make out the struggle between the two men for possession of the child's story. Freud is always scrupulously polite about the insight and capacity of Hans's father, but nevertheless there is a strong sense of a *devoir*, an exercise, duty and offering, in the texts generated by the father for Freud's survey. Hans's father is both the child's teacher and Freud's bright pupil, kept in his place by Freud's enjoyment of the fact that Little Hans gets ahead of his dad.

Previously his father was able to predict what was coming and Hans, following his hints, trotted along behind; now it is Hans who hurries confidently on ahead, while his father has trouble keeping up. (p. 103)

Perhaps, more generously, there is delight for Freud in identification with the robust invention and intelligence of Hans himself – Hans, like Freud, trammelled by the half-lies of his society but persistently breaking through them to the insight borne in fantasy. Freud hears with the ears of a child, enjoying the aural consonance between words that have no manifest semantic connection. So *wegen* means 'because of' in German but in Viennese pronunciation also sounds like 'waggon' or 'cart', *Wägen*. Playing with other children at horses and carts, Hans is often the horse and hears their talk about the cart as fixing responsibility on him, the horse: *'wegen dem Pferde'* ('because of the horse', see p. 46 and note 19, p. 81). Freud picks up Hans's alarm at his seeming responsibility and his phobic response to both horse *and* cart as an outcome:

We must never lose sight of the fact that children treat words much more concretely than adults do and consequently find great significance in words that sound the same. (note 20, p. 82)

With nice honesty, Freud then acknowledges that this particular example of verbal association yielded nothing more for the analyst though readers now, accustomed to Freud's methods, may fancy they can see connections onwards when Hans later asserts that buses, furniture-vans and coal-carts are all stork-box carts.

Like Lewis Carroll, Freud was alert to the ways in which words convert themselves into things, and things into words. Like Wordsworth, he knew that adults could press children into exasperated and seemingly captious invention by too zealous questioning: the five-year-old in Wordsworth's poem 'Anecdote for Fathers' replies 'in careless mood' to his father's question as to whether he would rather be at Kilve, or where he is now at Liswyn farm. The father relentlessly presses the question 'why':

> At this, my Boy hung down his head,
> He blush'd with shame, nor made reply;
> And five times to the child I said,
>
> 'Why, Edward, tell me why?'
> His head he raised – there was in sight
> It caught his eye, he saw it plain –
> Upon the house-top, glittering bright,
> A broad and gilded vane.
>
> Then did the boy his tongue unlock;
> And thus to me he made reply:
> 'At Kilve there is no weather-cock,
> And that's the reason why.'

The contingent triumphs. Yet, had Freud been listening to that conversation he would no doubt have observed again that in the psyche nothing is arbitrary and that the *absence* of the weather-cock is an interesting preference for the little boy.

The shape of the story that Freud has unfolded out of the materials, sometimes crabbed, offered by Hans's father, and out of the inventiveness of Hans himself, is one of heartening comedy – a comedy that at once reverses the fixities of Fate and affirms the Oedipus complex. The father writes:

30 April. Hans is again playing with his imaginary children, and so I say to him: 'How can your children still be alive? After all, you know that a boy can't have children.'

Hans: 'I know that. Before I was the Mummy, *but now I'm the Daddy.*'

I: 'And who is the children's Mummy?'

Hans: 'Mummy of course, and you're their Grandpa.'

I: 'I see, you'd like to be as tall as me, married to Mummy, and then she would have children.'

Hans: 'Yes, I would like that; and Lainz Grandmama (my mother) could be the grandma.' (p. 77)

Freud comments on this happy farrago of generation and gender:

All's well that ends well. Our young Oedipus has found a happier solution than that prescribed by Fate. Instead of eliminating his father, he bestows upon him the same good fortune that he desires for himself; he instates him as grandfather, and marries him to his own mother too. (p. 77)

Freud was never deluded about one important reason that sexual material was so consistently highlighted by his patients in their approach to him. As he remarks in his reflections on this case:

At the same time we must remind ourselves that it was his parents who, out of all the relevant pathogenic material, brought the topic of Hans's preoccupation with his widdler into the foreground. (p. 98)

At his first encounter with the 'Ratman', Freud asked him what caused him 'to put particular emphasis on information about his sexual life'. The man replied 'that that is what he knows about my theories'. (p. 128) However, it turns out that what then particularly drew him to Freud was Freud's work on puns and word association:

[W]hen leafing through one of my books recently [he] came across an explanation of bizarre associations of words that reminded him so much of his own 'mental efforts' with regard to his own ideas that he resolved to entrust himself to me for treatment. (p. 128)

Other than this 'leafing through' of *The Psychopathology of Every-day Life* (1901) he had read none of Freud's writing. Freud's capacity to knead language and to probe the significance of nonsense was of particular value in this case of obsessive-compulsive disorder. The one condition he placed on his patient was that he should tell everything that came into his mind 'even if the thoughts seemed *unimportant, irrelevant, or nonsensical*' (Freud's emphasis, p. 129) or even if they were '*unpleasant*' to him. The young chatter of Hans, even when its topic was prompted by his parents, gave Freud access to a field of thought more open than he could rely on entering with an adult patient, hence his emphasis, above, on complete disclosure.

The analysis of Little Hans concluded in May 1908 and the case was published in the following year; already in 1907 Freud had published an essay on the sexual enlightenment of children invoking some of the earliest material about Hans, there called 'Little Herbert' – a less fairy-tale-hero name. In that same year, 1907, Freud began his analysis of the 'youngish man with a university education', now stuck with the grim name the 'Ratman' in endless memorial of what the unfortunate man himself most wished to forget ever having heard about. Again, as with Little Hans, there is the suggestion of folktale or *Märchen* in the naming that accords with the sense that these people are our driven or totemic representatives. Freud suggested that in obsessional neurosis we encounter a symbolic language that is closer to conscious linguistic processes than is that of hysteria. Indeed, the patient himself, describing his obsessional idea as a child that his parents could hear his thoughts, explained it to himself at the time by supposing that he must have spoken his thoughts aloud without hearing them himself. That notion he sees as the onset of his illness. The form of the illness was his dread that harm would befall people he loved if he countenanced certain compulsive ideas and desires: the first of them, quite early in his childhood, was to see girls – particularly his nurses and carers – naked. Specifically, he feared that such wishes would bring about the death of his father. The two love objects he presented in his recital of his life story were his father and a certain lady. Freud was astonished to discover, a little way into the analysis, that the father of whom the Ratman spoke with such immediacy and whose welfare so absorbed him had in fact been dead for a number of years. The lady he had wooed, but had been rebuffed.

The temporal order of disclosure by the patient, and of life-events, is particularly complicated in this case. It brings out the degree to which time is inherently kaleidoscopic in recall. Memory comes unbidden and is not stacked in orderly receding units. In the case of a person with obsessional thoughts, that effect of immanence, of a limitless presence of past events in this moment now, is exaggerated and threatening. It is barely controllable. In the case of this young man it could be controlled only by making a bargain with performative language. He must at all costs keep to the exact terms of an agreement he has made. Read from the outside there appears to be a mismatch between content and enactment. And both are at a curious angle to the episode that precipitated the bargain he must keep. The frame narrative is of an inconvenient but relatively trivial loss: the young man has left behind his pince-nez and must send for another pair. The pince-nez are picked up from the post office and brought to him and he owes a small amount of money for their collection. We will return to that level of the story.

The inner and appalling episode, as it occurs in this narrative, has become also a difficult and fragmented dialogue between the young man and Freud. The young man recounts an experience just after the loss of the pince-nez, during his time as a military officer. This is not an episode of battle-trauma or of neurasthenia brought on by the sights of war. Indeed, there is no record of any military engagement whatsoever within the case history itself. The experience is that of listening to a story. The story is told by a particularly disagreeable captain who, the young man recounts, '*obviously took pleasure in cruelty*' (Freud's emphasis here and below). He tells the appalled listener of a 'particularly terrible form of punishment practised in the Orient' (p. 134). Excess and a kind of fictionality are indicated by that term 'the Orient'. The punishment involves rats. It is still painful to read the struggles by the young man to disclose to Freud, at Freud's urging, the nature of this punishment. The punishment is disgusting indeed: rats bore into the anus of the victim. What makes the episode still scarifying to the reader is not only the murmured hesitations of the speaker reluctant to communicate a pornographic anecdote he cannot be rid of, but Freud's description of the young man's expression as he tells it:

[A] very strange compound expression is visible on his face, which I can only interpret as *horror at the pleasure he does not even know he feels*. (p. 134)

Coupled with this is the young man's acknowledgment that 'the idea flashed through my mind that *this might happen to someone who was dear to me*' (p. 134). More, it turns out that he is thinking not only of a threat to his lady but to his father, despite his being already dead. To ward off this threat (which has been conjured by himself) he proposes to himself a vow that he must repay Lieutenant A. for having picked up his pince-nez and paid the fee: this might seem a small matter to accomplish. But a fugue of events and mistaken identities sets in that gives a certain light-operatic flourish to the ensuing picaresque story: trivial, absurd and desperate are his attempts, which founder when he discovers that neither of his fellow-officers paid the fee but the young woman at the post office herself. All that matters to him is the strict wording of his vow and its performance. The tight and distorted plotting he has manufactured has, in fact, produced a vow that was from the start incapable of being properly fulfilled. But it takes months of telling and re-telling before he can bring himself to know – let alone acknowledge – the whirl of contradiction by whose means he has sought to shield himself from perversity within. Words in a vow have an obdurate performativity; they must be fulfilled. For this patient, they have also acted as bulwarks against chaos and Freud has much work to overcome the resistances that have both imprisoned and held together the Ratman: the patient himself comes to feel that nothing short of disintegration and reintegration of his personality is needed to gain his freedom.

Could he succeed in reintegrating his personality? If so he was confident that he could achieve a great deal, perhaps more than other people. (p. 142)

Freud clearly enjoyed the intelligence of his patient and the opportunity to open out with him the theoretical implications of his personal dilemmas. They talk together quite discursively, even, on Freud's part too, unguardedly. When he records their conversation about the 'wicked' unconscious and its relation to the infantile, and about splits in the personality, Freud feels obliged to add a footnote later:

All this is admittedly only very roughly correct, but will do in the first instance as an introduction. (p. 173)

The ingenuity of patient and analyst is well matched and, in the later phases of Freud's account, a return is made to the impulse that first drew the young man to him: namely, the fascination with word-play and allusion. For example, the word 'rat' is secreted in the German for 'to marry', *heiraten*, and together Freud and his patient draw in the figure of the Rat-Wife in Ibsen's *Little Eyolf* (herself a figure, as Freud notes, based on the Pied Piper of Hamelin who frees the town of rats but lures away the children). The association of rats with children is established. When, in Goethe's *Faust*, Mephistopheles needs to get through a door guarded by a magic pentagram he conjures up a rat to help him cross the threshold into the forbidden zone (p. 177). The rat breaks through magically. Other associations are with syphilis, with anal eroticism and with childhood intestinal worms. Whatever the subject-matter, the pleasure of intellectual work in common thrives between Freud and the young man, particularly through the pursuit of allusion and punning signification. The young man's 'compulsion to understand' here takes a benign role (p. 152). These varying perceptions help to solve the rat idea and to restore the patient to psychic health. The partial form of the narrative 'Some Remarks on a Case' also gave Freud the chance to explore a variety of as yet incomplete insights, such as his discussion of how smell forms part of erotic experience and of memory gained in childhood. The subtle explorations and the emergence into lucidity recorded in this case history make the footnote at the end, added by Freud in 1923, extraordinarily poignant:

The patient, who had recovered his psychic health as a result of the analysis described here, was – like so many other promising and estimable young men – killed in the Great War. (p. 202)

That fate also affirmed Freud's analysis as an ungainsayable success: he 'had recovered his psychic health as a result of the analysis described here'. No loose ends or setbacks in a long life remained to be recorded. In this way, the Ratman differs from two other of Freud's most famous patients: Dora, who broke off the analysis, and the Wolfman who suffered further bouts of mental ill health at intervals after his analysis was completed. By June 1914, just before the opening of the First World War, the Wolfman felt himself restored to health after an analysis of four and a half years, and by November of that year Freud had written the case history. But he held back publication until after the war had ended. In 1919 the Wolfman had become a refugee from Russia and had lost his family fortune. He then briefly re-entered analysis with Freud and, wrote Freud in a final footnote to the 1924 edition:

since then the patient, deprived by the war of his home, his fortune and all his family relations, had felt normal and conducted himself impeccably. Perhaps the very misery he felt had contributed to the stability of his recovery by providing some satisfaction for his sense of guilt. (p. 320)

Perhaps also, a worldly predicament that put him on a level with the circumstances suffered by so many others of his generation stabilized for a time the Wolfman's sense of normality. He was later to experience further analysis and further trials, outward and inward, and in several chapters of autobiography offered his own assessment: *The Wolfman and Sigmund Freud* (ed. Muriel Gardner, London: Hogarth Press, 1971). Most surprising is the realization that through the years of his first analysis he was totally preoccupied by his love for Thérèse and then their difficult marriage, matters that do not enter Freud's account. The Wolfman, by sheer longevity, raises in an acute form the question of what success can mean in analysis when individual lives are the site of such vicissitudes over time.

Although the Wolfman seemed stabilized by world events after the First World War, he was shattered by the oncoming of the Second. Thérèse killed herself shortly after the entry of Hitler into Austria in 1938.

In the essay 'Some Character Types' Freud brilliantly pinpoints the wishful belief of each person that she or he is an exception to ordinary rules:

For this very reason, however, it is necessary for an individual to produce a special justification, one not available to everyone, if he announces himself to be a genuine exception and behaves accordingly. There may be more than one such justification; but in the cases I have investigated it was possible to prove that they had one characteristic in common, namely *the fate which had befallen them early in life.* (p. 325)

The example he offers in the essay is of physical disability ratifying exceptional behaviour: Shakespeare's *Richard II*I is quoted: 'Cheated of feature by dissembling nature'. Freud comments on the 'secret background of sympathy' (p. 327) created for this villain-hero, and his point is not just that we are to feel sorry for a cripple, however badly he behaves, but rather that the claim to be exceptional is a universal one. It is normal and inordinate at once. In that sense, the people he studies are both ordinary and aberrant. They are at once odd and 'like us'. It is crucial for him to explore this paradox because of the need to work across from the single example – the peculiar formation of each particular life, with which he so deeply empathizes – and his claim to uncover the general principles that govern the growth of consciousness and its roots in the unconscious. The single 'case' will not suffice for argument unless he can unfold generative conditions common to all.

In 'The "Wolfman"', with its extreme and sometimes vertiginous reversals of meaning, Freud brings into play a further argument, one derived from views then common but not at present much countenanced. He calls on the correspondence between ontogeny and phylogeny (the growth of the single organism and the growth of the species) that had been popularized in the wake of Darwin and that supplied the vocabulary for Victorian discussions of 'survivals'. Remote tribes were held to be 'survivals' from a primitive phase of human experience, and the symptoms of neurotics, Freud argued, called on buried strata of communal primitive recollections. *Totem and Taboo* (1912–13) is subtitled 'Some Points of Agreement between the Mental Lives of Savages and Neurotics'. Above all, childhood was seen as briefly giving access to such phylogenetic resources, through what Freud calls in 'The "Wolfman"' 'the pre-history of the patient's childhood' (p. 215). The development of civilizations could be paralleled to the development of the single life. The unconscious could be assigned a temporal as well as a geological description: that is, it is present not only in the depths of each present life but constituted from materials generated in a common proto-history of the race. This case history is entitled 'From the History of an Infantile Neurosis' and (as that 'From' indicates) is deliberately incomplete, concentrating exclusively on the infantile neurosis and, despite the patient's own request, setting aside 'a complete history of his illness, treatment and recovery' (p. 205).

The emphasis on childhood has also to do with the extraordinarily complex web of temporalities with which Freud must engage both in his encounter with the stories told by his patients and in his own structuring and telling of the process of analysis. In the Wolfman case, moreover, dreams play a central role. These are dreams and thoughts recounted by an adult to an adult but dating from the experiences of a child of four and a half or five. Any night's experience reminds us how much material is lost from a dream at the point of waking, how branching episodes and images drop away, how much confusion is falsely stabilized if we recount the dream to another, its clutter confined and pointed in the interests of narrating. It is no wonder then that Freud feels tonic disbelief at the time of his first encounters with the patient's version of his early experiences and dreams. Freud's description of his initial disbelief is also in itself tactical in convincing the reader to stay by his side as the account unfolds. He acknowledges ruefully at the outset 'that no way has yet been found to embed the convictions that are gained through analysis within any account of the analysis itself' (p. 211). There remains an experiential, even magical, residue that cannot be represented by the narrative: that residue is the actual encounter, its length, its silences, its timelessness, here curtailed into a slow-moving but progressively unfolding story. And there is more: even that difficulty of describing is concerned only with the dialogue between patient and analyst, and then with the analyst's communication to a reader. Beyond, within, beneath and behind that are the experiences, half understood, half recalled, distorted in their passage from unconscious to consciousness, deflected as well as condensed by obsession – childhood experiences that generated the belated encounter between these two grown men. The case history of the Wolfman, perhaps most of all the case histories, communicates to the reader the perturbing intricacy of all these interactions across time and interpretation. That is also its strength as a record of what analysis can mean, and perhaps accounts for the degree to which it has become the chosen site of further interpretation by a host of commentators analytic and literary.

The boy is represented as subject to seduction by his older sister in their earliest infancy, a girl whose later sad history is recounted in summary by Freud with a bleak and disquieting composure: a brilliant young woman gifted in both the study of natural sciences and as a poet, she falls into depression in her early twenties and 'On a second journey which took place soon afterwards she poisoned herself and died a long way from home' (p. 219). Freud diagnoses this as probably 'the onset of dementia praecox', not a diagnosis with which anyone now can be content. This narrative-niche does uncover the ethical problems generated by intense concentration on the single life: all others must give way before it and yield up their meaning to it. The girl-child who had played with the boy's penis in their infancy rejects his advances in adolescence; he turns from her to a little peasant girl who is a servant in the house. The story belongs to the boy becoming young man, not to either of these young women, each of whom is jettisoned from the story save in so far as they enter the constitution of his neurosis.

The story takes as its central motif the four-year-old's dream of the white wolves sitting quite still in the walnut tree ('The Dream and the Primal Scene', section IV). Freud recognized, and had already written on, the extent of fairy-tale materials in this dream, which left the child afraid of seeing something terrible when dreaming right up to his eleventh or twelfth year. The analysis of the dream was prolonged over several years and in the course of it emerged materials that caused Freud himself to demur at the probability of his own interpretation and (at least rhetorically) to fear that the reader would desert him (p. 234). The dream preserved and muffled, Freud came to think, long-forgotten memory traces of the child's observing his parents in the act of coitus, 'the primal scene'. Freud emphasizes that though the position the young couple adopted might be now unusual (though 'the phylogenetically older form', p. 238), the act was quite ordinary – and tender – and that they had simply forgotten the presence in the room of an eighteen-month-old child. He asserts, however, that for the child it acted as a second seduction with the threat of castration in it.

Freud, in this case history, is above all seeking to demonstrate that 'postponed understanding' draws on the events of early childhood and is repudiating the view that all neuroses are the products of later conflicts and that:

the significance of childhood is simply a sham created in analysis by the neurotic's tendency to express present interests by means of involuntary memories and symbols drawn from his infant past. (p. 248)

Yet he was always alert to the discordance between inner and outer events and declared that 'previously unconscious memories do not even have to be true; they may be true, but their truth is often distorted and interspersed with fantasized elements' (p. 250). Patience is Freud's tool for understanding and for helping his patient to understand. It is also his method for convincing his reader. He remains alert and responsive to difficulties in his theory (as throughout this section 'Some Matters for Discussion'). He jokes at times about the improbability of the transformations he is observing. He listens again, and then again, to his patient's account. He reads the dreams and reflects on them: 'To dream is, after all, to remember'. He reaches by slow process a state in which he can both observe and share the memories that generate dream-formation. He explicates – unpleats – hidden folds in the fan of recollection. He explores annexes to the patient's own knowledge of his story. He waits. He makes the reader wait. In 'The "Wolfman"' it is only late on that we come fully to know the third element in the child's seduction: religion and its homosexual imagery. And only after that long discussion are we given the simple imputed event through which the child interrupted his parents: he passed a stool.

How can Freud refute the charge that the analyst supplies both unremembered events and their interpretation to further the coherence of his story? In the section of this case history on 'Supplementary Material from Earliest Childhood', Freud produces an example that helps him counter the suggestion that it is the analyst's own fantasies that control interpretation. It is also a beautiful example of his method of reading materials, unreeling more and more effulgent memory-lore from the association made by his patient between butterflies and women (pp. 288–90). I shall not attempt to summarize it here. Each reader needs to read it for herself or himself, rather than in summary, gradually disclosing as it does both the vivid intimacy of a single life recalled and the associative processes common across time to the human mind and its emotions. What makes the case histories so engrossing is the way they combine attention to a particular irreplaceable 'exceptional' person and yet reveal the lives of others, through theory.

Gillian Beer, 2002

Translator's Preface

All translation is to some extent misrepresentation, and translating Freud is no exception. Any new attempt to make Freud's work accessible to an English-speaking audience must inevitably stand in the shadow of Strachey's monolithic accomplishment, the 'standard' edition and 'authorized' translation of Freud's collected works. It is fashionable to deprecate Strachey's achievement, and in some respects such criticism is justified, but it would be churlish and inappropriate to dismiss out of hand a translation which remains an invaluable source of reference. The sheer magnitude of the undertaking commands our respect, as does the fact that Strachey was able to refer problems of interpretation to Freud himself.

Like the Authorized Version of the Bible, though, Strachey's translation of Freud has enshrined certain inaccuracies that only determined iconoclasm can now dispel. And, unlike the Authorized Version, Strachey's translation does not have rolling and majestic periods to recommend it: indeed, it dismantles Freud's elegant, dignified German prose and replaces it with something very worka-day indeed. In order to convey the sense of what Freud has written, Strachey cuts, simplifies and interprets, sometimes using a number of short sentences to render a single sentence of Freud's. I have attempted to reflect the internal structure of Freud's writing, even where there is a risk of appearing convoluted, and to mirror his careful use of balance and repetition in my translation.

The key to Freud's writing lies in his subtle manipulation of everyday German, his sustained deployment of familiar metaphors to convey unfamiliar and remarkable ideas. Freud was *not* the father of psychobabble: very few of the terms he coined require a dictionary to make them comprehensible to the ordinarily educated reader. To take a well-known example: in the original German, those three continents in Freud's map of the mind for which Strachey coined the terms the 'id', the 'ego' and the 'superego', are simply the 'it', the 'I' and the 'above-I',[1] a delineation which is readily accessible to any thoughtful reader. The great distortion of Freud's terminology for which Strachey is responsible is the second reason why a new translation of Freud is urgently necessary, a point of view that Bruno Bettelheim argues eloquently in *Freud and Man's Soul* (1982). In the remainder of this preface I shall sketch out the main areas in which I have revised Strachey's terminology, explaining on what grounds I have done so.

Freud does occasionally use abstruse, scholarly terminology and when this occurs I have made no attempt to simplify it. 'Endopsychic', 'phylogenetic', 'affectivity' all render the equivalent German terms. (*Affekt*, however, I have translated in accordance with its usual sense of '[strong] emotion'.) The last section in the case history of 'Little Hans' is headed *Epikrise* in the German: the term is a specifically medical one, only to be found in loan-word dictionaries at the end of the nineteenth century, and means 'critical evaluation of the course of an illness'. After some thought I have retained the heading 'Epicrisis' in English where Strachey has simply 'Discussion'.

More usually, however, we find that Freud's terms are deceptively simple, and the difficulty faced by the translator is that of finding an equally simple – and grammatical! – equivalent, which can be deployed in the same wide variety of contexts and which retains at least something of the metaphorical range of meanings that adhere to the German term. Freud is remarkable for the consistency with which he manipulates a relatively small set of key terms, most of which carry the directness of everyday language; this no doubt contributes to the density and vividness of his writing. At the same time, he is able to introduce distinctions and variations that are quite possible and normal in German but that occasionally stretch the English language to its limits. A useful example of this is provided by the German word *Trieb*, which Strachey invariably translates as 'instinct' but which in fact means 'drive'. Its root sense is that of driving sheep or cattle; or of being driven to do something. Hence the individual 'drives', the forces which motivate us; the energy with which they do so is their *Triebkraft*, but collectively they might be referred to as the *Triebkräfte* (driving forces) or as the *Triebleben* (literally, 'drive life') of the individual. Still more problematic is the adjective *triebhaft* for which there is no single satisfactory English equivalent; for this and for the compound noun *Triebregung* (literally 'an impulse or stirring of the drive') I have opted to use the adjective 'involuntary'.

Closely related to the concept of drive is that of compulsion, which looms large in the case histories of both the Ratman and the Wolfman. Here the term *Zwang* ('compulsion'; from *zwingen*, to force) and its compound forms recur frequently; its translation poses problems only in the compound term *Zwangsneurose*, which Strachey renders as 'obsessional neurosis'. This term has passed into common usage, yet to translate it in this way is not only a mistranslation, but also obscures the connection with the element of compulsion present in all the related terms. For this reason I have opted for 'obsessive-compulsive neurosis', which reflects both the correct sense and the commonly accepted one, and at the same time echoes the designation now in general use, 'obsessive-compulsive disorder (OCD)'.

Freud confronts the translator with a further series of problems by using a number of near-synonyms which are nevertheless clearly used in contradistinction to one another. One example is provided by the names he gave to the process on which he was engaged, which he calls variously *Analyse* (analysis), *Behandlung* (treatment) and *Kur*. *Kur*, a word which is clearly related to the English word 'cure', was commonly used to designate the spa treatments that were so fashionable across Europe from the mid-nineteenth century until the Great War (the modern equivalent would probably be a health farm). Its broad sense is thus something like 'restoration', but as this would be somewhat recondite in the context, I have chosen instead to use the term 'therapy', since to a present-day reader this has the same breadth of scope and familiarity as the notion of 'taking the waters' to a contemporary of Freud's.

Equally central in any description of psychoanalysis are the various terms pertaining to the 'analysis of the soul'. Nowadays we readily overlook the fact that 'psyche' is the Greek word for 'soul' and that 'psycho-analysis' is, as it were, an oxymoron, but this root sense persists in the cognate German term *Seelenkunde* (knowledge of the soul). Freud normally uses *Psychoanalyse* and *psychoanalytisch*, but refers as often to the individual's *Seelenleben* (literally, 'soul-life') as to his *Psyche*. Where Strachey consistently translates *Seele* and its cognates in a very narrow sense as 'mind' or 'mental' I have opted for the adjective 'inner', translating *Seelenleben*, for example, as 'inner life'. Freud makes a further distinction between *psychisch* (pertaining to the psyche) and *psychologisch* (pertaining to psychology, i.e. the theory of the psyche); the former I translate 'psychic', the latter 'psychological'.

A further cluster of terms centres – unsurprisingly – on the concept of memory. The usual word is *Erinnerung*; but Freud also uses the terms *Eindruck* (impression) and *Reminiszenz* (reminiscence), one of a number of words found in his writing which has a strong Austrian colouring. In certain contexts (see pp. 234, 247, 249, 301) *Eindruck* seems to acquire the highly specific sense of what I have called a 'memory imprint', that is, a powerful impression that is retained but not processed, like a kind of internal snapshot. *Reminiszenz* I have translated, after discussion with Dr Nicola Luckhurst, as 'involuntary memory'. The term *Deckerinnerung*, misleadingly rendered by Strachey as 'screen memory', I have translated literally as 'cover-memory', by analogy with such concepts as a 'covering letter'. For the recovery in analysis of what may or may not be memories Freud uses the term *konstruieren*, meaning 'to construct'. My own rendering, 'to reconstruct', modifies the sense of the original German in the interests of intelligibility: in most contexts 'construct'/'construction' was felt to be ambiguous.

A final area in which one must treat Freud's near-synonyms with caution is that of psychic defences. The notion of 'defence mechanisms' has passed into current usage, but in fact Freud only occasionally uses a term such as *Schutzmaßregeln* (defensive measures). Much more common is the word *Abwehr*, used either on its own or in compounds. This indicates 'fending off', or more exactly 'parrying', and I have translated it accordingly, even though its use is sometimes a little clumsy.

There are a number of single terms used by Freud that merit closer examination. One that is of central importance to the essay 'Some Character Types Encountered in Psychoanalystic Work' is that of *Versagung*. In a key work on Freudian terminology Laplanche and Pontalis discuss the word at some length before concluding somewhat lamely that Strachey's 'frustration' will probably have to do. This is wrong, however: the German term points rather to a withholding of services, a refusal to oblige. (I am indebted to Professor John Reddick, incidentally, for pointing out that intransitive use of the verb is a linguistic development which postdates Freud.) *Versagung* thus implies that one part of the psyche, the I, is refusing to oblige another part, the it, so that 'refusal', though imperfect, is probably the best way to translate the term.

The term 'fixation', beloved of psychobabble, is Strachey's rendering of the perfectly common German word *Fixierung*. *Fixieren* means to stare at someone or something, to 'fix one's gaze' upon them. It is admittedly difficult to find a single translation that will fit all the contexts, but the word is a striking example of the way in which we have 'jargonized' Freud out of all recognition. In this particular case, I have opted for a variety of renderings but, where possible, I have retained the key sense of the 'fixed gaze'.

Ichgerecht, a Freudian coinage which Strachey renders with the hair-raising neologism 'ego-syntonic', can be translated straightforwardly enough 'acceptable to the I'. *Schaulust*, translated by Strachey as 'scopophilia', means simply 'the sexual pleasure derived from looking or watching'. *Besetzung*, too, is a common German term which Strachey mangles to produce 'cathexis'. The German *besetzen* has a variety of meanings including 'occupy' (in all senses), 'possess' and 'fill'; it has been suggested that Freud's particular sense of the term could be rendered as 'invest' or 'charge [with energy]'. I have followed Professor Joyce Crick in opting for the latter, as it seems to me to accord well with Freud's overall concept of psychic energy.

It is a guiding principle of this new translation of Freud that each translator should respond to Freud's writing in his or her own way, and that there should be no 'party line' on the translation of technical terms. While this obviously has considerable advantages as regards freshness and accuracy, it inevitably obscures the fact that, throughout his work, Freud is remarkably consistent in his choice of terms; moreover, some readers who are already familiar with psychoanalytic jargon may wish to know how particular key terms have been translated. For this reason, where my translation of such terms differs from the standard terminology, the German term will be found in square brackets after its first occurrence in each essay.

The names of people and some places have also been left in German, with an explanatory gloss where appropriate. I acknowledge a debt to D. J. Smith, whose book *Discovering Horse-drawn Vehicles* (1994) helped me out of some tricky vehicular corners with regard to the case history of Little Hans; and to Dr Almut Suerbaum and Mrs Regina Prince for their assistance with certain impenetrable words and phrases. (*Forschung*, as Freud himself makes clear, is an activity that combines notions of research, inquiry and exploration in more or less equal measure!) I am particularly grateful to my husband Ian Huish for his critical scrutiny of my typescript; any errors or infelicities that remain are my own responsibility.

Note

1. The simplicity of the terminology has been retained in all the other major European languages.

Analysis of a Phobia in a
Five-year-old Boy
['Little Hans']

I

Introduction

The history of illness and recovery in a very young patient that will be recounted in the following pages is not, strictly speaking, the product of my own observation. While I myself supervised the overall plan of treatment and also intervened personally on one occasion by talking to the lad myself, the treatment itself was carried out by the little boy's father; and I wish to express my profound gratitude to him for allowing me access to his notes for the purposes of this publication. The father's contribution goes further than this, however: in my view, no one else could have persuaded the child to admit so freely to his feelings and nothing could replace the expertise with which the father was able to interpret the utterances of his 5-year-old son: the technical difficulties of carrying out the psychoanalysis of so young a patient would have been insurmountable. Only by uniting in one person the authority of the father and that of the doctor, only because affectionate interests coincided with scientific ones, was it possible in this one case to apply a method that would normally have been quite unsuitable.

The particular value of observing this patient may be explained as follows. The physician who treats an adult suffering from neurosis by means of psychoanalysis – by painstakingly uncovering psychic formations layer by layer – eventually arrives at certain assumptions about infantile sexuality, in whose components he believes he has found the driving force behind all neurotic symptoms in later life. I have presented these assumptions in my *Three Essays on the Theory of Sexuality* (pub. 1905); I know that to anyone less familiar with

3

such matters they appear as distasteful as they appear irrefutable to the psychoanalyst. But even the psychoanalyst may admit to the desire for more direct, more immediate proof of these fundamental principles. Is it really so impossible to gain direct evidence from the child in all the freshness of youth of those sexual stirrings and fantasies, which in the case of an older person we must excavate so assiduously from the earthworks thrown up to conceal them; particularly since we assert that they are common to the constitution of all human beings and occur in the neurotic individual only in a more pronounced or distorted form?

To this end I have for years encouraged my pupils and friends to collect observations on the sexual life of children, which is normally either skilfully overlooked or deliberately denied. Among the material which came into my hands as a result of this request, pride of place was soon taken by the continuing story of little Hans. His parents, who were both among my closest followers, had agreed to bring up their first child with no more constraint than proved necessary to maintain decent behaviour, and as the child developed into a cheerful, good-natured and bright little boy, they proceeded quite happily with their attempt to let him grow and express himself without intimidation. I reproduce here the father's jottings on little Hans just as they were given to me, and I shall naturally refrain from any attempt to pervert and misrepresent the naivety and straightforwardness of the nursery, merely for the sake of convention.

The first information about Hans dates back to a time when he was not quite three years old. At that time he expressed in various remarks and questions a particularly lively interest in that part of his anatomy which he called his 'widdler'. Thus he once asked his mother:

Hans: 'Mummy, have you got a widdler too?'

Mummy: 'Of course I have. Why?'

Hans: 'I just wondered.'

At the same age he once went into a cowshed and saw a cow being milked. 'Look, milk comes out of the cow's widdler.'

These very first observations arouse the expectation that a great deal, if not most, of what little Hans shows us will prove typical of the sexual development of children. I have argued elsewhere[1] that we should not be too horrified if we encounter in a female the fantasy of sucking on the male organ. This shocking impulse is harmless in origin, for it is derived from sucking at the mother's breast; the cow's udder performs a useful mediating function here, for it is mammary in nature, but in form and position a penis. Little Hans's discovery confirms the last part of my theory. At the same time his interest in widdlers is not just theoretical: as we might surmise, it stimulates him to touch that organ as well. At the age of 3½ his mother catches him with his hand on his penis. She threatens him: 'If you do that, I'll tell Dr A. to come and he'll cut off your widdler. What will you do then when you need to widdle?'

Hans: 'I'll use my botty.'

He responds without any sense of guilt as yet, but acquires on this occasion the 'castration complex' that is so often to be inferred from the analysis of neurotics, even though without exception they strenuously resist any acknowledgement of it. There is much of importance that could be said about the significance of this element of child development. The 'castration complex' has left conspicuous traces in mythology (not just in Greek mythology, moreover); I have touched on the part it plays in a passage in *Die Traumdeutung* [*The Interpretation of Dreams*] (2nd edition, p. 385; 7th edition, p. 456) and elsewhere.[2] At about the same age (3½), standing in front of the lion's cage at Schönbrunn, he cries out with joyful excitement: 'I saw the lion's widdler.' The importance of animals in myth and fairy-tale is due in no small measure to the openness with which they display their genitalia and their sexual functions to the curious young child. There is no doubt as to Hans's sexual curiosity, but it also makes a research scientist of him, allows him to make real conceptual discoveries. At 3¾ he watches water being drained off from an engine at the station. 'Look, the engine's doing a widdle. But where's its widdler?' After a while he goes on thoughtfully: 'Dogs and horses have widdlers; tables and chairs don't.' Thus he has discovered a crucial characteristic that allows him to distinguish animate from inanimate. Intellectual curiosity and sexual curiosity appear to be inextricably linked. Hans's curiosity is directed towards his parents in particular.

Hans, aged 3¾: 'Daddy, have you got a widdler too?'

Father: 'Of course I have.'

Hans: 'But I've never seen it when you get undressed.'

On another occasion he watches with fascination while his mother undresses at bedtime. She asks 'Whatever are you looking at?'

Hans: 'I'm just looking to see if you've got a widdler too.'

Mummy: 'Of course I have. Didn't you know that?'

Hans: 'No, I thought because you're so big you must have a widdler like a horse's.'

We must bear in mind little Hans's expectation; its significance will become apparent later on.

The great event in Hans's life was the birth of his little sister Hanna when he was exactly 3½ years old (April 1903–October 1906). His behaviour on this occasion was noted down at the time by his father:

When labour begins at 5 a.m. Hans's bed is moved next door; he wakes up there at 7 a.m. and hears the groans of his mother in labour, whereupon he asks 'Why is Mummy coughing?' – After a pause – 'I expect the stork is coming today.'

Over the last little while we have often told him, of course, that the stork will be bringing a baby girl or boy, and so he quite correctly associates the unfamiliar groaning with the arrival of the stork.

Later he is taken into the kitchen; in the hall he sees the doctor's bag and asks 'What's that?' to which we reply 'A bag'. Quite convinced now, he says 'The stork's coming today.' After the birth the midwife comes into the kitchen and Hans hears her give orders for a cup of tea; then he says 'Oh I see, Mummy's got a cough and so they're making her tea.' He is then called into the bedroom, but doesn't look at his mummy, only at the bowls of bloody water still standing in the room, and pointing at the bloody bedpan he remarks, taken aback: 'My widdler doesn't make blood come out.'

Everything he says shows that he connects the unusual circumstances with the arrival of the stork. He is on tenterhooks, looks askance at everything, and there is no doubt that the first stirrings of doubt about the stork are gaining a foothold.

Hans is very jealous of the new arrival and as soon as anyone praises her, finds her pretty, etc., he replies scornfully: 'But she hasn't got any teeth yet.'[3] *For when he saw her for the first time he was astonished that she was unable to speak and assumed that the reason she could not speak was because she did not have any teeth.*

In the early days after the birth he finds himself having to play second fiddle, of course, and suddenly comes down with a very sore throat. In his fever he is heard to say: 'But I don't want a little sister!' It takes about six months for him to get over his jealousy, after which he becomes as affectionate towards Hanna as he is conscious of his own superiority.[4]

Shortly after this Hans watches his week-old sister being given a bath. He remarks: 'Goodness, her widdler is really tiny still; and adds, by way of consolation: 'When she grows up it's bound to get bigger'.[5]

At the same age, 3¾ years old, Hans relates a dream for the first time. 'When I was asleep today I thought I was in Gmunden with Mariedl.'

Mariedl is the landlord's 13-year-old daughter, who often played with him.

When Hans's father tells his mother the dream in his presence Hans corrects him: 'Not with Mariedl, *on my own* with Mariedl.'

Some background information:

Hans spent the summer of 1906 in Gmunden, where he used to spend the whole day in the company of the landlord's children. When we left Gmunden we thought he would find it hard to say goodbye and go back to town. To our surprise this was not the case. He obviously enjoyed the change and for several weeks said very little about Gmunden. Only weeks later did animated memories quite frequently come to the surface of the time he had spent in Gmunden. For about the last four weeks he has been transforming these memories into fantasies. He fantasizes that he is playing with the children, Berta, Olga and Fritzl, talks to them as if they were there with him and is capable of amusing himself for hours in this fashion. Now that he has a sister and is obviously preoccupied with the problem of where babies come from, he calls Berta and Olga 'his children' and adds on one occasion, 'My children, Berta and Olga, were brought by the stork too.' It is now six months since we left Gmunden, and the dream is obviously to be understood as the expression of his yearning to go back again.

This is what his father has to say; I will anticipate myself by observing that with his last remark about the children the stork is supposed to have brought him, Hans consciously contradicts a feeling of doubt lurking inside him. Luckily his father noted down quite a number of things that acquire an unexpected value later on.

I draw a giraffe for Hans, who has recently quite often been to Schönbrunn. He says to me, 'You must draw his widdler.' I reply, 'Draw it on yourself.' At this he adds a new line to the picture of the giraffe (see the accompanying drawing), which at first he leaves short but then adds another line to it, remarking, 'His widdler is longer than that.'

FIG. I

Hans and I walk past a horse which is urinating. He says, 'The horse's widdler is down below, like mine.'

He watches his 3-month-old sister being bathed and says pityingly, 'Her widdler is really really tiny.'

He is given a doll to play with, and undresses her. He looks at her carefully and says, 'Her widdler is only really tiny.'

We already know that this formula makes it possible for him to maintain the validity of his discovery (cf. p. 5).

Every researcher runs the risk of getting something wrong now and again. It may be of some comfort to him if, like Hans in the next example, he is not alone in his mistake, but can look to linguistic usage to excuse himself.[6] For in his picture book he sees a monkey and points to its upward-curling tail: 'Look Daddy, there's his widdler.'

In his fascination for widdlers he has thought up a very special game.

Off the hall are the WC and a dark storeroom for wood. For some time Hans has been going into the storeroom, saying: 'I'm going to use my lavatory.' One day I look in to see what he is doing in the dark storeroom. He is exposing himself and says, 'I'm having a widdle.' That is to say: he is 'playing' lavatories. It is clear that he is playing, not only because he is merely pretending to widdle, and not actually doing so, but also because he does not go to the lavatory, which would actually be a great deal easier, but prefers the wood store, which he refers to as 'his lavatory'.

It would be unfair to Hans to pursue only the auto-erotic aspects of his sexual life. His father offers detailed observations concerning his relationships with other children, which point to an 'object choice' such as we find with adults. Also, admittedly, to a quite remarkable changeableness and a polygamous disposition.

In the winter (he is 3¾) I take Hans with me to the skating-rink and introduce him to my colleague N.'s little daughters, who are both about 10 years old. Hans sits down next to them: they, conscious of their greater maturity, look down with some contempt on the little squirt, while he gazes at them reverentially, which has next to no effect on them. Nevertheless, Hans refers to them now only as 'his girls'. 'Where have my girls gone? When are my girls coming?', and for several weeks at home pesters me continually with 'When can I go skating with my girls again?'

Hans's 5-year-old cousin is here on a visit. Hans, now 4, embraces him continually and during one of these tender embraces says, 'Oh, I do love you.'

This is the first instance of homosexuality that we shall encounter in Hans, but certainly not the last. Our little Hans is apparently the epitome of all the vices!

We have moved to a new apartment. (Hans is 4.) A door leads from our kitchen to a narrow balcony, from which one can see into the apartment on the opposite side of the courtyard. Here Hans has discovered a little girl of 7 or 8. Now he sits on the step leading to the balcony waiting to adore her, and will sit there for hours. At 4 o'clock in particular, when the little girl comes home from school, we cannot keep him in the room, nor stop him from taking up his observation post. On one occasion, when the little girl does not appear at the window at the usual time, Hans becomes very agitated and plagues the servants with questions: 'When is the little girl coming home? Where is she?', etc. When she finally appears he is ecstatic and cannot take his eyes off the apartment opposite. The passion with which Hans embarked on this 'love at a distance'[7] can be explained by the fact that Hans has no little playmate, boy or girl. Frequent contact with other children is obviously a necessary part of a child's normal development.

Shortly afterwards we leave to spend the summer in Gmunden and Hans (4½) now has company. His playmates are our landlord's children: Franzl (about 12), Fritzl (8), Olga (7), Berta (5), as well as the next-door children, Anna (10) and two other little girls whose names I cannot recall, who are about 9 and 7. His favourite is Fritzl, whom he often embraces and assures of his love. On one occasion he is asked, 'Which of the little girls do you like best?' and answers 'Fritzl'. At the same time he is very aggressive towards the girls, swaggers and acts the man, embraces them and smothers them with kisses, which Berta for one very much enjoys. One evening, as Berta is coming out of the room he puts his arms round her neck and says in the sweetest of voices, 'You're so lovely, Berta'; however, this does not stop him from kissing the others and assuring them of his love too. He is also very fond of Mariedl, another of the landlord's daughters who plays with him; she is about 14, and one evening as he is being put to bed he says, 'I want Mariedl to sleep with me.' When he is told, 'She can't do that', he says, 'I want her to sleep with Mummy or Daddy, then.' He is told, 'She can't do that either, Mariedl must sleep downstairs with her parents', and the following dialogue ensues:

Hans: *'I'll go downstairs and sleep with Mariedl, then.'*

Mummy: *'Do you really want to leave Mummy and sleep downstairs?'*

Hans: 'Well, I'll come back up again in the morning, to have breakfast, and to do a wee.'

Mummy: 'All right then, if you really want to leave Daddy and Mummy: don't forget your jacket and trousers – bye-bye!'

Hans really does pick up his clothes and starts towards the stairs to go and sleep with Mariedl, but of course is fetched back.

(Behind the words 'I want Mariedl to sleep with us' there lies the other wish of course, that Mariedl, whose company he so enjoys, should become a part of our family. No doubt the fact that his mother and father allowed Hans to come into their bed, albeit only occasionally, awakened erotic feelings in him, and the desire to sleep with Mariedl can also be taken in an erotic sense. For Hans, as for all children, lying in bed with his father or mother is a source of erotic excitement.)

When challenged by his mother little Hans behaved like a real man despite his homosexual leanings.

On the following occasion, too, Hans said to his Mummy, 'You know, I should so like to sleep with that little girl.' The occasion gives rise to great amusement, for Hans behaves just like a grown-up in love. For some days a pretty little girl, about 8 years old, has been coming into the restaurant where we have lunch, and Hans has of course immediately fallen in love with her. He is constantly turning round on his chair to look at her out of the corner of his eye; he goes over to stand near her and flirt as soon as he has eaten, but goes bright scarlet if anyone catches him at it. If the little girl returns his glance he immediately looks in the opposite direction, covered in shame. His behaviour occasions hilarity, of course, in all the restaurant guests. Every day when we take him into the restaurant he asks, 'Do you think the little girl will be here today?' When she finally comes he goes as red as any adult in the same situation. On one occasion he comes over to me, quite blissful, and whispers in my ear: 'I know where the little girl lives. I've seen her go up the steps in such and such a place.' While he may behave aggressively towards the little girls at home, here he is altogether the platonically languishing beau. This may have something to do with the fact that the girls at home are village children, while this one is a lady of refinement. I *have already mentioned that he once said he would like to sleep with her.*

As I have no wish to prolong the state of emotional distress into which Hans has been thrown by his love for the little girl, I have effected an introduction and invited her to come and play in the garden one afternoon after Hans's nap. Hans is so excited by the thought that the little girl is coming to see him that for the first time he cannot get to sleep, but tosses and turns restlessly. His mummy asks him, 'Why can't you sleep? Is it because you are thinking about the little girl?' to which he replies happily, 'Yes.' When we left the restaurant after lunch he told everyone at home, 'Listen, my girlfriend's coming today', and 14-year-old Mariedl reports that he asked her again and again, 'Do you think she'll be nice to me? Do you think she'll give me a kiss if I kiss her?', and so on and so forth.

But that afternoon it rained and so the visit was put off, and Hans had to be content with Berta and Olga for company.

Further observations made during the summer spent in Gmunden suggest that there are all sorts of new developments in the little boy's world.

Hans, 4¼ years old. This morning his mummy gives Hans a bath, as she does every day, then dries him and pats him with talcum powder. As she puts talcum powder around his penis, taking care not to touch it, Hans says, 'Why don't you touch me there?'

Mummy: *'Because that's dirty.'*

Hans: *'What? Dirty? Why?'*

Mummy: *'Because it's not decent.'*

Hans *(laughing): 'It's fun, though.'*[8]

There is a striking contrast between the boldness Hans showed here towards his mother and a dream dating from around the same time. It is the first occasion when the content has been disguised by distortion, but the solution did not elude his father's quick wits.

Hans, 4¼. Dream. This morning Hans came in and said: 'Daddy, I thought something in the night. Someone says, "Who wants to come to me?" Then someone says, "Me." Then he has to make him have a widdle.'

Further questions made it clear that there was no visual element in this dream, which falls into the category of type auditif. *For the past few days Hans has been playing parlour games, including forfeit games, with the caretaker's children, among them his friends Olga (7) and Berta (5). (A: Whose is this forfeit I hold in my hand? B: Mine. Then they decide what B has to do.) The dream follows the model of the forfeit game, except that Hans doesn't want the person with the forfeit sentenced to the usual kiss, or box on the ears, but to a widdle; more precisely, someone has to make him do a widdle.*

I get him to tell me the dream again; he uses the same words but replaces 'then someone says' with 'then she says'. Translated, then, the dream goes as follows: I am playing forfeits with the girls. I ask, 'Who wants to come to me?' She (Berta or Olga) answers: 'Me.' Then she must make me do a widdle (i.e. help me urinate, something which Hans clearly finds agreeable).

Being helped to do a widdle, which involves unfastening the child's trousers and taking out his penis, is obviously a pleasurable activity for Hans. When they are out on a walk it is of course mainly his father who helps Hans in this way, which provides an opportunity for his homosexual tendencies to become fixed [Fixierung] *on his father.*

Two days earlier, as noted, when his mother was washing and putting talcum powder on the genital area, he asked her, 'Why don't you touch me there?' Yesterday, when I took Hans for a wee he asked me for the first time to take him behind the house so that no one could see, and added, 'Last year, when I did a widdle, Berta and Olga watched me.' I take this to mean that last year he enjoyed it when the girls watched him, but doesn't any more. The pleasure of exhibitionism is now being repressed. The repression in real life of his desire to be seen – or helped – by Berta and Olga when he is doing a widdle, explains why it has turned up in his dreams, in the charming guise of a forfeit game. – Since then I have repeatedly observed that he does not wish to be seen when doing a widdle.

I remark here merely that this dream conforms to the rule formulated in *Die Traumdeutung* [*The Interpretation of Dreams*] (p. 283f., 7th edition), namely that speech which occurs in dreams can be traced back to speech uttered or heard in the days immediately preceding the dream.

A further observation was noted by Hans's father in the weeks immediately following their return to Vienna:

Hans (4½) is again watching his little sister being bathed and starts to laugh. Asked, 'Why are you laughing?' he replies, 'I'm laughing at Hanna's widdler.' 'Why?' – 'Because her widdler's so lovely.'

Obviously this is not what he means. Hanna's widdler actually struck him as funny. This is incidentally the first time he acknowledges the difference between male and female genitals, instead of denying it.

Notes

1. 'Bruchstuck einer Hysterie-Analyse' ['Fragment of an Analysis of a Case of Hysteria'] (1905).

2. [*Addition 1923:*] Since the publication of this essay the theory of the castration complex has been further developed by contributions from Lou Andreas, A. Stärcke, F. Alexander and others. It has been asserted that the infant must experience every withdrawal of the mother's breast as a kind of castration, i.e. as the loss of a significant body part that is felt to belong to the infant itself; that the regular passing of stools must be interpreted in exactly the same way; that the very act of birth, the separation from the mother with whom the infant previously formed a single whole, is the archetype of all castration. While recognizing all these as roots of the complex, I have nevertheless argued that the name 'castration complex' should be limited to those excitations and consequences that are bound up with the loss of the penis. Anyone who has become convinced that the castration complex is inevitably present in the analysis of adults will naturally find it difficult to trace it back to a chance threat, which does not after all occur all that frequently, and must assume that the child reconstructs [*konstruiert*] this dangerous possibility for itself on the basis of the vaguest hints, which are never in short supply, after all. This was also the thinking that provoked a search for the deeper roots of the complex in general experience. Thus it is all the more valuable that in little Hans's case the threat of castration was reported by the parents, and that it occurred at a time when there was no question of any phobia.

3. Typical behaviour again. In the same situation another little boy, only 2

years older than his sibling, used to fend off admiring comments with the words 'Too li'l, too li'l'.

4. 'The stork can take him back again': thus another rather older child welcomed his baby brother. Compare my remarks in *Die Traumdeutung* [*The Interpretation of Dreams*] on dreams concerning the death of close relatives (p. 173f., 8th edition).

5. I have been told of two other little boys who, on being allowed a first curious look at their baby sister's body, passed the same judgement as Hans using identical words and followed up by the same expectation. One might regard this premature corruption of the child's intellect with horror. Why do these youthful researchers not acknowledge what they really see, namely that there is no widdler present? In little Hans's case we can at least provide a full explanation for his deficient powers of observation. We know that through careful induction he had arrived at the general principle that all animate beings, by contrast with inanimate ones, possess a widdler; his mother reinforced this conviction by providing corroboration of it with regard to people whom he was unable to observe himself. He is now utterly incapable of ceding this hard-won position because of a single occasion on which he had observed his little sister. And so he judges that there is a widdler present in this case too, just a very small one; but it will grow until it is as big as a horse's.

Let us go further to save little Hans's honour. As it happens, he has behaved no worse than a philosopher of the Wundt school. The latter considers consciousness to be the essential quality of the soul, just as Hans considers the widdler to be the indispensable characteristic of all living things. Should the philosopher now come across inner processes that must be inferred, but where no trace of consciousness can be detected – i.e. one knows nothing of them but has no choice but to infer them – he does not say that these are *un*conscious inner processes but calls them *faintly* conscious. The widdler is just really tiny still! And as far as this comparison goes, little Hans still has the advantage. For here too, as is so frequently the case in children's sexual research, a piece of correct knowledge is concealed behind the error. It is indeed true that the baby girl possesses a little widdler, which we call the clitoris, although it will not grow but remains stunted. (Cf. my short paper 'Über infantile Sexualtheorien' ['The Sexual Theories of Children'] [1908].)

6. [*Translator's note*: The German word *Schwanz* (tail) is also a slang word for *penis*.]

7. W[ilhelm] Busch: *Und die Liebe per Distanz, Kurzgesagt, missfällt mir ganz.* [Love at a distance, I must say/Is not for me, is not the way.]

8. I was told of a similar attempt at seduction by a three-year-old girl, whose mother – herself neurotic – refused to believe in infantile masturbation. She had had knickers made for the little girl and was checking that the crotch was not too tight by stroking upwards on the inner thigh. Suddenly the child closed her legs over her mother's hand and begged, 'Mummy, leave your hand there. It feels so nice.'

II

Case History and Analysis

Esteemed Professor Freud,

I am sending you another instalment of Hans, but this time, alas, notes for a case history. As you will gather, he has been suffering recently from a nervous disorder, which greatly concerns my wife and myself as we can see no way of dealing with it. I beg leave . . . to call on you tomorrow, but . . . enclose written notes on the available material.

Sexual over-excitement caused by his mother's caresses is no doubt at the root of the problem, but I am at a loss to identify the immediate cause of the disorder. The fear that a horse will bite him on the street seems connected in some way to fear of a large penis – you will recall from my earlier notes that he was aware at a very early stage of the horse's large penis and came to the conclusion that, as she is so big, his mother must have a widdler like a horse's.

I cannot make any useful sense of this. Has he perhaps seen someone expose himself? Or is it all to do with his mother? We are not at all happy to find that he is already posing us problems. Incidentally, apart from his fear of going out in the street and his evening moods he has not changed, and remains as cheerful and good-humoured as ever.

Let us leave on one side both the understandable concern expressed by Hans's father and his first attempts at explanation, and contemplate first of all the material he has provided. There is no sense in which our task is to 'understand' a medical case straight away; this can only happen later, once we have formed sufficiently clear impressions of the subject. We must suspend judgement for the time being and consider all the relevant material with the same degree of attention.

The first information dates from early January this year, 1908:

This morning Hans (4¾) comes into our room crying, and when his mother asks why he is crying he says, 'When I was asleep I thought you'd gone away and I didn't have a mummy any more to nuzzle (= cuddle).

An anxiety dream, then.

I had already noticed something similar in Gmunden this summer. At bedtime he tended to be rather tearful and once said something along the lines of: If I didn't have a mummy, if you went away, or something of the kind; I cannot remember the exact words. When he was in this elegiac mood his mummy unfortunately always took him into bed with her.

On about 5 January he got into bed with his mother in the morning and said to her, 'Do you know what Auntie M. said: "What a sweet little willy he's got."'[1] (Aunt M. stayed with us about four weeks ago; she was there once when my wife gave the boy his bath and did indeed make the aforementioned remark in a whisper to my wife. Hans heard and hoped to turn it to good account.)

On 7 January he sets off as usual with his nursery-maid to the Stadtpark (Public Gardens), bursts into tears in the street and asks to be taken home, because he wants a 'nuzzle' with his mummy. When asked at home why he did not want to go any further and why he was crying he will not reply. He is as cheerful as ever until the evening; at bedtime he becomes visibly anxious, cries, and cannot be persuaded to leave his mother; again he wants to nuzzle. Then he cheers up again and has a good night's sleep.

On 8 January my wife decides to take him for a walk herself to see what is going on; she plans to go to Schönbrunn, a favourite outing of his. Once again he starts to cry, refuses to leave the house, is frightened. In the end he does go but is visibly anxious when they are in the street. As they are coming back from Schönbrunn he says with great reluctance to his mother: I was afraid a horse would bite me. (He was indeed worried when they saw a horse at Schönbrunn.) In the evening he apparently has a similar attack to the day before,

*and again demands nuzzles. When reassured he says, crying, 'I know
I shall have to go for a walk again tomorrow', and then later, 'The
horse will come into my bedroom.'*

*The same day his mother asks, 'Do you sometimes touch your
widdler with your hand?' He replies, 'Yes, every night when I'm in
bed.' The next day, 9 January, before his afternoon nap, he is told
not to touch his widdler. Afterwards, when questioned, he says he
did touch it for a little bit, actually.*

This, then, would constitute the beginning of the anxiety and the
beginning of the phobia. It is clear that we have good reason to
distinguish the one from the other. There appears to be quite enough
material, moreover, to enable us to orientate ourselves, and no
moment is more propitious to our understanding than this early
stage, which is, alas, generally neglected or passed over. The disorder
begins with anxious, loving thoughts and an anxiety dream. Content:
losing the mother, so that he can no longer nuzzle. His affectionate
feelings for his mother must therefore have increased enormously.
This is the phenomenon underlying his state of mind. Let us confirm
this by recalling the two attempts to seduce his mother that he
undertakes, the first of which takes place in the summer, the second
– just before his fear of going out into the street erupts – consisting
merely in admiration of his genitals. It is the increase in affection
for his mother, suddenly translated into anxiety, that, as we would
say, underlies the repression. We do not yet know what is causing
the repression: it may simply be the result of an intensity of emotion
that the child is unable to control, or there may be other forces at
work too, which we have not yet identified. This we shall discover
in due course. Hans's anxiety, which corresponds to a repressed
erotic yearning, is initially without an object; like all childish anxiety,
it is still anxiety rather than fear. The child cannot know [at first]
what it is that he is afraid of, and if, on that first walk with his
nursery-maid, Hans refuses to say what he is afraid of, that is because
he does not know. He says what he does know, that when he is out
he misses his mummy and wants to nuzzle her, and that he doesn't
want to leave Mummy. Thus he is quite straightforward in revealing
the primary reason for his dislike of outings.

His state of mind before bedtime on two consecutive evenings, anxious and still clearly dominated by his loving feelings, demonstrates that at the beginning of his illness there is no question of a phobia of going out into the street or for a walk, or indeed of horses. In that case, his evening state of mind would be inexplicable: who thinks about the street and going for a walk at bedtime? It is transparently obvious, on the other hand, that he becomes anxious in the evening because his libido overwhelms him more strongly at bedtime, a libido whose object is his mother and whose aim might be, say, to sleep in the mother's bed. It was his experience *in Gmunden*, after all, that his mother could be persuaded by such moods to take him into her bed, and he would dearly like to bring about the same result here in Vienna. Let us not forget, moreover, that at times in Gmunden he was alone with his mother, since his father was unable to spend the whole of the holiday there, and also that there he was able to spread his affections over a whole series of playmates, boys and girls, whom he must now do without, so that his libido, now undivided, is focused entirely on his mother.

Anxiety, then, corresponds to repressed longing, but it is not entirely the same thing as the longing; the repression also stands for something. Longing can be transformed entirely into satisfaction if the longed-for object is supplied, whereas in the case of anxiety this therapy no longer works: the anxiety remains even when the longing could be satisfied, and can no longer be transformed back entirely into libido; something holds the libido back in the state of repression.[2] In Hans's case this is apparent when he next goes for a walk with his mother. He is now with his mother and yet still suffers from anxiety, that is, from an unsatisfied longing for her. Admittedly, the anxiety is less: he can be persuaded to go for a walk, whereas he forced the nursery-maid to take him home; moreover the street is not the right place for 'nuzzling', or whatever the young lover has in mind. But the anxiety has stood the test and must now find itself an object. While they are on their walk Hans expresses his fear that a horse will bite him for the first time. Where does the material for this phobia come from? Probably from those as yet unknown complexes that have contributed to the repression and that maintain his libidinal feelings towards his mother in a repressed state. This is another puzzling aspect of the case, the subsequent development of which we must now follow in order to find the solution. The father has already provided certain pointers, which we may take to be reliable: Hans had always taken a particular interest in horses because of their large widdlers, and assumed Mummy would have a widdler like a horse's, etc. But what does it mean when Hans expresses a bedtime fear that a horse will come into his room? A silly, childish anxiety, one might say. But neurosis does not express silly ideas, any more than a dream does. We criticize what we do not understand. And in doing so, we make things easy for ourselves.

We must resist this temptation on another count as well. Hans has admitted to playing with his penis every night for pleasure, before he goes to sleep. Now this, the average family doctor likes to say, this explains everything. The child masturbates, and that is why he is anxious. Not so fast! The fact that the child gives himself pleasure by masturbating does nothing to explain his anxiety, but on the contrary makes it all the more puzzling. A state of anxiety is not created by masturbation, still less by satisfaction. At the same time we can assume that young Hans, now 4¾ years old, has indulged in this pleasure every night for at least a year (cf. p. 5), and we shall learn that it is precisely at this time that he is struggling to resist the habit, which is more in keeping with the advent of anxiety and repression.

We must also speak out on behalf of that good lady, Hans's mother, doubtless very worried about her boy. His father, not without some semblance of justice, accuses her of bringing about the neurosis by her too great affection and all too frequent willingness to take the child into her bed; we could equally well reproach her with having precipitated his feelings of repression by her energetic rejection of his attempts at seduction ('That's dirty'). But she plays the part Fate intended for her, and hers is a difficult role.

Hans's father and I agree that he should say to Hans that the horse business was just silly, and there was an end to it. The truth was that he loved Mummy very much and wanted her to take him into bed with her. He was afraid of the horses now because he found the horse's widdler so interesting. He had said himself that it was wrong to be so preoccupied with widdlers, his own included, and that was quite right. I further suggested to Hans's father that we should choose the path of sexual enlightenment. Since we could assume, given the boy's past history, that his libido was attached to the desire to see Mummy's widdler, he should remove this objective by telling him that Mummy, like all females, as he should know because of Hanna – doesn't have a widdler. This last piece of information is to be imparted to Hans on an appropriate occasion in response to some question or remark.

The next reports on Hans cover the time from 1 to 17 March. An explanation of the month-long gap will soon be forthcoming.

After his father has explained matters to him,[3] there follows a less troubled period, during which Hans can be persuaded without undue difficulty to go for a daily walk in the Stadtpark. His fear of horses is gradually transformed into the compulsive desire to look at them. He says, 'I have to look at the horses, and then I feel scared.'

After an attack of influenza, which obliges him to keep to his bed for two weeks, his phobia is again so strong that he cannot be persuaded to go out; at the very most he sits on the balcony. On Sundays he goes with me to Lainz,[4] as there are only a few carriages to be seen in the streets then, and it is only a short distance to the station. In Lainz he refuses on one occasion to leave the garden and go for a walk because there is a carriage just outside the garden. After another week spent at home because he has had his tonsils out, his phobia gets even worse. He will go out on to the balcony but not for a walk; that is, as soon as he gets to the street door he turns round and goes straight back inside.

On Sunday 1 March, on the way to the station, the following conversation takes place: I try to explain to him again that horses don't bite. He says: 'But white horses bite; in Gmunden there's a white horse that bites. If you hold out your finger, it bites you.' (I notice that he says 'finger' rather than 'hand'.) He then tells me the following story, which I reproduce here in more coherent form: 'When Lizzi had to go away they had a carriage with a white horse outside their house to take the luggage to the station. (He tells me that the little girl Lizzi had been living nearby.) Her father was standing close to the horse and the horse turned its head (to touch him) and he said to Lizzi: 'Don't touch the white horse or it will bite you.' I reply, 'Do you know, I don't think you're talking about horses really, but about widdlers that shouldn't be touched.'

He: *'But widdlers don't bite.'*

I: *'Well perhaps they do'; whereupon he tries emphatically to prove that it really was a white horse.*[5]

On 2 March, when he gets frightened again, I say, 'Do you know what? Your silly nonsense – this is how he describes his phobia – will get better if you go out for a walk more often. It is so bad at the moment because you haven't been out of the house, because you've been ill.'

He: *'Oh no, it's so bad because I keep on touching my widdler every night.'*

Doctor and patient, father and son are unanimous, therefore, in ascribing the principal role in the pathogenesis of Hans's present state of mind to the habit of masturbation.[6] But there is also no lack of indication of other significant factors.

On 3 March a new girl came into service with us, whom he is particularly taken with. As she lets him climb up on her back when she is doing his room he now refers to her only as 'my horsey' and holds on to the back of her skirt shouting 'Gee-up!' On about 10 March he says to this new nursery-maid, 'If you do such and such a thing then you'll have to take all your clothes off, even your chemise.' (He means, as a punishment, but it is easy to discern the wish behind the remark.)

She: *'And what of it? I'd just say to myself that I haven't any money for new clothes.'*

He: *'But it would be an absolute disgrace, everyone would see your widdler.'*

The old curiosity, transferred to a new object, and appropriately enough in a phase of repression, disguised as an inclination to moralize!

On the morning of 13 March I say to Hans: 'Do you know, if you don't touch your widdler any more the silly nonsense will get better.'

Hans: *'But I don't touch my widdler any more.'*

I: *'But you still want to.'*

Hans: *'Maybe, but "wanting to" isn't the same as "doing" and "doing" isn't the same as "wanting to".'* (!!)

I: *'To stop you wanting to, you're going to have a bag to sleep in tonight.'*

After this we go outside. Although he is scared, he says, visibly cheered by the prospect of something to make the struggle easier, 'Now then, tomorrow when I have the bag to sleep in, the silly nonsense will go away.' And indeed he is much less scared of the horses and watches fairly calmly as the carriages go past.

The next Sunday, 15 March, Hans had promised to go with me to Lainz. At first he is reluctant, but in the end he goes with me. As there are only a few carriages on the streets he is visibly at ease, saying, 'Clever old God, sending the horses off early.' On the way I explain to him that his sister doesn't have a widdler like his. Girls and women don't have widdlers. Mummy doesn't, Anna doesn't, etc.

Hans: *'Have you got a widdler?'*

I: *'Of course I have, whatever did you think?'*

Hans (thinks for a moment): *'How do girls widdle if they haven't got a widdler?'*

I: *'They don't have the same kind of widdler as you do. Haven't you noticed that when Hanna has her bath?'*

All day long he is very cheerful, goes tobogganing, etc. Only towards evening does he seem out of sorts and appears to be frightened of horses.

In the evening the attack of nerves and the need for nuzzling is less pronounced than on previous days. The next day his Mummy takes him into town and in the street he is really scared. The next day he stays at home and is very cheerful. The following morning he comes upstairs at about 6 o'clock, very anxious. When we ask what is wrong, he tells us, 'I touched my widdler just a teeny bit. Then I saw Mummy with no clothes on, she had her chemise on and you could see her widdler. I showed Grete, my Grete[7] what Mummy was doing and I showed her my widdler. Then I took my hand away from my widdler.'

When I object that it must be either: in her chemise, or with no clothes on, Hans says, 'She was in her chemise but the chemise was so short I could see her widdler.'

The whole thing is not a dream but a masturbation fantasy, the equivalent, incidentally, of a dream. What he makes Mummy do clearly justifies his actions: 'If Mummy shows her widdler, then it's all right for me to do the same thing.'

From this fantasy we can deduce two things, first, that his mother's reprimand has had a powerful effect on him, and, second, that initially he does not accept the explanation that women do not have a widdler. He regrets that this should be the case and will not let go of the idea in his fantasy life. Perhaps he has his own reasons, moreover, for declining to believe what his father says.

Weekly report by Hans's father:
Esteemed Professor,

I enclose the next instalment of Hans's story, an interesting little tale. Perhaps I might take the liberty of calling on you on Monday during consultation hours and if possible I shall bring Hans with me – provided he will come. I asked him today, 'Would you like to come with me on Monday to see the Professor who can sort out the silly nonsense for you?'

He: 'No.'

I: 'But he has a very pretty little girl.' Whereupon he agreed cheerfully and willingly.

Sunday 22 March. To broaden the scope of our Sunday programme I suggest to Hans that we should go first to Schönbrunn and then go on to Lainz at lunchtime. In this way he has not only to cope with the walk from our apartment to the Stadtbahn [metropolitan railway] stop at the Central Customs House, but also the walk from Hietzing station to Schönbrunn and from there on to the steam tramway station at Hietzing, all of which he manages by looking away quickly if horses are coming, as he is clearly in an anxious mood. Looking away is Mummy's advice.

In the park at Schönbrunn he appears frightened of animals which he is normally able to look at quite fearlessly. And so he absolutely refuses to enter the house where the giraffe is; the same goes for the elephant, which he usually finds great fun. He is afraid of all the large animals, but enjoys the little ones. As for the birds, this time he is afraid of the pelican, which was never the case before, clearly also because of its size.

At this I say, 'Do you know why you are afraid of the big animals? Big animals have big widdlers and it is the big widdlers you are really afraid of.'

Hans: 'But I've never seen the widdler on any of the big animals.'[8]

I: 'But you've seen one on a horse, and horses are big animals too.'

Hans: 'Oh, I've often seen one on a horse. Once in Gmunden, when the carriage stopped in front of the house, once in front of the Central Customs House.'

I: 'When you were little you probably went into a stable, in Gmunden . . .'

Hans (interrupting): 'Yes, I went into the stables in Gmunden every day, when the horses came home.'

I: '– and you were probably frightened once when you saw the horse's great big widdler, but there's no need to be frightened. Big animals have big widdlers and little animals have little widdlers.'

Hans: 'And all human beings have widdlers and when I get bigger my widdler will grow too; it's taken root, after all.'

The conversation ended here. In the days that follow his fear seems greater again; he scarcely dares go out of the main entrance to the house, where we take him after lunch.

Hans's last words of reassurance to himself throw some light on the situation and allow us to correct some of his father's assertions. It is true that he is afraid of the big animals because he is thinking about their big widdlers, but one cannot actually say that he is afraid of the big widdlers themselves. Previously the thought of them had decidedly pleasurable associations and he had tried eagerly to catch a glimpse of them. But his enjoyment has since been spoilt by the general reversal of pleasure into its opposite, which – in a way that is not yet clear – has affected all aspects of his sexual exploration; spoilt, too, as we can see more clearly, by certain experiences and considerations which have had unhappy results. From the comforting remark: 'When I get bigger my widdler will grow too', we may conclude that he has constantly made comparisons in the course of his observations and remains deeply dissatisfied with the size of his own widdler. He is reminded of this defect by the big animals, which he dislikes for that reason. Since he is probably unable to become fully conscious of this whole train of thought, the painful feeling is transformed into anxiety, so that his present anxiety builds as much on his earlier pleasure as on his present aversion. When once a state of anxiety has been created, anxiety devours all other feelings; as repression takes its course and those once-conscious ideas to which strong feelings have become attached move more and more into the unconscious mind, all the associated emotions may be transformed into anxiety.

As a way of reassuring himself, Hans's odd remark, 'It's taken root, after all' allows us to guess at much that he is unable to express, that he did not express even in this analysis. I am supplementing my account here with material acquired during the analysis of adults, but I hope that this interpolation will not be considered forced or arbitrary. 'It's taken root, after all': given that this is intended to comfort and fortify, it calls to mind his mother's ancient threat to have his widdler cut off if he continues to play with it. At the time, at the age of 3½, that threat had no effect. He replied, unconcerned, that he would widdle through his bottom. It would be entirely typical behaviour if the threat of castration now took *belated* [*nachträglich*] effect, so that fifteen months later Hans is living in fear of sacrificing that precious part of his own self. It is possible to observe the belated effect of childhood commandments and threats in other cases, where the time lapse extends to as many years and more. Indeed I know of cases in which *belated obedience* to repression has been the major factor in determining the symptoms of illness.

The enlightenment recently offered to Hans, that women really do not have widdlers, can only have had a devastating effect on his self-confidence, by awakening the castration complex. This is the reason why he resisted the information, and why it failed to have any therapeutic effect: can there really be living creatures who don't possess a widdler? If so, it would no longer be so incredible if someone were to take away his widdler and turn him, as it were, into a woman![9]

In the night of the 27th to the 28th Hans surprises us by leaving his own bed in the pitch dark and coming into our bed. His room is separated from our bedroom by a closet. We ask him what the matter is, if he was afraid, perhaps. He says, 'No, I'll tell you in the morning', falls asleep in our bed and is carried back to his own.

Later the next day I question him closely as to why he came in to us in the night and after some reluctance the following conversation ensues, which I immediately note down in shorthand:

He: 'In the night there were two giraffes in my room, a big one and a squished one and the big one made a noise because I took the squished one away from it. Then it stopped making a noise and then I sat on the squished one's back.'

I, *at a loss:* 'What? A squished giraffe? What was it like?'

He: 'Yes.' (*Quickly fetches a piece of paper, crumples it up and says to me*) 'Squished, like that.'

I: 'And you sat on the squished giraffe's back? How did you do that?' *Again he shows me, sits down on the ground.*

I: 'Why did you come into our room?'

He: 'I don't really know.'

I: 'Were you frightened?'

He: 'No, not at all.'

I: 'Were the giraffes in your dreams?'

He: 'Not in my dreams, no; I thought it – I thought the whole thing – I'd already come up to your room.'

I: 'A squished giraffe: I wonder what that could be. You know you can't crumple up a giraffe as if it were a piece of paper.'

He: 'I know. In my head it was like that. There's not really anything like that in the whole wide world.[10] The squished one was lying on the floor and I picked it up in my hands and took it away.'

I: 'You mean you picked up a great big giraffe like that?'

He: 'I picked up the squished one.'

I: 'And where was the big one?'

He: 'The big one was standing a bit further away.'

I: *'What did you do with the squished one?'*

He: *'I held it in my hands for a bit, until the big one had stopped making a noise, and when the big one had stopped making a noise I sat on its back.'*

I: *'Why was the big one making a noise?'*

He: *'Because I took the little one away from it.'* (Notices that I am making notes and asks: *'Why are you writing everything down?')*

I: *'Because I send it to a professor who can take the "silly nonsense" away.'*

He: *'Oh I see, so you wrote down that Mummy took her chemise off as well, and you'll give that to the professor too.'*

I: *'Yes, but he won't understand how you can believe that there are such things as squished giraffes.'*

He: *'Just tell him I don't know myself and then he won't ask; but if he asks what a squished giraffe is he can write to us, and we'll write back, or shall we write now, I don't know.'*

I: *'But why did you come in to us in the night?'*

He: *'I don't know.'*

I: *'Tell me quickly what you are thinking about.'*

He (being funny): *'A glass of raspberry juice.'*

I: *'What else?'* } *His desires*

He: *'A gun to shoot people dead.'*[11]

I: *'You didn't dream it?'*

He: *'I'm sure I didn't; no, I know I didn't.'*

He continues: *'Mummy kept asking me to tell her why I came in to you in the night. Only I didn't want to, because at first I was ashamed of saying anything to Mummy.'*

I: *'Why was that?'*

He: *'I don't know.'*

My wife had indeed questioned him all morning before he would tell her the giraffe story.

Hans's father solves the giraffe fantasy the very same day.

The big giraffe is me, or more precisely, my big penis (the long neck), the squished giraffe my wife, more precisely, her sexual member: this is the consequence of the sexual enlightenment I had offered Hans.

Giraffe: see outing to Schönbrunn. Incidentally, he has a picture of a giraffe and an elephant above his bed.

The whole thing reproduces a scene which has taken place virtually every morning for the last few days. Hans always comes in to us early in the morning and my wife cannot resist taking him into bed with her for a few minutes. At this I always begin to warn her against taking him in with her ('the big one made a noise because I took the squished one away from it') and she interjects that this is nonsense, a couple of minutes will not make any difference, etc. Hans then stays in her bed for a little while ('Then the big giraffe stopped making a noise and then I sat on the squished one's back').

This marital scene, transposed into the giraffe world, may therefore be interpreted as follows: in the night he is overcome with longing for his Mummy, for her caresses and her sexual member and so he comes into our bedroom. The whole thing is the continuation of his fear of horses.

To this perceptive interpretation I can only add: 'Sitting on the giraffe's back' is probably Hans's image of taking *possession*. The whole thing is a fantasy of defiance, linked to his satisfaction at having triumphed over paternal resistance. 'You can shout as much as you like, Mummy takes me into bed with her all the same and Mummy belongs to me.' We are justified, then, in guessing that behind this, as his father suspects, lies Hans's fear that Mummy doesn't love him because his widdler will not stand comparison with his father's.

The next morning Hans's father receives corroboration of his interpretation of the dream.

On Sunday 29 March I go to Lainz with Hans. On the doorstep I bid my wife a joking farewell: 'Adieu, big giraffe.' Hans asks me, 'Why do you say giraffe?' I reply, 'Mummy is the big giraffe', to which Hans replies, 'Yes, and Hanna is the squished giraffe, isn't she?'

On the train I explain the giraffe fantasy to him, and he tells me, 'Yes, that is right', and when I say I am the big giraffe, because its long neck reminded him of a widdler, he says, 'Mummy has a neck like a giraffe's too, I saw that when she was washing her white neck.'[12]

On Monday 30 March, early in the morning, Hans comes to me and says, 'Daddy, today I thought two things. The first one was that I was in Schönbrunn with you looking at the sheep and then we crawled under the ropes and then we told the policeman at the entrance to the park what we'd done and he grabbed us.' He has forgotten what the second thing was.

I should mention here that on Sunday, when we wanted to go and look at the sheep, the area was closed off with a rope, and we could not get in. Hans was amazed that an area could be closed off simply with a rope, since, after all, one could easily duck underneath it. I told him that respectable people don't crawl underneath ropes. He remarked how easy it would be to do, to which I replied that if he did a policeman might come and take him away. There is an imperial guard who stands at the entrance to Schönbrunn, and I once told Hans that he arrests naughty children.

After we had returned from our visit to you, Professor, which occurred on the same day, Hans confessed another little desire to do what is forbidden. 'Daddy, this morning I had another thought.' 'What was that?' 'I went for a ride on a train with you and we smashed a window and the policeman took us away.'

The true continuation of the giraffe fantasy. He senses that it is forbidden to take possession of his mother; he has come up against the incest barrier. But in his view it is something which is forbidden by its very nature. When it comes to the forbidden pranks of his fantasy his father is there too and is also taken away and locked up. In his view his father also does that mysterious and forbidden thing with his mother for which he substitutes in his own mind something violent like smashing a window or penetrating a closed-off area.

That afternoon father and son visited me during my consultation hours. I had already made the little chap's acquaintance and had always enjoyed seeing him, as for all his self-confidence he was a charming, funny little fellow. I do not know if he remembered me, but he behaved impeccably, like a perfectly reasonable member of human society. Our consultation was brief. The father began by remarking that despite all efforts at enlightenment Hans's fear of horses had not diminished. We were also obliged to admit that the connections between the horses which frightened him and the tender feelings towards his mother that we had identified were not actually very substantial. Such details as I now learnt, things that particularly bothered him – what the horses had over their eyes and the black around their mouths – could certainly not be explained on the basis of what we knew. But watching the two of them sitting there and hearing the description of these anxiety-horses, I had a further intimation of what the solution could be, and understood very well why it might elude Hans's father in particular. I asked Hans in a joking way whether his horses wore spectacles, to which he replied that they did not, and then whether his father wore spectacles, to which despite the evidence he also replied in the negative; I asked whether by black around the 'mouth' he might mean a moustache, and then revealed to him that he was afraid of his father because he was so fond of his mother. He must think that his father was angry with him because of that, but that was not true, his father loved him, he need not be afraid to admit everything to him. I told him that for a very long time, even before he was born, I had known that a little Hans would come, who would love his mother so much that it would make him afraid of his father, and I had already told his father so. 'What makes you think that I am angry with you?' his father interrupted at this point, 'Have I ever shouted at you or hit you?' 'Oh yes, you have hit me', Hans corrected him. 'That isn't true. When?' 'This morning' the boy reminded him, and his father recalled that Hans had quite unexpectedly butted him in the stomach, whereupon he had smacked him almost as a reflex action. It was interesting that he had not registered this detail in the context of the boy's neurosis; now, however, he understood it to be an expression of his hostility towards him, perhaps also as an expression of his need to be punished.[13]

On the way home Hans asked his father: 'Does the Professor talk to the good Lord, since he knows everything before he is told?' I should have been extraordinarily proud of this accolade from a child's mouth if I had not provoked it myself with my playful bragging. After this consultation I received almost daily reports on the changes in our young patient's state. It was hardly to be expected that after what I had told him he would lose his fears at a single stroke, but it became apparent that he had now been given the possibility of bringing the products of his unconscious mind to the surface and unravelling his phobia. From this point onwards he was following a programme that I was able to communicate to his father in advance.

On 2 April we saw the first substantial improvement. *Up until then he could never be persuaded to spend long at the street door, and if horses came past he would always run back into the house with every sign of terror; this time he stood for an hour at the street door, even when carts and carriages came past, which is a not infrequent occurrence where we live. Now and again, if he sees a carriage coming in the distance, he runs back into the house, but turns round again straight away, as if he thinks better of it. In any case there appears to be only a residual anxiety and the improvement since your enlightening conversation with him is unmistakable.*

In the evening he says: 'If we can stand at the street door, we can go to the Stadtpark too.'

On 3 April he comes into my bed early in the morning, whereas for the past few days he has not come, appearing proud, indeed, of his self-restraint. I ask him, 'What made you come in this morning?'

Hans: *'I shan't come any more until I'm not scared.'*

I: *'So you come in because you are scared?'*

Hans: *'When I'm not with you I'm scared; when I'm not in bed with you, then I'm scared. I shan't come in until I'm not scared any more.'*

I: *'So you love me and you're afraid when you are alone in bed in the morning, and that's why you come in to me?'*

Hans: *'Yes. Why did you say it's* Mummy *that I love, when I'm afraid because it's* you *that I love?'*

The level of clarity the boy demonstrates here is really quite sophisticated. He discloses that love for his father is battling inside him with hostility towards his father as a result of their rivalry for the mother, and he reproaches his father with not having made him aware of this power play, which must ultimately give rise to fear. The father does not yet fully understand him, for during this conversation he becomes convinced for the first time of the boy's hostility towards him, a hostility whose existence I asserted during our consultation. The following material, which I reproduce in unabridged form, is actually more significant in terms of the father's understanding than that of my young patient.

Unfortunately I did not immediately grasp the significance of Hans's objection. Because of his love for his mother he obviously wants me out of the way, so that he can take his father's place. The repression of this hostile desire is transformed into anxiety about his father, and so he comes in early in the morning to see if I have gone away. Unfortunately I did not fully understand this at that moment and said:

'*When you are on your own you are frightened and want me, and then you come in to me.*'

Hans: '*When you aren't there I am afraid that you won't come home again.*'

I: '*Have I ever threatened not to come home?*'

Hans: '*You haven't, but Mummy has. Mummy said she wouldn't come home any more.*' *(He had probably been naughty, and she threatened to go away and leave him.)*

I: '*She said that because you were naughty.*'

Hans: '*Yes.*'

I: '*So you are afraid that I will go away because you were naughty, and that's why you come in to me.*'

At breakfast time I get up from the table, whereupon Hans says: '*Daddy, don't* race *off!*' *I am struck by the fact that he says 'race' rather than 'run', and I reply:* '*Aha, you're afraid of the horsey racing off.*' *He laughs.*

We know that this instance of Hans's fear is double-edged: he feels both fear *of* his father and fear *for* his father. The former derives from hostility towards his father, the latter from the conflict between that hostility and his affection for him, which is exaggerated here in reaction.

The father continues:

This is without doubt the first sign of something important. The fact that he will go as far as the street door but will not leave the house, and that at the first attack of anxiety he goes halfway back home, is motivated by fear of not finding his parents at home because they have gone away. At home he sticks to his mother like glue, his hostile feelings towards me make him afraid of my going away, because then he would be the father.

Last summer I had to leave Gmunden on numerous occasions to go back to Vienna, because of my work, and then he was the father. I remember that the horse phobia began with his experience in Gmunden when a horse came to fetch Lizzi's luggage and take it to the station. The repressed wish that I too should go to the station so that he could be alone with his mother ('the horse should go away') is translated into fear at the horse going away, and indeed nothing creates a greater state of anxiety in him than a carriage leaving the courtyard of the Central Customs House opposite our apartment, when the horses start to move.

This new information (hostile feelings towards the father) could only emerge once he knows that I am not angry with him because he is so fond of his mother.

In the afternoon I again go with him to the street door; once again he goes out onto the pavement and stays there even when carriages go past, only the occasional carriage makes him afraid so that he runs back into the entrance hall. He explains to me that 'Not all white horses bite', i.e. as a result of the analysis some white horses have already been recognized as 'Daddy', and they don't bite any more, but there are still some that do bite.

The situation outside our street door is as follows: opposite us is the warehouse of the Office of Consumer Tax, where there is a

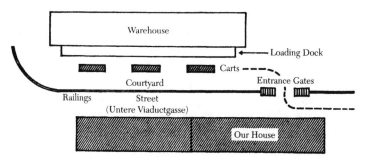

FIG. 2.

loading ramp which carriages and carts drive up to all day to collect packing cases and the like. The courtyard is closed off with railings. Opposite our apartment is the main entrance to the courtyard (Fig. 2).

For some days now I have noticed that Hans is particularly anxious when carts and carriages drive in or out of the courtyard, for in doing so they have to swing round quite sharply. I asked him on one occasion why he was so anxious and he replied: 'I'm afraid that the horses will fall over when the cart has to turn the corner (A).' *He is equally frightened when carts standing by the loading ramp suddenly start up and move off (B). Moreover he is more afraid (C) of big carthorses than of small horses, and more afraid of farm horses than of smart horses (the kind that pull cabs, for example). He is also more frightened if a carriage goes past at speed (D) than if the horses are trotting along slowly. Of course it is only in the last few days that these distinctions have become clear.*

I am tempted to say that as a result of his analysis, not only the patient but his phobia too has become bolder and dares to be more visible.

On 5 April Hans comes into the bedroom again and is sent back to his own bed. I say to him: 'As long as you carry on coming into our bedroom in the morning, your fear of horses won't get any better.' *He stands up to me, however, and replies:* 'I'm going to come anyway, even if I am still afraid.' *So he will not be stopped from coming to see his mother.*

After breakfast we are to go down to the street. Hans is looking forward to this, and instead of staying by the street door as usual plans to cross over to the courtyard, where he has seen street urchins playing often enough. I tell him I shall be pleased if he crosses the road, and seize the opportunity to ask why he is so afraid when the loaded carts standing at the loading ramp start up (B).

Hans: *'I'm afraid that I'll be standing by the cart and the cart will suddenly drive off and I'll be standing on the cart and trying to get on to the boards (the loading ramp) and I'll be driven off on the cart.'*

I: 'And if the cart is standing still? You're not afraid then?'

Hans: 'If the cart is standing still I'll quickly climb up on the cart and get on to the boards.' (Fig. 3.)

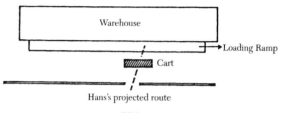

FIG. 3.

(Hans is planning, then, to climb on to a cart and then up on to the loading ramp and is afraid that the cart will drive off while he is on top of it.)

I: 'Perhaps you are afraid that you won't get home again if you're driven off on the cart?'

Hans: 'Oh no; I can always get back to Mummy, on the cart or in a hansom cab. I can tell him the number of our house.'

I: 'So what is it that you are afraid of, then?'

Hans: 'I don't know, but the Professor will know. Do you think he'll know?'

I: 'Why do you want to get up on the boards, anyway?'

Hans: 'Because I've never been over there, and I really wanted to go, and do you know why I wanted to? Because I wanted to load things and unload them and I wanted to climb all over the boxes. I'd really like to climb all over everything. Do you know who I learnt to climb all over things from? Some boys climbed all over the boxes and I've watched them and I want to do it too.'

Hans was not to have his wish, for even though he dared to go out on to the street, he felt too great a resistance to taking the few steps over the road into the courtyard, as carts were continually driving in and out.

The Professor knows only that the game Hans plans to play on the loaded carts must have acquired a symbolic connection with another wish, not yet mentioned, which it has come to represent. If it were not to seem too outrageous, however, it would already be possible to reconstruct what that wish was.

In the afternoon we go out on the street again, and after we have come back I ask Hans:

'*Which horses are you most scared of?*'

Hans: '*All of them.*'

I: '*That isn't true.*'

Hans: '*I'm most scared of the horses that have a sort of thing on their mouths.*'

I: '*What do you mean? The bit that they have in their mouth?*'

Hans: '*No, they have something black on their mouths (covers his mouth with his hand).*'

I: '*Do you mean a moustache, perhaps?*'

Hans: *(laughs): 'No, not that.*'

I: '*Have they all got one?*'

Hans: '*No, just some of them.*'

I: '*And what is it that they have on their mouths?*'

Hans: '*Something black.*' – *I think what he actually means are the broad leather straps on the muzzles of the dray horses (Fig. 4).*

FIG. 4.

'*And I'm most scared of the furniture vans.*'

I: '*Why is that?*'

Hans: '*If a furniture horse is pulling a heavy van I feel it's going to collapse.*'

I: '*So you are not scared of little carts?*'

Hans: '*No, little carts and mail vans don't scare me. And if I see an omnibus, that scares me most of all.*'

I: '*Why is that, because it is so big?*'

Hans: '*No, because once a horse collapsed pulling a carriage like that.*'

I: 'When was that?'

Hans: 'Once when I was out with Mummy in spite of my "silly nonsense", when we bought the waistcoat.'

(His mother subsequently confirms this.)

I: 'What did you think when the horse collapsed?'

Hans: 'It will always be like that from now on. Every horse will collapse when it is pulling an omnibus.'

I: 'Any omnibus?'

Hans: 'Yes! And furniture vans too. Not so often with furniture vans.'

I: 'Had the silly nonsense already started?'

Hans: 'No, it started just then. When the horse pulling the omnibus collapsed it really frightened me, honestly it did! As I was walking along, that was when it started.'

I: 'But the silly nonsense was that you thought the horse was going to bite you and now you are saying you were afraid the horse would collapse.'

Hans: 'Collapse and bite.'[14]

I: 'Why were you so frightened?'

Hans: 'Because the horse went like this with its hooves (lies down and demonstrates the horse kicking its legs). I was frightened because its hooves made such a racket.'

I: 'Where did you go with Mummy that day?'

Hans: 'First we went skating, then we went to a café, then we bought a waistcoat, then I went to the confectioner's shop with Mummy and then in the evening we came home; we came back through the Stadtpark.'

(My wife confirms all of this, including the fact that Hans's anxiety began immediately afterwards.)

I: 'Was the horse dead when it collapsed?'

Hans: 'Yes!'

I: 'How do you know?'

Hans: 'Because I saw (laughs). No, it wasn't dead at all.'

I: 'Perhaps you thought it was dead.'

Hans: 'No, not at all. I was only joking.' *(But the expression on his face had been serious.)*

As he is tired, I let him run off and play. The only other thing he tells me is that at first he was afraid of omnibus horses, then of all the others, and only recently of horses pulling furniture vans.

On our way back from Lainz I ask a few more questions:

I: *'When the omnibus horse collapsed, what colour was it? White, chestnut, brown, grey?'*

Hans: *'Black, both the horses were black.'*

I: *'Was it big or little?'*

Hans: *'Big.'*

I: *'Fat or thin?'*

Hans: *'Fat, very big and fat.'*

I: *'When the horse collapsed, did it make you think of Daddy?'*

Hans: *'Maybe. Yes. Perhaps.'*

Hans's father may have probed in many areas without success; but it does no harm to acquaint oneself with the details of such a phobia, the true object of which one hopes to be able to name. In this way we discover how diffuse it actually is. It is directed towards horses and carts, towards the fact that horses collapse and also that they bite, towards horses of a particular kind, towards carts which are heavily laden. Let us reveal straight away that all these peculiarities stem from the fact that originally the anxiety had nothing to do with horses but was transposed on to them as a secondary event, and then became attached to aspects of the horse complex that lent themselves to particular transferences. We must acknowledge in particular one highly significant result of the father's cross-questioning. We have discovered the actual occasion that gave rise to the phobia. This was when the boy saw a large, heavy horse fall to the ground; and one interpretation at least of this event that impressed itself upon the boy's mind would appear to be the one emphasized by his father, namely that Hans experienced on that occasion a wish that his father might also fall to the ground – and be dead. His serious expression when recounting the event surely bears out this unconscious meaning, but perhaps behind all this there lurks another meaning again? And what is the racket made by the horse's hooves all about?

For some time now Hans has been playing horses in the house:

he runs around, falls over, kicks his legs in the air, neighs. Once he ties a little bag round his neck for a nosebag. He repeatedly runs up to me and bites me.

He is more definite in accepting his father's recent interpretations than he is able to be in words, but naturally also likes to exchange roles, since his game is also serving the purposes of a wish-fantasy. And so he is the horse and he can bite his father, but at the same time, of course, he can identify with his father in this way.

For two days now I have noticed that Hans is quite definitely defying me, not in an insolent way but in high spirits. Is this because he is no longer afraid of me, the horse?

6 April. In the afternoon down to the street door with Hans. Every time a horse goes by, I ask him if he can see 'black round its mouth'; every time he says no. I ask him what the black actually looks like; he says it is black iron. My original supposition, that he was thinking of the broad leather straps of the dray-horses' harness, is clearly incorrect. I ask him if the 'black' reminds him of a moustache; he says, only because of the colour. What it is in reality, then, I still do not know.

His fear is less strong; on this occasion he risks it as far as the next-door house, but quickly turns tail when he hears the distant trotting of hooves. When a carriage drives up to our entrance and stops, he becomes fearful, and when the horse paws the ground he runs into the house. I ask him why he is frightened, and whether he is perhaps scared because the horse went like that (stamping my foot). He says: 'Don't make such a racket with your feet!' Compare his remark about the omnibus horse that collapsed.

He is particularly scared when a furniture van drives past. He runs inside the house. Without making anything of it I ask, 'Doesn't that kind of furniture van look like an omnibus?' He says nothing. I repeat the question. He then says, 'Well of course it does, or else I wouldn't be so scared of furniture vans.'

7 April. Today I ask him again what the 'black round the horses' mouths' looks like. Hans says, like a muzzle. The odd thing is that no horse has passed by for three days now on which he can identify one of these muzzles; I myself have not seen a horse of this kind on any of my walks, although Hans insists that there are some. I suspect that some kind of bridle – perhaps the broad strap around the horse's mouth – reminded Hans of a moustache, and that when I hinted at this that fear too disappeared.

Hans's improvement is consistent, the radius of his circle of activity, with the street door as its central point, ever broader; he even performs the hitherto impossible trick of running across the road to the opposite pavement. Any fear that still remains is connected to the scene with the omnibus, the significance of which, I have to admit, is still not clear to me.

9 April. This morning Hans comes in while I am washing, my upper torso naked.

Hans: 'Daddy, how beautiful you are, you're all white!'

I: 'Yes, just like a white horse.'

Hans: 'Only your moustache is black (picking up the allusion). Or is it your black muzzle, perhaps?'

Then I tell him that I had been at the Professor's house on the previous evening, and say, 'There are one or two things he'd like to know', to which Hans replies, 'I wonder what they are.'

I tell him I know when it is that he makes a racket with his feet. He interrupts me: 'Yes, when I'm in a "paddy" or when I'm supposed to do a plop and I'd rather play. (When angry he does indeed tend to make a racket with his feet, i.e. he stamps them. – 'Doing a plop' is doing 'a big job'. One day when Hans was little he got up off the pot and said: 'Look at the plop.' [He meant to say sock, because of the shape and colour.][15] We still use the term today. – Very early on, when he was supposed to go on the pot and did not want to leave his game he would stamp his feet in fury, thrash with his arms and legs and sometimes throw himself on the ground.)

'You kick your feet when you are told to go and do a widdle, too, and you don't want to because you would rather play.'

He: 'Daddy, I need a widdle' – and off he goes, no doubt in confirmation of my remarks.

In the course of his visit Hans's father had asked me what Hans could have been reminded of by the horse which collapsed kicking its legs in the air, and I made the suggestion that this might have been his own reaction when suppressing the urge to urinate. Hans confirms this when the urge to urinate comes up in the conversation, and contributes other meanings again of making a racket with his feet.

Then we go down to the street door. When a coal cart comes by, he says: 'Daddy, I'm really scared of coal carts, too.'

I: *'Perhaps because they are great big things, like omnibuses.'*

Hans: *'Yes, and they are so full and the horses have so much to pull and could easily fall down. If it's an empty cart, I'm not scared.'* *It is indeed the case, as I noticed earlier, that he is frightened only by heavily laden vehicles.*

Nevertheless, the situation is certainly opaque. The analysis is scarcely progressing; I fear that my description of it will soon begin to tire the reader. And yet, in every psychoanalysis there are dark times such as these. We will soon find Hans going off in a wholly unexpected direction.

I have come home and am talking to my wife, who has been out shopping and is showing me her various purchases. Among them is a pair of yellow drawers. Hans says 'Ugh!' several times, throwing himself on the ground and spitting. My wife tells me he has already done this several times on seeing the drawers.

I ask: *'Why do you say "Ugh"?'*

Hans: *'Because of the drawers.'*

I: *'Why: because of the colour, because they are yellow and make you think of widdle or plop?'*

Hans: *'Plop isn't yellow, it's white or black.'* Then: *'Daddy, is it easy to do a plop when you eat cheese?'* (*I once said this to him when he asked me why I eat cheese.*)

I: *'Yes.'*

Hans: *'Is that why you always go and do a plop first thing in the morning? I'd really like some cheese with my bread and butter.'*

Yesterday, too, when he was jumping around in the street he asked me: 'Daddy, isn't it true that if you jump around a lot it's easy to do a plop?' He has always had difficulty in moving his bowels, and we often have recourse to aperients and enemas. At one stage his habitual constipation was so bad that my wife went to Dr L. for advice. He was of the opinion that Hans was eating too much, which was indeed true, and recommended a more moderate diet, which rectified Hans's condition immediately. Recently constipation has again become a frequent occurrence.

After the meal I say: 'Let's write to the Professor again', and he dictates: 'When I saw the yellow drawers I said, "Ugh, I'm going to be sick" and I threw myself on the ground, closed my eyes and wouldn't look.'

I: 'Why is that?'

Hans: 'Because I saw the yellow drawers, and I did the same sort of thing when I saw the black drawers.[16] The black ones are the same sort, but they were black.' (Breaking off.) 'Daddy, I'm so glad; I'm always glad when I can write to the Professor.'

I: 'Why did you say "Ugh"? Did you feel sick?'

Hans: 'Yes, because I saw them. I thought I was going to have to do a plop.'

I: 'Why?'

Hans: 'I don't know.'

I: 'When did you see the black drawers?'

Hans: 'It was once when Anna (our maid) had already been with us for ages – in Mummy's room – she had just bought them and brought them home.'

(My wife confirms this.)

I: 'And did they make you feel sick too?'

Hans: 'Yes.'

I: 'Have you seen Mummy wearing drawers like that?'

Hans: 'No.'

I: 'Perhaps when she was getting dressed?'

Hans: 'I'd already seen the yellow ones once when Mummy bought them. (A contradiction! He saw the yellow drawers for the first time after his mother had bought them.) And she's got the black ones on today (correct!), because I saw her take them off this morning.'

I: 'What? She took the black drawers off this morning?'

Hans: 'This morning when she went out she took the black drawers off, and when she came home she put the black ones on again.'

I put this to my wife, as it seems to make no sense. And indeed she tells me that it is not true; of course she did not change her drawers before going out.

I ask Hans about this straight away: 'You told me that Mummy put her black drawers on, and then when she went out she took them off and when she came back she put them on again. But Mummy says that isn't true.'

Hans: *'I think perhaps I might have forgotten that she didn't take them off. (Indignant.) Why don't you leave me alone?'*

A word of explanation regarding this story of his mother's drawers: Hans is obviously being hypocritical when he pretends to be pleased that he is being given the opportunity to talk about this matter. In the end he throws off the mask and is rude to his father. These are things that at one time gave him *great pleasure* and that make him ashamed now that he has reached the stage of repression, so that he pretends they make him sick. He goes so far as to lie in order to suggest that there are other reasons why he has watched his mother changing her drawers; in reality the putting on and taking off of drawers belongs in the context of 'plop'. His father knows exactly what this is all about and what Hans is trying to hide.

I ask my wife if Hans has often been present when she was using the lavatory. She says, "Yes, often", he 'goes on and on' until she agrees; all children do the same thing.

Let us keep in mind this desire of Hans's, already repressed, to watch his mother doing a 'plop'.

We go down to the street door. He is very cheerful, and constantly leaping about pretending to be a horse, as it were; I ask him, 'Who is the omnibus horse really? Me, you or Mummy?'

Hans *(immediately)*: *'Me; I'm a young horse.'*

At the worst period of his phobia, if he was frightened by the sight of horses prancing, and asked me why they did it, I would say, to reassure him: 'Do you know, those are young horses, they prance about just as young boys do. You like prancing about, and you're a boy.' Ever since then, if he sees a horse prancing, he says: 'That's right, they're young horses!'

As we go back upstairs I ask, almost without thinking: 'Did you play horsey with the children in Gmunden?'

He: 'Yes! (After a moment's thought.) I think that was when the silly nonsense started.'

I: 'Who was the horsey?'

He: 'I was, and Berta was the coachman.'

I: 'Did you ever fall over while you were being the horsey?'

Hans: 'No! When Berta said "Hup!" I ran quickly, sometimes I'd race along.'[17]

I: 'You never played omnibuses?'

Hans: 'No, just ordinary carts and horses without carts. Even if the horse does have a cart it can still go without its cart and the cart can stay at home.'

I: 'Did you often play horsey?'

Hans: 'Yes, a lot. Fritzl (another of the landlord's children, as I have already mentioned) was the horsey once and Franzl was the coachman, and Fritzl ran really fast and then he stepped on a stone and his foot bled.'

I: 'Did he fall over?'

Hans: 'No, he put his foot in some water and then he put a bandage round it.'[18]

I: 'Were you often the horse?'

Hans: 'Oh yes.'

I: 'And that was when the silly nonsense started.'

Hans: 'Because they were always saying, "We'll get the horse", "We'll get the horse"[19] (he emphasizes the word 'we'll') and maybe that was why, because they were always saying "We'll get the horse", maybe that was why the silly business started.'[20]

Hans's father tries other lines of inquiry for a while, but without success.

I: 'Did they talk about the horses at all?'

Hans: 'Yes!'

I: 'What did they say?'

Hans: 'I've forgotten.'

I: 'Did they talk about the horses' widdlers?'

Hans: 'Oh, no!'

I: 'Were you already scared of horses then?

Hans: 'Oh no, I wasn't scared of them at all.'

I: '*Did Berta perhaps say something about the way a horse . . .*'
Hans (*interrupting*): '*does a widdle? No.*'

On 10 April I take up the threads of the previous day's conversation and ask what was meant by 'We'll get the horse'. Hans is
unable to remember, he recalls only that early in the morning several
children stood outside the front door chanting 'We'll get the horse,
we'll get the horse'. He was there too. When I become more insistent,
he explains that they weren't actually saying 'We'll get the horse' at
all, he had misremembered.

I: '*You were all in the stable a lot, too, you must have talked about
the horses then.*' – '*We didn't say anything about them.*' – '*What
did you talk about?*' – '*We didn't talk about anything.*' – '*Even
though there were so many of you, you didn't talk about anything?*'
– '*Well, we did talk a bit, but not about the horses.*' – '*About what,
then?*' – '*I can't remember.*'

I drop the subject, as the resistance is obviously too strong,[21] and
ask: '*Did you like playing with Berta?*'

He: '*Yes, I did, but not with Olga; do you know what Olga did?
Grete in Gmunden once gave me a ball made out of paper and Olga
ripped it up. Berta would never have ripped my ball up. I really
liked playing with Berta.*'

I: '*Did you see what Berta's widdler looks like?*'

He: '*No, but I saw the horse's, because I was always in the stables,
and so I saw the horse's widdler.*'

I: '*And so you were curious to know what Berta's and Mummy's
widdler looked like?*'

He: '*Yes!*'

I remind him that he once complained that the little girls always
wanted to watch when he did a widdle.

He: '*Berta always used to watch (not at all offended, but with
great satisfaction), she did it a lot. You know where the little garden
is, where the radishes are, that was where I used to do a widdle and
she used to stand at the front door and watch me.*'

I: '*And did you watch her when she did a widdle?*'

He: '*She used to use the lavatory.*'

I: '*And were you curious?*'

He: *'I used to go into the lavatory with her.'*

(This is true: the servants told us about it once, and I remember that we told Hans not to do it any more.)

I: *'Did you tell her you wanted to go in with her?'*

He: *'I went on my own and Berta said it was all right. I wasn't being naughty.'*

I: *'And you would have liked to see her widdler.'*

He: *'Yes, but I didn't see it.'*

I remind him of the dream he had about Gmunden: *'Whose is the forfeit I hold in my hand'*, etc., and ask him: *'When you were in Gmunden, did you wish that Berta would help you do a widdle?'*

He: *'I never said so to her.'*

I: *'Why did you never say so to her?'*

He: *'Because I never thought of it. (Interrupting himself.) If I write everything down and send it to the Professor the silly nonsense will soon be over, won't it?'*

I: *'Why did you wish Berta would help you do a widdle?'*

He: *'I don't know. Because she was watching.'*

I: *'Did you think you would like her to touch your widdler?'*

He: *'Yes. (Changing the subject.) It was fun in Gmunden. In the little garden where the radishes are there is a little heap of sand and I played in it with my spade.'*

(This is the garden where he used to do a widdle.)

I: *'When you were lying in bed in Gmunden did you ever touch your widdler then?'*

He: *'No, not then. I slept so well in Gmunden that I never even thought about it. It was only in —— Street,[22] and now.'*

I: *'So Berta never touched your widdler, then?'*

He: *'No, she didn't, because I never asked her to.'*

I: *'When did you wish she would?'*

He: *'Oh, one day in Gmunden.'*

I: *'Just the once?'*

He: *'Quite often.'*

I: *'She always watched when you did a widdle; perhaps she was curious about how you do a widdle.'*

He: *'Perhaps she was curious about what my widdler looked like.'*

I: *'You were curious too; was that just about Berta?'*

He: *'About Berta and about Olga.'*

I: *'And who else?'*

He: *'Nobody else.'*

I: *'That isn't true. About Mummy, too.'*

He: *'Oh yes, about Mummy of course.'*

I: *'But now you're not curious any longer. After all, you know what Hanna's widdler looks like.'*

He: *'It'll get bigger though, won't it?'*[23]

I: *'Of course it will, but when it does, it won't look like yours.'*

He: *'Yes, I know. It'll be like that (he means, as it is at the moment), only bigger.'*

I: *'Did you feel curious in Gmunden when Mummy was undressing?'*

He: *'Yes, and when Hanna had her bath I saw her widdler.'*

I: *'And did you see Mummy's, too?'*

He: *'No!'*

I: *'You thought it was disgusting when you saw Mummy's drawers.'*

He: *'Only when I saw the black ones – when she bought them, I felt sick, but it doesn't make me feel sick when she puts her drawers on or takes them off.* I feel sick because the black drawers are black like plop and the yellow ones are like wee-wee and it makes me want to do a widdle. When Mummy is wearing her drawers I can't see them because her clothes are on top.'*

I: *'What about when she takes her clothes off?'*

He: *'That doesn't make me feel sick. When the drawers are new they look like plop. When they are old the colour fades and they get grubby. When she has just bought them they are all clean but at home they get grubby. When she has just bought them they are new, but when she hasn't just bought them they are old.'*

I: *'So the old ones don't make you feel sick?'*

He: *'When they are old they are much blacker than a plop, aren't they? Well, they're a bit blacker.'*[24]

I: *'Have you often been in the lavatory at the same time as Mummy?'*

He: *'Lots of times.'*

I: *'Did that make you feel sick?'*

He: *'Yes . . . No!'*

I: *'Do you like being there when Mummy is doing a widdle or a plop?'*

He: *'Yes, I do.'*

I: *'Why do you like it so much?'*

He: *'I don't know.'*

I: *'Because you think you'll see Mummy's widdler?'*

He: *'Yes, that too.'*

I: *'Why do you never want to use the lavatory in Lainz?'*

(When we go to Lainz he always begs not to be taken to the lavatory; he was once frightened by the noises which the water makes when it is flushed down.)

He: *'Perhaps because of the racket when you pull the chain.'*

I: *'So you're scared.'*

He: *'Yes!'*

I: *'And what about in our lavatory here?'*

He: *'No, not here. In Lainz I am scared when you flush the lavatory. If I am there when the water is going down that scares me too.'*

So that he can demonstrate that he is not frightened in our apartment he asks me to go into the lavatory and pull the chain. Then he explains:

'At first there is a real racket, and then it gets quieter (when the water is flowing through). When it is making a real racket I'd rather stay in the lavatory, but when it is quieter I would rather go out.'

I: *'Because you're scared?'*

He: *'Because I always like watching (correcting himself), hearing when there is a really loud racket and so I'd rather stay in the lavatory so I can hear it properly.'*

I: *'What does a real racket make you think of?'*

He: *'That I have to do a plop in the lavatory.'* (The same, then, as the black drawers.)

I: *'Why?'*

He: *'I don't know. Yes I do, a real racket is the sort of noise it makes when you do a plop. A real racket reminds me of plop, and when it's quieter it reminds me of wee-wee (cf. the black and yellow drawers).*

I: 'Hans, wasn't the horse that was drawing the stage-coach the same colour as a plop?' (He had told me it was black).

He: (very embarrassed): 'Yes!'

I must put in a few words here. Hans's father asks too many questions and is pursuing his own ideas rather than allowing the boy to express himself freely. In this way the process of analysis becomes opaque and uncertain. Hans goes his own way and does not respond well to any attempt to deflect him. He is clearly preoccupied at present with plop and wee-wee, although we do not know why. The business of the 'racket' is no more satisfactorily cleared up than is the question of the black and yellow drawers. I should imagine that Hans's sharp ears have already picked up the difference in the sound made when a man or a woman is urinating. The analysis has forced the material somewhat artificially into an opposition between the two urges, however. To the reader who has not yet undergone analysis himself, I can only offer the advice that he should not attempt to understand everything straight away, but should give a certain unbiased attention to everything that comes along and wait to see what will happen next.

11 April. In the morning Hans comes into our room and is sent out, as he has been every day recently.

Later he tells me: 'Daddy, I thought something: I am sitting in the bathtub[25] and the ironsmith comes to unscrew it.[26] He gets out a big screwdriver and jabs me in the belly with it.'

Hans's father translates this fantasy as follows.

'I am in bed with Mummy. Then Daddy comes and drives me away. He takes my place with Mummy with his great big penis.'

We will reserve judgement for the time being.

He goes on to tell me a second idea which he has had: 'We're on the train going to Gmunden. At the station we start to get dressed but we aren't ready in time and when the train starts up again we are still on it.'

Later I ask: 'Have you ever seen a horse doing a plop?'

Hans: 'Yes, lots of times.'

I: 'Does it make a real racket when it does a plop?'

Hans: 'Yes it does!'

I: 'What does the racket remind you of?'

Hans: 'It's like plop going into the pot.'

The omnibus horse that collapses, making a racket with its hooves, is thus probably – a plop falling and making a noise. Fear of defecation, fear of heavily laden carts, is in the end just the same as fear of an overfull belly.

In a roundabout way the truth of the matter is gradually dawning on Hans's father.

11 April. At lunchtime Hans says: 'If only we had a bathtub in Gmunden, then I wouldn't have to go to the public baths.' It was the case that in Gmunden he was always taken to the public baths which were situated quite close by, so that he could be bathed in warm water, something he always protested against vigorously and tearfully. In Vienna, too, he always screams when he is made to sit or lie in the big bathtub to be washed. We have to bathe him in a kneeling or standing position.

Hans is now beginning to provide material of his own volition to sustain the analysis; this remark of his furnishes the connection between his last two fantasies (the ironsmith who comes to unscrew the bathtub and the unsuccessful journey to Gmunden). His father had correctly concluded that the latter indicated a reluctance to visit Gmunden. Another useful reminder, incidentally, that we must seek to understand thoughts that surface out of the unconscious not on the basis of what has gone before, but of what follows.

I ask him whether he is scared, and if so, why.

Hans: 'Because I might fall in.'

I: 'But why were you never scared when we bathed you in the little bathtub?'

Hans: 'Well then I was sitting up, I couldn't lie down because it was too small.'

I: 'When you went out in a rowing boat in Gmunden, weren't you scared that you might fall in the water then?'

Hans: *'No, because I held on to the side and then I couldn't fall in. It's only in the big bathtub that I'm scared I might fall in.'*

I: *'It's Mummy who gives you your bath. Are you scared that Mummy might drop you into the water?'*

Hans: *'I'm scared that she'll take her hands away and then my head will go under.'*

I: *'But you know Mummy loves you, she isn't going to take her hands away.'*

Hans: *'Well, I just thought she might.'*

I: *'Why?'*

Hans: *'I don't really know.'*

I: *'Perhaps because you'd been a naughty boy and you thought she didn't love you any more?'*

Hans: *'Yes!'*

I: *'When you watched Mummy giving Hanna her bath, did you ever wish she would let her go so that Hanna would fall in the water?'*

Hans: *'Yes.'*

In our opinion, this was a most accurate guess on Hans's father's part.

12 April. Returning from Lainz in a second-class compartment, Hans sees the black leather upholstery and says: 'Ugh, that makes me want to be sick, I feel sick when I see black drawers and black horses too, because it makes me want to do a plop.'

I: *'Have you perhaps seen something black on Mummy that scared you?'*

Hans: *'Yes!'*

I: *'What was it?'*

Hans: *'I don't know. A black blouse, or black stockings.'*

I: *'Perhaps you saw black hair round her widdler when you felt curious and were watching her.*

Hans: *(apologetically): 'But I didn't see her widdler.'*

When once again he felt scared as a cart drew out of the courtyard gate opposite, I asked: 'Don't you think this gateway looks like a botty?'

He: 'And the horses are the plops!' Since then, whenever he sees a cart driving out, he says: 'Look, here comes a "plop-plop"!' He does not usually employ the form 'plop-plop', which has the ring of an endearment. My sister-in-law always calls her little boy 'Tom-Tom'.

On the 13 April he finds a piece of liver in his soup and says: 'Ugh, a plop.' He is visibly reluctant to eat meat croquettes as well, because of their shape and colour, which remind him of plop.

That evening my wife recounts that Hans had been out on the balcony and had then said to her: 'I thought something, I thought Hanna was out on the balcony and fell.' I had told him on many occasions that he should keep an eye on Hanna when she goes out on to the balcony, in case she gets too close to the railings, which were constructed most unskilfully by an ironsmith of Secessionist bent, with over-large spaces that I have had to have reduced by means of wire mesh. Hans's repressed desire is transparently obvious. His mother asks him if he would prefer it if Hanna were not there, and he replies in the affirmative.

14 April. The subject of Hanna remains very much to the fore. When she was born, as you may recall from my earlier notes, Hans felt a great aversion for this baby who had robbed him of a part of his parents' love; even now this has not entirely disappeared and is only partly overcompensated for by an exaggerated tenderness towards her.[27] He has remarked on many an occasion that the stork is not to bring any more babies and that we should pay him not to bring any more from the big box where he keeps the babies. (Cf. his fear of furniture vans. Doesn't an omnibus look rather like a big box?) He says that Hanna is always crying and that it gets on his nerves.

On one occasion he says suddenly: 'Do you remember when Hanna arrived? She lay in the bed next to Mummy and looked so sweet and good.' (Praise of this kind rings suspiciously false!)

Then we went down to the street door. There is once again great progress to be remarked. Even drays inspire less fear in him. Once he calls out, almost joyfully: 'Here comes a horse with black round its mouth' and I am at last able to ascertain that it is a horse with a leather muzzle. Hans is however not in the least afraid of this horse.

At one point he bangs the pavement with his stick and asks:

'Daddy, is there a man under here . . . someone buried . . . or does that only happen in graveyards?' He is preoccupied, then, not only with the mystery of life, but also that of death.

When we go back in I notice a box standing in the hall and Hans says: 'Hanna went with us to Gmunden in a box like that. Every time we went to Gmunden, she came too, in the box. Don't you believe me this time either? Really, Daddy. You must believe me. We got a big box and there were all these babies inside sitting in the bathtub. (A small bathtub had been packed in the box.) I put them in there, really I did. I remember very well.'[28]

I: 'What do you remember?'

Hans: 'That Hanna travelled in the box, because I haven't forgotten. Word of honour!'

I: 'But last year Hanna travelled in the compartment with you.'

Hans: 'But before that she always came with us in the box.'

I: 'Didn't Mummy have the box?'

Hans: 'Yes, Mummy had it!'

I: 'Where was it?'

Hans: 'At home in the attic.'

I: 'Did she carry it round with her, perhaps?'[29]

Hans: 'Oh, no. When we go to Gmunden this time Hanna will travel in the box again.'

I: 'How did she get out of the box, then?'

Hans: 'She was taken out.'

I: 'By Mummy?'

Hans: 'By me and Mummy, then we got in the carriage and Hanna rode on the horse and the driver said "Gee-up". The driver was up on the box. Were you there too? Even Mummy knows. Mummy doesn't know, she's forgotten all about it, but don't say anything to her!'

I ask him to repeat it all.

Hans: 'Then Hanna got out.'

I: 'But she hadn't even started to walk.'

Hans: 'Well, we reached her down, then.'

I: 'How could she have been sitting on a horse, last year she couldn't even sit up on her own.'

Hans: 'Oh, yes, she sat up and called "Gee-up" and cracked the whip, "Gee-up, gee-up", the whip that used to be mine. The horse didn't have any stirrups and Hanna rode him; I'm not joking, Daddy.'

What can he mean by obstinately repeating such nonsense? Ah, but it is not nonsense, it is parody, it is Hans's revenge on his father. It amounts to saying: *If you really expect me to believe that the stork brought Hanna in October, when I'd already noticed how big Mummy's tummy was in the summer when we went to Gmunden, then I can expect you to believe my pack of lies too.* What else can Hans mean when he asserts that Hanna had already gone with them to Gmunden the previous summer 'in a box', except that he knew about his mother's pregnant state? The fact that he envisages the repetition of this journey in the box in each successive year either corresponds to a common way in which unconscious thoughts from the past come to the surface, or else it has a particular basis and expresses his fear of seeing his mother in the same pregnant state at the time of the next summer journey. We have now also discovered in what sense his journey to Gmunden was spoiled, as his second fantasy indicated.

Later I ask him how Hanna actually got into Mummy's bed at the time of her birth.

This gives him an opportunity to really let go and pull his father's leg.

Hans: *'Well, Hanna just arrived. Frau Kraus (the midwife) put her in Mummy's bed. After all, she couldn't walk. But the stork carried her in his beak. She couldn't walk, after all. (All in one breath.) The stork came up the stairs, as far as the entrance, and then he knocked and everyone was asleep and he had the right key and unlocked the door and put Hanna in your*[30] *bed and Mummy was asleep – no, the stork put her in her bed. It was right in the middle of the night and the stork put her very gently into the bed, no kicking and screaming, and then the stork picked up his hat and went away again. No, he didn't have a hat.'*

I: *'Who picked up his hat? The doctor, perhaps?'*

Hans: *'Then the stork went away, went home, and then he rang the bell and then nobody in the house got any more sleep. But don't tell Mummy and Tinni (the cook). It's a secret!'*

I: *'Are you fond of Hanna?'*

Hans: *'Oh, yes, I'm very fond of her.'*

I: *'Would you rather Hanna had never been born, or are you glad that she was born?'*

Hans: *'I'd rather Hanna had never been born.'*

I: *'Why?'*

Hans: *'At least she wouldn't scream as much as she does and I hate it when she screams.'*

I: *'But you scream yourself.'*

Hans: *'Well Hanna screams too.'*

I: *'Why do you hate it so much?'*

Hans: *'Because she screams so loudly.'*

I: *'But she doesn't scream.'*

Hans: *'If you smack her and she's got a bare bottom, she screams then.'*

I: *'Have you ever smacked her?'*

Hans: *'When Mummy smacks her bottom she screams.'*

I: *'And you don't like that?'*

Hans: *'No . . . Why not? Because she makes such a racket when she screams.'*

I: *'If you'd rather Hanna had never been born, you can't be very fond of her at all.'*

Hans: *'Mmm' (agreeing).*

I: *'That was why you thought that if Mummy let go when she was giving her her bath, she might fall in the water . . .'*

Hans (*finishing the sentence*): *'– and drown.'*

I: *'And you would be all alone with Mummy. And a good boy wouldn't want that to happen.'*

Hans: *'But he's allowed to think it.'*

I: *'It's not a good thing, though.'*

Hans: 'If he does think it, it is a good thing, though, so that we can write and tell the Professor.'[31]

Later I tell him: 'You know, when Hanna gets bigger and is able to talk you will feel much fonder of her.'

Hans: *'No I won't. I am fond of her already. When the autumn comes and she's a big girl I shall take her to the Stadtpark all on my own and I'll explain everything to her.'*

When I embark on further explanations, he interrupts me, probably to explain that it is not so very awful if he wishes Hanna were dead.

Hans: *'Daddy, she'd already been alive a long time, even before she arrived. She was alive and living with the stork.'*

I: *'Well no, perhaps she wasn't living with the stork.'*

Hans: *'Who brought her, then? The stork had her with him.'*

I: *Well, where did he bring her* from?'

Hans: *'From his house.'*

I: *'Where did he keep her, then?'*

Hans: *'In the box, in the* stork-box.'

I: *'And what does the stork-box look like?'*

Hans: *'Red. It's painted red.' (Blood?)*

I: *'Who told you that?'*

Hans: *'Mummy – well I thought it myself – I read it in a book.'*

I: *'Which book is it in?'*

Hans: *'In my picture book.' (I ask him to bring me his first picture book. There is a picture of a stork's nest with little storks on top of a red chimney. There is Hans's box; oddly enough, on the same page there is a picture of a horse being shod. Hans has transferred the babies to the box, since he cannot find them in the nest.)*

I: *'And what did the stork do with her?'*

Hans: *'Then he brought Hanna here. In his beak. You know, the stork from Schönbrunn, the one that bites people's umbrellas?' (Recalling a little incident in Schönbrunn.)*

I: *'Did you see the stork bring Hanna?'*

Hans: *'Daddy, I was still asleep. The stork doesn't bring little baby girls and boys when it's morning.'*

I: *'Why not?'*

Hans: *'He can't. A stork can't do that. Do you know why not? Nobody must see, and then all of a sudden, when morning comes, lo and behold – a baby girl!'* [32]

I: *'But you must have wondered at the time how the stork had done it.'*

Hans: *'Yes, I did.'*

I: *'What did Hanna look like when she arrived?'*

Hans *(insincere)*: 'All sweet and white. Wasn't she lovely!'

I: 'Yet when you saw her for the first time, you didn't like her.'

Hans: 'Oh, I did.'

I: 'You must have been surprised that she was so tiny?'

Hans: 'Yes.'

I: 'How small was she?'

Hans: 'Like a baby stork.'

I: 'And what else? A plop, perhaps?'

Hans: 'Oh no, a plop is much bigger . . . a little bit smaller, yes, just like Hanna.'

I had told Hans's father my prediction that it would be possible to trace the lad's phobia back to the thoughts and wishes provoked by his little sister's birth, but I had omitted to draw his attention to the fact that in terms of a child's theory of sexuality, a baby is a 'plop', so that Hans would go through the experience of the excremental complex. The temporary obscuring of the cure may be ascribed to this negligence on my part. Following my clarification of these matters, Hans's father now attempts to question Hans for a second time on this important point.

The next day I get him to repeat the story he told me yesterday all over again. Hans tells me: 'Hanna went to Gmunden in the big box, and Mummy sat in the compartment and Hanna went in the luggage compartment with the box, and then, when we got to Gmunden, Mummy and I lifted Hanna out and put her up on the horse. The driver was on the box and Hanna had my old whip (the one from last year) and she beat the horse with the whip and said "Gee-up" over and over and it was really funny and the driver used his whip too. The driver didn't use his whip at all because Hanna had the whip. – The driver was holding the reins – Hanna had the reins too (we always had a carriage to take us from the railway station to the house; here Hans is trying to reconcile his fantasy with reality). In Gmunden we lifted Hanna down from the horse and she walked up the steps on her own.' (Last year, when Hanna was in Gmunden, she was 8 months old. The year before, the time to which Hans's fantasy obviously refers, his mother was 5 months into her pregnancy when they arrived in Gmunden.)

I: *'Last year Hanna had already arrived.'*

Hans: *'Last year she travelled in the carriage, but the year before, when she was already with us . . .'*

I: *'Already with us, you say?'*

Hans: *'Yes, you always used to come with me so that we could go in the rowing boat, don't you remember, and Anna was your servant.'*

I: *'But that wasn't last year, Hanna hadn't arrived then.'*

Hans: *'Yes she had arrived then. When she first travelled in the box she could already walk and say "Anna".'* (She has only been able to do this for the last 4 months.)

I: *'But she hadn't arrived to live with us then.'*

Hans: *'Yes she had, she was living with the stork.'*

I: *'How old is Hanna, then?'*

Hans: *'She'll be two in the autumn. Hanna was there, you know she was.'*

I: *'And when was she at the stork's in the stork-box?'*

Hans: *'A long time before she travelled in the box. A long, long time before.'*

I: *'How long has Hanna been able to walk? When she was in Gmunden she hadn't learnt how to walk.'*

Hans: *'Last year she couldn't, but she could the rest of the time.'*

I: *'But Hanna has only been to Gmunden once.'*

Hans: *'No! She's been twice; yes, that's right. I remember very well. Ask Mummy, she'll tell you.'*

I: *'But Hans, that just isn't true.'*

Hans: *'Yes it is. The first time she was in Gmunden she could walk and ride, and then later she had to be carried. – No, she only learnt to ride after that and last year she had to be carried.'*

I: *'But she has only been walking for a little while. She couldn't walk in Gmunden.'*

Hans: *'Yes she could, just write it down. I remember it really well. – Why are you laughing?'*

I: *'Because you're a cheat, because you know perfectly well that Hanna has only been to Gmunden once.'*

Hans: *'No, that's not true. The first time she rode on the horse . . . and the second time (clearly becoming uncertain).'*

I: '*Was the horse Mummy, perhaps?*'

Hans: '*No, it was a real horse, we had a pony and trap.*'

I: '*But we always took a carriage and pair.*'

Hans: '*Well it must have been a cab then.*'

I: '*What did Hanna have to eat in her box?*'

Hans: '*They put bread and butter and herrings and radishes in for her (the sort of supper we used to eat in Gmunden) and while Hanna was travelling she put the butter on her bread and she ate 50 times.*'

I: '*Didn't Hanna scream?*'

Hans: '*No.*'

I: '*What did she do, then?*'

Hans: '*She sat there as good as gold.*'

I: '*Didn't she try to kick?*'

Hans: '*No, she just went on eating and didn't move an inch. She drank two big bowls of coffee, right to the bottom – it was all gone by morning and the rubbish was left in the box, the leaves from the two radishes and a knife to cut the radishes with; she gobbled it all up just like a hare in one minute flat. It was so funny. I even travelled in the box with Hanna, I slept in the box the whole night (two years ago we did indeed travel overnight to Gmunden) and Mummy went in the compartment. We spent the whole time eating, in the carriage as well, we had such fun. – She didn't ride on the horse (he is unsure now, because he knows we were driven in a carriage and pair) . . . she sat in the carriage. That's how it was, but me and Hanna went on our own, Mummy was riding one horse and Karoline (the girl we had the previous year) was on the other . . . Daddy, what I'm telling you now isn't the tiniest bit true.*'

I: '*What isn't true?*'

Hans: '*The whole thing. Daddy, let's put her and me in the box*[33] *and I'll do a widdle in the box. I'll just do a widdle in my trousers, it doesn't bother me, there's nothing wrong with it. Daddy, that's not funny, but it does make me laugh!*'

He then tells me the story of the stork coming, just the same as yesterday except that when he goes away he doesn't take his hat.

I: '*Where did the stork keep the front door key?*'

Hans: *'In his pocket.'*

I: *'Where does a stork have a pocket?'*

Hans: *'In his beak.'*

I: *'He kept the key in his beak? I've never seen a stork with a key in his beak.'*

Hans: *'Well how could he get in otherwise? How does the stork get through the door and come inside? No, it isn't true and I was wrong; the stork rings the doorbell and someone opens the door.'*

I: *'And how does he ring?'*

Hans: *'He presses the bell.'*

I: *'How does he do that?'*

Hans: *'He gets his beak and presses it against the bell.'*

I: *'And does he close the door behind him?'*

Hans: *'No, a maid closes the door. She was already up, so she opens the door and closes it.'*

I: *'Where is the stork's home?'*

Hans: *'Where is it? In the box where he keeps the baby girls. In Schönbrunn, perhaps.'*

I: *'I've never seen a box in Schönbrunn.'*

Hans: *'I expect it's just a bit further away. – Do you know how the stork opens the box? He gets his beak – there's a key to the box, too – he gets his beak and lifts one bit (one half of his beak) up and then he opens it up like this (demonstrates using the lock on my writing-desk). It works as a handle, too.'*

I: *'Isn't a baby girl a bit heavy for him?'*

Hans: *'Oh, no!'*

I: *'Listen, doesn't an omnibus look rather like a stork-box?'*

Hans: *'Yes, it does.'*

I: *'What about a furniture van?'*

Hans: *'And a little monkey cart (referring to a colloquial word for naughty children) does too.'*

17 April. Yesterday Hans fulfilled his long-held intention of going into the courtyard across the road from our house. Today he would not go, because there was a cart at the loading ramp right opposite the entrance gates. He told me: *'When there is a cart there I'm afraid*

I'll rag the horses *and they'll collapse and make a racket with their feet.'*

I: *'How do you rag horses?'*

Hans: *'You rag them when you shout at them and yell "Hup! Hup!"'* [34]

I: *'And have you ragged horses?'*

Hans: *'Oh yes, lots of times. Actually I'm afraid I'll do it, but I don't really.'*

I: *'Did you used to rag horses in Gmunden?'*

Hans: *'No!'*

I: *'But you like ragging horses?'*

Hans: *'Yes, I love it!'*

I: *'Would you like to whip them, too?'*

Hans: *'Yes, I would!'*

I: *'Would you like to beat the horses the way Mummy smacks Hanna? You like that too.'*

Hans: *'Beating the horses doesn't hurt them.* (This is what I once told him, to calm his fear of horses being whipped.) *I did it myself once, really I did. I was once holding a whip and I whipped the horse and it collapsed and made a racket with its feet.'*

I: *'When was this?'*

Hans: *'In Gmunden.'*

I: *'A real horse? Harnessed to a carriage?'*

Hans: *'It wasn't in harness.'*

I: *'Where was it then?'*

Hans: *'I was holding it so it wouldn't run away.'* (This all sounded somewhat improbable, of course.)

I: *'And where was this?'*

Hans: *'By the water fountain.'*

I: *'Who let you? Had the driver left it there?'*

Hans: *'It was just a horse from the stables.'*

I: *'How had it got to the water fountain?'*

Hans: *'I led it there.'*

I: *'Where from? From the stables?'*

Hans: *'I led it out because I wanted to whip it.'*

I: *'Wasn't anybody in the stables?'*

Hans: *'Oh, yes, Loisl was there (the driver from Gmunden).'*

I: *'And did he say you could?'*

Hans: *'I talked to him nicely and he said I could.'*

I: *'What did you say to him?'*

Hans: *'I asked if I could take the horse out and whip it and yell at it. He said I could.'*

I: *'Did you whip it a lot?'*

Hans: 'What I'm telling you isn't true.'

I: *'How much of it is true?'*

Hans: *'None of it's true, I just said it for fun.'*

I: *'So you never led a horse out of the stables?'*

Hans: *'Oh, no!'*

I: *'You'd like to have done, though.'*

Hans: *'I'd like to have done; I've thought about doing it.'*

I: *'In Gmunden?'*

Hans: *'No, only after we came home. I thought about it in the mornings, when I'd got dressed; no, first thing, when I was still in bed.'*

I: *'Why didn't you ever tell me this?'*

Hans: *'I didn't think to.'*

I: *'You thought about it because you were watching the street.'*

Hans: *'Yes.'*

I: *'Who would you really like to beat: Mummy, Hanna, or me?'*

Hans: *'Mummy.'*

I: *'Why?'*

Hans: *'I'd just like to beat her.'*

I: *'When have you seen anyone hit a Mummy?'*

Hans: *'I've never seen anyone do it, never ever.'*

I: *'And yet you'd like to do it. How would you like to do it?'*

Hans: *'With the carpet beater.' (His Mummy has often threatened him with the carpet beater.)*

I had to break off our conversation at that point.

In the street Hans explained to me that omnibuses, furniture vans and coal carts were all stork-box carts.

Pregnant women, then. Hans's fit of sadism immediately before this cannot be unconnected with our subject.

°

21 April. This morning Hans tells me of a thought he had had: 'There was a train in Lainz and I took the train to the Central Customs House station with Lainz Grandmama. You hadn't come down from the bridge yet and the next train was already in St Veit. By the time you came down the train was already there and we got in.'

(Yesterday Hans was in Lainz. To reach the platform you have to cross a bridge. From the platform you can see along the railway track as far as the station at St Veit. The whole thing is rather unclear. Originally Hans presumably thought that he had gone on the first train, the one I missed, then, when a second train arrives from Unter-St Veit, that I had followed on that one. He has distorted a part of this runaway fantasy, so that in the end he can say: 'We both went on the second train, in fact.'

This fantasy is related to the previous one, which remained uninterpreted, where we had taken too long to put our clothes on in the train at Gmunden and the train had drawn out of the station before we could get off.)

In the afternoon, outside the house. Hans suddenly runs into the house when a carriage and pair comes along, but I can detect nothing out of the ordinary about it. I ask him what is the matter. He says: 'I'm scared because the horses look so proud that they are going to collapse.' (The horses were being held on a tight rein by the driver, so that they were trotting along with their heads held high – they did indeed have a proud look about them.)

I ask him who might be proud like that.

He: *'You are, when I come into bed with Mummy.'*

I: *'So you wish I would collapse, do you?'*

He: *'Yes, you ought to be bare (he means barefoot, as Fritzl was) and catch your foot on a stone and then it would bleed and then at least I could be on my own with Mummy for just a little while. When you come up to our apartment I can run away from Mummy quickly so that you don't see me.'*

I: *'Do you remember who it was who caught their foot on a stone?'*

He: *'Yes, Fritzl.'*

I: *'When Fritzl fell over, what went through your mind?'*[35]

He: *'That you ought to hit a stone and go flying.'*

I: *'You'd like to be with Mummy, then, would you?'*

He: *'Yes, I would!'*

I: *'Why do I tell you off, then?'*

He: *'I don't know.' (!!)*

I: *'Why, Hans?'*

He: *'Because you're jealous.'*

I: *'That just isn't true!'*

He: *'Yes it is true, you're jealous, I know you are. It must be true.'*

My explanation that only little boys get into bed with Mummy, and big ones sleep in their own beds, had obviously not impressed him greatly.

I suspect that the wish to 'rag' the horse, that is, to beat and yell at it, is not directed at his mummy, as he told me, but at me. He probably only put his mother in the front line because he did not wish to admit the other possibility to me. In recent days he has been particularly affectionate towards me.

With the superiority of 'hindsight', so easily acquired, let us point out to his father that Hans's desire to 'rag' the horse is double-edged, composed of obscure, sadistic desires towards his mother and a clear urge to revenge himself on his father. It was only possible to reproduce the latter once the former had been allowed to come to the fore in the context of the pregnancy complex. When unconscious thoughts come together to form a phobia a kind of compression takes place; for this reason the analytical route can never reproduce the developmental path taken by the neurosis.

22 April. This morning Hans thought something else: 'A street urchin was travelling on the little truck and the guard came and took all the boy's clothes off and made him stand there until morning, and in the morning the boy gave the guard 50,000 gulden so that he would let him go on the little truck.'

(The Northern Line runs over the way from our apartment. There is a trolley standing in a siding, and Hans once saw a street urchin riding on it, and wanted to do the same thing. I told him that it was not allowed, and that the guard would come if he did. A second element in the fantasy is the repressed desire for nudity.)

For some time now it has been apparent that Hans's fantasy is working under the aegis of traffic systems and has progressed logically from horse-drawn transport to the railway. And thus in time all his street phobias are augmented by a fear of the railway.

At lunch time I hear that Hans has spent the whole morning playing with a rubber doll which he calls Grete. Using the hole which at one time held the tiny tin squeaker, he had pushed in a small penknife and then held the doll's feet to rip the legs apart so that the knife could fall out again. To his nursery-maid he remarked, pointing up between the doll's legs: 'Look, there's her widdler!'

I: *'What game have you been playing with your doll this morning, then?'*

He: *'I held its feet and ripped its legs apart, do you know why? Because there was a little knife inside, one of Mummy's. I put it in the doll where the little button squeaks and then I ripped the legs apart and it came out here.'*

I: *'Why did you rip its legs apart? So that you could see its widdler?'*

He: *'It was there in the first place, so I could see it anyway.'*

I: *'Why did you put the knife inside?'*

He: *'I don't know.'*

I: *'What does the little knife look like?'*

He brings it to show me.

I: *'Did you imagine that it was a baby, perhaps?'*

He: *'No, I didn't imagine anything at all, but it seems to me the stork once had a baby – or someone did.'*

I: *'When?'*

He: *'Once upon a time. That's what I heard, or perhaps I didn't hear, or perhaps it was a slip of the tongue.'*

I: *'What do you mean, a slip of the tongue?'*

He: *'Well, it's not true.'*

I: *'Everything we say is a little bit true.'*

He: *'Well, yes, a little bit.'*

I *(moving on to another subject)*: *'How do you imagine that chickens come into the world?'*

He: *'Well the stork grows them, the stork grows the chickens – no, the good Lord does.'*

I explain to him that chickens lay eggs and new chickens come out of the eggs.

Hans laughs.

I: *'Why are you laughing?'*

He: *'Because I like the idea of what you're telling me.'*

He says that he has already seen it happen.

I: *'Where was that?'*

He: *'You did it!'*

I: *'Where did I lay an egg?'*

He: *'In Gmunden, you laid an egg in the grass and all of a sudden a chicken popped out. You once laid an egg. I know that, I know as sure as anything. Because Mummy told me.'*

I: *'I'm going to ask Mummy if that's true.'*

Hans: *'It isn't true at all, but I once laid an egg and a chicken popped out.'*

I: *'Where?'*

He: *'In Gmunden I lay down in the grass, no, I knelt down and the other children didn't even look at me and all at once one morning I said: Everyone, listen, yesterday I laid an egg. Let's all look for it! And all at once they looked and all at once they saw an egg and out popped a little Hans. Why are you laughing? Mummy doesn't know and Karoline doesn't know because no one was looking and all at once I laid an egg and all at once it was there. Honestly. Daddy, when does a chicken grow out of the egg? When you leave it alone? Do you have to eat it?'*

I explain to him.

Hans: *'Well then, let's leave it with the hen, then the chicken will grow. Then we'll pack it in the big box and send it to Gmunden.'*

With a single bold stroke Hans has seized control of the analysis, since his parents are still reluctant to offer him the enlightenment to which he has long been entitled, and in a brilliant symptomatic action he informs them: *'You see, this is how I imagine birth to be.'* He was less than candid in the way he explained his game with the doll to the maidservant; to his father, on the other hand, he is direct in denying that he merely wanted to see the doll's widdler. When, by way of partial recompense, his father tells him how chickens come out of eggs, his dissatisfaction, together with mistrust and a sense of his own superior understanding, combine to produce this marvellous pastiche, culminating in a clear reference to the birth of his sister.

I: *'What game did you play with your doll?'*

Hans: *'I said Grete to her.'*

I: *'Why did you do that?'*

Hans: *'Because I said Grete to her.'*

I: *'What sort of game did you play?'*

Hans: *'I looked after her as if she was a real baby.'*

I: *'Would you like to have a baby girl?'*

Hans: *'Oh yes, I would. Why not? I'd like to have one, but Mummy mustn't have one, I don't want her to.'*

(He has often expressed himself in similar terms. He fears that with a third child he would draw an even shorter straw.)

I: *'But only women can have babies.'*

Hans: *'I'm having a baby girl.'*

I: *'Where will you get her from?'*

Hans: *'From the stork, of course.* He'll get the baby girl out, *and all of a sudden the baby girl will lay an egg and out of the egg will come another little Hanna, and another Hanna. And out of Hanna there will come another Hanna. No, just one Hanna will come out.'*

I: *'You'd like to have a baby girl, then.'*

Hans: 'Yes, I'm going to have one next year, *and she'll be called Hanna too.'*

I: *'Why shouldn't Mummy have a baby girl?'*

Hans: *'Because I want to have a baby girl one day.'*

I: *'But you can't have a baby girl.'*

Hans: 'Oh yes I can, boys have baby girls and girls have baby boys.'[36]

I: *'Boys can't have children. Only women – mummies – can have children.'*

Hans: *'Why can't I?'*

I: *'Because that's the way the good Lord has arranged things.'*

Hans: *'Why can't you have a baby, then? I'm sure you will in the end, you've just got to wait.'*

I: *'I'll wait a long time, then.'*

Hans: *'I belong to you, though.'*

I: *'But Mummy brought you into the world. So you belong to Mummy and me.'*

Hans: *'Does Hanna belong to me or to Mummy?'*

I: *'To Mummy.'*

Hans: 'No, to me. Why can't she belong to me and to Mummy?'

I: *'Hanna belongs to me, to Mummy and to you.'*

Hans: *'There you are, you see!'*

Obviously, as far as his understanding of sexual relations is concerned the child is missing an essential piece of information as long as he remains in ignorance of the female genitals.

On 24 April my wife and I enlighten Hans up to a point by explaining that babies grow inside the mummy and then are brought into the world like a 'plop' by pushing them out, and that this causes great pain. In the afternoon we go out in the street. He is clearly much relieved, running after carts and carriages, and his residual anxiety is betrayed only by the fact that he does not dare to venture far away from the main entrance, and cannot be persuaded to go for a longer walk at all.

On 25 April Hans charges me in the stomach, head down, something he did once before. I ask him if he is a goat.

He says: 'Yes, a ramb (ram).' *I ask him where he has seen a ram.*

He: 'In Gmunden, Fritzl had one.' *(Fritzl had had a real baby lamb as a pet.)*

I: *'Tell me about the lamb, what did it do?'*

Hans: 'Well, do you know, Fräulein Mizzi (a teacher who lived in the house) was always putting Hanna on the lamb's back, but it couldn't stand up when she did and it couldn't butt anyone. If you went up to it it used to butt you, because it had horns. Fritzl used to lead it on a piece of rope and tie it up to a tree. He always used to tie it up to a tree.'

I: *'Did the lamb butt you too?'*

Hans: 'It used to jump up at me, Fritzl once made me go up to it . . . I went up to it once, I didn't know, and all of a sudden it jumped up at me. It was ever so funny – I wasn't a bit frightened.'

This is most certainly not true.

I: 'Do you love your Daddy?'

Hans: 'Oh, yes.'

I: 'But perhaps sometimes you don't?'

Hans (*playing with a toy horse. Just then the horse falls over. He yells*): 'The horse has collapsed! Look what a racket it's making!'

I: 'One thing about Daddy that makes you cross is that Mummy loves him.'

Hans: 'No.'

I: 'Why do you always cry, then, when Mummy gives me a kiss? Because you're jealous.'

Hans: 'Yes, I know.'

I: 'So what would you like to do, if you were the Daddy?'

Hans: 'And you were Hans? – I'd like to take you to Lainz every Sunday, no, every day of the week. If I were the Daddy, I'd be ever so good.'

I: 'What would you like to do with Mummy?'

Hans: 'I'd take her to Lainz too.'

I: 'And what else?'

Hans: 'Nothing.'

I: 'Why are you jealous, then?'

Hans: 'I don't know.'

I: 'Were you jealous in Gmunden, too?'

Hans: 'Not in Gmunden (*this is not true*). In Gmunden I had my things with me, there was a garden I could play in, in Gmunden, and children to play with.'

I: 'Can you remember how the cow got her little calf?'

Hans: 'Yes, I can. It came in a little cart (– *no doubt he was told this at the time, in Gmunden; a further contradiction of the stork-theory –*) and another cow pushed it out of her bottom.' (*The first fruits of enlightenment, which Hans strives to bring into line with his 'cart theory'.*)

I: 'But it isn't true that it came in a cart, is it? It came out of the cow that was in the cowshed.'

Hans disagrees, and says that he saw the cart in the early morning. I point out that he was probably told that the calf came in a cart. In the end he agrees: 'Probably Berta told me, or – no, perhaps the landlord told me. He was there, and it was night-time and so it's true, what I told you, or no – I think perhaps no one told me anything, I thought it myself in the night.'

The calf, if I am not mistaken, was taken away in a cart; hence the confusion.

I: *'Why did you not think that the stork had brought it?'*

Hans: *'I didn't want to think that.'*

I: *But you did think that the stork had brought Hanna?'*

Hans: *'First thing in the morning (on the day of my wife's confinement), that's what I thought.'*

Daddy, was Herr Reisenbichler (the landlord) there when the calf came out of the cow?'[37]

I: *'I don't know. Do you think he was?'*

Hans: *'Yes, I think so ... Daddy, have you noticed how quite often horses have something black round their mouths?'*

I: *'I have quite often noticed it on the street in Gmunden.'*[38]

I: *'Did you often come into Mummy's bed when you were in Gmunden?'*

Hans: *'Yes.'*

I: *'And then you thought you were Daddy?'*

Hans: *'Yes.'*

I: *'And then you were frightened of Daddy?'*

Hans: 'You know it all, I didn't know any of that.'

I: *'When Fritzl fell over, you thought, if only Daddy would fall over like that, and when the lamb butted you, you thought, I wish it would butt Daddy. Do you remember the funeral in Gmunden?'* *(The first funeral Hans had ever seen. He often recalls it, no doubt because it is a cover-memory [*Deckerinnerung*].)*

Hans: *'Yes, what about it?'*

I: *'Perhaps you thought that if Daddy were to die you could be Daddy instead.'*

Hans: *'Yes.'*

I: *'Which carts and carriages still make you feel scared?'*

Hans: *'All of them.'*

I: *'That isn't true, is it?'*

Hans: *'Not a cab, or a pony and trap. Omnibuses and luggage carts, but only when they're loaded up, not when they're empty. When there's one horse and the cart is loaded up, I'm scared, but when there are two and it's loaded up, I'm not.'*

I: *'Do omnibuses scare you because there are so many people inside?'*

Hans: *'No, because there is so much luggage on the roof.'*

I: *'Mummy was loaded up too, wasn't she, just before she had Hanna?'*

Hans: *'Mummy will be loaded up again, when she has another baby, when another one grows, when there's another one inside her.'*

I: *'You'd like that, wouldn't you?'*

Hans: *'Yes.'*

I: *'You said you didn't want Mummy to have another baby.'*

Hans: *'Then she won't be loaded up any more. Mummy said, if Mummy doesn't want another baby, then the good Lord won't want her to have one either. If Mummy doesn't want one, she won't have one.'* (Of course, Hans also asked yesterday if Mummy still has babies inside her. I said no, if the good Lord doesn't want babies to grow inside her, they won't.)

Hans: *'But Mummy said, babies won't grow if she doesn't want them to, and you're saying it's if the good Lord doesn't want them to.'*

I told him that it is as I said, to which he replied: *'Were you there too? Then you must know better than me.'* And so he took his mother to task and she resolved the matter by explaining that if she didn't want a baby, the good Lord would not want one either.[39]

I: *'I think you do wish Mummy would have another baby after all.'*

Hans: *'But I don't really want it to happen.'*

I: *'But you can still wish.'*

Hans: *'Wish, yes.'*

I: *'Do you know why it's something you wish? Because you'd like to be the Daddy.'*

Hans: *'Yes . . . How does it go?'*

I: *'How does what go?'*

Hans: *'Daddies can't have babies, so how does it go if I'd like to be the Daddy?'*

I: *'You'd like to be the Daddy and be married to Mummy, you'd like to be as tall as me and have a moustache and you'd like Mummy to have another baby.'*

Hans: *'And when I get married, Daddy, I'll only have a baby if I want to, when I'm married to Mummy, and if I don't want to have a baby, the good Lord won't want me to either, when I'm married.'*

I: *'Would you like to be married to Mummy?'*

Hans: *'Oh yes.'*

It is evident that Hans's pleasure in his fantasy is still marred by uncertainty as to what role the father plays and doubts as to whether he would have any control over whether he had a baby or not.

That same day in the evening, as he is being put to bed, Hans says to me: 'Daddy, do you know what I'm going to do now? I'm going to talk to Grete until 10 o'clock, because she's here in bed with me. I always have my children in bed with me. Can you tell me why that is?' As he is already very drowsy I promise him that we will write this down in the morning, and he goes to sleep.

My previous notes show that ever since his return from Gmunden Hans has been fantasizing continually about his 'children', holding conversations with them, etc.[40]

And so on 26 April I ask him why he always talks about his children.

Hans: *'Why? Because I'd so like to have children, but I'd never wish for any, I shouldn't like to have any'.*[41]

I: *'Have you always imagined Berta, Olga and the rest to be your children?'*

Hans: *'Yes, and Franzl and Fritzl and Paul (his playmate in Lainz), and Lodi too.' A made-up name. His favourite child, the one he talks about most often. – I must emphasize here that the character of Lodi has existed for more than just a few days, since before the day we last tried to explain things to Hans (24 April).*

I: *'Who is Lodi? Is she in Gmunden?'*

Hans: *'No.'*

I: *'Does Lodi really exist?'*

Hans: *'Yes, I know her.'*

I: *'Who is she, then?'*

Hans: *'My Lodi, this one here.'*

I: *'What does she look like?'*

Hans: *'Look like? Black eyes, black hair . . . I met her once with Mariedl (in Gmunden) when I went into town.'*

When I ask for details, it turns out that the episode is invented.[42]

I: *'So you thought you were the Mummy, did you?'*

Hans: *'I really was the Mummy.'*

I: *'What did you do with your children?'*

Hans: *'I let them all sleep with me, the girls and the boys.'*

I: *'Every day?'*

Hans: *'Yes, of course.'*

I: *'Did you talk to them?'*

Hans: *'If the children didn't all fit in the bed I put some on the sofa and some in the pram, if there were any left over I took them up to the attic and put them in the box, but there were still children left over and I put them in the other box.'*

I: *'So the stork-boxes with the children in were up in the attic?'*

Hans: *'Yes.'*

I: *'When did you have your babies? Was Hanna already born then?'*

Hans: *'Yes, she'd been born for ages.'*

I: *'But who did you think you had got your babies from?*

Hans: *'From me, of course.'*[43]

I: *'But at the time you didn't even know that babies come from inside people.'*

Hans: *'I thought the stork had brought them.'* (A palpable lie, to sidestep the question.)[44]

I: *'Yesterday Grete was with you, but you know that boys can't have babies, don't you.'*

Hans: *'Well yes, but I think they can anyway.'*

I: *'What made you think of the name Lodi? That isn't a girl's name. Do you mean Lotti, perhaps?'*

Hans: *'No, it's Lodi. I don't know, I just think it's a nice name.'*

I: *(jokingly)*: *'Are you thinking of choccy-lodi, perhaps?'*

Hans (responding immediately): 'No, of Saffalodi[45] . . . *because I like sausages so much, and salami.'*

I: *'Don't you think Saffalodi looks a bit like a plop?'*

Hans: *'Yes!'*

I: *'What does a plop look like, then?'*

Hans: *'It's black. You know (pointing to my eyebrows and moustache), like that – and that.'*

I: *'And what else? Is it round like a Saffaladi?'*

Hans: *'Yes.'*

I: *'When you were sitting on the pot and you had to do a plop, did you think that you were going to have a baby?'*

Hans *(laughing): 'Yes, when we lived in —— Street, and here, too.'*

I: *'You know when the omnibus horses collapsed? The carriage looked like a baby-box, and when the black horse collapsed, it was like . . .'*

Hans *(completing the sentence): 'Like when a baby is born.'*

I: *'And what did it remind you of when it was making a racket with its hooves?'*

Hans: *'Well, when I don't want to sit on the pot and would rather play, I make a racket like that with my feet.' (He stamps his feet.)*

That is why he is so interested in whether people like *having babies or not.*

Today Hans has been playing 'packing cases' all day, loading them on and off carts, and says he would like to have a toy handcart with boxes like that. When we visited the courtyard of the Customs House over the way he used to be particularly interested in watching carts being loaded and unloaded. And it would scare him most when a cart had been loaded up and was about to drive off. 'The horses will collapse.'[46] *He used to call the doors of the Customs House outbuildings its 'holes' (first hole, second hole, third hole). Now he calls them 'poo holes'.*

His anxiety has almost completely disappeared, but he likes to remain in the vicinity of the house so that he can retreat if he gets frightened. However, he no longer bolts into the house itself and always remains outside. As you know, his state of illness began when he turned back in tears halfway through a walk, and then when he was forced to go out for a walk on a subsequent occasion he would only go as far as the Central Customs House station, from which it is still possible to see our house. During my wife's confinement he was of course separated from her, and his present anxiety, which prevents him from venturing beyond the vicinity of the house, is still a way of expressing the yearning he felt at that time.

30 April. Hans is again playing with his imaginary children, and so I say to him: 'How can your children still be alive? After all, you know that a boy can't have children.'

Hans: *'I know that. Before I was the Mummy,* but now I'm the Daddy.'

I: *'And who is the children's Mummy?'*

Hans: *'Mummy, of course, and you're their* Grandpa.'

I: *'I see, you'd like to be as tall as me, married to Mummy, and then she would have children.'*

Hans: *'Yes, I would like that; and Lainz Grandmama (my mother) could be the grandma.'*

All's well that ends well. Our young Oedipus has found a happier solution than that prescribed by Fate. Instead of eliminating his father, he bestows upon him the same good fortune that he desires for himself; he instates him as grandfather, and marries him to his own mother, too.

On 1 May Hans comes to me at lunchtime and says: 'D'you know what, Daddy? Let's write something down for the Professor.'

I: *'And what's that?'*

Hans: *'This morning I took all my children to the lavatory. First of all I did a plop and a widdle and they watched me. Then I sat them on the lavatory and they did a widdle and a plop and then I wiped their bottoms with paper. Do you know why I did that? Because I'd so much like to have children and I'd do everything for them, I'd take them to the lavatory and wipe their bottoms and do all the things you have to do for children.'*

When Hans admits to such a fantasy it would hardly be appropriate to deny the pleasure that for him is bound up with the excretory functions.

That afternoon, for the first time, he plucks up courage to go to the Stadtpark. As it is the first of May there are probably fewer carriages than usual, but enough, nevertheless, of the kind that up until now have always deterred him. He is very proud of his achievement and after tea I have to go to the Stadtpark with him once again. On the way we encounter an omnibus which he points out with the words: 'Look, a stork-box carriage!' If he will go with me to the Stadtpark again tomorrow morning, as we have planned, then we can probably say that he has made a full recovery.

On the morning of 2 May Hans comes to find me: 'Daddy, I thought something today.' At first he forgets what it was; later, although with considerable resistance, he tells me: 'The plumber came and he had a pair of pliers and first of all he took my bottom away and gave me a new one and then my widdler. He said "Let's see your bottom" and I had to turn round and he took it away and then he said "Let's see your widdler".'

Hans's father immediately grasps the nature of this wish-fantasy and feels not a flicker of doubt as to the only acceptable interpretation.

I: *'He gave you a* bigger *widdler and a* bigger *bottom.'*

Hans: *'Yes.'*

I: *'Like Daddy's, because you'd like to be the Daddy yourself?'*

Hans: *'Yes, and I'd like to have a moustache like yours, too, and hair like that.'* (Pointing to the hair on my chest.)

My interpretation of the fantasy that Hans related some time ago – the plumber came to unscrew the bath and then stuck a gimlet into my belly – therefore requires some correction: the big bathtub stands for the 'bottom', the gimlet or screwdriver, as I suggested at the time, for the widdler.[47] They are identical fantasies. This provides us with a new angle on Hans's fear of the big bathtub, too, which has, incidentally, also already diminished. He dislikes the fact that his 'bottom' is too small for the big tub.

Over the next few days it is Hans's mother's turn to put pen to paper, recording her delight at her boy's recovery.

°

A week later, I receive a final instalment from Hans's father:

Esteemed Professor Freud,

Permit me to amplify my account of Hans's illness with the following remarks:

1. After my first attempts to enlighten Hans the remission of his symptoms was not as great as I may perhaps have implied. It is true that Hans would accompany me on a walk, but only if he was made to, and even then he was extremely fearful. On one occasion he went with me as far as the Central Customs House station, from where you can still see our apartment, and refused to go any further.

2. Re: raspberry juice, gun. Hans is given raspberry juice when he is constipated. He frequently confuses the two words 'shot' and 'shit'.

3. When Hans was moved out of our bedroom into his own room he was about 4 years old.

4. There is still a residual uncertainty, which he expresses not through fear but in the normal urge to ask questions. His questions mostly concern such matters as what things are made of (trams, machines, etc.) and who makes things, etc. It is characteristic of most of his questions that Hans asks them even though he already knows the answer. He just wants to make doubly sure. Once, when he had thoroughly worn me out with questions I said to him: 'Do you think I know the answer to every question you ask me?' to which he replied: 'Well, I thought, since you knew all about that business with the horses, you'd know the answer to this, too.'

5. Hans now only refers to his illness as an historical event: 'Back then, when I had the silly nonsense.'

6. What remains unresolved is that Hans is racking his brains to discover what fathers have to do with children, since it is mothers who bring children into the world. This is the conclusion to be drawn from such questions as 'I belong to you too, don't I?' (He means, not just to his mother.) In what way he belongs to me is not clear to him. On the other hand, I have no direct proof that he might have observed parental coition, as you suggest.

7. In treating this subject it might be necessary to draw attention to the intensity of Hans's anxiety, as otherwise the reader might remark: *'If they had just given him a good spanking he would have gone for a walk soon enough.'*

In conclusion, I would add: his last fantasies show that Hans has also overcome the anxiety that arises from the castration complex, and given a heartening turn to his terrible expectations. The doctor, plumber, etc. does indeed come and take his penis away, but only in order to give him a bigger one instead. Let us hope that our young researcher happens early upon the discovery that all knowledge is piecemeal, and that at every stage something remains unresolved.

Notes

1. Verbal, and indeed actual caressing of the child's genitals on the part of affectionate relatives, and sometimes by the parents themselves, are among the most common events related in psychoanalysis.

2. To be frank, we regard that feeling of anxious longing as a pathological anxiety from the moment it can no longer be relieved by supplying the longed-for object.

3. About the reason for his anxiety; nothing as yet about the female widdler.

4. Viennese suburb [just beyond Schönbrunn], where Hans's grandparents live.

5. Hans's father had no reason to doubt that the boy was describing something that genuinely took place. – Itching sensations on the glans, which lead children to touch themselves, are, incidentally, commonly described with the words: Something has *bitten* me.

6. [In pre-1924 editions the wording here was 'resisting the habit of masturbation'.]

7. Grete is one of the Gmunden girls, whom Hans fantasizes about at the moment: he talks to her and plays with her.

8. This is not true. Compare his exclamation in front of the lion's cage, p. 5. Probably forgetfulness setting in as a result of repression.

9. I cannot interrupt the course of my narrative further, in order to demonstrate how far the unconscious trains of thought that I attribute here to little Hans are typical in their nature. The castration complex is the deepest unconscious root of anti-Semitism, for even in the nursery boys hear that Jews have something cut off their penis – a bit of the penis, they suppose – and this gives them the right to despise the Jews. Likewise, there is no stronger unconscious root to men's superiority over women. Weininger, that highly gifted and sexually disturbed young philosopher, who after writing his remarkable book *Geschlecht und Charakter* [*Gender and Character*] ended his own life by committing suicide, referred, in a chapter of his book that was much remarked upon, to Jews and women with the same hostility and heaped abuse on both in exactly the same terms. A neurotic individual, Weininger was entirely ruled by infantile complexes, thus in his view the characteristic shared by Jews and women is their relation to the castration complex.

10. Hans tells us quite clearly in his own language that this was a fantasy.

11. Unsure how to proceed, Hans's father here uses the classic technique of psychoanalysis. This does not get him very far, but what Hans does say proves to have a meaning in the light of subsequent disclosures.

12. Hans only confirms the interpretation of the two giraffes as father and mother, not the sexual symbolism according to which the giraffe itself represents the penis. This symbolism is probably correct, but one really cannot expect more of Hans.

13. The lad later repeated this reaction to his father more clearly and more completely by first hitting his father's hand and then giving that same hand a tender kiss.

14. Hans is right, however improbable this combination might seem. The connection, as we shall see, is namely, that the horse (the father) will bite him because of his desire that it (the father) should collapse.

15. [*Translator's note*: This is not an editorial explanation. Freud himself used square brackets here, to indicate a parenthesis within the parenthesis.]

16. A few weeks ago my wife acquired a pair of black drawers (of a design promoting natural movement) to wear on cycling tours.

17. He also had a pretend harness with little bells on. [*Father's comment*.]

18. More on this later. The father is quite right in supposing that Fritzl fell over.

19. [*Translator's note*: The German phrase is *wegen dem Pferde*, literally 'because of the horse'. Freud points out in note 20 that there is an aural connection between the word *wegen* and the Austrian pronunciation of the word for cart or carriage; I have tried to approximate to this with a play on 'we'll' and 'wheel'.]

20. A word of clarification: Hans does not mean that the silly nonsense started *at that time*, but *in that connection*. For it must surely be the case – according to the theory – that only something that was once a matter of great desire can be the object of a present phobia. And I would add – for this is something the boy cannot know himself – that it was the little word *wegen* that opened up the possibility of extending his phobia from the horse on to the cart (a word that Hans is used to pronouncing and hearing pronounced as *Wägen*). We must never lose sight of the fact that children treat words much more concretely than adults do and consequently find great significance in words that sound the same.

21. There is nothing to be gained from it in fact except the verbal link that eludes Hans's father. A good example of the conditions under which the analytical endeavour comes to nothing.

22. In the previous apartment, before the family moved house.

23. He is asking for reassurance that his own widdler will get bigger.

24. Hans is struggling here with a topic for which he cannot find the words, and it is difficult to know what he means. Perhaps he is saying that the drawers only awaken the memory of disgust when he sees them as a separate object; as soon as they are on his mother's body he no longer connects them with plop or wee-wee, now they interest him for a different reason.

25. Hans's mother gives him his bath. [*Father's note.*]

26. To take it away for repair. [*Father's note.*]

27. When we find the subject of Hanna following on directly from the subject of 'plop', the reason for this finally becomes clear. Hanna herself is a 'plop', babies are 'plops'!

28. He is now beginning to fantasize. We discover that box and bathtub mean the same to him and are representations of the space in which babies are to be found. Notice his repeated protestations!

29. The box is of course the womb. Hans's father wants him to know that he understands this. This is also the meaning of the chests in which the heroes of mythology are abandoned, from King Sargon of Agade onwards. – [*Note added in 1923:*] Cf. the study by Rank, *Der Mythus von der Geburt des Helden* [*The Myth of the Hero's Birth*] 1909 (2nd edition 1922).

30. Hans is obviously making fun of his father! Just as when he later begs his father not to betray the secret to his mother.

31. Bravo, little Hans! I could not hope for a better understanding of psychoanalysis from an adult.

32. We should not be unduly concerned by Hans's lack of consistency. In the previous conversation his doubts about the stork emerged from his unconscious mind linked with feelings of bitterness about his father's secretiveness. Now he is calmer he responds with the official answers, in which he has fashioned explanations for himself of the many difficulties raised by the stork hypothesis.

33. The box where we put anything we want to take to Gmunden, which stands in the hall. [*Father's note.*]

34. It often used to terrify him when drivers struck their horses and yelled 'Hup'.

35. Fritzl did indeed fall over, then, although earlier he [Hans] denied this.

36. Another fragment of infantile sexual theory whose meaning can only be guessed at.

37. Here Hans, who has every reason to feel suspicious of what adults tell him, weighs up whether the landlord is more reliable than his father.

38. The connection is this: for a long time his father would not believe Hans's notion of horses having something black round their mouths, until he was at last able to verify it for himself.

39. 'Ce que femme veut Dieu veut.' Young Hans, perceptive as ever, has once again uncovered a very serious problem.

40. There is no need to assume that Hans's longing to have children is an indication of any feminine trait. Since as a child his happiest times have been experienced with his mother, he is now reproducing this in active form, and so he himself must take the role of the mother.

41. This striking contradiction is the contradiction between fantasy and reality – between wishing and having. He knows that in reality he is a child, and that other children would only be a nuisance, but in his fantasy he is a mother and needs children with whom he can reproduce the affectionate warmth he himself has experienced.

42. It might be the case that Hans has idealized a chance encounter in Gmunden, and drawn, moreover, on his mother's colouring for eyes and hair.

43. Hans is only able to respond in terms of auto-eroticism.

44. That is, they are fantasy children – a masturbation fantasy.

45. Saffaladi = cervelat [a kind of salami]. My wife is fond of telling people that her aunt pronounces it 'Soffilodi' [i.e. with a strong Viennese accent]; Hans might have overheard this. [*Father's note.*]

46. Do we not use the term 'drop' to denote animals giving birth? [*Translator's note*: Freud uses the verb *niederkommen*, 'to be delivered', literally 'to come down'].

47. We might add that the choice of a boring tool is not without some connection to the word 'born'. A child would make no distinction between the words 'gebohrt' [bored] and 'geboren' [born]. While I accept this supposition voiced to me by a knowledgeable colleague, I could not say whether we are dealing here with a more profound general connection or whether this merely exploits a chance linguistic occurrence peculiar to German. Etymologically speaking, Prometheus (Pramantha), the creator of mankind, is also the 'borer'. Cf. Abraham, *Traum und Mythus* [*Dream and Myth*], vol. 4 of *Schriften zur angewandten Seelenkunde* [*Writings on Applied Psychology*], 1909.

III

Epicrisis[1]

There are three key questions to be borne in mind while examining this account of the development and resolution of a phobia in a boy not yet five years old: first, to what extent it bears out the assertions I made in *Drei Abhandlungen zur Sexualtheorie* [*Three Essays on the Theory of Sexuality*] (1905); second, what it might contribute to our understanding of this frequently encountered form of illness; and, third, whether it might cast some light on the inner life [*Seelenleben*] of children and cause us to review our intentions in educating our children.

1

My broad impression is that the picture of the sexual life of children which emerges from observation of little Hans corresponds very closely to the outline given in my *Theory of Sexuality*, which is based on the psychoanalytical examination of adults. But before I go on to examine this correspondence in detail, I must address two reservations that might be expressed as to the use made of this analysis. According to the first of these, little Hans is not a normal child, but predisposed to neurosis, as events, that is his illness, suggest; he is a 'chip off the old block' and it is not therefore permissible to apply conclusions that might be valid in his case to other, normal children. I shall consider this objection at a later stage, for while it may limit the value of what has been observed, it does not negate it entirely. The second, more rigorous objection claims that the analysis of a child by his own father, who is steeped in *my* theoretical views and tainted with *my* prejudices, *is altogether lacking in objective value*. A child is of course suggestible to a very high degree, as regards his father, perhaps, more than any other figure; he will allow any words to be put in his mouth out of gratitude to a father who pays him so much attention; his statements have no value as evidence and what he produces by way of ideas, fantasies and dreams naturally tend in the direction to which they have been pushed by every means at his father's disposal. In a word, the whole thing is another case of pure 'suggestion', which is merely somewhat easier to see through in the case of a child than in the case of an adult.

This is strange: 22 years ago, when I first became embroiled in the conflict of scientific opinions, I remember the scorn with which the older generation of neurologists and psychiatrists greeted attempts to establish the concept of suggestion and its effects. Since then the situation has altered fundamentally: reluctance has been transformed into an all too willing acceptance, not merely as a result of the influence enjoyed by the work of Liebeault, Bernheim and their followers in the course of the past two decades, but also because so many have discovered meanwhile that they can spare themselves the effort of thinking by employing that useful catchword, 'suggestion'. Of course, no one knows, and no one cares to know, what suggestion is, where it comes from and when it comes into play; it is enough to be able to label anything uncomfortable in the realm of the psyche 'suggestion'.

I do not share the view, much-favoured at present, that what children say is entirely arbitrary and unreliable. Nothing is arbitrary when it comes to the psyche; the unreliability of what children say is derived from the power of their fantasy, just as the unreliability of what adults say is derived from the power of their prejudices. Otherwise, a child never lies without good cause, and on the whole is more inclined to love truth than adults are. It would be a grave injustice indeed to little Hans to reject what he says out of hand; it is possible to discern quite clearly when resistance forces him to falsify or withhold, when, himself undecided, he accepts what his father says, so that we cannot accept this as proof; and when, no longer oppressed, his own inner truth comes bubbling out, a truth which up until that moment no one knew but himself. What adults say offers us no greater degree of certainty. It is only to be regretted that no depiction of the process of psychoanalysis can accurately convey the impressions that one receives while it is being carried out, that one can never be completely convinced by reading about it, but only by experiencing it oneself. But this deficiency is equally true of adult analysis.

His parents portray little Hans as a cheerful, straightforward child, as well he might be, given the way his parents brought him up, which was essentially to avoid the usual sins we commit in bringing up our children. As long as he could pursue his investigations in happy naivety with no suspicion of the conflicts which they would soon bring in their wake, he had no hesitation in communicating his thoughts and feelings, and the observations which date from before the time of his phobia are open neither to doubt nor to complaint. At the time of his illness and during the analysis we begin see inconsistencies between what he says and what he thinks, partly because unconscious material is coming to the surface that he is unable to master immediately, and partly because he withholds certain aspects of the content because of its bearing on his relationship with his parents. I protest my impartiality when I pronounce these difficulties to be no greater than in many cases of adult analysis.

It is true that many things had to be said to Hans during the analysis that he was not capable of saying himself, thoughts had to be fed to him that he had not shown any sign of thinking himself, his attention had to be turned in the direction from which his father was expecting something to come. That weakens the value of the analysis as evidence; but this is what happens in every analysis. For psychoanalysis is precisely not an objective scientific procedure, but a therapeutic intervention; it does not in itself attempt to prove anything, but merely to change something. In psychoanalysis the physician will always, to a greater or lesser extent, give the patient conscious expectations, which will enable him to recognize and get a grip on the unconscious. For in some cases more support is needed and in others less. But no one can manage without such help entirely. If something can be brought to a close without outside intervention, then it is only a mild disorder, never a neurosis, which sets itself up in opposition to the I [*Ich*] as if it were a foreign body; to overcome something like this one needs the help of another person, and the neurosis can only be cured to the extent that another person is able to help. If it is in the nature of a neurosis to turn from the 'other', as appears to be the case in those conditions that come under the heading of dementia praecox, then for that very reason such conditions are not to be healed by our endeavours. Now admittedly a child, by virtue of its less highly developed intellectual system, requires particularly intensive support. But what the physician communicates to his patient is itself drawn from analytical experience, and it is surely proof enough when, as a result of the physician's interventions, we are able to understand the logic of the pathogenic material and to arrive at a solution.

On the other hand our young patient showed sufficient independence of mind even during the analysis to acquit him of any accusation of 'suggestibility'. Like all children, he applies his sexual theories to the material available, without encouragement from anyone. And they are very far away from the adult mind; indeed, in this case I almost omitted to prepare Hans's father for the fact that Hans must needs arrive at the subject of birth by way of the excretion complex. What then became an obscure part of the analysis due to overhastiness on my part did at least provide positive testimony to the genuine and independent nature of Hans's thinking. All at once he became preoccupied with 'plop', and yet the father who was apparently guilty of suggestion had no idea where this had come from or where it might lead. In the same way, we cannot ascribe much of a role to Hans's father in developing the two fantasies about the plumber that proceed from the 'castration complex' Hans acquired at a young age. Here I must confess to having said nothing to Hans's father, out of theoretical interest, of my expectation that this connection would emerge, so that the value of a piece of evidence that is normally very hard to obtain should not go to waste.

If we were to go more deeply into the detail of the analysis, we would find ample further proof that young Hans was not dependent on any form of 'suggestion'; but I shall break off discussion of this first objection here. Even by means of such analysis I know I shall not convince a single person who does not wish to be convinced and so I shall continue to work through this account in the interest of those readers who are already convinced of the objectivity of unconscious pathogenic material, though not without emphasizing my agreeable feeling of certainty that the latter are increasing in number all the time.

The first characteristic that we can attribute to young Hans's sexual life is a particularly lively interest in his 'widdler', as this organ is called after what is hardly the less important of its two functions, and the one that is unavoidable as far as the nursery is concerned. This interest turns him into a research scientist, and thus he discovers that one may distinguish between the animate and inanimate according to the presence or absence of the widdler. He assumes that this significant bodily organ is to be found on all living creatures that he judges to be like himself, studies it on big animals, supposes it to be there on both his parents and cannot be prevented even by the evidence of his own eyes from observing its presence on his newborn sister. We might say that it would be too massive a blow to his 'world view' if he had to make up his mind to forego its presence in a being like himself, it would be as if he himself had had it snatched from him. Probably for that very reason his mother's threat, which contained nothing less than the loss of his widdler, is quickly pushed to the back of his mind, and can only take effect much later on. His mother's intervention occurred because he enjoyed giving himself pleasurable sensations by touching this organ; the little boy has thus embarked upon the most common – and the most normal – form of auto-erotic sexual activity.

In a manner which Adolf Adler aptly describes as 'a *confluence of drives*',[2] pleasure in one's own sexual organ becomes bound up with voyeurism [*Schaulust*] in its active and passive forms. The boy attempts to catch sight of other people's widdlers, develops a sexual curiosity and enjoys showing his own widdler to other people. A dream from the early period of repression has as its content the wish that one of his little friends should help him to do a widdle and so share in the sight herself. The dream attests to the fact that up until that time this wish had remained unrepressed, just as later statements confirm that he had been accustomed to satisfying it. The active direction taken by his voyeurism is soon associated with a definite theme. If he repeatedly expresses his regret to his father as well as his mother that he has not yet seen their widdlers, he is probably driven to do so by the need to *compare*. The I remains the standard by which we measure the rest of the world; by constantly making the comparison with our own self, we learn to understand it. Hans has observed that big animals have widdlers that are that much bigger than his own; he then presupposes the same proportional relationship in his parents' case and seeks to prove that this is indeed so. His mother's widdler, he thinks, is surely 'as big as a horse's'. He can then readily console himself with the fact that his widdler will grow as he does; it is as if the child's desire to grow bigger has all been channelled towards his genitals.

Right from the beginning, then, in little Hans's sexual constitution, the genital zone is the erogenous zone from which he derives the most intense pleasure. Apart from this we have evidence only of excremental pleasure, connected to the orifices of micturition and the evacuation of the bowels. If, in the last happy fantasy, which marks the overcoming of his illness, he has children whom he takes to the lavatory, supervises while they do a widdle and whose bottoms he wipes, for whom, in short 'he does all the things you have to do for children', it is surely irrefutable that these same tasks, performed by those whose duty it was to care for him in infancy, were to him a source of pleasurable sensations. The pleasure associated with the erogenous zones was obtained with the help of the person caring for him, his mother, and thus already leads to a choice of object; it is possible, however, that earlier still he was accustomed to procure this pleasure auto-erotically and was one of those children who like to hold excreta back until evacuation is accompanied by a voluptuous delight. I repeat that this is merely a possibility, for the analysis does not make it clear; the 'racket he makes with his feet' (thrashing about), which he later so greatly fears, points in this direction. Incidentally, these sources of pleasure are not conspicuously emphasized, as is often the case among children. He quickly became clean and neither bedwetting nor daytime incontinence were a feature of his early years; there was no sign of the tendency to play with his excrement, so distasteful in adults, which often recurs at the outset of any process of psychic regression.

It should be emphasized at this point that, during his phobia, there is unmistakable repression of both of these well-developed components of sexual activity. He is ashamed of urinating in front of others, accuses himself of touching his widdler, struggles to give up masturbation and is disgusted by 'plop', 'wee' and anything that reminds him of them. In his fantasy of looking after children himself, this repression is reversed again.

A sexual constitution like that of young Hans would not appear to be predisposed to develop perversions or their negative manifestations (let us restrict ourselves to the mention of hysteria). In my experience (though I must express myself here with great caution) the congenital constitution of the hysterical patient – and, as is more or less self-evident, in the case of perverts – is distinguished by the fact that other erogenous zones are favoured over the genital zone. We must single out one sexual 'deviation' as an exception to this rule. We find that the same overriding importance is attributed to the genital zone, and in particular to the penis, in the infancy of those who later become homosexual, who, according to my expectations and the observations of J. Sadger, all go through an amphigen phase during childhood. Indeed, the high value set on the penis by the homosexual male seals his fate. Such men may choose women as sexual objects in childhood, as long as they can assume that the part of the body which they regard as indispensable is also to be found in women; as they become convinced that women have deceived them in this particular, the woman becomes an unacceptable sexual object. They cannot dispense with a penis in the person who is to excite them to sexual intercourse and so in favourable circumstances they attach their libido to 'the woman with a penis', the youth whose appearance is decidedly feminine. Homosexuals are thus people for whom the erogenous significance of their own genitalia makes it impossible to manage without a sexual object corresponding to their own person. In the process of development from auto-eroticism to object-love they remain fixed at a point that is closer to auto-eroticism.

It is quite inappropriate to single out one particular homosexual drive; it is not a peculiarity of his drives that distinguishes the homosexual, but his choice of object. I refer to the fact, which I have discussed in detail in my *Theory of Sexuality*, that we have wrongly supposed the merging of drive and object in sexuality to be more complete than is in fact the case. The homosexual, whose drives are perhaps quite normal, cannot break free of an object that is characterized by one particular condition; in childhood, since that condition is automatically taken to be fulfilled everywhere, he can behave like young Hans, who makes no distinction in his affection for boys and girls and sometimes refers to his friend Fritzl as 'his most precious girl'. Hans is homosexual, as all children may very well be, quite in accordance with the undeniable fact that he only *knows of one kind of genitalia*, genitalia like his own.[3]

Our young eroticist does not develop further in the direction of homosexuality, however, but assumes an energetic masculinity that is polygamous in expression and whose various female objects call forth different types of behaviour, so that on one occasion he will boldly take the initiative and on another languish in yearning and shame. When there is a paucity of other objects of love he reverts to a preference for his mother, from whom he had turned away in pursuit of others, only to fall into neurosis on his return. It is only then that we learn of the intensity of the love he felt for his mother and what the fate of that love had been. The sexual objective he pursues with his playmates, namely to *sleep* with them, is derived from his experience with his mother; it is contained in the words themselves, which retain their meaning in later life, even if the content of those words undergoes an enrichment. The boy had found the usual route to object-love, by way of the care given him as an infant, and a new experience of pleasure, that of sleeping next to his mother, had become decisive for him; of its various components we would emphasize the pleasure of skin contact, which is constitutionally appealing to us all (according to Moll's nomenclature, which strikes us as somewhat artificial, we would have to describe this as the satisfaction of the contrectation drive).

In his relationships with his father and mother Hans provides the most graphic and concrete confirmation of all the claims I make in my *Interpretation of Dreams* and *Theory of Sexuality* as to the sexual relations of a child to its parents. He really is a young Oedipus, who wants his father 'out of the way', eliminated, so that he can be all alone with his beautiful mother, and sleep with her. This wish arose during the summer months in Gmunden, when his father's alternating presence and absence drew his attention to the conditions that determined that longed-for intimacy with his mother. At the time he was content with a version of the story in which his father 'was driven away', to which he was subsequently able to attach his fear of being bitten by a white horse, thanks to an accidental impression formed by another person's departure. Later, probably only after the return to Vienna, when Hans could no longer count on his father's going away, the wish was intensified until its content was that his father should go away for good, should be 'dead'. The fear of his father, arising out of this desire for his father's death, and thus quite normally motivated, constituted the greatest barrier to the analysis until it was removed by being articulated in my consulting room.[4]

And yet our Hans is in truth no villain, nor even a child in whom the cruel and violent tendencies of human nature are still exhibited without restraint at this stage of his life. On the contrary, he is unusually good-natured and affectionate in character: his father notes that the transformation of aggressive tendencies into feelings of sympathy took place in Hans at a very young age. Long before the phobia developed he would become uneasy if he saw someone whipping a horse on a merry-go-round, and he could never remain unmoved by the sight of someone crying. At one point in the analysis we glimpse a moment of repressed sadism in a particular context;[5] but repressed it was, and we shall later have to make a guess from the context at what it stands for and what it was intended to replace.

Hans feels an intense love for the father against whom he harbours a death-wish, and while his intelligence may lead him to query this contradiction,[6] he is still obliged to demonstrate its reality by hitting his father and then immediately kissing the place where he had hit him. We must also be careful not to object to such a contradiction; human feelings in general are made up of such pairs of opposites;[7] indeed, were things to be otherwise, there would probably be no question of repression and neurosis. These contradictory feelings, of whose simultaneous presence adults normally only become aware when they are passionately in love, and which tend to suppress each other until one of them succeeds in covering up the presence of the other altogether, are able to coexist peacefully in the heart of a child for quite some time.

The birth of a little sister when he was 3½ years old was of the greatest significance for the boy's psychosexual development. This event brought his relationship with his parents into sharper focus and presented his intellect with insoluble difficulties, while, at the same time, watching his little sister being cared for revived faint memories of his own earlier experiences of pleasure. This influence, too, is typical in nature: an unexpectedly large number of life histories and case histories have as their starting-point the flaring up of sexual pleasure and sexual curiosity which accompanies the birth of the next child. Hans's behaviour towards the new arrival is just as I have described in my *Interpretation of Dreams*.[8] A few days later, in an attack of fever, he reveals how little he is in favour of this new addition to the family. Hostility came first, even if affection followed.[9] From then on, the fear that another child might come along finds a place in his conscious thinking. In the neurosis, the hostility which he has already suppressed is represented by a particular fear, that of the bathtub; in the analysis he expresses his desire for his sister's death quite openly and not merely by means of oblique references that his father has to complete. Looking critically at his own feelings, he does not consider this wish to be as dreadful as the analogous one towards his father; but in his unconscious mind he obviously treats both figures in the same way because they both take his Mummy away from him and prevent him from being alone with her.

Incidentally, this event, and what it awakens, moves his wishes in a new direction. His victorious final fantasy is the summation of all the wishes stirring inside him, those that arose during the auto-erotic phase as well as those connected with object-love. He is married to his lovely mother and has innumerable children whom he can look after in his own way.

2

Hans is seized by anxiety on the street one day and falls ill: he is as yet unable to say what it is he is afraid of, but at the very beginning of this state of anxiety he betrays the motive for his illness, what he hopes to gain from it, to his father. He wants to stay with his mother, to nuzzle with her; the memory of his separation from her at the time when the baby was born may well contribute, as his father believes, to this feeling of longing. It soon becomes clear that his anxiety can no longer be translated back into longing, for he is afraid even when his mother goes out with him. Meanwhile we have an indication of what the libido, now transformed into anxiety, has attached itself to. Hans expresses the very particular fear that a white horse will bite him.

We call a state of illness of this kind a 'phobia' and might class the boy's case as agoraphobia, if it were not characteristic of this affliction that an otherwise impossible spatial achievement rapidly becomes possible when the patient is accompanied by someone who has been chosen for that purpose, even, *in extremis*, by the physician. Hans's phobia does not conform to this condition: place ceases to be important and horses become ever more clearly the object of his fear; in the early days, at the height of his anxiety, he expresses the fear that 'the horse will come into the room', a remark which made it very much easier to understand the nature of his fear.

Up to now the position of 'phobias' in the system of neuroses has been uncertain. What does seem clear is that phobias afford us merely a glimpse of syndromes that could belong to a variety of neuroses, and we need not attribute to them the significance of a particular process of illness. To designate phobias of the kind suffered by our young patient, which are certainly the most common, 'anxiety-hysteria' does not seem wide of the mark to me: I made this suggestion to Dr W. Stekel when he was undertaking a review of nervous anxiety states and I hope that the term will pass into common usage.[10] It is justified by the fact that in terms of their psychic mechanism such phobias correspond exactly to hysteria, up to a certain – crucial – point, which allows us to distinguish one from the other. For libido that has been released from the pathogenic material by means of repression is not *converted* – drawn off from the inner sphere and channelled into physical enervation – but allowed to exist freely in the form of anxiety. In those cases of illness with which I am familiar, 'anxiety-hysteria' and *'conversion hysteria'* can be mixed up together in varying proportions. We also find pure conversion hysteria without any anxiety, just as we find straightforward anxiety-hysteria, expressed through feelings of fear and phobias, without any conversion element: the case of little Hans is of the latter kind.

Anxiety-hysteria is the most common of all psychoneurotic illnesses; above all, cases of such hysteria occur in very early life and are in effect the neuroses of childhood. If a mother says of her child, for example, that he is very 'highly strung', we can assume in 9 out of 10 cases that the child is suffering from anxiety or from several kinds of anxiety at once. Unfortunately, the precise mechanism of this important illness has been insufficiently studied up to now; we have not yet established whether anxiety-hysteria, unlike conversion hysteria and other neuroses, is determined purely by constitutional factors or purely by chance experiences, or whether it is to be found in some combination of the two.[11] It appears to me to be the form of neurotic illness that least demands a particular constitution and consequently may be most readily acquired at any time of life.

We can easily identify one essential characteristic of anxiety-hysteria. Anxiety-hysteria develops ever further into 'phobia', so that in the end the patient may be free from anxiety, but only at the expense of subjecting himself to inhibitions and restrictions. From the very outset we find that the psyche works continuously to bind the anxiety that has been released back into the psyche, but such work is neither able to effect the re-transformation of anxiety into libido, nor to establish a connection with the complexes from which the libido stems. There is no alternative but to close off every possible opportunity for anxiety to develop by means of psychic stockades such as circumspection, inhibition or prohibition, and it is these fortifications that are manifested as phobias and, as we perceive it, constitute the essence of the illness.

We might say that, up until now, the treatment of anxiety-hysteria has been an entirely negative one. Experience has shown that it is impossible and, indeed, in some cases, positively dangerous to attempt to cure the phobia by violent means, by putting the patient in a situation where he is obliged to undergo delivery from his anxiety by having his cover taken away from him. He is thus obliged to seek refuge wherever he thinks he can find it, and encounters helpless contempt for his 'incomprehensible cowardice'.

From the very beginning of his illness the parents of our young patient were determined that he should be neither mocked nor bullied, but that they should seek access to his repressed desires by means of psychoanalysis. Hans's father was rewarded with success for his extraordinary efforts and his notes provide us with the opportunity to penetrate the structure of one such phobia and follow the course of the analysis that was undertaken in response to it.

It is not unlikely that the detailed and long-drawn-out nature of the analysis has made it difficult for the reader to understand in places. For that reason I shall begin by going over the material again in summarized form, omitting misleading detail and emphasizing the principal outcomes, as little by little they emerge.

We learn first of all that the eruption of Hans's state of anxiety was not as sudden as might at first appear. A few days earlier the child had awoken from a nightmare, the content of which was that his mummy had gone away and that he no longer had a mummy to nuzzle with. This dream alone points to a process of repression of disturbing intensity. We cannot explain it by saying, as we might in the case of many nightmares, that while dreaming the child experienced fear from some somatic source and then used that fear to satisfy an unconscious desire that was normally powerfully repressed (cf. *The Interpretation of Dreams*); on the contrary, this is a genuine dream of punishment and repression in which, moreover, the dream fails to serve its proper function, since the child awakens from sleep still fearful. We may readily reconstruct the actual process taking place in the unconscious. The child was dreaming of his mother's caresses, of sleeping with her, and all his pleasure is transformed into anxiety, all the imaginative content of the dream into its opposite. Repression has been victorious over the dreaming mechanism.

But the origins of this psychological situation lie even further back. The previous summer Hans had already experienced similar moods of yearning and anxiety in which he expressed the same kind of feeling; these then had the beneficial effect of causing his mother to take him into bed with her. We may assume a heightened sexual arousal in Hans from around this time, which has his mother as its object and whose intensity is expressed in two attempts to seduce his mother – the second of these very shortly before the eruption of his anxiety – an arousal which finds relief, moreover, in the daily satisfaction provided by masturbation. Whether the sudden transformation of this arousal takes place spontaneously or as a result of his mother's rejection or through the chance awakening of earlier impressions that will later be experienced as the 'cause' of his illness, we cannot say, and it is probably a matter of indifference, since the three possibilities cannot be construed as existing in opposition to one another. The important fact is the transformation of sexual arousal into anxiety.

We have already learned of the child's behaviour in the earliest stage of his anxiety and we know that the first content he gives to his fear is that a *horse* might bite him. At this point the first therapeutic intervention takes place. His parents suggest that his fear is a consequence of masturbation and instruct him in breaking the habit. I ensure that in his presence considerable emphasis is put on his loving feelings toward his mother, which he was attempting to replace with his fear of horses. A slight improvement brought about by this first attempt to influence events is rapidly lost to a period of physical illness. Hans's condition is unchanged. Soon after this Hans discovers the origin of his fear that a horse will bite him when he recalls an impression made on him in Gmunden. As she left, a father warned his child: 'Don't touch the horse or it will bite you.' The form of words which Hans chooses to express the father's warning recalls the way in which the warning against masturbation was expressed [literally, 'laying a finger on']. At first, then, his parents appear to be right in thinking that Hans is afraid of the satisfaction he is able to give himself by masturbating. However, the connection is fairly tenuous still, and the horse appears to have acquired his function as a bogey quite by accident.

I had put forward the conjecture that his repressed desire might now be expressed as wanting at all costs to see his mother's widdler. Since his behaviour towards a newly appointed house-maid appears to corroborate this, his father offers him a first piece of sexual enlightenment: women don't have widdlers. He reacts to this attempt to help him by telling his father of a fantasy in which he saw his mother showing her widdler.[12] This fantasy, together with a conversational remark that his widdler had 'taken root' after all, allow us the first insight into the patient's unconscious thought processes. His mother's threat to castrate him, made fifteen months earlier, was indeed belatedly having an effect on him, for his fantasy that his mother was doing the same as he was, the usual 'tit for tat' retort of children who stand accused, is intended to take some of the blame from his shoulders; it is a defensive fantasy, intended to parry feelings of guilt [*Schutz- und Abwehrphantasie*]. At the same time we must remind ourselves that it was his parents who, out of all the relevant pathogenic material, brought the topic of Hans's preoccupation with his widdler into the foreground. He has followed their lead in this but has not yet intervened independently in the analysis. No therapeutic success can be observed. The analysis has moved a long way away from horses, and the information that women don't have widdlers seems more likely to heighten his concern about keeping possession of his own widdler.

We are not concerned with therapeutic success in the first instance, however, but with putting the patient in a position where he can consciously understand his unconscious desires. This can be achieved, on the basis of veiled suggestions that he makes to us, by bringing the unconscious complex to his conscious attention with the help of our interpretative skills and *in our own words*. The element of similarity between what he hears and what he is looking for, which is itself attempting to force its way into consciousness despite his resistance, puts him in a position where he can locate what is unconscious. The physician is one step ahead of him in understanding; the patient follows along his own paths until they meet at the designated goal. Novices in psychoanalysis tend to conflate these two moments and to assume that the moment at which they recognize a patient's unconscious complex and the moment at which the patient himself grasps it, are one and the same. They expect too much if they hope to cure the patient by communicating their understanding to him, for he is only in a position to apply this information to locate *the place* in his unconscious mind where the unconscious complex *is embedded*. We now achieve a first success of this kind in Hans's case. Having partially overcome the castration complex, he is now in a position to express the desire he feels towards his mother, which he does, albeit in distorted form, in the *fantasy of the two giraffes*, one of which cries out unsuccessfully because Hans has taken possession of the other. Taking possession is represented by the image of sitting on top of. His father recognizes this fantasy as reproducing a scene which took place between parents and child that morning in the bedroom, and loses no time in stripping his desire of the distorting elements which still cling to it. He and Hans's mother are the two giraffes. Adequate determining factors for the giraffe fantasy in which they are clothed can be found in a visit to see these large animals in Schönbrunn a few days previously, the giraffe drawing which Hans's father had kept from an earlier occasion, and perhaps in an unconscious comparison occasioned by the giraffe's long, stiff neck.[13] We observe that the giraffe, a large animal interesting by virtue of its widdler, might have been a contender, along with the horse, for the role of bogey; the fact, moreover, that both father and mother are represented as giraffes provides a hint, so far overlooked, as to how we might interpret the anxiety-horses.

The interpretation of two lesser fantasies that Hans produces immediately after the poetry of the giraffe episode, namely forcing his way into a forbidden area in Schönbrunn and smashing a window in the metropolitan railway – where on both occasions the emphasis is on the culpable nature of the action and the father appears in the role of accomplice – unfortunately eludes his father. Hans therefore derives no benefit from telling them. What remains in the understanding, however, will come again; like an unredeemed ghost it will not be at peace until it is laid to rest and redeemed.

We encounter no difficulties in understanding Hans's two criminal fantasies. They are part of the complex associated with taking possession of the mother. It is as if the child is struggling with a faint intimation of something that he could do with his mother, something with which he could take possession of her completely, and he finds certain symbolic representations of what he cannot grasp; their common element is violence and transgression, and their content appears to accord remarkably well with the hidden truth. We can only say that they are symbolic coitus fantasies and it is far from irrelevant that his father is in the frame too: 'I want to do something with Mummy, something forbidden, I don't know what, but I know it's something you do too.'

The giraffe fantasy strengthened a conviction that Hans's remark, 'The horse will come into my room', had already implanted in me, and I thought it an appropriate moment to communicate to him what we might conjecture to be an essential element in his unconscious feelings: his fear of his father because of his jealous and hostile feelings towards him. At the same time I offered him a partial interpretation of his fear of horses: his father must be the horse, which he had good internal reason to fear. Certain details that aroused fear in Hans, the black around his mouth and in front of his eyes (moustache and spectacles, the prerogatives of the adult male), seemed to me to have been transferred directly from the father to the horses.

With this explanation I vanquished the most powerful resistance in Hans to conscious recognition of his unconscious thoughts, since it was his own father who was taking the role of his physician. From this moment on we had conquered the summit of his condition, the material flowed abundantly, the young patient showed courage in communicating the details of his phobia and soon intervened independently in the course of the analysis.[14]

Only now do we discover which objects and impressions Hans is afraid of: not merely horses, and the fact that horses bite, for we hear no more of this after a while, but carriages, furniture vans and omnibuses, whose common factor, it quickly emerges, is the heavy load they carry, horses that start to move, horses that are large and heavy in appearance, horses that move quickly. Hans himself then provides the key to these essential qualities: he is afraid that the horses will *collapse*, and thus everything that might make such a collapse more likely becomes part of the content of his phobia.

It is not at all rare for us to hear the actual content of a phobia, the true wording of a compulsion [*Zwangsimpuls*] and the like only after a period of psychoanalytical effort. Repression affects not only the unconscious complexes but is also continuously directed against anything that is derived from them, preventing the patient from recognizing the products of his illness. One is then in the curious position, as a physician, of coming to the assistance of the illness, of pleading for its recognition; but only those who completely misjudge the nature of psychoanalysis would linger over this phase of the analyst's endeavour, anticipating that damage will be inflicted by the analysis. The truth is that you cannot hang your thief until you have caught him, and some effort is required before one can get hold of the diseased formations that one intends to destroy.

I have already mentioned, in the glosses that accompany the case history, that it is highly instructive to allow oneself to become engrossed in the detail of a phobia, so as to form a clear impression that the connection between an anxiety and its objects is produced only at a secondary level. Hence the peculiarly diffuse and at the same time precisely determined nature of any phobia. Our young patient evidently found the material for his own particular key to the code in the impressions available to him all day long by virtue of the position of the family's apartment, opposite the Central Customs House. In this connection too he betrays a desire, now inhibited by anxious feelings, to play like the street urchins with the carts' loads, with the packages, barrels and boxes.

At this stage of the analysis he is able to retrieve the experience that immediately preceded the eruption of his illness, though it is not particularly significant in itself, an experience that we may undoubtedly regard as the occasion for that eruption. He went for a walk with his mother and saw an omnibus horse collapse, thrashing about with its legs. This made a great impression on him. He was violently afraid, believing the horse to be dead; from then on he thinks all horses are about to collapse. His father suggests that when he saw the horse fall over he had thought of him, his father, and must have wished that he too would fall over and be dead. Hans does not resist this interpretation; some time later, by means of a game in which he bites his father, he accepts the identification of his father with the much-feared horse, and from this time onward is relaxed and fearless, perhaps even a trifle over-confident in his behaviour towards his father. His fear of horses persists, however, and it is not yet clear by what connection the horse collapsing had touched on his unconscious desires.

Let us sum up what we have discovered so far: behind the original expression of anxiety, the fear that a horse would bite him, we have exposed a more profound anxiety, the fear that horses will collapse, and both of these, the biting horse and the falling horse, are the father who will punish him because of the wicked desires he harbours against him. In our analysis we have meanwhile lost sight of Hans's mother.

Quite unexpectedly, and certainly without Hans's father having said anything, Hans starts to be preoccupied with the 'plop complex' and to express revulsion at anything which reminds him of evacuating his bowels. In the middle of all this, his father, who is reluctant to go along with the new topic, continues to conduct the analysis along the lines that he prefers and causes Hans to remember an experience in Gmunden: the impression which it made lay hidden behind that of the omnibus horse which had collapsed. Fritzl, his beloved playmate, perhaps also his rival for the affection of their many girlfriends, had caught his foot on a stone when they were playing horsey; he had fallen over and his foot had bled. The incident with the omnibus horse that collapsed had reminded Hans of this accident. It is worth noting that Hans, who is preoccupied at this time with other matters, at first denies that Fritzl fell over – the event which produces the connection – and only admits it at a later stage of the analysis. For our purposes, however, it is of particular interest that the libido which has been transformed into fear is then projected on to the main phobic object, the horse. He found horses the most interesting of the large animals, and playing horsey was his favourite game with his childhood companions. Upon inquiry, Hans's father confirms my suspicion that it was he who had originally played the part of Hans's horse, and so it was possible to substitute Hans's father for Fritzl when the accident happened in Gmunden. Once the reversal caused by repression had taken effect, Hans found himself obliged to fear the horses that had previously had such strongly pleasurable associations for him.

As I have already mentioned, however, it is to the intervention of his father that we owe this last important illumination of the effectiveness of the event which triggered off Hans's illness. Hans himself is absorbed in his plop, and in the end we too must follow. We learn that Hans used to insist on accompanying his mother to the lavatory and that he did the same thing with Berta, who represented his mother at the time, until this was discovered and forbidden. The pleasure derived from watching a beloved person perform such functions corresponds to the 'confluence of drives' of which we have already seen one example in Hans's behaviour. Hans's father finally turns his mind to the symbolism of plop, and recognizes an analogy between a heavily laden cart and a body weighed down by faecal matter, between the way a cart drives out of the gateway and the way a stool is released from the body, and so on.

By comparison with the earlier stages, however, Hans's attitude to the analysis has altered significantly. Previously his father was able to predict what was coming and Hans, following his hints, trotted along behind; now it is Hans who hurries confidently on ahead, while his father has trouble keeping up. Hans quite unexpectedly brings us a new fantasy: the ironsmith or plumber has unscrewed the bathtub in which Hans is sitting and then jabbed him in the stomach with his big screwdriver. From now on our understanding limps along behind the material. Only later are we able to guess that this is the reworking of a procreation fantasy, in a form distorted by anxiety. The big bathtub where Hans is sitting in the water is the womb; the 'screwdriver', which Hans's father was quickly able to recognize as a big penis, is mentioned in the context of being born. It will sound very odd, of course, to interpret the fantasy thus: You 'bored' ('borned') me with your big penis and put me in my mother's womb. For the time being, however, the fantasy eludes interpretation and serves only as a connecting point for the communication of further material.

The anxiety that Hans feels at the prospect of bathing in the big tub is once again a composite one. One element still eludes us, but the other can immediately be explained with reference to the bathing of his little sister. Hans admits that he wishes his mother would drop the little girl while bathing her, and that she would drown; his fear of being bathed was the fear of being paid back for his wicked desires, of being punished by the same thing happening to him. He now abandons the subject of plop and moves on immediately to that of his little sister. We can guess, however, at the meaning of that discontinuity. Simply that little Hanna herself is a plop, that all babies are plops and are born like plops. Now we can see that the furniture vans, omnibuses and drays are nothing but stork-box carts, and that they are significant only as symbolic representations of pregnancy; to see a heavy, or heavily laden horse collapse was quite simply to see a woman in labour, the delivery of a child. The collapsing horse was thus not only his father dying, but his mother in labour.

And now Hans gives us a surprise that we had really not expected. He had been aware of his mother's pregnant state, which came to an end with the birth of the baby when Hans was 3½ years old, and he had reconstructed the true state of affairs, at least once the baby had been born, no doubt without saying a word to anyone, perhaps incapable of saying a word; all that could be observed at the time was that, immediately after the confinement, he manifested extreme scepticism with regard to those signs that were meant to indicate the presence of the stork. What this analysis demonstrates beyond the slightest doubt, however, is that *in his unconscious mind, despite what he officially claimed to know, he knew where the baby came from and where it had previously dwelt*; this is perhaps the most unshakeable aspect of it.

Conclusive evidence of this is provided by the elaborately detailed fantasy to which Hans so obstinately clings, that Hanna was with them in Gmunden the summer before she was born; how she arrived there, and how she was able at that time to do so much more than she could a year later, after she had been born. Hans's audacity in recounting his fantasy and the countless fantastic lies woven into it are far from nonsensical; it is all intended to enable him to take revenge on his father, whose attempts to mislead him with the stork fairy-tale have filled him with fury. It is exactly as if he wished to say: if you think I am so stupid that you can make me believe Hanna was brought by a stork, then in return I shall demand that you take my inventions for truth. The connection between this act of revenge against his father on the part of our young research scientist and the fantasy of ragging and beating the horses that follows is transparent. Once again it is double-edged, on the one hand following on from the ragging to which he has just subjected his father, on the other hand recalling the obscure sadistic desires towards his mother, which were expressed – though we did not at first recognize them – in the fantasies of forbidden action. He consciously acknowledges, moreover, the desire to beat his mummy.

We do not anticipate that there will be many more mysteries now. An obscure fantasy about missing the train seems to be a precursor of his later intention to settle his father with his grandmother in Lainz, since its subject is a journey to Lainz and Hans's grandmother appears in it. Another fantasy, in which a lad pays the guard 50,000 gulden to let him ride on the trolley, sounds almost like a plan to buy his mother from his father, whose strength after all lies partly in his wealth. Then, with a candour he has not previously summoned up, he admits to the desire to do away with his father and acknowledges the reason for this, the disruption of the intimate relationship with his mother. We should not be surprised to find that the same desires recur over and over again in the course of the analysis; the monotony arises only from the interpretations attached to them, but for Hans this is not a matter of repetition but of progression and development, from the first bashful intimations to an entirely conscious clarity, free from all distortion.

What follows is a confirmation on Hans's part of the results we have arrived at through analysis and which interpretation suggests are already secure. In an unambiguous symptomatic action, which Hans disguises in conversation with the maidservant but not with his father, he demonstrates what he imagines a birth to be; if we look more closely, however, he demonstrates more besides and shows us something which is not articulated any further within the analysis. He sticks a tiny knife belonging to his mother through a round opening in a doll's rubber body and makes it fall out again by tearing the doll's legs apart. His parents' subsequent explanation that babies do indeed grow in the mother's belly and are ejected from it like a plop comes too late; it does not teach him anything new. In another symptomatic action that occurs, as it were, by chance, he admits that he wishes his father were dead by making the horse he was playing with collapse, by knocking it over, that is, at the very moment when his father is speaking of just such a death-wish. He uses words to reinforce the notion that for him the heavily laden carriages represented his mother's pregnant state, and that the horse collapsing was like someone having a baby. The most delightful act of confirmation in this context, the invention of the name 'Lodi' for his favourite child, by which Hans proves that children are 'plops', only comes belatedly to our attention, for we learn that he had been playing with this sausage-child for some time already.[15]

We have already acknowledged Hans's last two fantasies, which show his recovery to be complete. The one about the plumber who gives him a new and, as his father rightly surmises, bigger widdler is not, however, merely a repetition of the earlier one that was concerned with the plumber and the bathtub. It is a victorious wish-fantasy in which he overcomes his fear of castration. The second fantasy, which acknowledges his desire to be married to his mother and to have lots of children with her, does not just exhaust the content of those unconscious complexes that were stirred into life by the sight of the collapsing horse and brought such fear in their wake – it also serves to correct what was quite simply unacceptable about such thoughts, in that instead of killing the father, it renders him harmless by elevating him to marriage with Hans's grandmother. This fantasy legitimately marks the end of both illness and analysis.

During the analysis of any medical case it is difficult to gain an overall impression of the structure and development of the neurosis. This is a matter for the work of synthesis to which one must assent in due course. In undertaking such an attempt at synthesis in the case of young Hans's phobia we are building on the description of his constitution, his dominant sexual desires and his experiences up until the birth of his sister that we have documented in the previous pages of this study.

The arrival of his little sister brought with it many things that from now on would not let him rest. First, a measure of deprivation: initially a period of separation from his mother, and later a permanent lessening of her care and attention, which he now had to learn to share with his sister. Second, a reawakening of the pleasure he experienced in being tended as an infant, which was aroused by everything he watched his mother do to his little sister. These two influences together resulted in heightened erotic neediness, which he began to be unable to satisfy. He compensates for the loss created by the arrival of his sister with the fantasy that he himself has children; and as long as he was able to play with these children in reality in Gmunden (during his second visit there), he found sufficient diversion for his affections. On his return to Vienna, however, he again felt lonely, and focused all his demands on his mother, suffering further deprivation because, from the age of 4½, he had been banished from his parents' bedroom. His heightened erotic excitability was now expressed through fantasies, which conjured up his summer playmates to people his isolation, and through regular auto-erotic satisfaction by means of masturbatory stimulation of the genitals.

Third, however, the birth of his sister set in motion a train of thought that, on the one hand, could not be resolved and, on the other hand, entangled him in conflicting feelings. A great mystery presented itself – where babies come from – perhaps the first problem whose resolution made any great demand on the child's intellect, and of which the riddle of the Theban sphinx is probably only a distorted version. The explanation offered to him, that Hanna was brought by the stork, was one he rejected. He had after all noticed that months before the baby's birth his mother had developed a big belly; that she had gone to bed, groaned at the time of the baby's birth and that when she got up she was slim once again. He concluded, therefore, that Hanna had been in his mother's belly and had then come out like a 'plop'. He could imagine the act of birth to be a pleasurable one, when he thought about his own earliest experiences of pleasure in emptying his bowels, and so his desire to have children himself was then doubly motivated: by the pleasure of giving birth, and of looking after his children (repaying, so to speak, the pleasure he himself had received). There was nothing in any of this that might lead to doubt or conflict.

But there was something else here that could not but disturb him. His father must have had something to do with baby Hanna's *birth*, for he maintained that Hanna and Hans himself were his children. But it was certainly not he who had brought them into the world, but Hans's mummy. His father was in the way when he wanted to be with his mother. When he was there, Hans could not sleep with his mother, and when his mother wanted to take Hans into bed with her his father would get angry. Hans had learned how good life could be for him when his father was not there and his desire to get rid of his father seemed quite justifiable. And now this hostility was intensified. His father had told him those lies about the stork and so made it impossible for him to ask for enlightenment in such matters. He did not merely prevent him from getting into his mother's bed, but also withheld from him the knowledge he longed for. He was putting him at a disadvantage in both respects, evidently in a way that was to his own advantage.

The fact that he loved and continued to love this same father whom he was obliged to detest as a rival, that he provided him with an example to follow, had been his first playmate and at the same time had cared for him in his early years, led to the first conflict of feelings, which Hans was initially unable to resolve. Given the way in which his nature had developed, love prevailed for the time being, suppressing feelings of hatred but without cancelling them out, since they were continually fuelled by his love for his mother.

His father, however, not only knew where babies come from but was able to put into practice that whatever-it-was that Hans himself had only the vaguest intimations of. Widdlers must have something to do with it, since excitement there accompanied all these thoughts, but the widdler would have to be a big one, bigger than Hans considered his own to be. If he were to follow the hints which his own responses provided, then it must have something to do with an act of violence perpetrated against Mummy, with smashing, opening up, penetrating a closed space, for the child was aware of such impulses within himself; but although, taking the sensations in his own penis as his starting-point, he was half way to postulating the existence of the vagina, he was unable to solve the riddle because, as far as he knew, something of the kind needed by a widdler simply did not exist; indeed, his conviction that his mother possessed a widdler just like his was a barrier to arriving at any solution. The attempt to solve the question of what you would have to do with Mummy so that she would have children sank into his unconscious, and neither the hostile active impulse towards his father nor the sadistic-loving one towards his mother were acted upon, the one because of the love that existed alongside the hatred, the other because of the helplessness that resulted from the boy's infantile theories of sexuality.

On the basis of what emerged in analysis this is the only way in which I am able to reconstruct the unconscious complexes and wishful impulses whose repression and re-awakening caused young Hans's phobia to appear. I know that I am assuming a great deal as regards the reasoning powers of a child of four or five, but I am allowing myself to be guided by recent discoveries and do not consider myself bound by the prejudices of ignorance. Perhaps we could have used Hans's fear of 'making a racket with his feet' to fill in one or two further gaps in our evaluation of the evidence. It is true that, according to Hans, it reminded him of the way he would thrash about if he was made to interrupt a game in order to do a plop, and so this element in the neurosis can be related to the problem of whether his mother liked having children, or was obliged to have them, but it is not my impression that this entirely explains 'making a racket with one's feet'. We might conjecture that the child has some memory of having observed his parents in the act of sexual intercourse in the bedroom; but his father is unable to confirm this. Let us be content, therefore, with what we have learned for ourselves.

What influence tipped the scales, in the situation we have described, transforming libidinal yearning into anxiety, and from which direction repression set in is a difficult question to answer and could no doubt only be decided by comparing this case with several similar analyses; whether the decisive factor was the child's intellectual inability to solve the problem of procreation, or to put the aggressive impulses released in coming so close to a solution to positive use, or whether it was a somatic incapacity, a constitutional intolerance of the regular practice of masturbation; or whether the simple prolongation of sexual excitement at such a high pitch of intensity led to the sudden reversal in his feelings are questions that must remain unanswered until new experience is able to help us.

Given the timing of events, we should not ascribe too great an influence to the occasion on which Hans's phobia broke out, for signs of anxiety could be observed in Hans long before the day on which he saw the omnibus horse collapse in the street.

Nevertheless, his neurosis came to be directly attached to this chance experience and a trace of it was retained in the elevation of the horse into an object of anxiety. We cannot ascribe 'traumatic force' to this influence in itself; only the previous significance of the horse as an object of special liking and interest and its direct connection with the incident of Fritzl falling over in Gmunden (which was more likely to have been traumatic in nature), together with the simple path of association from Fritzl to the father, endowed the chance observation of the mishap with such great power. Indeed, even these connections might have been insufficient had not the same impression, a versatile and ambiguous image, also proved able to touch on the second of the complexes lurking in Hans's unconscious, that of the confinement of his pregnant mother. From this moment on the way was opened up to the return of the repressed material, which took place in such a way that *the pathogenic material appears to have been adapted to (transposed on to) the horse complex, and the accompanying affects transformed uniformly into anxiety.*

It is remarkable that the imaginative content of the phobia as it stood had to undergo further distortion and substitution before it could be registered in the conscious mind. The first way Hans found to phrase his anxiety was: the horse will bite me; this arises from another scene in Gmunden, which is related on the one hand to his hostile wishes concerning his father and on the other hand recalls the warning he received against masturbation. A diversionary influence asserted itself at this point, which perhaps came from the parents; it is not clear to me whether the reports on Hans were completed carefully enough at the time to allow us to decide whether he expressed his anxiety in this form *before or only after* his mother had taken him to task over his masturbation. I would differ from the account in the case history by supposing the latter to be the case. It is unmistakable, moreover, that at every point the hostile complex towards the father conceals the libidinous one towards the mother, just as in the analysis this was the first one to be uncovered and dealt with.

In other medical cases there would be far more to say about the structure of a neurosis, its development and diffusion, but in young Hans's case the preceding history is very short and is superseded almost immediately by the account of his treatment. If the phobia appeared to develop further during the course of the treatment, drawing new objects and new conditions into its sphere, the father, who had undertaken the treatment himself, was perceptive enough, of course, to recognize that this merely brought to light things that had already taken place and was not some new product that could be blamed on the treatment. We are not always able to rely on such insight in the treatment of other cases.

Before I declare this synthesis of the results complete, I must acknowledge another point of view, consideration of which brings us to the very heart of the difficulties that accompany the understanding of neurotic states. We observe the way in which our young patient finds himself in the grip of an important repressive urge, which strikes at precisely those sexual components which dominate him.[16] He relinquishes the habit of masturbation and rejects in disgust anything that reminds him of excrement and the observation of bodily functions. Yet these are not the components that are stimulated at the outbreak of his illness (when he sees the horse collapse) and that provide the material for his symptoms, the content of his phobia.

This provides us with the opportunity to make an important theoretical distinction. We shall probably arrive at a more profound understanding of the case if we examine other components that do fulfil the two last-named conditions. In Hans's case these are impulses that had previously been suppressed and that, as far as we know, he had never been able to express without inhibition: hostile and jealous feelings towards his father and sadistic impulses towards his mother, which corresponded to intimations of the act of coitus. Perhaps it is in this early process of suppression that we find the disposition for his later illness. Such aggressive tendencies in Hans never find an outlet and so, as soon as they seek to break out in an intensified form at a time of deprivation and heightened sexual excitement, they ignite the struggle which we term a 'phobia'. In the course of this some of the repressed ideas manage to force their way into consciousness as the content of the phobia, but in a distorted form and assigned to another complex; and there is no doubt that this is a pretty miserable form of success. Repression still carries the day, *taking the opportunity to encroach on components other than those that press most urgently*. This does not alter the fact that the essence of the morbid state remains entirely bound up with the nature of those drive components [*Triebkomponente*] which it was necessary to reject. The purpose and content of the phobia is a substantial limitation on freedom of movement and thus a powerful reaction against those obscure impulses towards movement that were directed in particular towards the mother. To the boy, the horse was always an image of the pleasure of movement ('I'm a young horse' Hans says, prancing about), but since this pleasure in movement includes the impulse towards coitus, such pleasure in movement is curtailed by the neurosis and the horse is elevated to a symbol of terror. It would appear that in neurosis there remains nothing for the repressed drives but the glory of providing a pretext for the anxiety in consciousness. Yet while it is clear that in the phobia rejection of sexuality has won the day, the compromise nature of the illness will not allow there to be no other gain from repression. Hans's phobia about horses is after all another way of preventing him from going out into the streets, and provides him with a means of remaining at home with his beloved mother. His tender feelings for his mother have successfully asserted themselves; phobia enables the lover to cling to the object of his love, while ensuring, admittedly, that he remains innocuous. Taken together, these two effects reveal the true nature of neurotic illness.

In a recent and most original piece of work,[17] from which I borrowed the term 'confluence of drives' earlier, Adolf Adler argued that anxiety arises from the suppression of what he calls the 'aggressive drive', ascribing to this, in a broad-ranging synthesis, the principal role in what happens both 'in life and in neurosis'. If this particular case of phobia leads us to the conclusion that Hans's anxiety is to be explained as the repression of certain aggressive tendencies, namely hostile feelings towards the father and sadistic feelings towards the mother, then it would seem that we have furnished striking confirmation of Adler's views. And yet I cannot agree with what I regard as a misleading generalization. I cannot bring myself to accept a separate aggressive drive that exists alongside the sex drive and that of self-preservation [*Selbsterhaltungstrieb*], with which we are already familiar, and that is equal in importance to them.[18] It seems to me that Adler has incorrectly hypostasized as a separate drive what is a general and essential characteristic of all drives, namely their compulsive, 'driving' quality, what we might describe as their ability to stimulate motility. Nothing would then remain of the other drives except their relation to a particular goal, once their relation to the means of achieving that goal had been appropriated by the 'aggressive drive'; for the time being, despite the lack of clarity and certainty in our understanding of the drives, I should prefer to adhere to the usual view, whereby each drive is allowed its own capacity to be aggressive,[19] and to identify both the repressed drives in Hans as familiar components of sexual libido.

3

Before I proceed to a more detailed discussion, which I intend to keep short, of what we might learn from little Hans's phobia which is of general value for our understanding of childhood and children's upbringing, I must consider the objection, held over from the beginning of this section, which urges that Hans is neurotic, degenerate, subject to hereditary weakness, and hence not a normal child whose experiences might apply to other children. It has caused me some considerable distress to think of how all those adherents of 'normality' will vilify poor little Hans when they learn that he may indeed be said to have inherited a certain frailty. I had been able to provide assistance to his lovely mother when she developed a neurotic illness caused by the conflicts of girlhood, and this was indeed the beginning of my relationship with Hans's parents. I offer the following tentative remarks in Hans's favour.

First that, according to the strictest definitions, Hans does not conform to the image of a degenerate child with an inherited tendency to nervous disorder, but is in fact a prepossessing, cheerful fellow, well-proportioned and intellectually lively, a delight to others besides his father. There is no doubt as to his sexual precocity, it is true, but we do not have much material for the purposes of comparison that would allow us to arrive at a fair judgement of this. An investigative survey from an American source suggests, for example, that it is not unusual to encounter feelings of love and object-choice at a similarly early age, and we know the same thing to be true from the childhood reminiscences of men later held to be 'great', which leads me to think that sexual precocity is customarily present as a correlate of intellectual precocity and is thus more frequently encountered in gifted children than one might expect.

Having freely acknowledged a bias in favour of little Hans, I would further maintain that he is not the only child to have been overcome by phobias at some time in his childhood. It is well known that such afflictions are quite extraordinarily common, even in children whose upbringing leaves nothing to be desired in the way of strictness. Later, the children in question either become neurotic or remain healthy. Their phobias are given short shrift in the nursery, because they are inaccessible to treatment and no doubt something of an embarrassment. With the months or years they diminish in intensity and to all appearances are cured; but we have no insight into the psychic changes that such a cure necessitates, nor of the changes in character that result from it. When we then accept an adult sufferer from neurosis for psychoanalytic treatment, assuming that his or her illness has only manifested itself in maturity, we regularly discover that the neurosis is directly connected with that childhood anxiety and represents a continuation of it, and that this psychic work has continued to weave its web incessantly and without interruption throughout the patient's whole life, from the time of those childhood conflicts onward, regardless of whether the first symptom persisted or was withdrawn under the pressure of circumstances. Thus in my view Hans's illness was no worse than that of many children who are not branded as 'degenerates', but since the aim of his upbringing had been not to intimidate him, to handle him with the greatest possible care and the least possible constraint, his anxiety was able to manifest itself more boldly. Motives of bad conscience and fear of punishment were absent; these would otherwise undoubtedly have played their part in minimizing the anxiety. It seems to me that we pay too much attention to symptoms and give too little consideration to what causes them. In bringing up children we want nothing better than to be left in peace, to be spared any difficulty, in short to raise well-behaved children without undue concern as to whether the children themselves profit from such a procedure. I can imagine, therefore, that it might have been beneficial to Hans to produce his phobia, for it drew his parents' attention to the difficulties the child was inevitably going to experience in the process of learning to be a civilized member of society, in attempting to overcome inborn drive components, and this disorder of his brought his father to his assistance. Perhaps now he has the advantage over other children, in that he no longer carries within him the seed of repressed complexes that must always be of significance for later life, since it always distorts the development of character to some extent and possibly creates a predisposition to neurosis later on. I am inclined to think so, though I do not know whether many others will share my view, nor whether experience will prove me right.

I must also ask in what way Hans might have been damaged by our bringing to light those complexes which children repress and parents fear. Were the boy's claims on his mother perhaps given the force of reality, or did actions take the place of his intentions to harm his father? Many will no doubt have feared this, misunderstanding the nature of psychoanalysis and believing that we only strengthen evil drives by making them conscious. These wise gentlemen are then only acting consistently when they advise – for goodness' sake – against having any dealings with the wickedness lurking behind the neuroses. They forget, it is true, that they are doctors, displaying a fatal similarity to Dogberry in Shakespeare's *Much Ado About Nothing*, who advises the Watch in a similar vein to keep well away from any thieves or burglars they might encounter: 'for such kind of men, the less you meddle or make with them, why, the more is for your honesty.'[20]

The sole consequences of the analysis are, however, that Hans gets better and is no longer afraid of horses, and that he behaves rather familiarly towards his father, as the father himself tells me with some amusement. But what his father may have forfeited in respect he has gained in trust: 'I thought you knew everything since you knew all about the horses.' For analysis does not reverse the *outcome*, that of repression; the drives which were suppressed remain suppressed, but this is achieved in a different way, with the help of the highest inner authorities [*seelische Instanzen*] the process of repression, which is automatic and excessive, is replaced by moderate and purposeful mastery – in a word, *repression is replaced by condemnation*. This would seem to furnish proof of what we have long suspected, namely that consciousness has a biological function and that when it comes into play it brings with it significant advantages.[21]

If it had been solely up to me I should have taken the risk and given the child the one further explanation that his parents withheld. I should have confirmed his instinctive hunch and told him of the existence of the vagina and of coitus, diminishing still further what remained unresolved and putting an end to his urgent questioning. I am convinced that neither his love for his mother nor his childlike nature would have suffered as a result of such explanations, and that he would have understood that his preoccupation with these important, awe-inspiring matters must be laid to rest until his wish to get bigger had been fulfilled. But the pedagogical experiment was not taken as far as this.

That it is wrong to draw a sharp distinction between 'neurotic' and 'normal' children and adults; that 'illness' is a purely pragmatic summation concept, and that predisposition and experience must coincide for the threshold to be crossed and this summation to be reached; that as a result there is a constant reclassification of many healthy individuals who are deemed to be suffering from neurotic illness, whereas far fewer are reclassified in the opposite direction; these are all things which have been said so often and with such resonance that I surely cannot be alone in making such claims. That the way in which we bring up our children can have a powerful influence in bringing about the predisposition to illness described here, or in preventing it, is at the very least highly probable, but what still appears to be in doubt is what we should aim to achieve in bringing up our children, and where we should intervene. Up until now the task has been seen as that of controlling the drives and sometimes indeed that of suppressing them; the result was not a satisfactory one and when it did succeed it was to the benefit of a small number of privileged people who were not required to suppress their own drives. No one asked the question, moreover, in what way and at what cost the repression of these inconvenient drives had been achieved. If we were to substitute another task for this one, namely to make the individual capable of civilized behaviour and useful to society while sacrificing as little as possible of his own activity, then whatever light psychoanalysis can shed on the origin of pathogenic complexes, and on what lies at the heart of each and every neurosis, deserves to be recognized by educationalists as invaluable guidance for dealing with children. The practical conclusions that may be drawn from this, and the extent to which experience will justify their application in the present social context, I must leave it to others to put to the test and decide.

I cannot take my leave of our young patient's phobia without giving voice to a conjecture that makes the analysis that brought about his cure particularly valuable to me. Strictly speaking I learnt nothing new from this analysis, nothing that I had not already been able to deduce – though less directly and with less clarity – from my treatment of other, older patients. And since on each occasion the neuroses of these other patients could be traced back to the same infantile complexes that underlay Hans's phobia, as we were able to reveal, I am tempted to claim a typical and exemplary importance for this childhood neurosis, and to suggest that the variety of manifestations of neurotic repression and the richness of the pathogenic material do not prevent us from deducing them all from a very small number of processes, all concerned with the same complexes of ideas.

(1909)

Notes

1. [*Translator's note*: Freud's term '*Epikrise*' was not in common usage: it does not appear, for example, in Grimm's dictionary, the equivalent of the *OED*. It appears in an 1870 lexicon of foreign loan-words [*Kaltschmidt*], defined as 'assessment (of an illness)'; a contemporary definition [*Duden*] gives 'critical evaluation of the course of an illness made by the doctor at the close of treatment'. I have retained the Greek term to reflect its abstruseness for Freud's readers.]

2. A. Adler, 'Der Aggressionstrieb im Leben und in der Neurose' ['The Aggressive Drive in Life and Neurosis'] (1908).

3. [*Addition 1923:*] I emphasize later (1923) that the period of sexual development in which our young patient finds himself is characterized in general by the fact that it only recognizes one kind of genitalia, the male; in contrast to the later period of maturity we find not the primacy of the genitals, but the primacy of the phallus.

4. Hans's two notions: 'raspberry juice and a gun to shoot people dead' will certainly not have been determined by a single factor. They probably have as much to do with his hatred for his father as with his constipation complex. The father, who himself guessed at the latter derivation, also thinks of 'blood' when he thinks about 'raspberry juice'.

5. Wanting to beat and 'rag' the horses.

6. Cf. the critical questions addressed to his father (p. 33 above).

7.

> *Das macht, ich bin kein ausgeklügelt Buch*
> *Ich bin ein Mensch mit seinem Widerspruch.*

[I am, you see, no cunningly-contrived fiction but a human being with all his contradictions.] C. F. Meyer, *Huttens letzte Tage* [*Hutt's Last Days*].

8. P. 172, 8th edition.

9. Cf. what he has in mind once the little girl has learnt to talk (p. 57 above).

10. W. Stekel, *Nervöse Angstzustände und ihre Behandlung* [*States of Nervous Anxiety and their Treatment*], 1908.

11. [*Addition 1923:*] The question posed here has admittedly not been pursued. There is, however, no reason to assume that anxiety-hysteria forms any exception to the general rule that in the aetiology of a neurosis there must be a combination of predisposition and experience. Rank's notion of the effects of the birth trauma would appear to throw particular light on the particular susceptibility to anxiety-hysteria that is found in childhood.

12. [*Addition 1924:*] In the context we should add: and touching it as well (p. 24). He, after all, cannot show his widdler without also touching it.

13. This is in keeping with Hans's later admiration for his father's neck.

14. Fear of the father, even in those analyses where the patient is a stranger to the physician, is one of the most significant contributory factors where there is resistance to the reproduction of unconscious pathogenic material. Such resistance is partly in the very nature of these [stereotypical] 'motifs', but it is also possible, as in this example, that an element of the unconscious material is able *by virtue of its content* to inhibit the reproduction of another element.

15. An initially disconcerting idea on the part of the brilliant cartoonist Th. Th. Heine – whose drawings for *Simplizissimus* show how the master butcher's child falls in the sausage machine and then, mourned by his parents as a sausage, is blessed and flies up to heaven – can thus be traced back, as a result of the Lodi episode in our analysis, to infantile roots.

16. His father even observed that an element of sublimation set in at the same time as the repression. His state of anxiety was accompanied by an increased interest in music and the development of the musical gifts he had inherited.

17. See above [note 2].

18. [*Addition 1923:*] This was written at a time when Adler still appeared to be working within the boundaries of psychoanalysis, before he put forward the idea of male protest and denied the notion of repression. Since then I have also had to acknowledge the existence of an 'aggressive drive', which is, however, not the same as that put forward by Adler. I prefer to call it a 'destructive or death drive' (*Jenseits des Lustprinzips* [*Beyond the Pleasure Principle*], *Das Ich und das Es* [*The I and the It*]). Its opposition to the libidinal drives finds expression in the familiar polarity of love and hate. My objection still stands, moreover, to the fact that Adler's concept diminishes a general characteristic of all the drives in favour of one particular one.

19. [Earlier editions contained the words 'without being directed towards a particular object', which were deleted in 1924.]

20. Here I cannot resist asking in bewilderment where those who oppose my views derive the knowledge that they parade so confidently, as to whether repressed sexual drives have a part to play – and if so, what part – in the aetiology of neurosis, if they silence their patients the moment they begin to say anything about their complexes and what follows on from them. In that case, the reports produced by my followers and myself are the only scientific evidence accessible to them.

21. [*Addition 1923:*] Throughout this passage I use the word 'consciousness' in a sense that I have later avoided, for the normal processes of thought that are capable of becoming conscious. We know that such thought processes may also take place *pre*consciously and we do well to evaluate such 'consciousness' in purely phenomenological terms. This does not of course contradict the expectation that the process of becoming conscious also fulfils a biological function.

IV

Postscript to the Analysis of Little Hans

A few months ago – in the spring of 1922 – a young man introduced himself to me, saying that he was the 'little Hans' whose childhood neurosis I had written about in 1909. I was very glad to see him again, for I had lost sight of him some two years after the completion of his analysis and for more than ten years had had no idea what had become of him. The publication of this first case of child analysis had caused something of a stir and provoked a storm of indignation and predictions of disaster because the boy had 'lost his innocence' at such a tender age, and had been sacrificed on the altar of psychoanalysis.

None of these fears had been realized, however. Little Hans was now a strapping youth of nineteen. He declared that he was in excellent health and not suffering from any kind of problem or inhibition. He had not only passed through puberty unscathed but had also been able to cope with the strain of one of the hardest trials of his emotional life. His parents had divorced and had each entered into a new marriage. As a result he lived alone but was on good terms with both his parents; his only regret was that the disintegration of his family had brought about a separation from the younger sister of whom he was so very fond.

One thing Hans told me was particularly remarkable, and I will not venture to offer any explanation for it. He told me that when he read his own case history it was like reading about a stranger: he did not recognize himself, could not remember anything of what was related, and only when the journey to Gmunden was mentioned did a glimmer of memory dawn and he thought he might have been this boy. Thus, far from preventing him from forgetting these events, the analysis itself had been forgotten. Something similar occurs sometimes to those familiar with psychoanalysis when sleeping. Awakened by a dream, one determines to analyse it without delay, then, satisfied with the results of one's efforts one falls asleep once more, and the next morning both dream and analysis are forgotten.

(1922)

Some Remarks on a Case of Obsessive-compulsive Neurosis [The 'Ratman']

The following pages will contain material of two different kinds: first, fragmentary notes on the medical history of an instance of obsessive-compulsive neurosis [*Zwangsneurose*], which, in terms of its length and its damaging consequences, and in the patient's own estimation, could be accounted a moderately severe case, the year-long treatment of which brought about the complete restoration of the patient's personality and the lifting of inhibitions. Second, however, arising directly from this case and drawing on others that I have analysed previously, I make a number of aphoristic statements on the genesis and the more subtle mechanisms of psychological compulsion [*Zwang*], which aim to provide a continuation of my first accounts of the subject, published in 1896.[1]

Such a summary of the contents of my essay seems to require some justification, for I would not wish anyone to think that I consider this particular way of conveying information to be beyond criticism, worthy of emulation: in reality I am merely paying proper attention to inhibitions regarding both external circumstances and content, and would willingly have provided more information, if that had been only possible and permissible. To be precise, I cannot provide a complete treatment history because this would require too detailed an account of my patient's circumstances. The irksome attentions of a city that focuses quite particularly on my activities as a physician preclude the possibility of any entirely faithful account; I find the kind of distortions, however, to which one normally has recourse increasingly inappropriate and reprehensible. If they are only minor ones they do not fulfil their intended purpose of protecting the patient from indiscreet curiosity, and if they are more substantial then the sacrifice is too great, for they ruin our understanding of the overall logic of the case, which derives precisely from the petty realities of everyday life. This last circumstance gives rise to the paradoxical state of affairs whereby one may far more readily divulge to the public a patient's most intimate secrets, since he will then remain unrecognized, than the most harmless and banal features that distinguish his personality, as in this he is known to everyone and will thereby be rendered recognizable to all.

If I may thus excuse the terrible truncation of the medical and treatment history given here, I am obliged to provide a still more convincing explanation for the fact that I have limited myself to individual findings from the psychoanalytical investigation of obsessive-compulsive neurosis. I admit that I have not yet succeeded in comprehending the complex structure of a *severe* case of obsessive-compulsive neurosis in its entirety and that I should be unlikely to succeed in making such a structure, discerned or dimly perceived by the exercise of analytical thought through the masses of material deposited during treatment, apparent to others by reproducing the analysis in full. It is my patients' resistance and the forms in which this is expressed that make this latter task so difficult; but it must be said that, by its very nature, the understanding of obsessive-compulsive neurosis is not simple, but in fact more difficult than a case of hysteria. One would really expect the opposite to be true. The means by which obsessive-compulsive neurosis gives expression to its secret thoughts, the language of obsessive-compulsive neurosis, is merely a dialect, so to speak, of the language of hysteria, but it is a dialect whose meaning we ought to find it easier to sense because it is more closely related to the expression of our conscious thought than hysterical language is. Above all, it does not contain that leap from the spiritual domain into somatic enervation – hysterical conversion – which we can never manage to follow ourselves by grasping it intellectually.

Perhaps also it is only our lesser degree of familiarity with obsessive-compulsive neurosis that is to blame for the fact that reality does not confirm our expectations. Patients suffering from a severe degree of obsessive-compulsive neurosis present themselves for analytical treatment far less often than those afflicted by hysteria. They also dissimulate their condition in everyday life as long as they can and frequently only visit a doctor at a stage of suffering so advanced that if they were afflicted with tuberculosis, for example, it would exclude the possibility of admission to a sanatorium. I draw such a comparison because with straightforward cases of obsessive-compulsive neurosis, or severe ones that we are able to combat early enough, just as with that chronic infectious disease, we can point to a series of dazzlingly successful cures.

In such circumstances no other possibility remains but to offer an account of things that is imperfect and incomplete enough to reflect our knowledge and what it is permissible to say. The fragments of understanding offered here, which were arduous enough to bring to light, may not be very satisfactory in themselves, but other investigators may still use them as a starting point for their work, and common endeavour may succeed in an undertaking that perhaps exceeds the powers of the individual.

Note

1. 'Weitere Bemerkungen über die Abwehr-Neuropsychosen' ['Further Remarks on Neuropsychoses with a Parrying Function'] (1896). (II 'Wesen und Mechanismus der Zwangsneurose' ['The Nature and Mechanisms of Obsessive-compulsive Neurosis'].)

I *Case History*

A youngish man with a university education introduces himself with the information that he has been suffering from compulsive ideas since childhood, but that this has been particularly severe over the past four years. The main content of his suffering is his *fear* that something will befall two people whom he greatly loves, his father and a lady whom he admires. In addition he experiences *compulsive urges*, for example to cut his throat with a razor, and imposes *prohibitions* on himself relating to matters of indifference. He says that he has wasted years of his life struggling with these notions and as a result has been held back in life. None of the cures he has attempted have done him any good except for one course of hydropathic treatment in a clinic in ——, but this was no doubt only because he struck up an acquaintance there that led to regular sexual intercourse. He has no such opportunities here and has intercourse rarely and at irregular intervals. Prostitutes are repugnant to him. His sex life has been altogether wretched, and masturbation has played only a minor role, when he was 16 or 17. His potency is normal, he claims; he first had intercourse at the age of 26.

He gives the impression of being clear-headed and perceptive. When I ask what causes him to put particular emphasis on information about his sexual life he replies that that is what he knows about my theories. Apart from this he has read nothing of what I have written, but when leafing through one of my books recently came across an explanation of bizarre associations of words[1] that reminded him so much of his own 'mental efforts' with regard to his own ideas that he resolved to entrust himself to me for treatment.

A. Induction into the Treatment

The next day, after he had agreed to abide by the only condition of the therapy, namely, to tell me everything that came into his mind, even if he found this *unpleasant*, and even if the thoughts seemed *unimportant, irrelevant* or *nonsensical*, I left it to him to decide on an opening topic; he began as follows:[2]

He has a friend for whom he feels exceptional regard. He goes to this man whenever he is troubled by some criminal impulse and asks him if he despises him for his criminal thoughts. The friend sustains him by reassuring him that he is blameless but has probably been used to examining his life from this point of view since earliest youth. Another man, a student of 19 as against his 14 or 15, had once exercised a similar kind of influence over him in earlier times; he had taken a great fancy to him and done wonders for his self-esteem, so that he had thought himself almost a genius. This student later became his private tutor and changed his attitude towards him quite suddenly, treating him like the worst kind of fool. Finally he realized that the man was in fact interested in one of his sisters and had only taken up with him in order to gain an entrée into the house. This was the first great shock of his life.

He then continues, with no apparent transition:

B. Infantile Sexuality

'My sexual life began very early. I remember a scene that took place when I was 3 or 4 years old (I can recall everything from the age of 5 onward), which came into my mind quite clearly years later. We had a pretty young governess called Fräulein Peter.[3] One evening she was lying on the sofa reading, quite scantily dressed; I was lying next to her and asked for permission to crawl under her petticoats. She said I could, provided that I did not tell anyone. She was not wearing very much, and I touched her genitals and her belly, which I found rather odd. Since then I have felt a burning, tormenting curiosity to see the female body. I can still remember with what feeling of suspense I waited at the Baths, where I was still allowed to go with my sisters and governess, for our governess to take off her clothes and enter the water. From the age of 5 I can remember more. We had another governess then, also young and pretty, who had abscesses on her bottom which she used to squeeze every evening. I would wait furtively for that moment to ease my curiosity. The same was true at the Baths, although Fräulein Lina was more reserved than the other one. (In answer to my interpolated question he replied: 'I did not sleep regularly in her bedroom, but mostly with my parents.') I remember a scene that took place when I must have been about 7 years old.[4] We were all sitting together one evening, the governess, the cook, another girl, my brother who was 18 months younger, and myself. I suddenly caught a snatch of the girls' conversation and heard Fräulein Lina say: "You could do that with the little one, but Paul (that is, me) is too clumsy, he would be bound to get it wrong." I did not understand very clearly what was meant, but did understand that the remark was a disparaging one, and began to cry. Lina comforted me and told me that a girl who had done something similar with a little lad in her care had been locked up for several months. I do not think she got up to any mischief with me, but I was allowed to take all sorts of liberties with her. When I came into her bedroom I would pull the covers off her and touch her and she would never try to stop me. She was not very intelligent and obviously very needy sexually. At 23 she had already had one child, whose father she later married, so that nowadays she has a title. I still meet her quite often on the street.

'At the age of 6 I was already troubled by erections and I know that I once went to my mother to complain to her about this. I remember too that I had to overcome certain scruples in order to do so, for I already sensed that there was some connection with my fantasies and my curiosity and for some time back then harboured a morbid notion that *my parents knew what I was thinking, which I explained to myself by saying that I had articulated my thoughts without hearing them myself*. I see this as the beginning of my illness. There were people, girls, that I liked the look of and whom

I had an urgent wish *to see naked*. These desires were accompanied, however, by *an uncanny feeling that something would happen if I allowed myself such thoughts and that I had to do all sorts of things to prevent this.'*

(When asked he gives as an instance of such fears: 'For example, that *my father would die.'*) 'From an early age I was preoccupied by thoughts of my father's death; this made me melancholy for a long time.'

On this occasion I learn with astonishment that the father, who, even today, is the object of his compulsive fears, has been dead for several years.

What our patient recalls, in this first consultation hour, of his life at the age of 5 or 6 is not merely the beginning of his illness, as he thinks, but the illness itself. A complete case of obsessive-compulsive neurosis, lacking none of its essential elements, at one and the same time the core of his later affliction and a model for it, the elementary organism, so to speak, whose study alone can convey to us the complicated topography of the present illness. We see the child dominated by one component of the sexual drive, voyeurism [*Schau-lust*], and as a result wishing repeatedly and with great intensity to see females whom he finds attractive without their clothes. This wish corresponds to the later compulsive idea; if it does not yet have its compulsive character this is because the I [*Ich*] has not yet set itself up in complete contradiction to it, does not yet sense it to be something alien, and yet something somewhere is already stirring to contradict that wish, for its emergence is regularly accompanied by feelings of painful embarrassment.[5] Clearly conflict is already present in the inner life of this libidinous young man; alongside the compulsive wish we find a compulsive fear which is intimately bound up with that wish: whenever he has thoughts of this kind he is obliged to fear that something terrible will happen. The nature of this terror is already veiled in a characteristic vagueness that from now on will never be absent from the expression of the neurosis. But with a child it is not difficult to discover what is veiled in such vagueness. If we are given an instance of any single one of the blurred generalities of the patient suffering from obsessive-compulsive neurosis we can be sure that the instance is the actual, original idea that generalization is intended to obscure. If we reconstruct the sense of the compulsive fear, therefore, it runs: 'If I harbour the wish to see a woman naked, my father must die.' Feelings of painful embarrassment clearly acquire an uncanny, superstitious tinge and already give rise to an urge to do something to avert disaster, which is realized subsequently in *defensive measures* [*Schutzmaßregeln*].

An erotic drive [*Trieb*] and the rebellious refusal of it, a (not yet compulsive) wish and the (already compulsive) fears that resist it, painful embarrassment as the accompanying emotion [*Affekt*] and an urge to perform parrying actions [*Abwehrhandlungen*]: the inventory of the neurosis is complete. Indeed, a further element is also present, the formation of a kind of *delirium* or *delusion* whose content is most peculiar: he believes that his parents know what he is thinking because he articulates his thoughts without being able to hear them himself. We shall hardly go wrong if we glimpse in this childlike attempt at explanation some intimation of those remarkable inner [*seelisch*] processes that we term unconscious and that we cannot dispense with if we wish to arrive at a scientific clarification of such obscure subject matter. 'I articulate my thoughts without hearing them' sounds like a projection on to the outside world of our assumption that he has thoughts which he does not know about, like an endopsychic perception of what has been repressed.

It may be clearly recognized that this elementary infantile neurosis already has its problem and its apparent absurdity just like any complex adult neurosis. What does it mean that the father must die if the child experiences the stirrings of libidinous desire? Is this pure nonsense, or are there ways of understanding these words, of comprehending them as the necessary product of earlier processes and assumptions?

If we apply insights gained elsewhere to this case of childhood neurosis we will conjecture that here too, before the child reaches the age of 5, there have been traumatic experiences, conflicts and repressions, which, though totally forgotten themselves, have left a residue behind which forms the content of the boy's compulsive fear. We shall later learn how far it is possible to recover these forgotten experiences or to reconstruct [*konstruieren*] them with some degree of confidence. In the meantime let us *emphasize* the coincidence, which is unlikely to be immaterial, that our patient's childhood amnesia comes to an end when he is precisely 5 years old.

That a chronic case of obsessive-compulsive neurosis should begin in this way in early childhood with libidinous desires that are closely linked to uncanny expectations and an inclination to parrying actions, is familiar to me from several other cases. It is absolutely typical, even if probably not the only possible type. A brief word as to the early sexual experiences of my patient, before we proceed to the content of the second session. No one is likely to dispute the fact that these could be described as particularly extensive and far-reaching in their effect. Yet this is also true of the other cases of obsessive-compulsive neurosis that I have been able to analyse. In contrast to hysteria, the characteristic feature of premature sexual activity is never absent. Obsessive-compulsive neurosis shows us, far more clearly than hysteria, that the significant moments that shape the psychoneurosis are not to be sought in the sexual experiences of the present day, but in those of infancy. To superficial inquiry, the sexual life of a patient suffering from obsessive-compulsive neurosis in the present may seem entirely normal; frequently it offers far fewer pathogenic moments and abnormalities than is the case with our present patient.

C. The Great Compulsive Fear

'I think I will begin today with the experience that was the direct cause of my seeking your advice. It was in August, during military exercises in ——. I had been miserable before this and had tormented myself with all kinds of compulsive ideas, which quickly receded, however, during the exercises. I was interested in showing the career officers that not only had I – a reserve officer – learned something, I was also capable of endurance. One day we undertook a short march from ——. During a halt I lost my pince-nez and, even though I could easily have found them again, I did not want to delay our departure and decided to manage without them; however I sent a telegram to my optician in Vienna, asking him to send me a replacement by return. During this same halt I sat down between two officers, one of whom, a captain with a Czech name, was to become a significant figure for me. I felt a certain fear of this man, *for he obviously took pleasure in cruelty*. I am not saying that he was a bad man, but in the officers' mess he had spoken repeatedly in favour of introducing whipping as a punishment, so that I had been obliged to oppose him quite forcefully. Now, during the halt we got into conversation and the captain told me that he had read about a particularly terrible form of punishment practised in the Orient . . .' At this point he breaks off, stands up and asks to be dispensed from any account of the details. I assure him that I have no liking for cruelty myself and certainly have no desire to torment him, but that naturally I cannot make him a gift of something that is not mine to give. He might just as well ask me to make him a gift of a couple of comets. The overcoming of resistance was a requirement of the therapy and we could not simply disregard it. (I had explained the concept of resistance to him at the beginning of the hour, when he told me that he had to overcome a great deal in himself in order to tell me about his experience.) I went on: whatever I could do, however, to guess the full meaning of something to which he could only allude, should be done. Did he perhaps mean impaling? No, not that, but the condemned man was tied up – (he expressed himself so unclearly that I could not immediately guess in what position) – with an upturned pot over his behind, into which *rats* were then put, which – once again he stood up, showing every sign of horror and resistance – *bored their way in*. Into the anus, I added, helping him out.

At all the more significant moments of his narration a very strange compound expression is visible on his face, which I can only interpret as *horror at the pleasure he does not even know he feels*. He continues with great difficulty: 'At that moment the *idea*[6] flashed through my mind that *this might happen to someone who was dear to me*.' When asked a direct question he indicates that he is probably not carrying out the punishment himself, but that it is being carried out in an impersonal way. After some guessing I am sure that it is the lady he admires to whom this 'idea' applies.

He interrupts his narrative to assure me how alien and hostile he finds these thoughts that confront him, and to express surprise at the astonishing speed with which everything connected with them is pouring out. At the very same moment as the idea the 'sanction' also appears, i.e. the parrying measure that must be adopted to prevent such a fantasy from being realized. As the captain was speaking of that awful punishment and the ideas surfaced inside him he was able to fend off *both* with his usual formula, a 'but' accompanied by a dismissive wave of the hand and the words 'Whatever are you thinking of?'

His use of the plural form took me by surprise, just as it will have been incomprehensible to my readers. After all, we have only heard of one idea so far, namely that the rat punishment should be carried out on the lady. Now he is forced to admit that at the same time there surfaced another idea, that the punishment should also be applied to his father. Since his father died many years ago, making this compulsive fear even more nonsensical than the first, the idea had sought to elude conscious acknowledgement for a while longer.

The next evening that same captain handed him a parcel that had arrived by post and said 'Lieutenant A.[7] paid the charges for you; you will have to pay him back.' The packet contained the pince-nez that he had ordered by telegram. At that moment, however, a 'sanction' took shape in his mind: *You must not pay back the money*, or it will happen (i.e. the rat fantasy would be realized on his father and the lady). And straight away, in accordance with a familiar pattern, there arose a command to combat this sanction, as incontrovertible as a vow: '*You must pay back the 3.80 crowns to Lieutenant A.*', words that he found himself speaking half out loud.

Two days later the military exercises came to an end. He filled up the intervening time with efforts to pay back the small sum of money to Lieutenant A. but found himself prevented from doing so by any number of difficulties of an apparently *objective* nature. At first he attempted to make the payment through another officer who was going to the post but was very pleased when this man brought the money back and explained that he had not bumped into Lieutenant A. at the post office, as this manner of keeping his vow did not satisfy him since it did not meet the form of words: 'You must pay back the money to Lieutenant A.' Finally he met the man A. who refused to take the money, however, remarking that he had not paid anything on his behalf, and did not deal with the post at all, it was Lieutenant B. who did so. It caused him some consternation to realize that he could not keep his vow because it was based on a false premiss and he dreamed up the most bizarre solutions to his problem: he would go to the post office with both A. and B., where A. would give 3.80 crowns to the girl who dealt with the post and the girl would give this money to B. so that he could pay A. back the 3.80 crowns according to the strict wording of his vow.

It would not come as any surprise if my reader ran out of patience at this point, for the detailed account given by my patient of the external events of those days and his reactions to them was marred by internal contradictions and appeared hopelessly confused. Only on the third time of telling did I succeed in giving him some insight into this lack of clarity and revealing to him the displacements and falsifications of memory that he had got himself into. There is no need for a detailed recapitulation, for the essential facts are quickly told; I shall remark merely that at the end of this second session my patient appeared dazed and confused. He repeatedly addressed me as 'Captain', probably because at the beginning of the hour I had remarked that I was not cruel like Captain M. and had no intention of tormenting him unnecessarily.

Apart from that, he explained in this consultation hour only that, from the very beginning, in all his earlier fears that something would happen to those he loved, he imagined that such punishments would take place not merely in this world, but also in the next, for all eternity. Up until the age of 13 or 14 he had been conscientious in his religious practice, but from this time on had started to develop the free-thinking attitudes that he still held today. He handles this contradiction by saying: 'What do you know about the afterlife?

What does anyone know? We cannot know anything, there is nothing to lose, so go ahead.' This man, normally so astute, considers such logic to be impeccable and exploits reason's uncertainty in questions of this kind to underpin the way in which he has overcome his pious outlook.

In the third session he finishes the highly characteristic tale of his efforts to keep his compulsive vow: in the evening there took place the final gathering of the officers before the close of the military exercises. It fell to him to reply to the toast to 'the gentlemen of the reserve'. He spoke well, but as if in a dream, for his vow was always at the back of his mind, troubling him. He passed a terrible night as arguments and counter-arguments fought it out; the principal argument, of course, being that the premiss underlying his vow, the assumption that Lieutenant A. had paid the money on his behalf, no longer held true. But he comforted himself that the matter was not yet closed, since A. would accompany them as far as a certain point on their ride to the station at P. the next morning, so that he would have time to speak to him on the subject of this small favour. He did not do so, however, and let A. ride off, but sent a message by his boy that he would call on him that afternoon. He himself arrived at the station at 9.30 a.m., deposited his luggage and undertook a number of errands in the little town, intending to call on A. after this. The village in which A. was stationed was about an hour away from the town of P. by carriage. To go by rail to the place where the post office was situated would have taken three hours, but in this way, he thought that he could just manage to carry out his complicated plan and still catch the evening train from P. to Vienna. His conflicting ideas were: on the one hand, that he was being a coward and obviously only wanted to save himself the discomfort of asking A. to make this sacrifice and of appearing a fool in his eyes, and so was ignoring the requirements of his vow; and on the other hand, that on the contrary he was being a coward in keeping his vow, since in doing so he was only seeking respite from his compulsive ideas. If, when he was trying to make up his mind about something, the arguments balanced one another out, he usually allowed chance events to determine the outcome as if they were divine judgements. This was why he said yes when a porter on the station asked him 'For the 10 o'clock train, sir?', left the town at 10 and effected a *fait accompli* which brought him considerable relief. He even accepted a token for the *table d'hôte* from the guard responsible for the restaurant car. At the first station it suddenly occurred to him that it was still possible to get out here, wait for the train in the opposite direction and take this as far as P., make his way to the place where A. was billeted, undertake the three-hour train journey with him to the post office, etc. Only the fact that he had told the waiter that he would be taking lunch prevented him from carrying out his intention; he did not give it up entirely, however, but postponed leaving the train until a later station. In this way he struggled on from station to station until he reached one where it seemed impossible to get out because he had relatives living there, and decided to travel through to Vienna, where he could call on his friend, explain the matter to him and, depending on his decision, return to P. after that on the night train. He countered my doubts as to whether that would have been feasible by assuring me that he would have had half an hour between the arrival of the one train and the departure of the other. Once in Vienna he found his friend, though not in the restaurant where he had expected to find him, did not arrive at his friend's apartment until 11 o'clock in the evening and explained the matter to him that same night. His friend threw up his hands in frustration that he could still doubt that he was in the grip of a compulsive idea, calmed him down sufficiently to enable him to sleep extremely well and went with him the next morning to the post office, so that he could dispatch the 3.80 crowns to the post office where the parcel containing the pince-nez had itself arrived.

This last piece of information gave me a point of reference from which to disentangle the distortions in his narrative. If, once his friend had brought him to his senses, he sent the small sum of money neither to Lieutenant A. nor to Lieutenant B. but directly to the post office, he must have known, and must already have known when he left, that he owed the delivery charges *to no one other than the post-office official*. It transpired that he had indeed known this even before the captain had challenged him and he had sworn his vow, for now he remembered that some hours *before* his meeting with the cruel captain he had had occasion to introduce himself to another captain who had explained the true state of affairs to him. This officer had told him, on hearing his name, that he had been in the post office shortly before and had been asked by the *young woman in the post office* whether he knew a Lieutenant H. (our patient) for whom a parcel had arrived on which delivery charges were due. He replied in the negative, but the young woman said that she would trust the unknown lieutenant and would pay the charges herself for the time being. In this way our patient came into possession of the pince-nez he had ordered. The cruel captain was in error when, on handing over the package, he urged him to pay back the 3.80 crowns to A. Our patient must have known that this was an error. Nevertheless he made a vow, based on this error, which was bound to torment him. In doing so he had suppressed the episode with the other captain and the existence of the trusting young woman in the post office both to himself, and also, in narrating the story, to me. I concede that in the light of this correction his behaviour appears even more unreasonable and incomprehensible than it did before.

After he had left his friend and returned to his family he was assailed by doubt all over again. His friend's arguments had not been any different from his own, after all, and he was under no illusion that this temporary reassurance was to be attributed only to his friend's personal influence. The decision to go to a doctor had been cunningly woven into his delirium as follows. He thought he would ask a doctor to prepare a statement certifying that he needed to perform an act such as he had thought of in connection with Lieutenant A. in order to restore his health, and A. would undoubtedly allow himself to be persuaded by such a statement to accept the 3.80 crowns from him. By playfully placing one of my books in his hands, chance led him to choose me. There was no question of my preparing any certificate for him, however, and he very sensibly asked only to be liberated from his compulsive ideas. Many months later, at the height of his resistance, the temptation surfaced once more to go to

P. after all, seek out Lieutenant A. and stage the little comedy of repaying the money.

D. Initiation into an Understanding of the Therapy

No one should expect to learn at this early stage what ideas of mine might cast light on these peculiarly odd compulsive ideas (about the rats); correct psychoanalytical technique requires that the physician suppress his curiosity, leaving the patient free to decide the order in which topics are addressed in psychoanalytical work. I greeted my patient therefore at the beginning of the fourth session with the question: 'How do you wish to continue?'

'I have decided to tell you something that I consider very significant and that has tormented me from the very beginning.' He goes on to tell me his father's medical history in considerable detail, his father having died 9 years ago of emphysema. One evening, believing his condition to be critical, he asked the doctor when he could consider his father to be out of danger. The reply came: the evening of the day after tomorrow. He did not imagine for a moment that his father might not live that long. He went to bed at 11.30 in the evening for an hour, and when he awoke at 1 a.m. he learnt from a friend who was a doctor that his father had died. He reproached himself for not having been at his father's deathbed, a reproach that was intensified when the nurse told him that his father had once spoken his name in the last days and had asked her, when she went to his bedside: 'Are you Paul?' He thought he had noticed that his mother and sisters reproached themselves similarly; but they did not speak of the matter. At first he was not tormented by this reproach; for a long time he could not take in the fact of his father's death; again and again it came about that when he heard a good joke he would say to himself: 'I must tell my father that.' His imagination played on the idea of his father, moreover, so that when there was a knock at the door he would often think: 'That will be my father', and would expect to see his father when he walked into a room; and although he was never able to forget the fact that he was dead, the expectation that his ghost would appear held no terror but was something for which he felt a deep longing. It was 18 months later when the memory of what he had failed to do re-awakened and began to torment him so horribly that he regarded himself as a criminal. The reason for this was the death of an aunt by marriage and his visit to the mourning household. From then on his thought patterns began to encompass the hereafter. The immediate consequence of this attack was a serious inability to work.[8] As he recounts how he was only sustained at that time by the comfort offered him by his friend, who rejected such reproaches as being terribly exaggerated, I take the opportunity to offer him a first insight into the basic premisses of psychoanalytical therapy. If we encounter a mismatch between idea-content and emotion [*Affekt*], that is, between the magnitude of the reproach and its cause, the layman would say that the emotion was too great for the cause, and hence exaggerated, so that the conclusion drawn from the reproach, that of being a criminal, was a false one. The physician, on the other hand, says: no, the emotion is justified, we should not spend our time criticizing the patient's sense of guilt, but it actually belongs to another content, which is unknown (*unconscious*) and which must first be sought. The idea-content that we know about has arrived here by means of inaccurate linking. We are not used, however, to sensing strong emotions in ourselves without idea-content, and so in the absence of a content we take a different one, which seems more or less to fit, as a surrogate, much as our police, if they cannot catch the real murderer, will arrest the wrong person in his place. The fact that inaccurate links are made also accounts in itself for the impotence of logic in combating the tormenting idea. I finish by admitting that this new way of looking at things leads at first only to further enigmas, for how is he to admit the justice of a reproach that says that he has acted like a criminal towards his father when he must know that he has never actually committed any sort of crime against him?

In the next session he expresses considerable interest in my explanations but permits himself to voice a number of doubts: how, he asks, could my suggestion that the reproach, the sense of guilt, is a true feeling help to bring about a cure? – It is not the suggestion that has this effect, I reply, but discovering the unknown content to which the reproach belongs. – Yes, that is precisely his question, he counters. – To illustrate my brief statements on the psychological *distinctions between what is conscious and what is unconscious*, and on the wear and tear to which all consciousness is subject, while the unconscious remains relatively unchanged, I refer to the antiquities displayed in my consulting room, remarking that they were in fact merely grave goods and that for them burial had meant preservation. Pompeii had only started to decay once it had been unearthed. – He goes on to ask whether there was any guarantee as to how one would react towards what one found out. One person might behave in such a way as to overcome the reproach, but another might not, he thought. – No, I reply, it is in the nature of things that the emotion is always overcome, usually while the work is still in progress. After all, people are making every effort to preserve Pompeii, but anyone would wish to be rid of such tormenting ideas. – He had said to himself that a reproach can only be the result of offending against one's own most personal moral laws, and not against external ones. (I confirm this, replying that someone who merely offends against *them* often feels that he is a hero.) Such a process could only be possible, then, in the case of a *complete disintegration of the personality*, present from the beginning. Could he succeed in reintegrating his personality? If so he was confident that he could achieve a great deal, perhaps more than other people. – To this I reply that I entirely agree with this idea of a split in his personality; all that he need do is weld this new opposition, between the moral person and the wicked one, together with the one we had discussed earlier, the opposition between the conscious and the unconscious. The moral person was the conscious part, the wicked one the unconscious part.[9] – He can remember that, although he regards himself as a moral person, he certainly did things in his *childhood* that had come from the other person. – I observe that he has discovered, incidentally as it were, one of the main characteristics of the unconscious, namely its relationship to the *infantile*. The unconscious is the infantile part, that bit of the personality that cut itself off back in infancy, did not continue to develop alongside the rest of the personality and was thus *repressed*. What issues from the repressed unconscious are the elements sustaining the involuntary thinking that constitutes his suffering? He might discover another characteristic of the unconscious even now; I would happily leave him free to do so. – He finds nothing further to say on this topic but instead expresses doubt as to whether changes that have been in existence for so long can be reversed. In particular, he asks, what can be done about the idea of the afterlife, which after all cannot be refuted by logic? – I do not dispute the seriousness of his case nor the significance of the constructs he has embraced, but suggest that his age is very much in his favour, as is the intactness of his personality: in saying this I am making a positive comment about him, and he is visibly cheered by it.

In the next session he begins by saying that he must relate an actual incident from his childhood. After the age of 7, as he had already told me, he experienced a fear that his parents could guess his thoughts, a feeling that has persisted, actually, all his life. At the age of 12 he loved a little girl, the sister of a friend (this was not sexual in nature, he told me when I asked him; he did not want to see her naked, she was too little), but she was not as affectionate as he would have liked. And then the idea occurred to him that she would be loving towards him if misfortune befell him; the death of his father came involuntarily into his mind as one such possibility. He rejected this idea immediately and forcefully, and defends himself even now against the possibility that this might have been the expression of a 'wish'. It was simply 'thought association'.[10] – I object: if it was not a wish, why the ruffled feathers? – Well, only because of the content of the idea, that his father might die. – I say that he is treating the formulation as if it were *lèse-majesté*, where, as is well-known, the same punishment is meted out whether one says 'The king is an ass' or whether the unmentionable words are couched in a sentence such as 'If anyone says . . . he will answer for it to me.' I could quite easily find a context in which the idea-content that he was so reluctant to accept would exclude any possibility of reluctance; e.g. 'If my father were to die, I should kill myself on his grave.' – He is shaken, but will not abandon his protest, so that I break off our disagreement by observing that the idea of his father's death did not make its first appearance on this occasion but clearly dates back much further, and that some time we must follow the trail back to its origin. – He goes on to tell me how a very similar thought came to him in a flash six months before his father's death. He was already in love with the lady he had mentioned,[11] but was prevented by material considerations from contemplating a closer connection. Then the idea came: *his father's death would perhaps make him rich enough to be able to marry her.* Defending himself against this thought he went so far as to wish that his father might leave him nothing at all, so that he should not be compensated by gain of any sort for what was to him such a terrible loss. The same idea came to him on a third occasion, but in a much less powerful form, the day before his father's death. He thought 'Now I may be going to lose what I love most in the world'; this was immediately contradicted: 'No, there is someone else whose loss would be far more painful to you.'[12] Such thoughts amaze him, he tells me, since he is quite sure that his father's death is something he could never have wished for, but only feared. – After he has said this in a very loud voice I think it useful to introduce a new bit of theory. Theory suggests that anxiety of this kind corresponds to an earlier *wish*, now repressed, so that we must assume that the truth is the exact opposite of what he has just asserted. This also fits in with the requirement that the unconscious should be in contradictory opposition to the conscious mind. He is very emotional, very sceptical, and is amazed that he could possibly have harboured such a wish when his father is, after all, the dearest person on earth to him. There is absolutely no doubt that he would have renounced any happiness for himself if he could have saved his father's life by doing so. I reply that it is just this intense love that is the condition of repressed hatred. In the case of people to whom he was indifferent he would no doubt easily succeed in allowing the motivation for moderate liking and a similar degree of antipathy to coexist – say, if he were a civil servant and thought of his head of department as a pleasant superior but a stickler for regulations and an inhumane judge. Shakespeare's Brutus says something similar of

Caesar (III, 2): 'As Caesar lov'd me, I weep for him; as he was fortunate, I rejoice at it; as he was valiant, I honour him; but – as he was ambitious, I slew him.' This speech already has a disconcerting effect, because we imagined Brutus to feel a more intense affection for Caesar than this. In the case of a person who was closer to him, his wife, say, he would strive for a greater uniformity of feeling and, as is only human, would fail for that reason to notice the faults which might stir up feelings of dislike, would ignore them, as if blinded. Thus it is precisely the magnitude of his love that prevents feelings of hatred (although the term is something of a caricature), which must after all come from somewhere, from remaining conscious. It is a problem to know where this hatred comes from, admittedly; his own evidence pointed to the time when he feared that his parents could guess what he was thinking. On the other hand we might also ask why his great love had not been able to blot out his feelings of hatred, as is customary when such impulses are in opposition. One can only assume that the hatred is bound up with a source, a trigger, which makes it indestructible. On the one hand, therefore, a connection of this kind protects the hatred he feels for his father from being destroyed, while on the other hand his great love prevents it from becoming conscious, so that the only thing left is precisely that existence in the unconscious from which it can force its way out now and again in lightning flashes.

He admits that this all sounds very plausible, but without a trace of conviction, of course.[13] He begs leave to ask how it is possible for an idea of this kind to come in fits and starts, to occur for a brief moment at the age of 12 and then again at 20 and once again two years later, and only then to persist. He cannot believe that the feelings of hostility had been extinguished in between, and yet there had been no sign of any reproach during the periods of respite. I reply: when someone asks a question of this kind they already know the answer. All they need do is carry on talking. When he continues there is apparently only a faint connection with what had gone before: he had been his father's best friend, and his father his; except in a few areas where fathers and sons tend to keep out of each other's way (I wonder what he means here?) the intimacy between them had been greater than he now felt for his best friend. It is true that he had greatly loved the lady for whose sake he had slighted his father in his own mind, but his wishes with regard to her had never been truly sensual, like the feelings that had filled his childhood; sensual impulses had been much stronger altogether in childhood than during puberty. – I suggest that he has now given the answer we had been waiting for, and at the same time discovered the third great characteristic of the unconscious. The nature of the source from which his hostility towards his father derives its indestructible quality is clearly that of *sensual desire*, and here he had somehow felt his father to be an *intruder*. A conflict of this kind between sensuality and filial love was entirely typical. He had experienced periods of respite because, after the first premature explosion of sensuality in him, these feelings had been quite considerably dampened down. Only when intense amorous desires set in once again did the analogous situation cause his hostility to re-emerge. I ask him to confirm, moreover, that I did not steer him on to the subject either of infancy or of sexuality, but that he had raised them of his own accord. – He goes on to ask why, at the time of his amorous attachment to the lady, he had not simply decided that his father's ability to intrude on this love was not worthy of consideration when compared with the love he felt for him. – I replied that it is hardly possible to strike someone dead *in absentia*. To make a decision of this kind it would have been necessary for this to be the first occasion on which he had experienced the wish he complains of; but that wish was in fact one that had been *long repressed*, towards which he could react no differently than he had done before and that therefore continued to evade annihilation. The wish (to eliminate the intrusive father) must have come about at a time when things were very different, when he perhaps did not love his father more than he loved the person who was the object of his sensual desires, or when he was not capable of a clear decision, in very early childhood, before the age of 6, before continuous recollection set in, and so it had remained fixed for all time. With this reconstruction of events our discussion came to an end for the time being.

°

In the next session, the seventh, he returns to the same topic once again. He cannot believe that he could ever have experienced the wish to harm his father. He recalls a novella by Sudermann that made a powerful impression on him: in it, one sister feels a murderous desire towards the other when visiting her sick-bed, because she would like to marry her husband. She then kills herself because, after recognizing such base motives in herself, she feels she does not deserve to live. He can understand this, and considers it quite all right if his thoughts destroy him, because he deserves no better.[14] I remark that it is well known that those who are ill derive a certain satisfaction from their suffering, so that they all in fact strive only partially to get well. He must not lose sight of the fact that a treatment of the kind we were undertaking would inevitably be accompanied by *constant resistance*; I should be reminding him of this fact over and over again.

He tells me that he now wishes to speak of a criminal action in which he is unable to recognize himself but which he remembers quite clearly. He quotes a saying of Nietzsche's: 'Das habe ich getan' sagt mein Gedächtnis, 'das kann ich nicht getan haben' – sagt mein Stolz und bleibt unerbittlich. Endlich – gibt das Gedächtnis nach. ['I did that', says my memory; 'I cannot have done that', says my pride and refuses to yield. Finally – memory gives way.'[15]] 'So my memory did not give way.' – 'Only because you derive pleasure from your reproaches in order to punish yourself.' 'My younger brother and I – we are good friends nowadays, he is giving me great cause for concern at the moment as he is contemplating a marriage that I consider to be folly; I have already thought of going there and murdering the female concerned so that he cannot marry her – we often used to fight when we were children. At the same time we were very fond of one another and were inseparable, but I was obviously ruled by jealousy, for he was the stronger, the better looking and for that reason the better loved.' 'You told me of one such jealous scene with Fräulein Lina.' 'Well, after one occasion of that kind, before I was 8 years old, I am sure, for I was not yet at school, where I went at the age of 8, this is what I did: we both owned toy guns of a well-known type; I loaded mine using the ramrod and told him if he looked down the barrel he would see something interesting, and when he was looking down it, I pulled the trigger. I hit him in the forehead and did not do him any harm, but my intention was really to hurt him. Afterwards I was beside myself, threw myself on the ground and asked myself: how could I possibly have done that? – But I did do it.' – I use the opportunity to plead my case. If he had retained the memory of such a deed, which now seemed so alien to him, he could not deny the possibility that at a younger age still he had experienced something similar, something he could no longer remember, directed against his father. – He could tell of other vengeful impulses against that lady whom he so greatly admires and of whose character he gives such an enthusiastic account. Perhaps she did not find it easy to love and was saving herself for the one man to whom she would one day belong; she did not love him. When this became clear to him a conscious fantasy took shape in his mind that he would become very rich, marry someone else and then call on the lady with his wife, in order to hurt her feelings. But at this point his imagination failed for he was obliged to admit that he was quite indifferent to the other woman, his wife, his thoughts became confused and in the end he realized that this other woman would have to die. This fantasy, just like his attack on his brother, he finds, is characterized by the *cowardice* that is so terrible to him.[16] – As our conversation continues I tell him that he must logically declare himself free of responsibility for all these traits of character, since all these reprehensible impulses go back to childhood and are effectively products of his childhood character, which live on in the unconscious, and he knows perfectly well that one cannot demand ethical responsibility from a child. Only as he develops does the ethically responsible human being emerge from the sum of a child's aptitudes.[17] He expresses doubt, however, that all his evil impulses have their origin in childhood. I promise to prove it to him in the course of the therapy.

He cites the fact that his illness has been so enormously aggravated since his father's death, and I agree with him inasmuch as I recognize that mourning for his father is the principal source of the illness's intensity. His mourning has found pathological expression, so to speak, in his illness. Whereas the course of mourning is normally completed in twelve months to two years, pathological mourning like his can last for an unlimited length of time.

This is as much as I am able to narrate of my patient's case history in detail and according to the order of events. It more or less corresponds to the exposition of the treatment, which continued for 11 months.

E. Some Compulsive Ideas and How to Translate Them

It is a well-known fact that compulsive ideas appear to be either without motivation or without sense, just like the phrasing of our nightly dreams, and our first task is to establish their foothold and meaning in the inner life of the individual so that their purpose is evident, self-evident in fact. One should never be misled in the exercise of translation by an appearance of insolubility; the wildest and most peculiar compulsive ideas can be solved when one is properly absorbed in the task. One arrives at such a solution, however, by bringing the compulsive ideas into temporal connection with the patient's experiences, that is, by examining when an individual compulsive idea first appeared and under what external circumstances it tends to be repeated. In the case of compulsive ideas that have not acquired a permanent existence, as is very often the case, the work of solution is simplified accordingly. We may quickly become convinced that once the connection between the compulsive idea and the patient's experiences has been uncovered, those other puzzling elements of the pathological formation that we desire to understand – its meaning, the mechanism which produced it, how it is derived from the psychic driving forces that determine its development – can all readily be comprehended.

I shall begin with a particularly transparent example of the *suicidal impulse* which so frequently occurs in our patient, which virtually analyses itself in description: he lost some weeks of study as a result of his mistress's absence, as she had gone away to care for her grandmother who was seriously ill. In the middle of the most zealous bout of studying the thought suddenly occurred to him: 'The command to accept the first possible examination date in the term would be tolerable. But what if one were visited by the command to slit one's throat with a razor blade?' Straight away he realized that the command had already been uttered and was hastening to the cupboard to fetch his razor when it occurred to him: 'No, it is not as simple as that. You must go there[18] and kill the old woman.' At this he fell to the ground, horror-struck.

Here the connection between this compulsive idea and our patient's life is contained in the opening remarks of the account. His lady was absent while he was studying strenuously for an examination that would make union with her a more realistic possibility. While studying he was overtaken by longing for his absent love and the thought of the reason for her absence. And then there came something that in a normal person might have been a stirring of ill-feeling towards the grandmother: 'Did the old woman really have to fall ill now, when I feel such dreadful yearning for *her*?' We must suppose something similar but far more intense to have taken place in our patient, an unconscious attack of rage that, together with his yearning, might have been couched in the exclamation: 'Oh, I should like to go there and kill the old woman who is keeping my beloved from me!' There follows the command: 'Kill yourself as a punishment for such murderous, angry cravings' and, accompanied by such vehement emotion, the whole process enters the consciousness of our compulsive patient *in reverse order* – the punitive command at the beginning, the reference to the punishable cravings at the end. I do not think there is anything forced in this attempt at elucidation, nor does it incorporate many hypothetical elements.

Another, more long-lasting impulse to indirect suicide, so to speak, was more difficult to explain because its relation to the patient's experience was hidden behind one of these external associations that seem so very offensive to our conscious minds. One day during the summer holidays the idea suddenly came to him that he was too fat and must *lose weight*. He now began to leave the table before dessert, to tear out on to the roads in the August heat without a hat and then to climb up mountains in double-quick time until the sweat was pouring off him and he was obliged to stop. A suicidal intention behind this obsession with losing weight became clearly apparent on one occasion when, at the top of a steep incline, he heard a command to throw himself off, which would have meant certain death. The solution to this illogical compulsive activity was revealed to our patient only when it suddenly occurred to him that the object of his affections had also been staying at the summer resort, but accompanied by an English cousin who showed her numerous little attentions and of whom he was very jealous. This cousin was called Richard and was known, as is generally the case in England, as *Dick*.[19] He wanted to murder this man, Dick, for the jealousy and rage he felt towards him was far greater than he was able to acknowledge, and so, to punish himself, he imposed on himself the torture of this reducing diet. As different as this compulsion may seem from the previous direct command to suicide, they have one significant feature in common, their genesis as a reaction to a monstrous rage, incomprehensible to consciousness, against someone whose presence intrudes upon a love affair.[20]

Other compulsive ideas, though also directed towards the beloved, reveal a different mechanism, however, and are derived from a different drive. During the period when his lady was present in the resort where he was spending the summer, he produced, quite apart from the obsession with losing weight that we have already mentioned, a whole series of compulsive activities relating, in part at least, to her. On one occasion, when he was with her on a boat and a sharp wind was blowing, he had to press her to put on his cap because the command had formed in his head that *nothing should happen to her*.[21] It was a kind of *protective compulsion* that bore other fruits besides. On another occasion, when they were together in a thunderstorm he suddenly felt the compulsion to *count* to 40 or 50 between lighting and thunderclap, something that he was quite unable to comprehend. On the day of her departure he caught his foot on a stone lying in the road and *had* to move it to the edge because the idea came to him that in a few hours her carriage would be passing along the same stretch of road and might perhaps be damaged by this very stone, but a few minutes later it occurred to him that this was nonsense and he *had* to go back and restore the stone to its original position in the middle of the road. After she had left he was seized by a *compulsion to understand* that rendered him intolerable to everyone he knew. He forced himself to understand every single syllable that anyone spoke to him, as if otherwise some great treasure might elude him. He was continually asking: 'What did you just say?' And when it was repeated to him he said he thought they had said something different the first time, and his dissatisfaction remained.

All these products of his illness turn on an event which dominated his relationship with his mistress at that time. Before the summer, when he took his leave of her in Vienna, he interpreted something she said as meaning that she did not wish to be associated with him in present company, and this made him very unhappy. In the summer they found the opportunity to bring the matter out into the open and the lady was able to prove to him that her words, which he had taken the wrong way, had in fact been intended to protect him from the ridicule of others. Now he was again very happy. The clearest reference to this incident is contained in his compulsion to understand, the form of which is as if he had said to himself: 'After this experience you must never again misunderstand anyone if you want to spare yourself unnecessary torment.' But his resolution has not only been generalized from that single occasion but has also – perhaps because of his beloved's absence – been displaced from her esteemed person on to every other poor wretch. The compulsion cannot have been produced only by satisfaction at the explanation he received from her, either, but must express something else as well, for it modulates, after all, into doubt and dissatisfaction concerning the repetition of what he has heard.

We can track down this other element by examining the other compulsive commands the patient experienced. The significance of the protective compulsion can only be as a reaction – remorse and penitence – to an opposite, hostile impulse that had been directed, before matters had been resolved between them, against the beloved. In the light of accompanying material the compulsion to count during the thunderstorm can be interpreted as a measure to ward off fears that signified mortal danger. Analysis of the compulsive ideas that we discussed earlier has already prepared us to assess our patient's hostile impulses as particularly violent ones, of the kind that express themselves in senseless rage, and then we find that this rage against the lady contributes to his compulsive ideas even after the two have been reconciled. His obsessive doubts as to whether he has heard correctly represent his continuing doubt as to whether he has in fact understood his beloved correctly this time, whether he is justified in taking her words as proof of her tender affection for him. The doubt expressed in his compulsion to understand is doubt as to whether she loves him or not. A battle is raging in the lover between love and hate, both directed towards the same person, and the battle is depicted graphically in the compulsive action, which is also symbolically significant, of removing the stone from the road she is to take and then reversing this act of love, putting the stone back where it was so that her carriage will come to grief and she will be hurt. We misunderstand this second element of the compulsive action if we see it merely as the critical rejection of morbid behaviour that he himself makes it out to be. The fact that this too is enacted under a sense of compulsion reveals that it is itself part of the morbid behaviour and is determined by its opposition to what motivates the first element of his action.

Compulsive activity of this kind with two consecutive time-signatures, where the rhythm of the first cancels out the second, is a typical feature of obsessive-compulsive neurosis. It is of course misunderstood in the conscious thought processes of the patient and given a secondary motivation – i.e. *rationalized*.[22] Its true meaning lies in its depiction of the conflict between two more or less equally strong opposing impulses, opposites which, in my experience to date, are always those of love and hate. They deserve our particular theoretical interest because they reveal a new type of symptom formation. Instead of arriving at a compromise, as regularly occurs in cases of hysteria, where a single means of depiction suffices for both elements in the opposition, thus killing two birds with one stone,[23] here the two opposing elements each find satisfactory expression singly, first the one and then the other, though of course not without an attempt being made to produce some sort of logical connection between the two hostile elements – one that often defies all logic.[24]

Conflict between love and hate made itself known in our patient's case by means of other symptoms as well. At the time when his sense of piety was reawakened he devised prayers for himself that began to require up to an hour and a half to say because something always crept in to the pious formulations to turn them into their opposites. If he – a Bileam in reverse – were to say 'May God watch over him', an evil spirit would quickly slip in a 'not'.[25] On one occasion when this happened, the idea occurred to him to curse, thinking that a contradiction would certainly creep in then; in this notion the original intention, repressed by means of prayer, was able to force its way through. In his perplexity he arrived at a solution by giving up his prayers, replacing them with a short formula concocted out of the initial letters and syllables of various prayers. He then pronounced these so quickly that nothing could force its way in.

He once brought me a dream that contained a representation of the same conflict transposed on to the figure of the physician: My mother has died. He wishes to offer his condolences but is afraid that in doing so he will break into the same *impertinent laughter* that he has already produced repeatedly in cases of bereavement. For this reason he chooses to write a card instead with the letters 'p.c.', but these are changed, as he writes them, into 'p.f.'[26]

The conflicting nature of his feelings for his mistress was too obvious to have eluded his conscious perception entirely, even if we may conclude from the compulsive way in which he expressed them that he was unable to assess correctly quite how profound his negative impulses towards her were. When he had first wooed her ten years previously the lady had refused him. Since then periods of time during which he believed he loved her passionately had alternated, to his conscious mind, with others during which he felt indifferent to her. When, in the course of his treatment, he was to take a step which brought him closer to the objective of asking for her hand, his resistance was normally expressed in the initial conviction that he was not really so very fond of her; this was, however, quickly overcome. On one occasion, when she was seriously ill in bed, a fact that aroused his extreme sympathy, he was looking at her when the wish burst out of him that she should lie there forever. This notion he interpreted to himself, with an over-subtle lack of comprehension, as expressing the wish that she should be ill all the time so that he might be released from the fear of repeated attacks of illness, which he found unbearable![27] From time to time he found himself preoccupied in imagination with daydreams that he himself recognized as 'revenge fantasies', and of which he felt ashamed. Because he thought that she would place great value on the social standing of any suitor, he would fantasize that she had married a man of this kind, who was in government office. He now finds a position in the same department and enjoys greater advancement, so that the other man becomes his subordinate. One day this man performs a dishonest action. The lady falls at his feet, begging him to save her husband. He promises to do so and reveals that it was only out of love for her that he had taken this position in the first place, having foreseen a moment of this kind. Now that he has saved her husband his mission is complete and he intends to resign his office.

In other fantasies whose content was that he did the lady a great service, or some such, without her discovering his identity, he recognized only tender affection, failing to appreciate that the nobility he displayed, in the manner of Dumas' Count of Monte Cristo, was intended to repress the desire for revenge, and evaluating the origin of the emotion, and its purpose, accordingly. He admitted, incidentally, that from time to time he experiences quite explicit impulses to do some harm to the lady he adores. These impulses are generally subdued in her presence and come to the fore only in her absence.

F. Immediate Cause of the Illness

One day our patient made brief mention of an incident in which I could not but recognize the cause of his illness, or at least the recent trigger, some six years ago, for the attack of illness that persists into the present day. He himself had no idea that he had uttered something of significance; he could not remember ever having set any store by the incident, which, by the way, he had never forgotten. Such behaviour calls for some theoretical evaluation.

It is the rule in hysteria that the recent causes of illness fall prey to amnesia in exactly the same way as those infantile experiences with whose help the energy generated by the emotion is converted into symptoms. Where it is impossible to forget completely, amnesia nevertheless gnaws away at the recent traumatic trigger and, at the very least, robs it of its significant components. In this amnesia we find proof of the repression that has taken place. As a rule this is not the case in obsessive-compulsive neurosis. The infantile preconditions of neurosis may have fallen prey to amnesia – though this is often an incomplete process; the recent causes of the illness, on the other hand, remain in the memory. Here the process of repression uses a different mechanism, which is actually more straightforward; instead of forgetting the trauma, it deprives it of the emotion with which it is charged [*Affektbesetzung*] so that all that remains in the conscious mind is an idea-content which is neutral and reckoned to be without significance. The distinction lies in the psychic event that can be reconstructed behind the phenomenon; the outcome of the process is almost the same in both cases, for a neutral memory-content is only rarely reproduced and plays no part in a person's conscious intellectual activity. In order to distinguish between the two kinds of repression we can initially only make use of the patient's protestation that he feels on the one hand that he has always known something, or on the other that he forgot it a long time ago.[28]

Thus it is not at all rare for people suffering from obsessive-compulsive neurosis and afflicted by self-reproaches, who have connected the emotion from this with the wrong causes, to communicate the right ones to their physician without the slightest suspicion that the reproaches have merely become detached from them. Astonished, almost boastful even, they may perhaps comment: 'But I think nothing of it.' So it was in the first case of obsessive-compulsive neurosis I encountered, many years ago, which opened my eyes to the nature of that illness. My patient was a civil servant afflicted by apprehensions without number, of whose compulsive action over the branch in the park at Schönbrunn I gave an account earlier; he engaged my attention by virtue of the fact that, after visiting me for a consultation, he always handed me clean, uncreased notes. (At that time there were no silver coins in Austria.) When once I remarked that one could recognize the civil servant by the brand new florins that he drew from the public purse, he informed me that on the contrary, the florins were not new at all but had been ironed in his own home. It was a matter of conscience to him not to hand anyone dirty paper notes; they carried bacteria of the most dangerous sort, which might harm the recipient. At that time I already had some faint sense of the connection between the neuroses and sexuality and so on another occasion I took the risk of asking my patient how he felt about this matter. 'Oh, everything's fine in that department', he answered lightly, 'I don't go short. There's more than a few good families where I play the kindly old uncle and now and again I take the opportunity to invite a young girl on an outing to the country. Then I arrange things so that we miss the train and have to spend the night in the country. I do things very handsomely; I always take two rooms, but when the girl is in bed I go in to her and masturbate her.' – 'Are you not afraid of doing her some harm when you use your dirty hand to work on her?' – At this he exploded, however: 'Harm? What do you mean, harm? I didn't do any of them any harm, and they all liked it. Some of them are married already and it didn't do them any harm.' He took my query in very bad part and never came back. I could only explain the contrast between his anxiety with regard to the paper florins and his complete lack of concern in abusing the girls in his care, however, as a *displacement* of the emotion aroused by the reproach. The intention behind such displacement was clear enough; if he left the reproach where it belonged he would be obliged to renounce a sexual satisfaction that was probably urged upon him by powerful determining forces going back to infancy. Displacement thus secured him a considerable *gain from illness*.

Now, however, I must discuss the cause of illness in our patient in greater detail. His mother was brought up in a rich family to which she was distantly related; this family owned a large industrial enterprise. His father entered the service of this enterprise when he married and thus, effectively as a result of his choice of marriage partner, achieved a reasonable degree of affluence. Teasing banter between his parents, who enjoyed an excellent marriage, revealed to their son that some time before he made the mother's acquaintance the father had paid court to a pretty but poor girl of modest family. This, then, was the background history. One day, after his father's death, his mother told him that she and her rich relatives had been talking about his future, and one of her cousins had expressed a willingness to give him one of his daughters in marriage, once he had finished his studies; this business connection with the firm would then also open up brilliant professional prospects. The family's plan sparked off an internal conflict as to whether he should remain faithful to his beloved, who was poor, or follow in his father's footsteps and take to wife the rich, well-born and attractive girl intended for him. He resolved this conflict, which was actually the conflict between his love and the continuing effect of his father's will, by means of illness, or more precisely: he used his illness to escape the task of resolving it in reality.[29]

The proof of this interpretation lies in the fact that the principal outcome of the illness was a persistent inability to work, which caused him to defer the conclusion of his studies for years. The outcome of an illness, however, is part of the intention behind that illness; what is apparently the consequence of illness is in reality its cause, the motive for becoming ill.

At first, not surprisingly, my patient was reluctant to acknowledge the truth of my explanation. He could not imagine the marriage plan having had such an effect on him, and claimed that it had not made the slightest impression on him at the time. As the therapy continued, however, he was persuaded in a curious manner that my supposition was correct. With the help of a transference fantasy he experienced all over again in the present things that he had forgotten from the past or that had only taken place in his unconscious mind. A confused and difficult period of treatment work eventually produced the information that he had elevated a young girl whom he had once met on the steps of my house to the status of my daughter. He was attracted to her and started to imagine that I was only being so kind and unbelievably patient with him because I wanted him for a son-in-law; and that through this marriage he would enhance the wealth and refinement of my house to a level that would correspond to his own aspirations. Inside him, however, this temptation battled with his inextinguishable love for his mistress. After we had overcome instance after instance of the most powerful resistance and the most bitter insults, he could not escape the persuasive effects of the complete analogy between transference fantasy and past reality. I give as an example one of his dreams from this period as a sample of the representational style: *he sees my daughter standing in front of him, but instead of eyes she has two filthy splodges*. Anyone who understands the language of dreams will have no difficulty in translating this: *he is marrying my daughter not for her lovely eyes, but for her money*.

G. The Father Complex, and the Rat Idea Solved

We can retrace the thread from the cause of illness in his later years to our patient's childhood. He found himself in a situation that he knew or supposed to be the same as the one confronting his father before his own marriage, and was able to identify with his father. In another way, too, his dead father had a part to play in his more recent illness. The conflict underlying the illness was essentially the clash between the continuing effect of his father's will and his own inclinations as a lover. If we consider what the patient told us in the first consultation hours we cannot dismiss the probability that this conflict goes way back into his past and was already present in his childhood years.

Our patient's father was by all accounts a most excellent man. Before his marriage he had been a non-commissioned officer and this period of his life was reflected in his bluff, soldierly air and a tendency to use crude expressions. Besides those virtues celebrated on every tombstone, he was distinguished by his hearty sense of humour and a generous forbearance towards his fellow men; it certainly does not contradict this characterization, but rather completes the picture, if we say that he could be abrupt and violent, something which occasionally, for as long as they were little and naughty, brought the children some very severe beatings. As the children grew up he was different from other fathers in the sense that he did not seek to make himself into a figure of inviolable authority but divulged to them with good-natured candour the small mishaps and misdemeanours of his life. His son was doubtless not exaggerating when he said that they had got on like the best of friends, except with regard to one particular matter (cf. p. 145). This one matter must have been the reason why the thought of his father's death preoccupied the small boy with unusual and excessive intensity (p. 131), why such thoughts found expression in the compulsive ideas of his childhood, and why he could wish that his father might die so that a certain young girl might be softened by pity and behave more tenderly towards him (p. 143).

It is undoubtedly the case that something stood between father and son in the area of sexuality and that in some way the father had come to oppose his son's prematurely awakened erotic sensibilities. Several years after his father's death, on first experiencing the pleasurable sensations of coitus, the idea forced its way into the son's mind: 'This is marvellous; it would be worth killing one's father for!' Here we find both an echo and a clarification of the compulsive ideas of his childhood. Shortly before his death, incidentally, the father had expressed a view that was directly opposed to the direction taken by our patient's affections, a direction that was later to dominate his thinking. He observed that his son sought out the company of the lady in question, and advised him against it, saying that it was imprudent, and that he would only compromise himself.

We find other material to amplify these solid indications when we turn our attention to the history of our patient's masturbatory sexual activity. In this area we find a disagreement between the views held by doctors and those of their patients that has not yet been adequately explored. The latter are united in regarding masturbation – by which they mean masturbation during puberty – as the source and fount of all their suffering; doctors have no general view on this matter, but in the light of experience, which shows that most of those whose later behaviour is entirely normal also masturbated for some time during puberty, the majority tend to dismiss their patients' testimony as gross exaggeration. Here too, in my view, the patients are more likely to be right than the doctors. The patients catch a glimpse of a genuine insight whereas the doctors are in danger of overlooking something essential. It is certainly not the case, as the patients themselves would have it, that masturbation in puberty, which we might almost call typical behaviour, can be held responsible for all neurotic disorders. Such a statement is in need of interpretation. Masturbation during puberty is in reality, however, merely the renewal of childhood masturbation, which has always been left out of account up to now; this normally reaches a climax of some sort between the ages of 3 and 4 or 5 and is undoubtedly the clearest expression of the child's sexual constitution and the place where the aetiology of later neurosis is to be sought. In a veiled way, then, our patients are actually laying the blame on their infantile sexuality, and they are quite right to do so. On the other hand, it is impossible to solve the problem of masturbation if we are determined to regard masturbation as an isolated clinical phenomenon, forgetting that it represents the discharge of the most diverse sexual components and the fantasies that they sustain. Only to a very slight extent is the harmful character of masturbation something autonomous, determined by its own nature. What is important is that it coincides with the pathogenic significance of the patient's sexuality as a whole. The fact that so many individuals tolerate the practice of masturbation, up to a point at least, without coming to any harm, shows us quite simply that in their case their sexual constitution and the course taken by developmental processes in their sexual life permits the exercise of the sexual function according to certain cultural conditions,[30] while others, in consequence of an unfavourable sexual constitution or distorted development, fall ill as a result of their sexuality, i.e. they are unable to fulfil the requirement to suppress and sublimate sexual components without recourse to inhibitions and substitute-formations.

Our patient's attitude to masturbation was a striking one: he did not practise masturbation in puberty and according to a certain view it would thus have been fair to anticipate that he would remain free from neurosis. The urge to masturbatory activity manifested itself, on the other hand, in his twenty-first year, *a short time after his father's death*. Each time, having achieved satisfaction, he was deeply ashamed and soon vowed to give up the habit. From then on he masturbated only rarely and for somewhat surprising reasons. He could be moved to do so when he experienced a particularly beautiful moment or read a particularly beautiful passage in a book. Thus, for example, when he heard the driver of a mail-coach blowing his horn so splendidly one lovely summer afternoon in the inner city until he was told to stop by a policeman because it was forbidden to sound horns in the city! Or, another time, when he read in *Poetry and Truth* of how, in an outburst of tender affection, the young Goethe freed himself from the effect of a curse spoken by a jealous young woman against the next woman his lips should kiss. Superstitious, he let the curse hold him back for a long time, but now he broke free from restraint and covered his love with kisses.

It puzzled him not a little that he should feel the urge to masturbate precisely on such lovely and uplifting occasions. I was obliged, however, to identify the common element in these two examples as prohibition and the flouting of a command.

We may place in the same context his strange behaviour at a time when he was studying for an examination and was playing with a fantasy that he had become very partial to, namely that his father was still alive and might come back at any moment. At the time he arranged his day so that his study was undertaken in the small hours of the night. He would break off his studies between midnight and 1 o'clock and open the front door of the apartment as if his father might be standing there; then, after he had come back in, he would unfasten his trousers and gaze at his penis in the hall mirror. It is easier to understand such antics if we assume that he was behaving as if he expected his father to visit him at the witching hour. When his father was alive he had been a somewhat lazy student, a fact that his father had often lamented. Now, if he returned as a ghost he should find him at his studies and be pleased with him. His father was most unlikely to take pleasure in the other aspect of his behaviour, however; in this way he defied him and gave simultaneous expression, by means of a compulsive action that he did not understand, to the two sides of his relationship with his father, just as he did to the lady he loved in his later compulsive action over the stone on the road.

Basing myself on these and similar indications I ventured to reconstruct the possibility that as a child of 6 he had committed some sexual misdemeanour relating to masturbation and received a painful beating from his father. While his punishment had put an end to the masturbation it had left him, on the other hand, with an ineradicable grudge against his father and fixed him for all time in the role of an intruder upon sexual pleasure. (Cf. similar conjectures in one of the first sessions, p. 146.) To my great astonishment the patient now told me that his mother had recounted such an incident from his early childhood on many occasions, and that it had obviously not been forgotten because it had such remarkable associations. He, on the other hand, had retained no trace of it in his own memory. However, the story was as follows: when he was still very young – it would be possible to determine the exact point in time because it coincided with the fatal illness of one of his older sisters – he was supposed to have done something awful for which he received a beating from his father. The little chap apparently got into a fearful rage and abused his father even as he was being beaten. Since he was not yet familiar with any terms of abuse, however, he called him by the names of all the objects which came into his mind, such as 'You lamp, you towel, you plate', etc. Shaken by this elemental outburst his father paused in mid-blow and remarked: 'This boy will either be a great man one day, or a great criminal!'[31] He thought this scene had had a permanent impact both on himself and on his father. His father had never beaten him again; he himself attributes some part of the change in his character to this experience. From then on, terrified by the magnitude of his rage, he had become a coward. His whole life long, moreover, he had had a terrible fear of being beaten and would creep away, horrified and outraged, whenever one of his brothers or sisters was being caned.

When he questioned his mother again she provided both confirmation of this narrative and also the information that he was aged between 3 and 4 at the time and had been punished because he had *bitten* someone. Even his mother could not remember any more; she thought – though with considerable uncertainty – that the person to whom the boy had caused injury might have been the children's nurse; nothing she said suggested that the offence might have been sexual in nature.[32]

A discussion of this childhood scene will be found in the footnote below; here I will merely say that as a result of its re-emergence he started to falter for the first time in his refusal to believe in feelings of rage against his beloved father, acquired prehistorically and subsequently lying dormant. I had expected the scene to have a more powerful effect, if anything, since he had been told of this event so often, by his father as well, that there was no doubt as to its reality. With a capacity to flout logic that is always particularly disconcerting in highly intelligent patients suffering from a compulsive disorder, he denied the value of the scene as evidence, protesting over and over again that he himself could not remember a thing about it. He was obliged therefore to come by the conviction that his relationship to his father did indeed need to be amplified by material from the unconscious by the painful route of transference. It soon came about that in dreams, daytime fantasies and arbitrary notions he would insult me and mine in the most coarse and offensive manner, yet at the same time he never intentionally showed me anything but the greatest respect. His behaviour when relating these insults to me was that of a desperate man. 'Most honoured Professor, how can you allow yourself to be insulted in this way by filthy scum like me? You ought to throw me out; I don't deserve any better.' He would get up from the couch and walk around the room as he spoke, claiming at first that this was motivated by tact: he could not bear to say such terrible things while lying there in comfort. Soon he himself hit upon the more convincing explanation, however, that he was putting himself at arm's length for fear that I would strike him. If he remained seated, he would conduct himself like a man seeking to protect himself in desperate anxiety from an intemperate beating: he would bury his face in his hands, cover his face with his arm, or run away suddenly, his features distorted with pain, etc. He recalled how his father would fall into sudden rages and in the violence of his feelings would no longer have any sense of how far he could go. In this school of suffering he gradually gained the conviction he had been lacking, which would have seemed obvious to anyone who was not personally involved; and then the way was open to the solution of the rat idea. At the highpoint of the therapy a wealth of factual material that had previously been withheld now became available, so that everything fell into place.

In my discussion I shall, as previously indicated, reduce and summarize as far as possible. The first puzzle, clearly, was why the two things the Czech captain said to our patient, the rat story he told and the admonition to give the money back to Lieutenant A., should have had such an agitating effect on him and induced such violent pathological reactions. It was reasonable to assume that this was a case of 'complex-sensitivity' and that the captain's words had grated on hyperaesthetic areas of his unconscious mind. This was indeed the case; as always happened in military contexts, he was unconsciously identifying with his father, who had himself served as a soldier for a number of years and often told stories of his soldiering days. Now, as chance would have it – chance contributing to symptom-formation in much the same way as the phrasing of a joke – one of his father's little adventures had had an important element in common with the captain's challenge. His father once lost a small sum of money, money that was his responsibility as a non-commissioned officer, in a game of cards called *Spielratte*, or 'Gambling Rat', and he would have been in desperate straits had not one of his comrades advanced him the money. After he had left the army and become a prosperous man he sought out the comrade who had helped him, intending to give him back the money, but was unable to find him. Our patient was not sure whether he had ever been able to return the money; he was embarrassed by the memory of his father's youthful misdeed because, after all, his unconscious mind was filled with hostile evidence of his father's character. The captain's words, 'You must pay back the 3.80 crowns to Lieutenant A.', sounded like a reference to his father's unpaid debt.

The information that the young lady from the post office in Z. had herself paid the charges, at the same time making a flattering remark about him,[33] had however strengthened his identification with his father on another front. He now told me that in the village where the post office was situated the innkeeper's pretty daughter had also responded warmly to the smart young officer, and he had resolved to return after the exercises were over and try his luck with this girl. Now she had a rival in the form of the young lady from the post office; and just like his father and the story of his marriage, he could now vacillate over which of the two he should favour once he had dispatched his military duties. Now, all of a sudden, we can see that his extraordinary indecision as to whether he should travel on to Vienna or return to the place where the post office was, the constant temptation to turn back in his journey (cf. p. 137), were not as absurd as they necessarily first appeared. The conscious motivation for his attraction to Z., the little place where the post office was situated, was the need to fulfil his vow with the help of Lieutenant A. In reality the object of his longing was the young lady from the post office, who was to be found in the selfsame place, and the lieutenant was merely a good substitute, since he had lived in the same place and even carried out the military post duties. Then, when he heard that it was not Lieutenant A. but another officer, B., who had done post duty on that particular day, he added him to the combination too and was now able to reproduce his vacillation over the two young women who were favourably inclined towards him in his delirious fantasies concerning the two officers.[34]

In attempting to elucidate the effects of the captain's rat story we must adhere more closely to the sequence of events in the analysis. At first this produced a remarkable wealth of associative material, but failed to render the situation created by the compulsive forma-

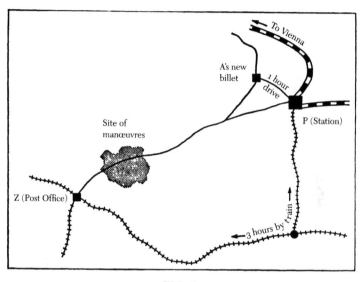

FIG. 1

tion any more transparent. The thought of the punishment carried out by the rats stimulated a number of drives and awakened any number of memories, so that, in the short interval between the captain's story and his exhortation that the money should be repaid, the rats had acquired a whole series of symbolic meanings, to which new ones were subsequently added. My account of all of this can admittedly only be a partial one. Most importantly, the rat punishment reawakened the *anal eroticism* that had played an important part in his childhood, and that had gone on for years, prolonged by the constant irritation caused by worms. The rats thus acquired the meaning of money,[35] a connection that the patient indicated to me by associating the word 'rate' to the word 'rat'. In his compulsive delirious fantasies he had inaugurated a formal rat currency; e.g. when I answered his question as to the cost of an hour's treatment I discovered six months later that for him this meant 'So many florins, so many rats'. The whole complex of financial interests connected to his inheritance from his father was gradually converted into this language, i.e. all the ideas that belonged to this area of his thinking were carried over the verbal bridge *rate–rat* into the realm of compulsion and subjected to the power of the unconscious. The significance of the rats as money was further supported, by means of the verbal bridge *Spielratte*, or 'Gambling Rat', by the captain's admonition to pay back the money due on his postal packet; whence it was possible to discover the connection with his father's misdemeanour over the game of cards.

He was also familiar, however, with the rat's significance as a carrier of dangerous infections and could therefore use it as a symbol of the fear of *syphilitic infection* that is so justifiably to be found in military circles; behind this were hidden all kinds of doubts as to his father's lifestyle at the time when he was serving in the army. Put another way, the carrier of syphilitic infection was the penis itself, so that the rat could become the sexual member, and was entitled for another reason to be so regarded. The penis, particularly that of a small boy, could easily be described as a *worm*, and in the captain's narrative the rats were burrowing in the anus, just like the great roundworms of his childhood. Thus the rats' meaning as penis was again grounded in anal eroticism. The rat is in any case a dirty animal, which feeds on excrement and lives in sewers that carry waste.[36] It is probably unnecessary to spell out how much further the rat delirium could spread in the light of this new meaning. 'So many rats – so many florins' might for example be an excellent way of characterizing a female profession which he greatly despised. On the other hand, it is doubtless not without significance that the substitution of penis for rat in the captain's narrative produces a situation involving intercourse *per anum*, which must have appeared particularly repugnant to him with reference to his father and his mistress. And when we consider that this situation recurred in the compulsive threat which formed in his mind after the captain's admonition it would unmistakably recall certain curses used by the Southern Slavs, the phrasing of which can be read in *Anthropophyteia*, edited by F. S. Krauß. This and other material all came into the rat discussion, incidentally, under cover of the notion of '*marriage*', and contributed to the structuring of it.

The way in which the tale of the rat punishment threw into turmoil those prematurely suppressed impulses to selfish and sexual cruelty in our patient is confirmed by his own description and by the expressions on his face when retelling the story. And yet, despite all this wealth of material, we could shed no light on the meaning of his compulsive idea until one day the Rat-Wife in Ibsen's *Little Eyolf* came up in conversation and led us to the irrefutable conclusion that in many of the forms of expression taken by his compulsive delirious fantasies rats also signified *children*.[37] In seeking to understand how this new meaning had come about we immediately discovered its oldest and most significant roots. Once when visiting his father's grave he had seen a large animal, which he took to be a rat, scampering past the low mound.[38] He assumed that it had come out of the grave itself and had just been feeding on his father's corpse. It is an inseparable part of our notion of the rat that its sharp teeth gnaw and bite;[39] but its voracious, filthy and vicious nature does not go unpunished: he had often watched, horror-struck, as a rat was cruelly hunted down and ruthlessly killed by human beings. He had often felt sympathy with these poor rats. Now he himself had been just such a repulsive, filthy little fellow, capable of biting those around him in his fury, and fearfully beaten for doing so (cf. p. 164). He could indeed see in the rat 'a living likeness of himself'.[40] In the captain's story, Fate had thrown him a word designed to grate, so to speak, on the complex of his feelings and he was quick to react to it with his compulsive idea.

Rats were children, then, according to his earliest experiences and their painful consequences. And now he provided a piece of information that he had withheld from its proper context for long enough, but which fully explained his interest in children. As a result of a gynaecological operation, the removal of both ovaries, the lady whose admirer he had been for so many years and yet could not bring himself to marry was condemned to childlessness; this was indeed the principal reason for his hesitation, since he was extraordinarily fond of children.

Only now did it become possible to understand the inscrutable process that had formed his compulsive idea: drawing on the assistance of infantile theories of sexuality and the symbolism familiar to us from the interpretation of dreams, a meaningful translation of the whole could be made. When the captain told him the story of the rat punishment during the midday halt in the course of which he lost his pince-nez, he was at first struck only by the cruelty and lasciviousness of the imagined situation. But he immediately made a connection with that scene from his childhood in which he had been the one to bite; the captain, who had voiced his support for punishments of that kind, took the place of his father in his eyes and attracted part of the bitterness that he had felt rising up in him at the time against his cruel father, and which now recurred. The momentary emergence of the idea that something of the kind could happen to someone dear to him we might translate as the wishful impulse: 'Someone should do something like that to you', directed in the first instance towards the narrator, but in fact against his father. When, a day and a half later,[41] the captain hands him the packet that has arrived COD, reminding him to pay Lieutenant A. back 3 crowns and 80 hellers, he already knows that his 'cruel superior' is in the wrong and that he is indebted to no one other than the young lady from the post office. It is on the tip of his tongue, then, to frame a scornful reply such as 'Whatever are you thinking of?' or 'And pigs might fly', or 'A fig[42] for paying him back', replies that were not a matter of compulsion. But, out of the father complex that has meanwhile been stirred up again, and the memory of that scene from early childhood, the reply forms on his lips: 'Yes, I will give A. the money back on the day my father and that lady have children', or, 'As surely as my father and that lady are able to have children, I will pay him back the money.' Scornful assurance, then, linked to an absurd condition that cannot be fulfilled.[43]

But now the crime had been committed and he had reviled the two people he held most dear, his father and his beloved; this called out for punishment and the sentence consisted in imposing a vow on himself which it was impossible to carry out, one that kept to the wording of his obedient reply to his superior's unjustified reminder: '*Now you really must give A. back the money.*' In convulsive obedience he repressed his better knowledge, the fact that the captain's admonition had been based on a false premiss: 'Yes, you must give the money back to A., as your father's representative demands. Your father cannot be mistaken.' The crown cannot be mistaken either, and if the sovereign addresses a subject with a title which is not his, it is henceforth his entitlement.

Only vague rumours of this process penetrate his conscious mind, but his rebellion against the captain's command and its transformation into its opposite find some representation in consciousness. (First of all: 'I must *not* give back the money or it [the rat punishment][44] will happen', and then its metamorphosis into the opposite task imposed by his vow as a punishment for his rebellion.)

We must try to imagine the constellation of circumstances in which this great compulsive idea was formed. Long abstinence, together with the friendly response from women that the young officer can count on, had made him libidinous, and he had, moreover, reported for military duty in a state of some estrangement from his mistress. This heightened libido meant that he was inclined to take up the ancient struggle against his father's authority once more, and dared to think of finding sexual satisfaction with other women. Doubts as to his father's memory, and misgivings as to the worth of his beloved had both grown stronger; in this state of mind he let himself be carried away into expressing derision for them both, and then punished himself for doing so. He was thus repeating an old pattern. When he hesitates for so long, once the military exercises are over, as to whether he should travel to Vienna or stay and fulfil his vow, he is demonstrating at a stroke the twin conflicts that had been troubling him for as long as he can remember: should be remain obedient to his father, should he remain true to his beloved?[45]

A further comment on how we are to interpret the content of the sanction 'otherwise the rat punishment will be carried out on both of these people': it is based on the validity of two infantile theories of sexuality, which I have written about elsewhere.[46] The first of these theories supposes that children come out of the anus; the second draws the conclusion consistent with this, that men are just as able to have children as women. According to the technical rules of dream interpretation 'coming out of the bowel' can be represented by its opposite, a 'crawling into the bowel' (as in the case of the rat punishment), and vice versa.

There is no real justification for expecting to find simpler solutions to such severe compulsive ideas, or indeed solutions by any other means. With the emergence of this solution the rat delirium went away.

Notes

1. *Zur Psychopathologie des Alltagslebens* [*On the Psychopathology of Everyday Life*] (1901).

2. An edited version of the notes I took the evening after treatment, using as far as possible what I can recall of the actual words used by the patient. – I can only warn against using the treatment hour itself to write down what one has heard. The damage done to the patient by the distraction of the doctor's attention is greater than can be excused by any gain with regard to faithfulness of reproduction in the case history.

3. Dr Alfred Adler, who previously practised as an analyst, once recalled in a private lecture the particular significance we may attribute to the *very first* things a patient tells us. A piece of supporting evidence: the patient's opening words emphasize the influence exercised over him by men, the role of the homosexual object-choice in his life, and immediately afterwards allow us to discern a second motif that will later come to the fore, the conflict between man and woman, their clash of interests. It is in this context also that we must place the fact that he recalls his first pretty governess by her surname, which happens to resemble a male Christian name. In well-to-do Viennese society it is more usual to call a governess by her Christian name, which is thus more likely to stick in the memory.

4. He later acknowledges that this scene probably took place a year or two later.

5. Let us not forget that the attempt has been made to explain compulsive ideas without any consideration of affectivity!

6. He uses the word 'idea'; the stronger and more significant term 'wish', or perhaps 'fear', has obviously been covered up by a process of censorship. I am unfortunately unable to reproduce the characteristic imprecision of all that he says.

7. Here the names are of no great moment.

8. We arrived at a better understanding of the effect of this episode subsequently, when the patient described it in greater detail. His widowed uncle had cried out in distress: 'Other men indulge themselves in every possible way, but I lived only for this woman!' Our patient took this to be a reference to his father, casting suspicion on his conjugal fidelity, and although his uncle contested this interpretation of his words in the strongest possible terms their effect could not be reversed.

9. All this is admittedly only very roughly correct, but will do in the first instance as an introduction.

10. It is not only those who suffer from obsessive-compulsive neurosis who derive satisfaction from toning down their language like this.

11. Ten years ago!

12. One cannot fail to recognize the opposition that is indicated here between the two people he loves, his father and the 'lady'.

13. Such discussions are never intended to convince. They are only intended to introduce the repressed complexes into the conscious mind, to arouse dispute about them in the sphere of conscious inner activity and to make it easier for new material to emerge from the unconscious. Only after the patient has processed the material that has been recovered in this way can we speak of conviction, and as long as the patient remains unconvinced we may judge that the material has not yet been exhausted.

14. This consciousness of guilt embodies the clearest contradiction of his refusal to accept at the outset that he had ever had any desire to harm his father. It is a type commonly met with in the reaction to repressed material which has leaked out: the initial No of refusal is immediately followed by a confirmation, indirect in the first instance.

15. *Jenseits von Gut und Böse* [*Beyond Good and Evil*], IV, 68.

16. This is something that will be explained later on.

17. I present these arguments only to have their impotence confirmed all over again. I find it incomprehensible when other psychotherapists report that they are successful in combating neurosis using such weapons.

18. We must supply the word 'first'.

19. [*Translator's note*: *Dick* is the German word for *fat*.]

20. The use of names and particular words to establish a connection between unconscious thoughts (impulses, fantasies) and the patient's symptoms occurs far less frequently and indiscriminately in obsessive-compulsive neurosis than it does in hysteria. Yet I can recall another example, precisely concerning the name Richard, in the case of a patient who was in analysis with me some time ago. After a quarrel with his brother he began to brood as to how he could be rid of his wealth, wanting nothing more to do with money, etc. His brother was called Richard (in French, *richard* means *a wealthy man*).

21. We must supply the words 'which might be his fault'.

22. Cf. Ernest Jones ['Rationalization in Everyday Life', *J. Abnorm. Psychol.*] (1908).

23. Cf. 'Hysterische Fantasien und ihre Beziehung zur Bisexualität' ['Hysterical Fantasies and their Relation to Bisexuality'] (Freud, 1908).

24. Another patient suffering from compulsive disorders once told me that when walking in the park at Schönbrunn he had hit his foot on a branch that was lying across the path, which he then flung into the hedge which bordered the path. On the way home he was suddenly overcome with concern that in its new position the branch, which was now perhaps protruding somewhat, might cause an accident to someone passing the place after him. He was obliged to jump down from the tram, hurry back to the park, find the place and put the branch back in its original position, although it would have been clear to anyone except my patient that the original position was bound to be more dangerous for any passer-by than the new one in the bushes. The second, hostile, action which prevailed as an act of compulsion was dressed up in the motivation of the first, philanthropic, action, to make it acceptable to conscious thought.

25. Compare the similar mechanism determining those familiar sacrilegious slips [*Einfälle*] made by pious individuals.

26. ['P.c.', 'pour condoler': 'condolences'. 'P.f.', 'pour féliciter': 'congratulations'.] This dream offers an explanation for the compulsive laughter that is so commonly encountered at times of bereavement and is considered to be so mysterious.

27. We cannot overlook the possibility that there is another motive contributing to this compulsive notion: the desire that she should be defenceless in the face of his intentions.

28. Thus we must recognize that in obsessive-compulsive neurosis there are two kinds of knowledge, a superficial kind and one that goes deeper, and we have just as much right to affirm that a patient suffering from a compulsive disorder 'knows' what his traumas are as we do to affirm that he does not 'know'. For he knows, inasmuch as he has not forgotten them, but does not know, because he does not see their significance. It is often much the same in everyday life. There is a certain sense in which the waiters who used to wait on the philosopher Schopenhauer in the restaurant he frequented 'knew' him, at a time when he was not otherwise known in Frankfurt or outside it, but they did not know him in the sense that we talk today about 'knowledge of Schopenhauer'.

29. It should be emphasized that the flight into illness was made possible by the identification with his father. The emotions were then permitted to regress to remnants left over from childhood.

30. Cf. *Drei Abhandlungen zur Sexualtheorie [Three Essays on the Theory of Sexuality]* (1905).

31. The alternatives were incomplete. The most common outcome of such a passionate nature in one so young, that of neurosis, did not enter the father's mind.

32. In psychoanalysis one is frequently concerned with events of this kind from the early years, in which infantile sexual activity appears to peak and frequently comes to a catastrophic end through accident or punishment. Such events occur as a shadowy presence in dreams and often come to be so clear that they seem almost tangible, but they elude definitive clarification, and if one does not proceed with particular caution and skill it is impossible to come to any conclusion as to whether such a scene actually took place. The knowledge that we can often track down more than one version of such scenes in the patient's unconscious imagination, often very diverse in character, enables us to find the correct interpretative trail. If we do not wish to go astray in the judgement of reality we must remember above all that people's 'childhood memories' are only laid down at a later age (usually in puberty), when they undergo a complicated process of revision, entirely analogous to the way in which a race creates the sagas of its ancient history. We can see clearly that the adolescent attempts to *blur the memory of auto-erotic activity* by bringing remnants of memory [*Erinnerungsspuren*] up to the level of object-love, thus attempting, like a true historiographer, to see the past in the light of the present. Hence the superabundance of seductions and assassinations in these fantasies, while reality confines itself to auto-erotic activity and its stimulation by means of tender caresses and punishments. One becomes aware, moreover, that the person fantasizing about his childhood *sexualizes his memories*, i.e. creates a connection between banal experiences and sexual activity, extending his sexual interest to them too, and is probably following the trace of a genuine connection by doing so. It will be clear to anyone who remembers my 'Analysis of a Phobia in a Five-year-old Boy' that it is not the intention of these remarks belatedly to diminish the significance I have claimed for infantile sexuality by reducing it to an aspect of the sexual interest of puberty. My intention here is merely to provide some technical instructions for clearing up those fantasy formations whose purpose it is to distort our picture of infantile sexual activity.

Only rarely, as is the case with our patient, are we in the happy position of being able to establish the factual basis for these poetic evocations of times long past by referring to the unshakeable testimony of an adult. Nevertheless his mother's statement leaves the way open to a variety of possibilities. The fact that she did not proclaim the misdemeanour for which the boy was punished to be sexual in nature may be attributed to her own censorship, which in all parents endeavours to eliminate precisely this element from their children's past. It is equally possible, however, that the child was rebuked by the nurse or by the mother herself for some banal habit that was not sexual in nature, and was then disciplined by the father because of his violent reaction. In such fantasies the more distinguished figure of the mother regularly stands in for the nurse or another servant. A more far-reaching attempt to interpret the patient's dreams on this subject produced the clearest indications of a poetic fantasy, which we might term epic in scope, which brought sexual desire for his mother and sister and the premature death of that sister into connection with the father's punishment of our young hero. The attempt to unpick this tissue of concealing fantasies thread by thread was unsuccessful; we were prevented from doing so by the success of the therapy itself. The patient was back on his feet and life required him to tackle various tasks, in any case too long delayed, that were incompatible with the continuation of the treatment. It would thus be inappropriate to reproach me for this gap in the analysis. Scientific inquiry on the basis of psychoanalysis is at present merely a by-product of therapeutic endeavour, after all, and for that reason the yield is often greatest in the case of patients whose treatment is unsuccessful.

The content of childhood sexuality consists in the auto-erotic activation of the dominant sexual components, in traces of object-love and in the formation of that complex which we might term the *core complex* [*Kernkomplex*] *of the neuroses*, containing the first impulses, both tender and hostile, towards parents and siblings, once the curiosity of the young child has been awoken, usually by the arrival of a new brother or sister. The uniformity of the content and the consistency of later modifying effects readily explains the fact that in general we always find the formation of the same fantasies about childhood, regardless of how much or how little actual experience has contributed to this. It is entirely consistent with the infantile core complex that the father takes on the role of sexual opponent and intruder upon auto-erotic sexual activity, and this is usually borne out by reality.

33. We should not forget that he heard about this before the captain demanded (quite unjustifiably) that he should pay back the money to Lieutenant A. Our understanding of the incident turns on this point, the

suppression of which led to the most unholy confusion and prevented me for a while from grasping the significance of the whole affair.

34. [*Addition 1923:*] The patient having done everything in his power to obscure this little incident of paying back the charges due upon the pince-nez, I have perhaps not succeeded in my attempt to clarify every detail. I am therefore reproducing here a little map with which Mr and Mrs Strachey attempted to elucidate the situation at the end of the military exercise. My translators correctly observe that the patient's behaviour remains incomprehensible unless it is expressly pointed out that Lt A. had previously been living in Z., where the post office was, and had been responsible for the military post, but in the last days of the exercise had handed this duty on to Lt B. and been transferred to A. The 'cruel' captain knew nothing of this change, hence his mistake about paying the money back to Lt A.

35. Cf. 'Charakter und Analerotik' ['Character and Anal Eroticism'] (1908).

36. Let me remind anyone who is inclined to shake his head over such leaps of the neurotic imagination of similar capriccios with which the artist sometimes indulges his imagination, e.g. the 'diableries érotiques' by Le Poitevin.

37. Ibsen's Rat-Wife is surely derived from the legendary rat catcher of Hamelin, who first lures the rats into the water and then by the same means steals away the children of the town, never to come back again. Little Eyolf, too, throws himself into the water under the spell of the Rat-Wife. In legend the rat appears not so much a repulsive creature as an uncanny one, one might almost say chthonic, and is used to portray the souls of the dead.

38. One of the weasels so commonly found in the Zentralfriedhof [Main Cemetery] in Vienna.

39. Goethe, *Faust I* (Scene 3):

> *Doch dieser Schwelle Zauber zu zerspalten*
> *Bedarf ich eines Rattenzahns.*
>
> . . .
>
> *Noch einen Biss, so ist's geschehn!*

[But to break through the magic of this threshold I need a rat's tooth. (*He conjures up a rat.*) . . . Another bite, and it is done!]

40. Goethe, *Faust I* (Auerbach's Cellar):

> *Er sieht in der geschwollnen Ratte*
> *Sein ganz natürlich Ebenbild.*

[For in the bloated rat he sees a living likeness of himself.]

41. Not the next evening, as he said at first. It is quite impossible for the pince-nez he ordered to have arrived on the same day. He shortens the interval in his memory, because the decisive thought connections were made in that time and because he is repressing the encounter with the officer who told him of the friendly behaviour of the young lady from the post office, which also occurred during this time.

42. A Viennese expression [*einen Schmarren*].

43. In the language of compulsive thinking, then, just as in dreaming, absurdity signifies derision. See *Die Traumdeutung* [*The Interpretation of Dreams*] (1900, Chapter VI, G).

44. The square brackets are Freud's own.

45. It is perhaps interesting to underline the way in which obedience to the father once again coincides with a loss of interest in the beloved. If he stays to give A. back the money he has atoned to his father and at the same time abandoned his mistress in favour of another magnet's attraction. Victory in this conflict goes to the lady, at any rate when the patient's normal state of mind is restored.

46. Cf. 'Über infantile Sexualtheorien' ['On the Sexual Theories of Children'] (1908).

II *Theoretical Remarks*[1]

A. *Some General Characteristics of Compulsive Formations*[2]

The definition I gave in 1896 of compulsive ideas, namely that they are 'reproaches that have been repressed but now return transformed, always related to a sexual act from childhood that brought pleasure when carried out',[3] seems to me today to be arguable in formal terms although the elements of which it is composed are of the best. My definition was too concerned to impose unity, modelling itself on the procedure of compulsive patients themselves, who, with the tendency to imprecision that is characteristic of them bundle together the most diverse psychic formations under the name 'compulsive ideas'.[4] In fact it is more correct to speak of 'compulsive thinking' and to emphasize the fact that compulsive structures may be equivalent to the most diverse psychic actions. These may be defined as wishes, temptations, impulses, reflections, doubts, commands and prohibitions. Patients generally endeavour to diminish this certainty of definition and to use the content, denuded of its emotional index, as a compulsive idea. In one of the first sessions our patient provided an example of a wish treated in just this way by the attempt to reduce it to the level of a mere 'thought association' (p. 143).

We must also acknowledge that it has not even been possible up until now to show due appreciation for the phenomenology of compulsive thinking. In the secondary parrying struggle that the patient conducts against the 'compulsive ideas' that have penetrated his consciousness, certain formations come into being that merit a particular designation. Consider, for example, the chains of thought that preoccupy our patient on his journey home after the military exercises. These are not purely reasonable deliberations that are in opposition to his compulsive thoughts, but hybrids, as it were, of both types of thought, absorbing certain assumptions that belong to the compulsion they are fighting and thus placing themselves (by rational methods) within the sphere of diseased thinking. Such formations, it seems to me, merit the term *delirious fantasies* [*Deliria*]. One example, which should be placed in its proper context in the case history, will serve to make the distinction. When for a time during his studies our patient gave himself up to the antics we have described, working late into the night, then opening the door to meet his father's ghost, then looking at his genitals in the mirror (p. 162), he attempted to set himself straight by asking himself sternly what his father would have to say if he really were still alive. But the argument had no force as long as it was framed in such reasonable terms; the haunting only came to an end once he had expressed the same idea in the form of a delirious threat: if he indulged in such nonsense once more, something dreadful would happen to his father in the world beyond.

The value of making a distinction between primary and secondary parrying struggles, entirely justified in itself, is unexpectedly limited by the recognition that *the patient does not know himself how his own compulsive ideas are worded*. Paradoxical as this sounds, it makes perfectly good sense. In the course of psychoanalysis it is not only the patient who gains in courage, but also the illness, as it were, which ventures upon more explicit expression. Leaving this metaphorical image on one side, it is no doubt the case that the patient, who up until now has turned away in fear from knowledge of his own morbid productions, now turns his attention upon them and experiences them in greater clarity and detail.[5]

Beyond this, there are two particular ways in which we can acquire a more exact knowledge of compulsive formations. In the first place, we learn that dreams can provide us with the actual text of compulsive commands and the like, whereas in his waking hours the patient's knowledge of them is distorted and garbled, as if read off from a mutilated dispatch. These texts appear in the dream as *spoken material*, contradicting the rule that what is spoken in a dream is derived from spoken material heard during the day. Second, when following the trail of a case history in analysis, one often arrives at the conviction that several compulsive ideas, which follow on from one another but are not identical in their wording, are basically one and the same. The compulsive idea has been successfully dismissed the first time and now returns in a disguised form in which it is not recognized, so that it can perhaps hold its own more effectively in the struggle to throw it off precisely as a result of that disguise. However, the original form is the true one, often revealing its meaning without recourse to a mask. Having gone to great lengths to clarify an incomprehensible compulsive idea, it is not uncommon to hear a patient say that an idea, wish or temptation such as the one I have reconstructed did indeed occur once before the compulsive idea took hold, but had not lasted. Suitable examples from our patient's history would unfortunately involve me in too many elaborate explanations.

What we officially designate a 'compulsive idea' thus bears the traces of the primary parrying struggle, although the original wording has been distorted. This distortion enables it to survive, for conscious thought is obliged to misunderstand it in the same way as it does the content of dreams, itself a product of compromise and distortion, which continues to be misunderstood by daytime thinking.

Proof of the misunderstandings of conscious thought can be found not only in the compulsive ideas themselves, but also in the products of the secondary parrying struggle, e.g. in protective formulae [*Schutzformeln*]. I should like to offer two good examples of this. As a parrying formula our patient employed the word '*but*', spoken quickly and accompanied by a dismissive wave of the hand. On one occasion he told me that this formula had changed recently so that he now put the emphasis on the second syllable of the German word '*aber*'. Asked why this change had taken place, he told me that the neutral *e* of the second syllable offered him no protection against the interference he feared from something alien and opposed to him, so that he had decided to accentuate the *e*.

This explanation, though entirely in keeping with the style of those suffering from obsessive-compulsive neurosis, proved incorrect, its value at best that of a rationalization; in reality the pronunciation *'abér'* brought the word into alignment with *'Abwehr'* [parrying], a term that had become familiar to him as a result of our theoretical conversations on the subject of psychoanalysis. The therapy had thus been used improperly and deliriously to reinforce a parrying formula. On another occasion he told me of his special magic word, constructed as a means of protection against all temptation by taking the initial letters of all the most powerfully restorative prayers, and rounding them off with the word *'amen'*. I cannot give the word itself here for reasons that will immediately become apparent. For when I learned what the word was I could not help noticing that it was in fact the name of the lady he admired, in anagrammatic form; this name contained an *s* that he had placed at the end, immediately before the word *'amen'* [*Samen:* semen]. He had thus – let us say – brought together his mistress and his semen, i.e. masturbated over a fantasy of her. He himself, however, had not noticed this glaringly obvious connection: the repressed material had duped his defences. A good example, incidentally, of the dictum that whatever one tries to fend off will always eventually infiltrate whatever is being used to fend it off.

If we maintain that compulsive thoughts have undergone a distortion similar to that of dream thoughts before they become dream-content, then the technique by which distortion is achieved will be of interest to us; there would be nothing to prevent us from demonstrating various means of achieving distortion, taking as examples a number of compulsive ideas that have been translated and comprehended. Given the limitations of this publication, however, I can provide only a few individual examples. Not all of our patient's compulsive ideas were as complex in their construction and as difficult to unlock as the great rat idea. In other cases a very simple technique was used, that of distortion by means of omission – *ellipsis* – which is employed to such excellent effect in jokes, but serves its turn here, too, as a means of defending oneself against understanding.

One of his oldest compulsive ideas, for example, a favourite (with the value of an exhortation or warning) was: *'If I marry the lady, something terrible will happen to my father'* (in the afterlife). If we insert the missing links, now familiar to us from the analysis, the thought process runs as follows: 'If my father were still alive my intention to marry the lady would make him as furious as he was in that childhood scene long ago, so that once again I would be over-come with fury towards him and would wish every kind of evil upon him, and because of their omnipotence[6] my wishes would come true.'

Or another case of an elliptical solution, once again a warning or ascetic prohibition: He had a sweet little niece, of whom he was very fond. One day the idea came to him: *'If you allow yourself to engage in intercourse, something terrible will happen to Ella'* (death). Let us put back what has been taken out: 'Every time you engage in intercourse, even with someone else, you must remember that in your marriage sexual intercourse will never result in the birth of a child' (because of the lady's sterility). 'This will cause you such distress that you will become jealous of little Ella and begrudge your sister the child. The consequence of these jealous feelings must be the death of the child.'[7]

This technique of elliptical distortion appears to be typical of obsessive-compulsive neurosis: I have encountered it in the compul-sive thoughts of other patients as well. A particularly transparent example, interesting by virtue of a certain similarity with the struc-ture of the rat idea, is provided by a case of doubt in a lady who was afflicted essentially by a tendency to actions of a compulsive nature. In Nuremberg she went for a walk with her husband, and he accompanied her into a shop where she bought various items for her child, among them a comb. The husband, wearied by the time she was taking over selecting her purchases, told her that on the way there he had seen some coins in an antique shop that he wished to buy, and that after he had bought them he would come back to collect her. In her opinion, however, he was away far too long. When he returned she asked him where he had been, to which he replied 'In the antique shop I told you about', and at that very moment she felt a tormenting sense of doubt as to whether she had not in fact always possessed the comb that she had just bought for the child. Of course she was unable to uncover the straightforward connection. We have no alternative but to explain her doubt as displacement and to reconstruct the complete, unconscious thought as follows: 'If it is true that you have only been in the antique shop, if I am supposed to believe that, I might just as well believe that this comb, which I have just bought, has been in my possession for years.' A derisive and ironic suggestion of parity, then, similar to our patient's notion: 'Yes, just as surely as the two of them (my father and the lady) will have children, I will give the money back to A.' In this lady's case her doubts were connected to an unconscious jealousy which caused her to assume that her husband had passed the time by visiting his mistress.

I shall not attempt on this occasion to undertake any psychological evaluation of compulsive thinking. It would provide extraordinarily valuable results, and would do more to clarify our understanding of the nature of the conscious and the unconscious than the study of hysteria and hypnotic phenomena. It would be highly desirable if those philosophers and psychologists who develop astute theories of the unconscious based on hearsay or conventional definitions were to go first to the phenomena of compulsive thinking for their decisive impressions; one might almost demand that they should, if only this did not require so very much more effort of them than their customary working methods. I will only mention here that in obsessive-compulsive neurosis unconscious inner processes may on occasion break through into consciousness in their purest, most undistorted form, that this breakthrough may take place at any one of various stages in the unconscious thought process, and that compulsive ideas can generally, at the moment when they break through, be recognized as formations which have long been in existence. Hence the striking phenomenon that, when one is attempting to trace the first appearance of a compulsive idea, the patient suffering from obsessive-compulsive neurosis will, in the course of the analysis, have to shift it further and further back and constantly find new 'first occasions' for it.

B. Some Psychic Peculiarities of Obsessive-compulsive Neurosis – The Patient's Relationship to Reality, Superstition and Death

It is my intention to discuss certain spiritual characteristics of obsessive-compulsive neurosis that appear unimportant in themselves but which pave the way for an understanding of more important matters. In my patient's case they were extremely pronounced – yet I know that they cannot be ascribed to his individual personality but to his illness and are typically to be encountered in other patients suffering from obsessive-compulsive neurosis.

Our patient was exceedingly superstitious, despite the fact that he was a highly educated, enlightened man of considerable shrewdness who assured me from time to time that he did not believe a word of all that nonsense. He was thus superstitious and yet not superstitious, and yet he clearly differed from those uneducated believers in superstition who are at one with their beliefs. He seemed to understand that his superstition was a result of his compulsive thinking, although at times he professed to have absolute faith in it. Such contradictory and uncertain behaviour is most readily explained from the angle of a particular attempt at explanation. I did not hesitate to assume that in respect of these things he held two different and opposing convictions, rather than that his mind was not yet made up. He then oscillated between these two viewpoints and was most evidently dependent on whichever attitude towards his compulsive disorder was uppermost at the time. As soon as he had mastered a particular compulsion he would smile at his gullibility with the superiority of understanding, and nothing could occur to unsettle him; and as soon as he found himself dominated once again by an unresolved compulsion – or resistance, which amounts to the same thing – he would experience the strangest coincidences, which appeared to bear out his credulous convictions.

His superstition was nevertheless that of an educated man and did not encompass such fatuous notions as fear of Fridays, the number 13 and the like. He did however believe in omens and prophetic dreams, was constantly encountering people whom he had just inexplicably been thinking about, and receiving letters from correspondents who had suddenly been brought to mind after a very long interval. At the same time he was honest enough, or perhaps sufficiently true to his official convictions, not to forget instances when the most powerful premonitions had come to nothing, e.g. the certain premonition, once when he was going away for the summer, that he would not return to Vienna alive. He also admitted that by far the greater number of portents concerned matters that had no particular importance for him personally, and that if he were to meet an acquaintance whom he had not thought of for a long time and had then suddenly thought about a few moments previously, nothing further would transpire between him and the person so miraculously glimpsed. He was of course also unable to deny that all the most significant events of his life had occurred unaccompanied by portents, such as the way his father's death had taken him, unsuspecting as he was, by surprise. But all these arguments had no effect on the contradictory nature of his convictions and demonstrated only the compulsive character of his superstition, already clearly apparent from the vacillation that followed the fluctuations of resistance.

I was not of course in a position to find rational explanations for all his tales of past marvels, but as far as similar events during the period of treatment were concerned, I was able to prove to him that he himself contributed constantly to the fabrication of these marvels, showing him what means he employed when doing so. His tools were indirect seeing and reading, forgetting and, above all, delusions of memory. In the end he himself helped me to uncover the little sleights of hand that brought about these marvels. On one occasion, uncovering an interesting infantile root of his belief in the efficacy of premonitions and predictions, he was able to remember that his mother had very often said, when it was a matter of fixing a date: 'That day and that day won't do; I shall have to lie down then.' And on the day in question she would indeed always have taken to her bed!

Unmistakable, this wish to find support for his superstition in his own experience; hence the close attention he paid to those familiar inexplicable everyday coincidences and the unconscious assistance he would render when they did not go quite far enough. I have found the same need in many other patients suffering from obsessive-compulsive neurosis and suspect its existence in still more. It seems to me to be easily explained by the psychological characteristics of obsessive-compulsive neurosis. As I made clear earlier (p. 156), in this disorder repression does not take place through amnesia, but through the destruction of causal connections consequent upon the withdrawal of the accompanying emotion. It would seem that these repressed relationships retain a certain warning power – which I have compared elsewhere to an endopsychic perception[8] – so that they are made to enter the outside world by means of projection and there bear witness to what has failed to occur in the psychic sphere.

Another inner need common to those suffering from obsessive-compulsive neurosis, and having a certain affinity with the one we have just mentioned, the pursuit of which takes us deep into an exploration of the drives, is the desire for *uncertainty* in life, or for *doubt*. The creation of uncertainty is one of the methods that neurosis employs to draw the patient out of *reality* and isolate him from the world, which is after all a tendency of all psychoneurotic disorder. Once again it is all too obvious to what extent the patient contributes to this state of affairs in order to avoid certainty and remain in doubt; in some patients, indeed, this tendency finds vivid expression in a dislike of – clocks, which ensure that the time, at least, can be determined, and in the little tricks that they perform unconsciously to render harmless any instrument that excludes the possibility of doubt. Our patient had developed a particular skill in avoiding information that might have helped him towards a decision that would resolve his inner conflict. Thus he had not allowed himself to be enlightened with regard to his mistress's state of health, the crucial factor in his decision to marry, and was apparently unable to say who had carried out the operation and whether one ovary had been removed or both. He was obliged to recall what had been forgotten and to establish what he had neglected to find out.

The particular fondness that the patient suffering from obsessive-compulsive neurosis feels for uncertainty and doubt provides him with a motive for allowing his thoughts to return constantly to topics where uncertainty is a general human response and where our knowledge and judgement must necessarily remain a matter of doubt. Such topics are pre-eminently paternity, life expectancy, the afterlife and memory – to which we generally give credence without possessing the faintest proof of its reliability.[9]

Obsessive-compulsive neurosis makes substantial use of the uncertainty of memory in symptom formation; the role played by life expectancy and the afterlife in the content of the patient's thinking is something we shall shortly discover. First, though, as the most appropriate transition to that topic, I shall discuss the characteristic tendency to superstition in our patient, my earlier reference to which (p. 183) will no doubt have disconcerted more than one reader.

I am referring to the *omnipotence* he claims for his thoughts and feelings, his good and evil wishes. It is certainly no small temptation to declare this idea to be a delusion that goes far beyond the limits characteristic of obsessive-compulsive neurosis; except that I have encountered this same conviction in another patient suffering from compulsive disorders who has long since recovered and now leads a normal, active life, and in fact all those suffering from obsessive-compulsive neurosis conduct themselves as if they shared this conviction. Our task will be to shed some light on this over-estimation of their powers. Let us quite simply assume that in this belief the patient is freely acknowledging an element of the ancient megalomania of the child, and let us ask our patient what his conviction is based on. He cites two experiences in response. The second time he visited the hydropathic establishment where he had enjoyed the first and only positive influence on the course of his illness, he asked to be put in the same room as before, the position of which had favoured his relations with one of the nurses. In reply he is told that the room is already occupied, an old professor having taken it, and he reacts to this news, which greatly reduces his therapeutic prospects, with the unkind words: 'Let's hope he drops dead, then.' Two weeks later he wakes in the middle of the night troubled by the idea of a corpse, and in the morning he learns that the professor has indeed suffered a stroke and that he was brought up to his room at around the time our patient had woken up. The other experience concerned a spinster lady, advanced in years and hungry for love, who had responded to him with great warmth and had once asked him straight out if he might not be able to love her. His answer was evasive; a few days later he learned that she had thrown herself out of the window. Now he told himself reproachfully that it would have been in his power to keep her alive by offering her his love. In this way he acquired the conviction that his love and hatred were omnipotent. While we would not wish to deny the omnipotent power of love, let us emphasize that we are dealing here with death in both cases, and accept the explanation that suggests itself, namely that our patient, like others suffering from compulsive disorders, is compelled to over-estimate the effect of his hostile feelings in the outside world because a significant part of the inward psychic effect eludes his conscious knowledge. His love – or rather, his hatred – are indeed both excessively powerful, for they create those compulsive thoughts whose origins he does not understand and which he is quite unable to fend off.[10]

Our patient had a very particular attitude to the business of death. He took a warm interest in mortalities of every kind and was a respectful presence at every funeral, so that his brothers and sisters referred to him derisively as 'the vulture'; and yet he was also constantly killing people off in his imagination so that he could express his cordial sympathy with the bereaved relatives. The death of an older sister when he was somewhere between 3 and 4 years old played an important role in his fantasies and was regarded as having a direct bearing on the childhood misdemeanours committed during those years. We know, moreover, at what an early age he was preoccupied with the thought of his father's death, and we may even interpret his illness as a reaction to this event, which, 15 years previously, he had compulsively desired. The disconcerting way in which he extends his compulsive fears to the 'afterlife' is quite simply a compensation for the death wishes he felt towards his father. Introduced some 18 months after his bereavement when his mourning for his dead father underwent a renewal, this was intended to cancel out the fact of his father's death, in the teeth of reality and for the sake of the wish he had previously attempted to express in fantasies of every kind. We have on several occasions (p. 180 and p. 183.) learned to translate the rider 'in the afterlife' with the words 'if my father were still alive'.

And yet other patients suffering from a compulsive disorder do not behave so very differently from our patient, even where Fate has not decreed that their first encounter with the phenomenon of death should take place at such an early age. Their thoughts are unceasingly preoccupied with the life expectancy of others and the possibility of their death; initially their superstitious tendencies had no other content and perhaps have no other origin whatsoever. They need the possibility of death above all, however, in order to resolve conflicts which they have left unresolved. Their essential characteristic is the inability to make decisions, particularly in affairs of the heart; they endeavour to put off every decision and, consumed with doubt as to which person they should decide for, or what measure they should resort to against someone, they take the court of the ancient German empire as their model, where trials were usually ended by the death of the litigants before the judge had reached his decision. And so in all the conflicts of life they have an eye on the possibility that someone who is important to them, generally someone they love, will die, whether it be one of their parents, a rival, or one of the objects of their love, between whom they waver in their affections. In thus acknowledging the death complex in obsessive-compulsive neurosis we are already touching on the question of the drives in those suffering from compulsive disorders, a matter to which we shall now turn our attention.

C. The Drives, and the Derivation of Compulsion and Doubt

If we wish to arrive at an understanding of the psychic forces whose interplay built up this neurosis we must go back to what we learned from our patient about the immediate cause of his illness in maturity and in childhood. He fell ill in his twenties, when faced with the temptation of marrying a woman other than the one who had long been the object of his affections, and avoided making any decision in this conflict by postponing all the activities required to arrive at such a decision, his neurosis providing him with the means of doing so. We can reduce the inability to decide between the object of his love and the other woman to the conflict between his father's influence and his love for his mistress, and thus to a conflict of choice between father and sexual object such as already existed in his early childhood, according to the evidence supplied by memory and by his compulsive notions. We cannot mistake the fact, moreover, that his whole life long he had entertained conflicting feelings of love and hatred towards his beloved just as he had towards his father. Revenge fantasies and compulsive phenomena such as his compulsion to understand or his tinkering with the stone on the highway bear witness to these contradictory feelings, which were normal and understandable up to a point, since his mistress had given him grounds for hostility in her initial dismissal of him and her later coolness towards him. However, the same contradiction in his feelings dominated his relationship with his father, as we discovered by translating his compulsive thoughts, and his father must also have given him grounds for hostility during his childhood, as we were almost definitely able to establish. He was conscious to a considerable extent of the way in which his relationship to his beloved was composed of tenderness and hostility. At most he was deluded as to the extent of his negative feelings and the manner of their expression, whereas his hostility towards his father, once intensely conscious, had left him and could only be brought back into his conscious mind to the accompaniment of the most violent resistance. In the repression of his infantile hatred towards his father we catch a glimpse of the process which forced everything that happened subsequently into the framework of neurosis.

These conflicts of feeling in our patient, which we have enumerated separately, do not exist independently of one another, but are welded together in pairs. His hatred towards his mistress was always found together with his attachment to his father, and vice versa. But the two currents of conflict we are left with after this simplification, the opposition between his father and his mistress and the contradictory feelings of love and hatred to be found within each of these relationships, have nothing to do with one another, in terms of either their content or their genesis. The first of the two conflicts corresponds to the vacillation between man or woman that normally occurs in the choice of love-object; it is first brought home to the child in the famous question: 'Whom do you love more, Daddy or Mummy?' and then accompanies him through life regardless of the differing intensity of feeling he may develop towards one or other parent, and different choices concerning his definitive sexual objectives. Normally, however, this opposition quickly loses its characteristic sharp edge of contradiction, its merciless either/or quality, and room is found for the unequal claims of the two sides, although even in the normal individual the high esteem in which one sex is held is always greater when the other sex is disparaged.

The other conflict, between love and hatred, strikes us as a stranger thing. We know that at the beginning of a love affair feelings of love are frequently perceived as hatred, or that love which is denied satisfaction easily turns into hatred, at least in part, and we learn from the poets that in the stormy phases of passion these opposing feelings can exist alongside one another for a time, each struggling to gain the upper hand. But we are astonished when we encounter love and hatred towards the same person in chronic coexistence, both experienced with the greatest intensity. We should have expected true love to have overcome hatred long ago, or else to have been consumed by it. In truth the continued existence of this opposition is only possible under particular psychological conditions and with the collusion of the unconscious state. Love has not been able to extinguish hatred but only to force it into the unconscious, and in the unconscious, protected against the neutralizing influence of consciousness, it is able to survive and even to grow. Under these circumstances conscious love tends to swell up in reaction and assume a particular intensity in order to remain equal to the continuously imposed task of holding the opposing force back in the repressed state. A separating-out of the opposites, taking place at a very early age in childhood pre-history and leading to the repression of one part, usually hatred, would appear to be the precondition for the disconcerting way in which the individual's erotic life is constellated.[11]

Looking over a number of analyses concerning cases of compulsive disorder, we form the impression that a relation between love and hatred such as we find in our patient is one of the most frequent, most obvious and hence probably one of the most significant characteristics of obsessive-compulsive neurosis. However enticing a prospect it might be, however, to relate the problem of 'neurosis choice' to the drives, we have good reason to avoid this temptation; we must tell ourselves that in all the neuroses it is always the same repressed drives that are revealed as the symptom-carriers. After all, hatred that is held back in the unconscious mind and suppressed by love also plays an important part in the pathogenesis of hysteria and paranoia. We know too little of the essential nature of love to make any definite decision here; in particular the relationship of its *negative factors*[12] to the sadistic components of the libido remains entirely unexplained. It must therefore be regarded as a provisional explanation if we say that, in the cases of unconscious hatred we have discussed, the sadistic components of love have been particularly strongly developed from constitutional causes, and for that reason have been prematurely and all too thoroughly suppressed, so that the neurotic phenomena we have observed are now derived on the one hand from conscious feelings of affection, taken to an extreme in reaction, and on the other hand from the sadism that continues to function in the unconscious mind as hatred.

However we are to understand this curious relation of love and hatred, nevertheless, observation of our patient confirms its presence beyond a shadow of doubt, and it is agreeable to discover how readily we are able to comprehend the enigmatic processes of obsessive-compulsive neurosis by relating them to this one factor. If intense feelings of love are countered by and bound up with almost equally strong feelings of hatred, the immediate consequence must be a partial paralysis of the will, an inability to make decisions with regard to any action where love is to be the driving motive. But indecision does not remain limited to a single group of actions for long. For, in the first place, which of a lover's actions are not related to this principal motivation? Second, sexual behaviour fulfils an exemplary function that has a powerful modifying effect on an individual's other reactions; and, third, it is in the psychological character of obsessive-compulsive neurosis to exploit the mechanism of *displacement* as far as possible. The crippling of the ability to make decisions thus extends gradually to all areas of human action.[13]

Hence the controlling power of *compulsion* and *doubt* as we encounter them in the inner life of those suffering from compulsive disorders. *Doubt* corresponds to the internal perception of indecisiveness that seizes the patient in the face of every intended action, as a result of the inhibition of love by hatred. It is actually a doubting of love, which ought after all to be what is most certain in his own mind, diffused throughout everything else and displaced for preference on to the tiniest and most indifferent things. Whoever doubts his love might, nay, must doubt everything else, however small, as well.[14]

In the case of defensive measures, the same doubt leads to uncertainty and to continuous repetition intended to ward off that uncertainty, and eventually creates a situation where the defensive actions become just as impossible to implement as the decision over the love affair that was the original source of inhibition. When I started my research I had to assume that the uncertainty found in those suffering from compulsive disorders was derived from another and more general source, which appeared to conform more closely to the norm. If, for example, while I am drafting a letter another person disturbs me with constant questioning, I feel justifiable uncertainty afterwards as to what I might have written under the influence of such disturbances and am obliged to read the letter through again once I have finished it, just to be certain. I was thus also able to suppose that the uncertainty felt by those suffering from compulsive disorders, for example in their prayers, might stem from the fact that unconscious fantasies were constantly interfering with the activity of prayer and disrupting it. This assumption was correct, and yet it is easy to reconcile it with my previous assertion. It is true that uncertainty as to whether a defensive measure has been carried out or not is derived from unconscious, disruptive fantasies, but these fantasies contain precisely the opposing impulse that the act of prayer is intended to fend off. In our patient's case this was made abundantly clear on one occasion, when the disruption did not remain unconscious but distinctly made itself heard. While attempting to pray the words '*May God protect her*' a hostile '*not*' suddenly erupts from the unconscious and he guesses correctly that this constitutes the beginnings of a curse (p. 154). If that '*not*' had remained unspoken he too would have found himself in a state of uncertainty and would have gone on praying for longer and longer; but once it had been articulated he gave up prayer at last. Before doing so he tried all sorts of methods, like others suffering from compulsive disorders, to keep the interference of the opposing impulse at bay, shortening his prayers and saying them as quickly as possible; other individuals endeavour to '*isolate*' any such defensive action from everything else. In the long run, however, all these techniques are fruitless; if the loving impulse, displaced on to some trivial action, has been able to accomplish something, the hostile impulse will soon follow to cancel out what has been achieved.

If someone suffering from a compulsive disorder then discovers the weak point in the structure that safeguards our inner life, the unreliability of memory, he can, with its assistance, extend doubt to encompass everything, even completed actions which bore no relation to the love–hate complex, and thus the whole of the past. Let us recall the example of that lady who had just bought a comb for her little girl in the shop and who, after her suspicions towards her husband had been aroused, began to doubt whether she had not in fact been in possession of the comb for some time already: is this woman not saying quite candidly: 'If I can doubt your love' (and this is only a projection of her doubt as to her own love for him) 'I can doubt this too, I can doubt absolutely everything', thus exposing to our understanding the hidden meaning of neurotic doubt?

Compulsion is an attempt to compensate for doubt, however, and to correct the unbearable state of inhibition to which doubt bears witness. If, with the help of displacement, the individual succeeds in arriving at a decision with regard to any of his inhibited intentions, then it *must* be carried out; admittedly it is no longer the original intention, but the energy that has been dammed up behind it will no longer be denied the opportunity to find a channel in substitute action. Thus it finds expression in commands and prohibitions, as first the affectionate impulse and then the hostile one assumes control of the channel, allowing energy to be discharged. The tension created when the compulsive command cannot be carried out is unbearable and is experienced as intense anxiety. But even the route to a substitute action, one displaced on to the most trivial of things, is so hotly contested that it can usually only be implemented as a protective measure, and remains closely bound up with an impulse which must be fended off.

Moreover, by means of a kind of *regression*, preparatory actions take the place of any definitive decision, thinking replaces acting and any stage of thought preliminary to action asserts itself with compulsive force to replace substitute action. Depending on whether this regression from acting to thinking is more or less pronounced, an individual case of obsessive-compulsive neurosis assumes the character of either compulsive thought (compulsive ideas), or compulsive action in the strict sense of the word. True compulsive actions of this kind only become possible, however, because in them a kind of reconciliation takes place between the two conflicting impulses by means of compromise formations. For compulsive actions come ever closer – and this is increasingly apparent the longer the condition lasts – to infantile sexual activity of the masturbatory type. And so we do come to acts of love after all in this form of the neurosis, but only with the help of a new kind of regression: these are not acts involving a real person, the object of love and hatred, but auto-erotic activity of the kind that took place in childhood.

The first type of regression, from acting to thinking, is facilitated by another factor that contributes to the emergence of the neurosis. Something that almost always features in the history of those suffering from compulsive disorder is the early appearance and premature repression of the drive to visual experience and sexual knowledge, which also directed the infantile sexual activity of our patient in some measure.[15]

We have already considered the significance of the sadistic components in the genesis of obsessive-compulsive neurosis; where the drive to knowledge is dominant in the constitution of the sufferer, brooding becomes an important symptom of the neurosis. Thought processes themselves become sexualized as sexual desire, which would normally refer to the content of the patient's thoughts, is applied to the act of thinking itself, and the satisfaction felt in arriving at a certain intellectual outcome is experienced as sexual satisfaction. This relationship between the drive to knowledge and the intellectual process makes it particularly well suited, in the various forms of obsessive-compulsive neurosis where it has a part to play, to waylaying the energy that struggles in vain to force its way through to action and luring it in the direction of thought, which offers the possibility of a different kind of pleasurable satisfaction. In this way, with the help of the drive to knowledge, the substitute action can find further substitutes in preparatory acts of thought. The postponement of action soon finds a substitute in cerebration so that in the end the entire process is transferred to a new sphere while retaining all its particular characteristics, in the same way that Americans choose to move a house from one place to another, stone by stone.

Drawing on the above remarks I would now venture a definition of the psychological characteristic, long sought-after, which lends the products of obsessive-compulsive neurosis their 'compulsive' quality. Those thought-processes which (as a consequence of the inhibitions caused at the motor end of systems of thought by the existence of contradictory feelings) are undertaken with an expenditure of energy which – qualitatively as well as quantitatively – is normally reserved for actions, *thoughts*, that is, *which by a process of regression must stand for deeds*, become compulsive in nature. No one, surely, will question the assumption that for economic reasons thinking normally requires a lesser displacement of energy (probably at a higher level [of energy-charge]) than action, whose aim is to discharge energy and to alter the outside world.

What has penetrated consciousness with disproportionate force in the guise of a compulsive thought must now be safeguarded against the efforts made by conscious thought to dissipate it. We already know that this protection is achieved by means of the *distortion* to which the compulsive thought is subjected before it becomes conscious. This is not its only means of protection, however. Over and above this we find that the opportunity is rarely neglected of detaching the compulsive idea from the situation in which it arose, where, despite distortion, it would be most readily accessible to the understanding. With this in mind, an *interval* of time is *inserted*, on the one hand between the pathogenic situation and the compulsive idea that follows on from it, in order to mislead conscious thought in its attempt to establish some kind of causality; and on the other hand the content of the compulsive idea is detached from its particular connections by means of *generalization*.

One example of this is provided by our patient's 'compulsion to understand' (p. 152); a better one, perhaps, comes from another patient who would not allow herself to wear jewellery of any kind, although the reason for this went back to a single piece of jewellery that she envied her mother, hoping that it would eventually come to her by process of inheritance. And finally, if we may draw a distinction between this and the uniform act of distortion, the compulsive idea is protected against the conscious work of resolution by means of phrasing that is deliberately chosen for its vagueness or ambiguity. Having been misunderstood, the turn of phrase can now enter the patient's delirious fantasies and any further development or substitution of the compulsion will proceed from this misunderstanding rather than the correct wording. It is possible, nevertheless, to observe the way in which these delirious fantasies constantly strive to establish new connections to the content and phrasing of that compulsion that did not find its way into conscious thought.

For the sake of a single observation I should like to return to the subject of the drives in obsessive-compulsive neurosis. Our patient also turned out to have a *nose*, and on his own admission recognized people in his childhood according to their smell, like a dog; even now olfactory perceptions were more significant to him than they are to other people.[16] I have found the same to be true of others suffering from neurosis, compulsive disorders and hysteria, and have learnt to acknowledge the role played by pleasure in smell, lost since childhood, in the genesis of the neuroses.[17] I should like to raise the general question of whether it is possible that the diminishing of the olfactory sense, which became inevitable as mankind lifted its face up off the ground, and the organic repression of the pleasure in smell produced by this, might not play a significant part in mankind's ability to develop neurotic illnesses. This might result in greater understanding of the fact that, with the intensification of culture, it is precisely man's sexual life that must bear the sacrifice of repression. We have after all long been aware of the intimate connection between the sexual drive in the animal organism and the function of the olfactory organ.

In conclusion let me express the hope that these incomplete notes of mine – incomplete in every sense – might inspire others to immerse themselves further in the study of obsessive-compulsive neurosis and bring new material to light. The characteristic aspects of this form of neurosis, those aspects that distinguish it from hysteria, are not in my opinion to be sought in the drives, but in psychological relationships. I cannot leave my patient without articulating my impression that he had disintegrated, so to speak, into three personalities, one unconscious and two pre-conscious, I would say, between which his conscious mind oscillated. His unconscious personality encompassed prematurely suppressed impulses, which we might term passionate and wicked; in his normal state he was good, clever and enlightened, possessing a superior understanding and embracing life, but in a third mode of psychic organization he was in thrall to superstition and ascetism, so that he was able to hold two sets of convictions and embody two ways of looking at the world. The reaction formations to his repressed desires were contained predominantly in the pre-conscious personality and one could easily predict that, if his illness had persisted, it would have consumed his normal personality altogether. At present I have the opportunity of studying a lady who is suffering from a severe tendency to compulsive actions, who is similarly divided into two personalities, one tolerant and cheerful and the other ascetic and inclined to deep gloom, and who puts forward the former as her official self while remaining dominated by the latter. Both modes of psychic organization have access to her conscious mind, and we must uncover behind the ascetic personality the unconscious part of her being that is entirely unknown to her, consisting of ancient wishful impulses, long repressed.[18]

(1909)

Notes

1. [This heading was added in 1924.]

2. A number of the points discussed here and in the next section have already been touched on in the literature on obsessive-compulsive neurosis, as can be seen from L. Löwenfeld's exhaustive study *Die psychischen Zwangserscheinungen* [*Phenomena of Psychological Compulsion*], published in 1904, the standard work on this form of illness.

3. 'Weitere Bemerkungen über die Abwehr–Neuropsychosen' ['Further Remarks on Neuro-psychoses with a Parrying Function'].

4. This lack of definition is corrected within the essay itself, where we find the sentence: 'The reawakened memories and the reproaches formed from them never enter consciousness unchanged; on the contrary, whatever becomes conscious in the form of compulsive idea and compulsive emotion, pathogenic memory substituted for conscious life, are *compromise formations* between the repressed ideas and the ideas that repress them.' Particular emphasis should therefore be placed in my definition on the word 'transformed'.

5. In many cases the patient withholds his attention to the extent that he cannot give the content of a compulsive idea at all, nor describe a compulsive action which he has carried out on countless occasions.

6. On the matter of 'omnipotence' see [p. 188].

7. I will remind the reader of the use of techniques of omission in jokes by means of examples taken from one of my essays (*Der Witz und seine Beziehung zum Unbewußten* [*The Joke and Its Relation to the Unconscious*]). 'In Vienna there lives a quick-witted and pugnacious writer whose sharp invective has repeatedly earned him physical mistreatment from those he has attacked. Once, when the talk was of a new misdemeanour on the part of one of his habitual opponents, a third person remarked: "*If X hears that, he'll get his ears boxed.*" The contradiction is resolved once we fill in the gap: "*He will write such a vicious article against the man concerned that*", etc.' The content of this elliptical joke also corresponds to some extent with the first example above.

8. *Zur Psychopathologie des Alltagslebens* [*The Pyschopathology of Everyday Life*] (1901), Chapter XII, Section C (b).

9. Lichtenberg: 'Ob der Mond bewohnt ist, weiß der Astronom ungefähr mit der Zuverlässigkeit, mit der er weiß, wer sein Vater war, aber nicht mit der, woher er weiß, wer seine Mutter gewesen ist' [The astronomer knows if there is a man in the moon with about as much certainty as he knows who his father was, but not with so much certainty as he knows who his mother was.] – It marked great cultural progress when mankind decided to place logical conclusion on a par with the evidence of the senses and to pass from matriarchy to patriarchy. – Prehistoric figures in which a smaller figure sits on the head of a larger one depict patrilineal descent: the motherless Athene springs from the head of Zeus. In our language we still use the word *Zeuge* ['witness', literally 'generator'] to describe the person who produces evidence in court, after the male role in the business of reproduction, and in hieroglyphics 'witness' is written using the image of the male genitalia.

10. [*Addition 1923:*] Since the publication of this essay, the omnipotence of thoughts, or more precisely of wishes, has been recognized as an essential part of the inner life of primitive peoples. (See *Totem und Tabu* [*Totem and Taboo*], 1912–13.)

11. Cf. discussion of this subject in one of the first sessions. [*Addition 1923:*] The highly appropriate term 'ambivalence' was later coined by Bleuler to describe this constellation of feelings ('Vortrag über Ambivalenz' ['Lecture on Ambivalence'] *Zentbl. Psychoanal.*, vol. 1). Cf., incidentally, the subsequent continuation of this discussion in the essay 'Die Disposition zur Zwangsneurose' ['The Disposition to Obsessional Neurosis'] ([Freud] 1913).

12. 'Many a time have I wished that he were dead, and yet I know that I should be much more sorry than glad if he were to die: so that I am at my wits' end', says Alcibiades of Socrates in the *Symposium*.

13. Cf. depiction by means of tiny details as a technique in jokes.

14. Hamlet's lines of love to Ophelia:

> *Doubt thou the stars are fire;*
> *Doubt that the sun doth move;*
> *Doubt truth to be a liar;*
> *But never doubt that I love.* (Act II, Scene 2)

15. There is probably also a connection here with what are on average the quite considerable intellectual gifts of those suffering from compulsive disorders.

16. I might add that in his childhood he had been dominated by strong coprophiliac tendencies. In addition let us remember the anal eroticism emphasized earlier.

17. E.g. in certain forms of fetishism.

18. [*Addition* 1923:] The patient, who had recovered his psychic health as a result of the analysis described here, was – like so many other promising and estimable young men – killed in the Great War.

From the History of an
Infantile Neurosis
[The 'Wolfman']

I *Preliminary Remarks*

The case of illness that I shall document in the following pages[1] – once again only in fragmentary form – has a number of distinguishing peculiarities which demand some special comment before I embark on my account. The case concerns a young man who suffered a physical collapse in his eighteenth year following a gonorrhoeal infection; when, several years later, he came to me for psychoanalytic treatment he was completely dependent and incapable of autonomous existence. He had lived more or less normally during the decade of his youth which preceded the illness and had completed his secondary school studies without undue disruption. His earlier years, however, had been dominated by a serious neurotic disorder which began shortly before his fourth birthday as anxiety hysteria (animal phobia) and then turned into an obsessive-compulsive neurosis [*Zwangsneurose*], religious in content, the ramifications of which persisted into his tenth year.

I shall document only this infantile neurosis. Despite a direct demand to this effect on the part of my patient I have declined to write a complete history of his illness, treatment and recovery because I regard the exercise as technically impracticable and socially unacceptable. This deprives me of the possibility of demonstrating the connection between his childhood illness and the later, definitive episode. Of the latter I can say only that it caused our patient to spend long periods of time in German sanatoria where his case was classified by the highest authorities as 'manic-depressive psychosis'. This was an accurate diagnosis of the patient's father, whose life, rich in interests and activities, had regularly been disrupted by severe attacks of depression. As far as the son is concerned, however, I have been unable to observe, in the course of several years, any mood swings that go beyond what is consonant with the obvious psychic situation in terms of intensity and conditions of appearance. I have formed the impression that this case, like many others on which clinical psychiatry imposes a variety of changing diagnoses, is to be understood as a residual condition resulting from a case of obsessive-compulsive neurosis which has spontaneously run its course but where recovery has been incomplete.

My account will thus deal with an infantile neurosis analysed not during the course of the illness but fifteen years after it had come to an end. This situation has both advantages and disadvantages in comparison with the other. Analysis of the neurotic child himself will appear fundamentally more reliable but is unlikely to contain much by way of content; we have to put too many words and thoughts into the child's mouth and may perhaps find nevertheless that the deepest strata cannot be penetrated by consciousness. Analysis of a childhood illness via the medium of adult memory, where the individual is now intellectually mature, is free of such limitations; but we must take into account the distortion and adjustment that takes place when, at a later date, we look back at our own past. The former situation brings more convincing results, perhaps, but the latter is by far the more instructive.

In any case it is fair to say that the analysis of childhood neuroses can lay claim to a particularly high degree of theoretical interest. Such analyses do about the same for the proper understanding of adult neurosis as children's dreams do for the dreams of adults. Not that they can be seen through more easily or are composed of fewer elements; the difficulty of empathizing with the inner life [*Seelenleben*] of the child in fact makes such dreams particularly hard work for the physician. However, they dispense with so many of the subsequent layers that the essential elements of the neurosis emerge with unmistakable clarity. It is well known that resistance to the results of psychoanalysis has taken a new form in the present phase of the battle over psychoanalysis. Previously it was enough to challenge the reality of the facts asserted by analysis and to this end the best technique appeared to be to avoid any kind of verification.

Apparently, this procedure is gradually being exhausted and opposition now takes a different route, acknowledging the facts but disposing of the resulting conclusions by means of re-interpretation so that it is possible, after all, to fend off such offensive conclusions. The study of childhood neurosis shows that these attempts at re-interpretation, which are either shallow or forced, are entirely inadequate. It demonstrates that the libidinal drives which my opponents would so like to deny are of paramount importance in the formation of neurosis, while revealing the absence of any pursuit of distant cultural goals, about which the child knows nothing and which can therefore have no meaning for him.

Another feature that commends the analysis described here to the reader's attention relates to the severity of the illness and the length of treatment required. Those analyses that lead quickly to a favourable outcome are valuable for the therapist's self-confidence and demonstrate the medical significance of psychoanalysis; but they remain of scant importance in promoting our scientific understanding. We learn nothing new from them. They lead so quickly to success only because we already knew everything that was necessary to deal with them. We can only learn something new from analyses that present us with particular difficulties, which can only be surmounted after some considerable time. In these cases alone do we succeed in descending to the deepest and most primitive strata of inner development in order to retrieve solutions to problems which are posed by the forms assumed subsequently by that very development. Strictly speaking we might then say that only an analysis that has penetrated thus far is worthy of the name. Of course, a single case cannot enlighten us with regard to everything we should like to know. Or, more precisely, it could tell us everything if we were only in a position to comprehend it all and if the unpractised nature of our own perceptions did not oblige us to be content with just a little.

The case of illness that I shall describe in the following pages left nothing to be desired in terms of productive difficulties of this kind. The first years of treatment produced very little change. A fortunate constellation decreed that external circumstances made it possible, nevertheless, to continue with the therapeutic attempt. I can easily imagine that in less favourable circumstances the treatment would have been abandoned after a certain period of time. I can only say in favour of the physician's standpoint that he must be as 'timeless' in his approach as the unconscious itself if he wants to learn or achieve anything. In the end this can only happen if he is prepared to renounce any short-sighted therapeutic ambitions. There are few other cases in which one can expect the degree of patience, submissiveness, insight and trust that were required on the part of this patient and those closest to him. The analyst can tell himself, however, that the results achieved in one case by such lengthy endeavours will now help significantly to reduce the treatment time in another, equally severe case, and that in this way the timeless nature of the unconscious can progressively be overcome, once one has yielded to it on the first occasion.

The patient I am concerned with here maintained an unassailable position for a long time, entrenched behind an attitude of submissive indifference. He listened and understood but would allow nothing to come anywhere near him. One could not fault his intelligence, but it was as if it had been cut off by those involuntary [*triebhaft*] forces that determined his behaviour in the few human relationships left to him. He had to be educated for a long time before he could be persuaded to take an independent interest in our work and when, as a result of his efforts, the first moments of release occurred, he suspended the work immediately to prevent any further possibility of change and to maintain the comfortableness of the former situation. His timidity at the prospect of an independent existence was so great that it outweighed all the hardships of being ill. There was only one way of overcoming it. I had to wait until his attachment to me had grown strong enough to counterbalance it, and then I played off the one factor against the other. I decided – not without allowing myself to be guided by reliable signs that the timing was right – that the treatment would have to end by a certain date, no matter what progress had been made. I was determined to keep to this deadline; in the end my patient recognized that I was serious. Under the inexorable pressure of the deadline that I had set, his resistance, his fixed determination [*Fixierung*] to remain ill gave way, after which the analysis delivered up all the material which made it possible, within a disproportionately short length of time, to dissolve his inhibitions and eliminate his symptoms. It is from this last period of therapeutic work, during which the patient's resistance had at times completely disappeared and he gave an impression of the kind of lucidity normally only to be attained through hypnosis, that I derived all the explanations which enabled me to understand his infantile neurosis.

In this way the course of the treatment illustrated the dictum, long held to be true by the analytic technique, that the length of the road that the analysis must travel with the patient and the wealth of material that must be mastered on that road are as nothing compared to the resistance encountered during the work, and are only worthy of consideration in that they are necessarily proportional to that resistance. It is the same process as when a hostile army takes weeks and months to cross a stretch of land that an express train could cover in a few hours in peace time, and that one's own army had crossed in a matter of days a short time before.

A third peculiarity of the analysis in question only compounded the difficulty of deciding whether to write about it. On the whole the results are satisfactorily congruent with what we already knew, or else a clear connection can be established. However, many details appear so curious and incredible, even to me, that I hesitate to ask others to give them credence. I exhorted my patient to subject his memories to the most rigorous criticism but he found nothing improbable in what he had said and maintained that he was telling the truth. My readers can at least be sure that I am merely reporting something that arose as an independent experience and was not influenced in any way by my expectations. I could not do otherwise than recall those wise words that tell us there are more things in heaven and earth than are dreamt of in our philosophy. Anyone capable of screening out his acquired convictions even more thoroughly than I could no doubt discover still more of such matters.

Note

1. This case history was written up shortly after conclusion of the treatment in winter 1914/15, in the light of the recent attempts to re-interpret psycho-analytic material undertaken by C. G. Jung and Adolf Adler. It is to be taken in conjunction with the essay published in the *Jahrbuch der Psychoanalyse* [*Yearbook of Psychoanalysis*], VI (1916), 'Zur Geschichte der psychoanalytischen Bewegung' ['On the History of the Psycho-Analytic Movement', 1914] and supplements the essentially personal polemic which that essay contains with an objective evaluation of the analytic material. It was originally intended for the subsequent volume of the *Yearbook* but since its appearance in that journal was postponed indefinitely as a result of the retarding effects of the Great War, I decided to include it in this collection, organized by a new publisher. I had meanwhile been obliged to discuss much that should have found its first expression here in my *Vorlesungen zur Einführung in die Psychoanalyse* [*Introductory Lectures on Psycho-analysis*], given in 1916/17. There are no modifications of any note to the text of the first version; additional material is indicated in square brackets.

II *Survey of the Patient's Milieu and Medical History*

I can write neither a purely historical nor a purely pragmatic history of my patient; I can provide neither a treatment history nor a case history, but shall find myself obliged to combine the two approaches. It is well known that no way has yet been found to embed the convictions that are gained through analysis within any account of the analysis itself. Certainly nothing would be gained by providing exhaustive minutes of what took place during analytic sessions; moreover, the techniques of the treatment preclude the production of any such minutes. An analysis of this kind is not published, then, to command the conviction of those who have hitherto shown themselves to be dismissive and incredulous. We expect to offer something new only to those researchers whose experiences with patients have already sown the seeds of conviction.

I shall begin by describing the child's world and relating those aspects of his childhood story that I learned without any particular effort; essentially nothing was added to this material over several years, and it remained just as opaque during the whole of this time.

His parents married young; it was a happy marriage, but the first shadows were soon to be cast by illness on both sides, his mother suffering from gynaecological complaints, his father from attacks of moroseness which resulted in his absence from the family home. Only much later did our patient develop some understanding of his father's illness, of course, but his mother's ill-health was known to him from his earliest years. For this reason she had relatively little to do with her children. One day, certainly before the age of four, holding his mother's hand, he listens to his mother complaining to the doctor whom she is accompanying on his way, and commits her words to memory, later using them of himself. He is not the only child, but has a sister some two years older, lively, gifted and impetuously naughty, who is to play an important role in his life.

He is cared for by an old children's nurse as far back as he can remember, working-class, uneducated and untiringly affectionate towards him. For her he is a substitute for her own son, who died young. The family lives on a country estate which in the summer they exchange for another country estate. Neither is far from the city. It marks a turning-point in his childhood when his parents sell the estates and move to the city. Close relatives often come to stay on one or other estate for long periods of time, his father's brothers, his mother's sisters and their children, his maternal grandparents. In the summer, his parents used to go away for several weeks. In a cover-memory [*Deckerinnerung*] he sees himself standing with his nurse, watching his father, mother and sister being driven away in a carriage, and then going calmly back into the house. He must have been very small at the time.[1] The next summer his sister was left at home and an English governess appointed, whose responsibility it was to supervise the children.

In later years he was told a great many things about his childhood.[2] Much of it he knew himself but without being able to make connections, of course, in terms of chronology or content. One story handed down in this way, which had been repeated in his presence on countless occasions because of his later illness, introduces the problem to whose solution we shall devote our attention. He is said to have been a very gentle, obedient and rather quiet child at first, so that people used to say he should have been the girl and his sister the boy. But once when his parents came back from their summer holiday they found him transformed. He had become discontented and irritable, was constantly flying into a passion, and would take offence at the slightest thing, raging and yelling like a savage, so that when this condition persisted, his parents expressed concern that it would not be possible to send him to school later on. It was the summer when the English governess was there; she had turned out to be a silly, cantankerous woman, and, incidentally, a slave to drink. His mother was thus inclined to see a connection between the boy's changed character and the English woman's influence, and assumed that he had been provoked by her treatment of him. His grandmother, a shrewd woman who had also spent the summer with the children, was of the opinion that the boy's touchiness was the result of constant quarrelling between the English governess and the children's nurse. The governess had repeatedly called the nurse a witch and obliged her to leave the room; the little boy had openly taken the part of his beloved 'Nanja' and made clear his hatred of the governess. Whatever the case, the English woman was sent away soon after the parents' return, without the child's disagreeable behaviour changing one whit.

The patient has retained his own memories of this difficult time.[3] He thinks he made the first scenes when he did not receive two lots of presents at Christmas time, as he had a right to expect, Christmas Day being also his birthday. His beloved Nanja was not exempt from his demands or his touchiness, indeed she was perhaps the most relentlessly tormented of all. But this phase of character change is indissolubly linked in his memory to many other strange and morbid phenomena, which he is unable to bring into any kind of chronological order. He bundles together everything I shall be describing here, things that cannot possibly have occurred at the same time and that are full of internal contradictions, attributing them all to one and the same period of time, which he calls 'when we were still living on the first estate'. They left this estate, he thinks, when he was five years old. He is thus able to tell me that he suffered from an anxiety that his sister exploited in order to torment him. There was a particular picture book, which showed a picture of a wolf standing on its hind legs and stepping out. Whenever he set eyes on this picture he would start to scream furiously, fearing that the wolf would come and gobble him up. His sister, however, always managed to arrange matters so that he would have to see this picture and took great delight in his terror. At the same time he was also afraid of other animals, both large and small. On one occasion he was chasing after a lovely big butterfly with yellow-striped wings that had pointed tips, trying to catch it. (Probably a 'swallowtail'.) Suddenly he was seized by a dreadful fear of the creature and gave up his pursuit, screaming. He also experienced fear and disgust at the sight of beetles and caterpillars. And yet he was able to recall that at the same period he had tortured beetles and cut up caterpillars; horses also gave him an uncanny feeling. He would scream if a horse was beaten and once had to leave a circus for this reason. On other occasions he enjoyed beating horses himself. Whether these two conflicting attitudes to animals really held sway simultaneously, or whether one had not in fact supplanted the other – though if that were the case, in what order and when – his memory would not allow him to decide. He was also unable to say whether the difficult period was replaced by a period of illness or whether it had persisted throughout. In any case, in the light of what he went on to say, one was justified in making the assumption that in those childhood years he had gone through what could clearly be recognized as an episode of obsessive-compulsive neurosis. He told me that for a long period of time he had been very pious. He had had to pray at great length and cross himself endlessly before he could go to sleep at night. Every evening he would do the rounds of the holy pictures hanging in his room, using a chair to stand on, and bestow a reverent kiss on each one. It was somewhat out of keeping, then – or actually perhaps entirely in keeping – with this pious ritual that he recalled blasphemous thoughts coming into his mind, as if planted there by the devil. He was obliged to think: 'God – swine' or 'God – crud'. Once, journeying to a German spa, he was tortured by a compulsion to think of the Holy Trinity when he saw three piles of horse dung or other excrement lying on the road. At this time he used also to adhere to a peculiar ritual if he saw people who inspired pity in him, beggars, cripples, old men. He had to breathe out noisily in order not to become like one of them, and under certain conditions also had to inhale deeply. I was naturally inclined to assume that these clear symptoms of obsessive-compulsive neurosis belonged to a somewhat later period of time and a later stage of development than the signs of anxiety and the cruel behaviour towards animals.

Our patient's more mature years were characterized by a very unpromising relationship with his father, who after repeated depressive episodes could now no longer conceal the morbid aspects of his character. In the early years of his childhood it had been a most affectionate relationship, and this was how his son remembered him. His father was very fond of him and enjoyed playing with him. Even as a little boy he was proud of his father and would only ever say that he wanted to grow up to be a gentleman just like him. His Nanja had told him that his sister was his mother's child, but he was his father's, and this pleased him greatly. As his childhood came to an end he became estranged from his father. His father undoubtedly preferred his sister and he was very hurt by this. Later, fear of his father became the dominant emotion.

When he was getting on for eight all the symptoms the patient ascribed to the phase of existence which had begun with the difficult period disappeared. They did not disappear all at once but returned a few more times, finally ceding, in the patient's opinion, to the influence of the teachers and tutors who replaced his female carers. Put very briefly, then, the enigmas which yielded up their solutions in the course of the analysis are as follows: where did the boy's sudden change of character come from, what was the meaning of his phobia and his perversions, how did he acquire his compulsive [*Zwangs-*] piety and what was the connection between all these phenomena? Let me remind the reader once again that our therapeutic work was directed towards a later neurotic episode of recent occurrence and that information about those earlier problems could only emerge if the course of the analysis led us away from the present for a while, obliging us to take a detour through the pre-history of the patient's childhood.

Notes

1. 2½ years old. It later became possible to say quite definitely when most things had taken place.

2. As a general rule information of this kind can be regarded as material whose credibility is beyond question. An obvious possibility, requiring no effort, is therefore to fill in the gaps in a patient's memory by making inquiry of older family members; however I cannot warn strongly enough against

such techniques. The stories told by the patient's relatives when invited and exhorted to provide such information are open to all the critical misgivings that could possibly apply. One regularly regrets having made oneself dependent on such information, and in asking for it one has undermined the relationship of trust in the analysis and invoked a different authority. Everything that it is possible to remember will eventually emerge in the course of the analysis.

3. [*Translator's note*: The phrase used by Freud, '*schlimme Zeit*', refers both to the boy's naughtiness and to the fact that it was a painful period for him. I have attempted to convey this ambiguity by using the adjective 'difficult'.]

III *Seduction and its Immediate Consequences*

Understandably my suspicions fell first on the English governess, whose presence in the house had coincided with the change in the boy. He had retained two cover-memories relating to her, which in themselves were incomprehensible. Once, as she was walking ahead of them, she said to the children following behind: 'Look at my little tail!' On another occasion her hat blew away when they were out on a trip, to the great satisfaction of brother and sister. These pointed towards the castration complex and might allow us to reconstruct, say, a threat made by her against the boy, contributing significantly to the development of abnormal behaviour. It is not in the least dangerous to put such reconstructions [*Konstruktionen*] to the analysand: they do no harm to the analysis if they are erroneous and in any case one does not give voice to them if there is not some prospect of coming closer to the truth in the process. The immediate effect of putting forward these ideas was the appearance of dreams that it was not possible to interpret completely but which always seemed to play around with the same content. The subject of the dreams, as far as one could tell, was aggressive action on the boy's part towards his sister or the governess, which resulted in energetic rebuke and punishment. As if he had tried . . . after a bath . . . to expose his sister's nakedness . . . to tear off layers of clothing . . . or her veil . . . and the like. It was not possible, however, to arrive by means of interpretation at any definite content, and, once we had formed the impression that the same material was being processed in these dreams in ever-changing ways, it was clear how we were to understand what were apparently involuntary memories [*Reminiszenzen*]. It could only be a question of fantasies that the dreamer had once entertained about his childhood, probably during puberty, and which had now emerged again in a form so difficult to recognize.

We learnt what they meant in one fell swoop when the patient suddenly recalled the fact that his sister had seduced him 'when he was still very little, when they were living on the first estate' into sexual pursuits. First came the memory that on the lavatory, which the children often used together, she had issued the invitation: 'Shall we show each other our bottoms?' and had then suited the action to the word. Later we arrived at the more essential elements of the seduction and all the accompanying details of time and locality. It was in the spring, at a time when the father was away from home; the children were playing on the floor in one room while their mother was working in the next room. His sister had reached for his penis and played with it, saying incomprehensible things about Nanja all the while, as if by way of explanation. She said that Nanja did this all the time with everyone, the gardener, for example, she would turn him upside down and then take hold of his genitals.

This made it possible to understand the fantasies we had guessed at earlier. They were intended to erase the memory of an event which later offended the patient's sense of masculine pride, achieving this goal by replacing historical truth with its wished-for opposite. According to these fantasies he had not taken the passive role towards his sister, but on the contrary had been aggressive, had wanted to see his sister without her clothes on, had been rejected and punished, and had thus fallen into the rage recounted so insistently by domestic tradition. It was also expedient to weave the governess into this story, since his mother and his grandmother attributed most of the blame to her, after all, for his bouts of rage. His fantasies thus corresponded exactly to the creation of sagas, by means of which a nation which later becomes great and proud seeks to conceal the insignificance and misadventure of its origins.

In reality the governess could have played only the most remote part in the seduction and its consequences. The scenes with his sister took place in the spring of that same year in which the English governess arrived to take the parents' place during the midsummer months. The boy's hostility to the governess in fact came about in a different way. By calumniating the children's nurse and saying she was a witch the governess was following in his sister's footsteps, since it was she who had first told him those dreadful things about their nurse, and this gave him the opportunity to express the repugnance that, as we shall learn, he had come to feel for his sister after she had seduced him.

That his sister had seduced him was certainly no fantasy, however. Its credibility was strengthened by a piece of information he received in later, more mature years and had never forgotten. In a conversation about his sister, a cousin, more than a decade older, had told him that he could remember very well what a forward, sensual little thing she had been. As a child of four or five she had once sat down on his lap and unfastened his trousers to take hold of his penis.

I shall interrupt the story of my patient's childhood for a moment in order to speak of this sister, her development, her subsequent fate and the influence she had over him. She was two years older and always ahead of him. Boisterous and tomboyish as a child, she underwent a dazzling intellectual development distinguished by an acute and realistic understanding; she favoured the natural sciences as an avenue of study yet at the same time produced poems of which their father had a very high opinion. She was intellectually far superior to her numerous early suitors and used to make fun of them. In her early twenties, however, she grew morose, complained that she was not pretty enough and withdrew from all social contact. Sent away on a tour in the company of an older lady, a friend of the family, she told the most improbable stories on her return of how her companion had ill-treated her, yet her inward attention remained obviously fixed on the woman who had allegedly tormented her. On a second journey, which took place soon afterwards, she poisoned herself and died a long way from home. Her state of mind probably corresponded to the onset of dementia praecox. Her case was among those testifying to a considerable inherited tendency to neuropathic affliction in the family, but it was by no means the only one. An uncle on the father's side, who lived for many years as an eccentric, died with every indication of having suffered from severe obsessive-compulsive neurosis; among the more distant relatives a considerable number have been and are afflicted by more minor nervous disorders.

In childhood our patient saw his sister – leaving aside for a moment the matter of the seduction – as an uncomfortable rival for their parents' approval and found the superiority that she so ruthlessly demonstrated highly oppressive. He particularly envied her the respect that their father demonstrated for her mental capabilities and her intellectual achievements, while he, inhibited intellectually since the episode of obsessive-compulsive neurosis, had to accept being held in lesser regard. From the age of thirteen onwards his relationship with his sister began to improve; similar intellectual aptitudes and shared opposition to their parents brought them so close that they were on the best and friendliest of terms. In the turbulent sexual agitation of puberty he ventured to approach her with a view to physical intimacy. When she rejected him with as much determination as skill he immediately turned from her to a young peasant girl, a servant in the house who bore the same name as his sister. In doing so he took a decisive step as far as his choice of heterosexual object was concerned, for all the girls he later fell in love with, often with the clearest signs of compulsion, were also servant girls, whose education and intelligence necessarily lagged far behind his own. We cannot deny that if all these objects of his love were substitutes for the sister who had refused him, then a tendency to demean his sister, to neutralize the intellectual superiority which had once so oppressed him, played a crucial part in his choice of object.

Alfred Adler subordinates everything, including the individual's sexual attitudes, to motives of this kind, arising from the will to power and the drive to assert oneself [*Behauptungstrieb*]. Without for a moment wishing to deny the validity of such motives of power and prerogative, I have never been convinced that they are able to support the dominant, exclusive role he attributes to them. If I had not seen the analysis of my patient through to the end, my observation of this case would have obliged me to modify my prejudice in the direction of Adler's theories. The concluding stages of the analysis provided unexpected new material, however, from which it became evident that these power motives (in this case, the tendency to demean) had only governed the patient's choice of object in the sense that they had contributed to it, rationalized it, while the real, more profoundly determining element allowed me to hold fast to my earlier convictions.[1]

When news of his sister's death reached him, our patient told me that he felt barely a trace of pain. He forced himself into an outward show of mourning and was able coolly to rejoice in the fact that he was now the sole heir to the family fortunes. He had already been suffering from his more recent illness for some years when this occurred. I must admit, however, that this one statement made me hesitate in my diagnostic judgement of the case for some considerable time. True, it was to be supposed that his pain at the loss of the most beloved member of his family would be inhibited in its expression by continued jealousy towards her and the intrusion of his now unconsciously felt incestuous love, but I needed to find some kind of substitute for the outburst of pain that had failed to take place. I eventually found one in another expression of strong feeling, which had remained incomprehensible to him. A few months after his sister's death he had himself made a journey to the region where she had died; there he sought out the grave of a great poet whom at that time he idealized, and shed hot tears over the grave. He himself was perplexed by his reaction, for he knew that more than two generations had passed since the death of the poet he so admired. He understood what had happened only when he remembered that their father used to compare his dead sister's poems to those of the great poet. An error in his narrative had given me another indication as to the true meaning of this homage apparently paid to the poet, which I was able to draw his attention to at this point. He had repeatedly told me earlier that his sister had shot herself and then been obliged to correct himself, since she had taken poison. The poet, however, had been shot, in a duel.

I shall now take up the brother's story again, and for a while I must describe what actually took place. It turned out that at the time when his sister set about seducing him the boy was 3¼ years old. It happened, as I have said, in the spring of that same year in which his parents found him so radically changed on their return home in the autumn. It seems obvious, then, to assume that there was some connection between this transformation and the awakening of sexual activity that had taken place in the intervening period.

How did the boy react to his older sister's enticements? The answer is that he rejected her, but he rejected the person, not the thing. His sister was not acceptable to him as a sexual object, probably because rivalry for their parents' love had already determined his relationship with her as a hostile one. He avoided her and her advances soon ceased. In her place, however, he sought to win for himself another, more beloved person, and the things his sister herself had said, invoking Nanja as her model, guided his choice towards Nanja. He thus began to play with his penis in front of Nanja, something that must be taken, as in so many other cases where children do not conceal masturbation, as an attempt at seduction. Nanja disappointed him, telling him with a serious expression that that was a naughty thing to do. Children who did that would get a 'wound' there.

We can trace the effect of this remark, which was to all intents and purposes a threat, in various directions. His attachment to Nanja became less strong. He could have been angry with her; later, when the tantrums began, it became clear that she had indeed enraged him. Yet it was characteristic of him that initially he would stubbornly defend against anything new, whatever libido position he was having to give up. When the governess took the stage and insulted Nanja, driving her out of the room and trying to destroy her authority, he in fact exaggerated his love for the person under threat and behaved negatively and defiantly towards the attacking governess. Nevertheless he began secretly to look for another sexual object. The seduction had given him the passive sexual objective of having his genitals touched; we shall learn in due course the person with whom he hoped to achieve this and the paths that led to his choice.

It is entirely in accordance with our expectations to learn that his sexual inquiries began with his first experiences of genital arousal and that he soon came up against the problem of castration. At this time he had the opportunity to watch two girls urinate, his sister and her friend. He was bright enough to have been able to grasp the true state of affairs from this alone but instead behaved in the same way as we know other male children to behave. He rejected the idea that he was seeing confirmation here of the wound with which Nanja had threatened him, and explained it to himself as the girls' 'front bottom'. This decision did not mark the end of the subject of castration, however; he found new indications of it in everything he heard. Once, when sticks of barley sugar were handed out to the children, the governess, who was inclined to lurid fantasies, declared that they were chopped-up pieces of snake. This caused him to remember that his father had once come upon a snake when out for a walk and had chopped it into pieces with his walking-stick. He had been told the story (from *Reineke Fuchs [Reynard the Fox]*) where the wolf tried to catch fish in winter and used his tail as bait, whereupon his tail froze in the ice and broke off. He learnt the different names used for horses depending on the intactness of their sex. He was thus preoccupied with the thought of castration without believing in it or being frightened by it. Other problems relating to sexuality were posed by the fairytales with which he became acquainted at this time. In 'Little Red Riding Hood' and 'The Seven Little Kids' children were pulled out of the body of the wolf. Was the wolf female, then, or could men also carry children in their bodies? At this time he had not yet decided on the answer to that question. He had no fear of wolves as yet, incidentally, at the time of these investigations.

One remark made by our patient will clear the way to an understanding of the change in character that manifested itself during his parents' absence and that was distantly connected with his sister's seduction. He relates that soon after Nanja had rejected and threatened him he gave up masturbation. *The sexual life directed by the genital zone, which was beginning to stir, had succumbed to external inhibition, and this influence had flung it back into an earlier phase of pre-genital organization.* As a result of the suppression of masturbation, the boy's sexual life became anal-sadistic in character. He became irritable and took pleasure in tormenting animals and people, using this to achieve satisfaction. The principal object of torment was his beloved Nanja, whom he knew how to torture until she burst into tears. In this way he took his revenge for the rejection he had received at her hands, and at the same time satisfied his sexual desires in a form corresponding to this regressive phase. He started to be cruel to tiny creatures, catching flies so that he could pull off their wings, stamping on beetles; in his imagination he also enjoyed beating large animals, horses. These were entirely active, sadistic pursuits; we shall hear something of his anal impulses during this period in another context.

It is valuable to learn that fantasies of a quite different kind, contemporaneous with these, also surfaced in the patient's memory, the content of which was that boys were being punished and beaten, beaten in particular on the penis; and we can easily guess for whom these anonymous objects served as whipping-boys by looking at other fantasies, which took the form of the heir-apparent being locked in a narrow room and beaten. He himself was obviously the heir-apparent; in his imagination his sadism was turned against himself, veering into masochism. The detail of the sexual organ itself taking its punishment allows us to conclude that a sense of guilt, directed at his masturbation, was already at work in this transformation.

In analysis there could be no doubt that these passive aspirations [*Strebungen*] emerged at the same time as, or very soon after, the active, sadistic ones.[2] This is in keeping with an uncommonly distinct, intense and persistent *ambivalence* on the part of the patient, expressing itself here for the first time in the symmetrical development of contradictory pairs of partial drives. This behaviour was in future to remain as characteristic of him as the further trait that none of the libido positions which he achieved was ever in fact fully superseded by a later one. Each would exist alongside all the others, allowing him to vacillate unceasingly in a way that proved incompatible with the acquisition of a fixed character.

The boy's masochistic tendencies bring us to another point, which I have not mentioned up until now because it can only be firmly established through analysis of the subsequent phase of development. I have already mentioned the fact that, after Nanja rejected him, he broke away from her and focused his libidinal expectations on a different sexual object. This person was his father, then absent from home. He was guided towards this choice, no doubt, by the coincidence of various factors, including chance ones such as his memory of the dismembered snake; above all, however, he was renewing his first, original choice of object, which had been made, in accordance with the narcissism of the small child, by way of identification. We have already heard that his father had been a much-admired example to him, and that when asked what he wanted to be he used to answer: 'A gentleman like my father.' The object of identification in his active current [*Strömung*] now became the sexual object of a passive current in the anal-sadistic phase. We gain the impression that his sister's seduction of him had forced him into a passive role and given him a passive sexual objective. Under the continuing influence of this experience, he followed a path from sister to Nanja to father, from the passive attitude towards a woman to the same towards a man, and yet in doing so he was able to connect up with an earlier, spontaneous stage of development. The father was once again his object, identification having been succeeded by object-choice, as is appropriate at a higher stage of development; transformation of an active attitude into a passive one was both outcome and sign of the seduction that had taken place in the intervening period. Taking an active attitude towards the excessively powerful figure of the father during the sadistic phase would of course have been much less feasible. On his father's return, in late summer or autumn, his tantrums and furious scenes were put to a different use. They had served an active, sadistic purpose towards Nanja; now, towards his father, their purpose was masochistic. By parading his difficult behaviour he wanted to compel his father to punish and beat him and in this way gain from him the masochistic sexual satisfaction he desired. His screaming fits were nothing other than attempts at seduction. In accordance with the motivation behind masochism, he would also have found satisfaction for his sense of guilt in being punished. One memory had stored up a recollection for him of how, during one such exhibition of difficult behaviour, his screaming gets louder as soon as his father comes in;

yet his father does not beat him but attempts to calm him down by throwing the cushions from the bed up in the air and catching them again.

I do not know how many times, in the face of a child's inexplicable naughtiness, parents and mentors would have occasion to recall this typical connection. The child who is behaving so wildly makes a confession, intending to provoke punishment. In being punished the child is seeking both the appeasement of its sense of guilt and the satisfaction of its masochistic sexual aspirations.

We owe the further clarification of this case to a memory, which came to the patient with great certainty, that the symptoms of anxiety had only joined the other signs of character change once a certain incident had occurred. Before then there had been no anxiety; immediately after this occurrence he found himself tormented by anxiety. We can state with certainty that the point at which this transformation took place was just before his fourth birthday. Thanks to this clue, the period of childhood with which we are particularly concerned can be divided into two phases, a first phase of difficult behaviour and perversity which lasted from his seduction at the age of 3¼ until his fourth birthday, and a longer, subsequent phase dominated by the signs of neurosis. The incident that permits us to draw the dividing line was no external trauma, however, but a dream, from which he awoke beset with anxiety.

Notes

1. See below, p. 292.
2. By passive aspirations I mean those with a passive sexual objective, but what I have in mind is not a transformation of the drives but a transformation of their objective.

IV *The Dream and the Primal Scene*

I have already published this dream elsewhere[1] because of the fairy-tale elements it contains and so I shall begin by reproducing what I wrote at that time:

'I dreamed that it is night and I am lying in my bed (the foot of my bed was under the window, and outside the window there was a row of old walnut trees. I know that it was winter in my dream, and night-time). Suddenly the window opens of its own accord and terrified, I see that there are a number of white wolves sitting in the big walnut tree outside the window. There were six or seven of them. The wolves were white all over and looked more like foxes or sheepdogs because they had big tails like foxes and their ears were pricked up like dogs watching something. Obviously fearful that the wolves were going to gobble me up I screamed and woke up. My nurse hurried to my bedside to see what had happened. It was some time before I could be convinced that it had only been a dream, because the image of the window opening and the wolves sitting in the tree was so clear and lifelike. Eventually I calmed down, feeling as if I had been liberated from danger, and went back to sleep.

'The only action in the dream was the opening of the window, for the wolves were sitting quite still in the branches of the tree, to the right and left of the tree trunk, not moving at all, and looking right at me. It looked as if they had turned their full attention on me. – I think that was my first anxiety-dream. I was three or four at the time, certainly no more than five. From then on until I was ten or eleven I was always afraid of seeing something terrible in my dreams.'

He then drew a picture of the tree with the wolves sitting in it, too, which confirms the description he gave [Fig. 1]. Analysis of the dream brought the following material to light.

FIG. 1

He always related this dream to the memory that in those childhood years he would express a quite monstrous anxiety at the picture of a wolf that was to be found in his book of fairytales. His elder sister, highly superior, would tease him by showing him this very picture on some pretext or other, at which he would begin to scream in horror. In this picture the wolf was standing on his back paws, about to take a step forward, paws outstretched and ears pricked. He thought this picture was there as an illustration to the fairy-tale 'Little Red Riding Hood'.

Why are the wolves white? That makes him think of the sheep which were kept in large flocks quite near the estate. His father sometimes took him to visit the flocks of sheep and he was always very proud and happy when this happened. Later on – inquiries suggest that it could easily have been shortly before this dream took place – an epidemic broke out among the sheep. His father sent for one of Pasteur's disciples, who inoculated the sheep, but after the inoculation they died in even greater numbers than before.

How did the wolves get up in the tree? A story occurs to him that he had heard his grandfather tell. He cannot remember whether it was before or after the dream, but the content of the story strongly supports the first possibility. The story goes as follows: a tailor is sitting in his room working when the window opens and in leaps a wolf. The tailor hits out at him with his measuring stick – no, he corrects himself, he grabs him by the tail and pulls it off, so that the wolf runs away, terrified. Some time later the tailor goes into the woods and suddenly sees a pack of wolves coming towards him, and so he escapes from them by climbing up a tree. At first the wolves do not know what to do, but the maimed one, who is also there and wants his revenge on the tailor, suggests that one should climb on another's back until the last one can reach the tailor. He himself – a powerful old wolf – will form the base of this pyramid. The wolves do as he says, but the tailor recognizes the wolf who visited him, the one he punished, and he calls out suddenly, as he did before: 'Grab the grey fellow by the tail.' The wolf who has lost his tail remembers what happened, and runs away, terrified, while the others all tumble down in a heap.

In this story we find the tree that the wolves are sitting on in the dream. There is also an unambiguous link with the castration complex, however. It is the *old* wolf who loses his tail to the tailor. The foxtails which the wolves have in the dream are no doubt compensation for the absence of a tail.

Why are there six or seven wolves? It seemed that we could not answer this question, until I expressed some doubt as to whether his anxiety-image could in fact have referred to the tale of Little Red Riding Hood. That fairy-tale gives rise to only two illustrations, the meeting of Little Red Riding Hood and the wolf in the forest, and the scene where the wolf is lying in bed wearing Grandmother's nightcap. Another fairy-tale must therefore be concealed behind his memory of that picture. He soon found that it could only be the story of 'The Wolf and the Seven Little Kids'. Here we find the number seven, and also the number six, for the wolf gobbles up only six of the little kids while the seventh hides in the clock-case. We also find white in this story, for the wolf has the baker whiten his paws after the little kids recognize him on his first visit by his grey paw. The two fairy-tales have a great deal in common, incidentally. In both we find people being eaten up, the stomach being cut open, the people who have been eaten taken out again, heavy stones being put back in their place and finally the big bad wolf being killed in both cases. In the story of the little kids we find the tree as well. After he has eaten his fill the wolf lies down under a tree and snores.

I shall have a particular reason to concern myself with this dream in another context, where I shall evaluate it and consider its possible meaning in greater depth. It is a first anxiety-dream, remembered from childhood, the content of which gives rise to a very particular sort of interest in the context of other dreams which followed soon after, and certain incidents in the dreamer's childhood. Here we shall confine ourselves to the dream's relationship to two fairy-tales which have a great deal in common, 'Little Red Riding Hood' and 'The Wolf and the Seven Little Kids'. The impression left on the child dreamer by these fairy-tales found expression in a veritable phobia about animals, distinguished from other similar cases only by the fact that the animal that gave rise to the anxiety was not a readily accessible object (such as a horse or a dog) but one familiar only from stories and picture books.

I shall look at the explanation for these animal phobias and the significance that we should attribute to them on another occasion. Here, I shall anticipate myself only by remarking that this explanation is entirely in keeping with the main characteristic which the dreamer's neurosis reveals in later life. Fear of the father was the most powerful motive for his illness and an ambivalent attitude towards any father-substitute dominated his life, just as it dominated his behaviour in the consulting room.

If, in my patient's case, the wolf was merely the first father-substitute, the question arises as to whether the secret content of the tale of the wolf who gobbled up the little kids or the tale of Red Riding Hood is anything other than infantile fear of the father.[2] My patient's father, incidentally, had a characteristic tendency to '*affectionate scolding*', of the kind used by many people in dealing with their children, and the teasing threat 'I'll gobble you up' may have been uttered more than once when the father, later so strict, used to cuddle and play with his little son. One of my patients told me that her two children were never able to feel really fond of their grandfather because he used to frighten them, in the course of his affectionate games, by telling them he would cut open their tummies.

Leaving aside everything in this essay that anticipates how we might apply the dream, let us return to the immediate issue of how we should interpret it. I should point out that to arrive at an interpretation was an exercise that took several years. The patient told me about the dream very early on, and quickly embraced my conviction that it concealed the cause of his infantile neurosis. In the course of the treatment we often came back to the dream but only arrived at a complete understanding of it during the last months of the therapy, thanks to spontaneous work on the part of my patient. He had always emphasized that two moments in the dream had made the most powerful impression on him, first, the utter calm of the wolves, their motionless stance, and, second, the tense attentiveness with which they all stared at him. The sense of reality as the dream came to an end, which persisted after he had woken up, also seemed noteworthy to him.

Let us take up this last point. Experience of the interpretation of dreams tells us that there is a particular meaning to this sense of reality. It assures us that something in the latent material of the dream lays claim to reality in the dreamer's memory, and thus that the dream refers to an incident that actually took place and has not merely been fantasized. I am referring, of course, only to the reality of something unknown; the conviction, for example, that his grandfather really told him the story of the tailor and the wolf, or that the tale of 'Little Red Riding Hood' or 'The Seven Little Kids' had really been read to him could never be replaced by that sense of reality which outlasts the dream. The dream appeared to point to an incident the reality of which is emphasized by its very contrast with the unreality of the fairy-tales.

If we were to assume the existence of an unknown scene of this kind, concealed behind the content of the dream, i.e. a scene which had already been forgotten at the time of the dream, it must have occurred at a very early age. The dreamer tells us after all that 'when I had the dream I was three or four, certainly no more than five'. We might add, 'And the dream reminded me of something that must have taken place even earlier.'

Those aspects of the manifest dream-content singled out by the dreamer, the moments of attentive watching and motionlessness, had to lead us to the content of that scene. We naturally expect this material to be distorted in some way, perhaps even to be distorted into its opposite, as it reproduces the unknown material of the scene.

It was possible to draw a number of conclusions from the raw material provided by the first analysis, conclusions that could be fitted into the context we were seeking. Concealed behind the mention of sheep-breeding we could find evidence for his exploration of sexuality, interests that could be satisfied in the course of the visits he made together with his father; but there must also have been hints of a fear of death, since for the most part the sheep died in the epidemic. What stands out most in the dream, that is, the wolves in the tree, led directly to the grandfather's story, the most gripping aspect of which could hardly have been anything other than its connection with the topic of castration, the stimulus for the dream.

The first, incomplete analysis of the dream had further led us to infer that the wolf was a father-substitute, so that this first anxiety-dream had brought to light the fear of his father, which was to dominate his life from then on. It is true that even this conclusion was not yet a definite one. However, if we assemble the elements that can be deduced from the material provided by the dreamer, the results of the preliminary analysis, we find the following fragments, which could be used as the basis of a reconstruction:

An actual event – occurring at a very early age – watching – motionlessness – sexual problems – castration – the father – something terrible.

One day our patient took up the interpretation of the dream once again. He thought that the part of the dream in which 'suddenly the window opens of its own accord' is not entirely explained by its relation to the window at which the tailor is sitting and through which the wolf comes into the room. He thought it must mean: my eyes are suddenly opened. I am asleep then, and suddenly wake up, and then I see something: the tree with the wolves. There was nothing to object to here, but we could take it further. He had woken up, and had seen something. The attentive gaze, which in the dream he attributes to the wolves, is actually to be ascribed to him. At a decisive point a reversal [*Verkehrung*] had taken place, indicated, incidentally, by another reversal in the manifest content of the dream. For it is a reversal for the wolves to be sitting in the tree, whereas in the grandfather's story they are down below and are unable to climb up into the tree.

Now, what if the other moment emphasized by the dreamer had also been distorted by reversal or inversion [*Umkehrung*]? Instead of absence of motion (the wolves sit there motionless, gazing at him but not moving) we should have: violent movement. He woke up suddenly, then, and saw a scene of violent excitement which he watched with tense attentiveness. In the one case distortion consists in the exchange of subject and object, active and passive modes, being watched instead of watching; in the other case it consists in transformation into the opposite: calm instead of excitement.

Further progress in understanding the dream was made on another occasion by the abruptly surfacing notion that the tree was the Christmas tree. And now he knew that he had dreamed the dream shortly before Christmas, in anticipation of Christmas itself. Since Christmas Day was also his birthday it was now possible to establish a definite time for the dream and the transformation which it brought in its wake. It was shortly before his fourth birthday. He had fallen asleep in excited anticipation of the day that was to bring him two lots of presents. We know that, in circumstances like these, the child readily anticipates the satisfaction of his wishes in dreams. And so in the dream it was already Christmas, and the content of the dream showed him his presents, the gifts that were intended for him hanging on the tree. But instead of presents they had turned into – wolves, and the dream ended with his fear that the wolf (probably his father) would gobble him up, so that he sought refuge with his nurse. Our knowledge of his sexual development before the dream took place makes it possible for us to fill in the gap in the dream and explain the way in which satisfaction was transformed into fear. Among the wishes that informed his dreams, the strongest one that stirred must have been for the sexual satisfaction he longed to receive from his father. The strength of that wish succeeded in refreshing the long-forgotten memory trace [*Erinnerungsspur*] of a scene that could show him what sexual satisfaction from his father looked like, and the result was fright, horror at the satisfaction of his wish, repression of the impulse represented by the wish and therefore flight from the father towards the less dangerous figure of the nurse.

The significance of this Christmas date had been preserved in the alleged memory that his first tantrum had occurred because he had not been satisfied by his Christmas presents. This memory draws together true and false elements: it could not hold true without some modification since his parents had frequently repeated their assurance that his difficult behaviour had already been apparent after their return in the autumn and not just at Christmas, but the crucial aspect, the relationship between tantrums, Christmas and a lack of sexual satisfaction, had been established in this memory.

What was the image, however, conjured up by those sexual yearnings at work in the night, an image capable of scaring him away so powerfully from the fulfilment he desired? According to the material provided by the analysis there was one condition it had to fulfil: it had to be of a kind which would convince him of the existence of castration. Castration anxiety then became the driving force behind the transformation of his feelings.

We are now approaching the point at which I must abandon my attempt to draw on the actual course of the analysis. I fear that it will also be the point at which the reader will abandon his faith in what I have to say.

What was activated that night out of the chaos of unconscious traces left by a memory imprint [*Eindruck*] was the image of coitus between the boy's parents in conditions which were not entirely usual and which lent themselves to observation. It gradually became possible to find satisfactory answers to all the questions that might be prompted by this scene, given that that first dream was reproduced endlessly in countless variations during the therapy, and on each occasion the analysis provided the wished-for explanations. In this way we were first able to establish the child's age when he observed his parents, some 18 months.[3] At the time he was suffering from malaria, and the attacks recurred at a certain time each day.[4] From the age of nine onwards he was periodically subject to depressive moods, which would set in during the afternoon, reaching their lowest point at around five o'clock. This symptom was still present during the analytic treatment. The recurrent depression replaced the previous attacks of fever or lassitude; five o'clock was either the time when the fever reached its height or the time when he observed the coitus, supposing that the two did not coincide.[5] He was probably in his parents' bedroom precisely because he was ill. This episode of illness, which is also directly corroborated by tradition, suggests that the incident took place in the summer, so that we can assume an age of n + 1½ for the boy born on Christmas Day. He had thus been asleep in his cot in his parents' room and woke up, possibly as a result of mounting fever, in the afternoon, perhaps at five o'clock, the hour that was later to be marked by depression. It would be in accordance with our assumption that it was a hot summer's day if his parents had retired for an afternoon siesta, only half dressed.[6] On waking, he witnessed 'coitus a tergo' [from behind], repeated three times;[7] he could see his mother's genitals as well as his father's penis and understood what was happening as well as what it meant.[8] Eventually he disturbed his parents' intercourse in a way that will be discussed later.

Fundamentally, there is nothing out of the ordinary, nothing that gives the impression that we are dealing here with the product of wild imaginings, in the fact of a young married couple, married only a few years, allowing a siesta on a hot summer's day to evolve into tender relations, ignoring as they did so the presence of the 18-month-old boy asleep in his cot. I would say rather that it is entirely banal, an everyday occurrence, and even the coital position that we must infer does not alter this judgement in any way. Particularly since there is nothing in the evidence to suggest that coitus took place each time from behind. A single occasion would have sufficed, after all, to allow the spectator the opportunity to make observations that would have been rendered more difficult, impossible even, if the lovers had assumed a different position. The content of the scene itself is thus no argument against its credibility. The suspicion of improbability will be raised on three other counts: that at the tender age of 18 months a child should be capable of perceiving such a complicated event and retaining it so accurately in the unconscious; second, that it is possible at the age of 4 to process the memory imprints received in this way, belatedly advancing to an understanding of what was seen; and, finally, that the child should succeed by whatever method in making conscious the details of such a scene, witnessed and understood in such circumstances, in a way that is both coherent and convincing.[9]

Later I shall subject these and other misgivings to careful scrutiny; let me assure the reader that I am no less critical than he in my acceptance of the child's observation, and would ask him to join me in resolving to believe *provisionally* in the reality of this scene. Let us first continue to study the way in which this *'primal scene'* [*Urszene*] is related to the patient's dream, his symptoms and his life history. We shall then consider separately the effects proceeding from the essential content of the scene and from one of the visual imprints contained in it.

By this last I mean the positions he saw his parents assume, the man upright and the woman bent over, rather like an animal. We have already heard how his sister used to scare him during his period of great anxiety by showing him the picture in his fairy-tale book in which the wolf is depicted standing on his hind legs with one foot forward, paws outstretched and ears pricked. While in therapy with me he never tired of searching in antiquarian bookshops until he found his childhood picture-book and recognized in one of the illustrations to 'The Tale of the Seven Little Kids' the image that had so terrified him. He thought that the position assumed by the wolf in this picture might have reminded him of the position taken by his father in the primal scene we had reconstructed. At any rate, this picture was the starting-point for a further backwash of fear. On one occasion, at the age of six or seven, when he learned that he was to have a new teacher the next day, he dreamed the following night that this teacher was a lion and was approaching his bed, roaring loudly, in the stance taken by the wolf in the picture, and once again awoke in terror. By then he had already overcome the wolf phobia and so was free to choose another animal as the object of his anxiety; in this later dream he recognized that the teacher was a father-substitute. Each of his teachers played this same paternal role in the later years of his childhood and was vested with the influence wielded by his father for good and ill.

Fate gave him strange cause to renew his wolf phobia during his grammar school years, and to make the relationship underlying it a channel for serious inhibitions. The name of the teacher responsible for Latin instruction in his class was *Wolf*. He was intimidated by this man right from the start and was once resoundingly told off by him for making a stupid mistake in a Latin translation, after which he could not shake off the paralysing anxiety this teacher induced in him, soon transferred on to other teachers as well. The occasion on which he came to grief in his translation is not without significance, however. He had to translate the Latin word 'filius' and did so using the French word 'fils' instead of the corresponding word in his own tongue. The wolf was indeed still the father.[10]

The first of the 'transitory symptoms'[11] that the patient produced during treatment in fact went back to the wolf phobia and the tale of 'The Seven Little Kids'. In the room where the first sessions took place there was a large grandfather clock opposite the patient, who lay on a divan with his head turned away from me. I was struck by the fact that, from time to time, he would turn his face towards me, look at me in a very friendly way, as if to placate me, and then turn his gaze away from me towards the clock. At the time I thought this was an indication that he was longing for the end of the session. A long time afterwards the patient reminded me of this dumb-show and gave me the explanation, reminding me that the youngest of the seven little kids found a hiding-place in the case of the wall-clock while his six brothers were gobbled up by the wolf. And so what he wanted to say was: Be kind to me. Must I be afraid of you? Are you going to gobble me up? Should I hide from you in the clock-case, like the youngest of the seven little kids?

The wolf whom he feared was undoubtedly the father, but his fear of the wolf was conditional upon its being in an upright position. His memory told him quite definitely that pictures of the wolf where he was on all fours or, as in the story of 'Little Red Riding Hood', lying in bed, did not frighten him. No less significant was the position that, according to our reconstruction of the primal scene, he had seen assumed by the female; this significance was restricted, however, to the sexual sphere. Once he had reached maturity the most striking phenomenon in his erotic life were attacks of compulsive physical infatuation that occurred and disappeared again in mysterious succession, releasing enormous energy in him even at times where he was otherwise inhibited, and which were quite beyond his control. An especially valuable connection obliges me to delay a full evaluation of these compulsive love episodes a little longer, but I can state here that they were linked to a particular condition, hidden from his conscious mind, which we were first able to recognize during the therapy. The woman must have taken up the position attributed to his mother in the primal scene. From puberty onwards he felt a woman's greatest charm to be the possession of large, conspicuous buttocks; coitus in any position other than from behind gave him scarcely any pleasure at all. There is every justification, it is true, for the critical objection that a sexual preference of this kind for the rear parts of the body is a general characteristic of individuals inclined to obsessive-compulsive neurosis and that we are not justified in deriving this from any particular memory imprint from childhood. It is part of the structure of a disposition to anal eroticism and of the archaic features which distinguish such a constitution. Copulation from behind – 'more ferarum' [in the manner of beasts] – is after all certainly to be regarded as the phylogenetically older form. We shall return to this point, too, in later discussion, once we have noted down the material relating to his unconscious condition for sexual relations.

Let us now return to our discussion of the connections between the dream and the primal scene. According to our previous expectations, the dream should present the child, who is looking forward to having his wishes fulfilled on Christmas Day, with the image of sexual satisfaction received from his father, as seen in the primal scene, providing a model for the satisfaction which he himself longs to receive from his father. Instead of this image, however, there appears material from the story which his grandfather had told him a short time before: the tree, the wolves, the loss of the tail in the form of over-compensation, in the bushy tails of the creatures that are apparently wolves. A connection is missing, an associative bridge that would lead us from the content of the primal story to that of the wolf story. This connection is again provided by the position, and by the position alone. The tail-less wolf in the grandfather's story tells the others to *climb on top of him*. The memory of the image of the primal scene was awakened by means of this detail; in this way material from the primal scene could be represented by material from the wolf story and at the same time the number 2, denoting his parents, could be replaced in the desired manner by the larger number of wolves. The content of the dream underwent a further transformation as the material from the wolf story adapted itself to the content of the tale of 'The Seven Little Kids', borrowing from here the number 7.[12]

The transformation of the material – primal scene, wolf story, tale of 'The Seven Little Kids' – mirrors thought progression as the dream takes shape: longing for sexual satisfaction received from the father – understanding of the condition of castration attached to it – fear of the father. Only now, I think, have we arrived at a full explanation of the four-year-old boy's anxiety dream.[13]

As to the pathogenic effect of the primal scene and the alteration in sexual development that its resurrection produced: after all we have already touched on, I shall be brief in my remarks. We shall only follow up the particular effect to which the dream gives expression. At a later stage, we must make it clear to ourselves that the primal scene does not give rise to a single sexual current, but to a whole series of them, a positive splintering of the libido. We must keep in view, moreover, the fact that the activation of this scene (I am deliberately avoiding the word 'memory' here) has the same effect as if it were a recent experience. The effectiveness of the scene has been postponed [*nachträglich*], and loses none of its freshness in the interval that has elapsed between the ages of 18 months and 4 years. In what follows we may perhaps find grounds for supposing that it had certain effects even at the time when it was witnessed, from the age of 18 months on.

When the patient submerged himself in the situation of the primal scene, he brought the following perceptions to light from his own experience: he had previously assumed that the process he had observed was an act of violence, but this did not accord with the expression of pleasure he saw on his mother's face; he had to acknowledge that what was at issue here was satisfaction.[14] The essentially new fact that observation of his parents' intercourse brought him was the conviction that castration was a reality, a possibility which had already preoccupied his thoughts before then. (The sight of the two girls urinating, Nanja's threat, the governess's interpretation of the sticks of barley sugar, the memory of his father cutting a snake into pieces.) For now he could see with his own eyes the wound that Nanja had spoken of and understood that its presence was a condition of intercourse with his father. He could no longer confuse it, as he had done when watching the little girls, with the girls' bottoms.[15]

The dream ended in fear, which was only allayed once he had his Nanja with him. He thus sought refuge from his father with her. His fear was a rejection of his wish for sexual satisfaction from his father, the aspiration that had implanted the dream. The expression of that fear – being gobbled up by the wolf – was simply the reversal – a regressive one, as we shall hear – of the wish for coitus with the father, that is, for satisfaction such as his mother had experienced. His latest sexual objective, the passive attitude towards his father, had succumbed to repression; fear of his father, in the form of the wolf-phobia, had taken its place.

And the force which drove this repression? All the facts of the case suggest that it could only be narcissistic genital libido, which, in the form of concern for his male member, resisted a satisfaction that appeared to be conditional upon the sacrifice of that member. He drew from his threatened narcissism the masculinity to defend himself against the passive attitude towards his father.

At this point in our account we recognize the need to modify our terminology. During his dream he had reached a new phase of sexual organization. Up until then the sexual opposites for him had been *active* and *passive*. Since the seduction, his sexual objective had been a passive one, that of having his genitals touched, which regression to the previous stage of anal-sadistic organization then transformed into the masochistic objective of being disciplined, punished. It was a matter of indifference to him whether he achieved this objective with a man or a woman. He had moved on from Nanja to his father regardless of the difference in sex, asking Nanja to touch his penis, hoping to provoke his father into beating him. In this way the genital aspect was disregarded; in his fantasy of being struck on the penis this connection, which had been concealed by regression, was able to find expression. But now the activation of the primal scene in his dream led him back to the genital mode of organization. He discovered the vagina and the biological meaning of male and female. He now understood that active equalled male, passive female. His passive sexual objective would have had to be transformed into a female one, expressed as being taken in intercourse by the father instead of having his father strike him on the penis or the bottom. This feminine objective now fell forfeit to repression, and had to be replaced by fear of the wolf.

Here, we must break off discussion of his sexual development until new light can be shed back on to this earlier stage from later stages of his history. In evaluating the wolf phobia we might add that his mother and father were both turned into wolves. His mother played the castrated wolf, which let the others climb on to its back, his father the wolf who did so. We have heard him say, however, that his fear related to the wolf only when it was in a standing position, that is, to the father. We are also struck by the fact that the fear in which the dream ends is foreshadowed in the grandfather's story. In that story the castrated wolf who let the others climb on to its back is overcome by anxiety as soon as he is reminded of the absence of his tail. It would seem, then, that during the dreaming process he identified with his castrated mother and is now struggling to resist this outcome. Translated, I hope accurately, it is as if he is saying: if you want to be satisfied by your father you must accept castration as your mother has done; but I do not want that. A distinct protest in favour of masculinity! Let us be clear, incidentally, that the great disadvantage of the sexual development in this particular case is that it is not an undisrupted one. It was first crucially influenced by the seduction and is now sent off course by the observation of coitus, the postponed effect of which is like a second seduction.

Notes

1. 'Märchenstoffe in Träumen' ['Fairy-tale Material in Dreams'] (1913).

2. Cf. the similarity perceived by O. Rank between these two fairy-tales and the myth of Kronos (1912) [Völkerpsychologische Parallelen zu den infantilen Sexualtheorien' ('Parallels with Infantile Sexual Theories in the Psychology of Peoples'), *Zentbl. Psychoanal.*].

3. A less likely possibility, virtually untenable in fact, is an age of 6 months.

4. Cf. the way in which this element was later reworked in the obsessive-compulsive neurosis. In dreams during the therapy it was replaced by a strong wind. [*Added 1924*:] ('Aria' = air).

5. We should recall in this context that the patient only drew *five* wolves to illustrate his dream, although the text of the dream refers to 6 or 7.

6. In white underclothes, hence the *white* wolves.

7. Why three times? He once asserted quite suddenly that I had reconstructed this detail by means of interpretation. This was not the case. It was a spontaneous notion, eluding further criticism, which, as was his wont, he attributed to me, ensuring its reliability by means of this projection.

8. I mean that he understood it at the time of his dream, when he was 4 years old, not at the time he observed it. At the age of 18 months he acquired the memory imprints that he was able to understand later, at the time of his dream, thanks to his subsequent development, his sexual excitement and his sexual exploration.

9. The first of these problems is not resolved if we assume that the child was in fact probably a year older when he observed his parents, that is, 2½, so that he might have been entirely capable of speech. As far as my patient was concerned, the possibility of re-scheduling the event in this way was virtually excluded by the accompanying circumstances of the case. We should, incidentally, take into account the fact that it is not rare in analysis to uncover such scenes in which parental coitus is observed. The condition of doing so is precisely, however, that they take place in earliest childhood. The older the child, the greater the pains taken by the parents, at a certain social level, to deny the child any such opportunity for observation.

10. After he had been told off by the teacher-wolf, he discovered that his chums were all of the opinion that the teacher was expecting to be appeased with – money. We shall return to this point later. – I can imagine what a relief it would be to any rationalistic consideration of this childhood tale if we could assume that in reality all the boy's fear of the wolf could be attributed to the Latin teacher of the same name, projected back into childhood and giving rise, in conjunction with the illustration from the fairy-tale book, to this fantasy of the primal scene. Yet this is untenable; the evidence for the prior occurrence of the wolf phobia and its attribution to the childhood years on the first estate is all too certain. And the boy's dream at the age of 4?

11. Ferenczi (1912) ['Über passagère Symptombildungen während der Analyse' (On Transitory Symptom Formations during Analysis') *Zentbl. Psychoanal.*].

12. In the dream, 6 or 7. 6 is the number of children who were eaten up, the seventh takes refuge in the clock case. It remains one of the strictest laws of dream interpretation that an explanation can be found for every detail.

13. Now that we have succeeded in producing a synthesis of the dream I shall attempt to provide an overview of the relationship between the manifest dream-content and the latent dream-thoughts.

It is night and I am lying in my bed. This last is the beginning of the reproduction of the primal scene. 'It is night': a distortion of 'I was asleep'. The remark: 'I know that it was winter in my dream, and night-time' refers to the memory of the dream and does not form part of its content. The remark is correct: it was on a night before his birthday, or more precisely before Christmas Day.

Suddenly the window opens of its own accord. To be translated: suddenly I awake for no reason, memory of the primal scene. The influence of the wolf story, in which the wolf leaps in through the window, here acts to modify the material and transforms direct expression into metaphorical expression. At the same time, the introduction of the window serves to locate the dream content that follows in the present time. On Christmas Eve the doors are suddenly opened and there before our eyes is the tree with all the presents on it. Thus the influence of the boy's anticipation of Christmas asserts itself here, including the element of sexual satisfaction.

The big walnut tree. Represents the Christmas tree, thus topical; also the tree from the wolf story, where the tailor seeks refuge when chased by the wolves, and under which the wolves lie in wait. Experience has convinced me that the tall tree is also a symbol of observation and voyeurism. When sitting at the top of a tree one can see everything going on below without being seen oneself. Cf. the well-known story by Boccaccio and similar farcical stories.

The wolves. Their number: six or seven. In the wolf story, a pack of no particular number. The designated number shows the influence of the tale of 'The Seven Little Kids', six of whom were eaten. Replacing the number two found in the primal scene with a larger number, which would be absurd in the primal scene, provides a welcome means of distortion, which serves the purposes of resistance. In the drawing that the dreamer produced to illustrate the dream, he gives expression to the number 5 which is probably intended to correct his assertion that 'it was night'.

They are sitting in the tree. Initially they replace the Christmas presents hanging on the tree. They have also been transferred on to the tree because that could mean that they are watching. In the grandfather's story they are lying all around the bottom of the tree. In the dream, their relationship to the tree has thus been reversed, from which we may conclude that other reversals of the latent material are also present in the dream-content.

They are watching him with tense attentiveness. This aspect has come into the dream from the primal scene entire, at the cost of complete reversal.

They are completely white. A trivial feature in itself, strongly emphasized in the dreamer's narration, it owes its intensity to the way in which it fuses a considerable number of elements from every level of the dream and unites secondary details from the other dream sources with a more important element from the primal scene. The determining factor here is doubtless derived from the white of the bedlinen and the parents' underclothes; in addition there is the white of the flocks of sheep and the sheepdogs as an allusion to the sexual exploration carried out in the animal kingdom and the white in the tale of 'The Seven Little Kids', where the mother is recognized by the whiteness of her hand. Later we shall also have cause to see the white underclothes as an allusion to death.

They are sitting there motionless. A contradiction of the most conspicuous content of the scene observed by the boy: the violent excitement which, by virtue of the position to which it leads, forms the connection between the primal scene and the wolf story.

They have tails like foxes. This is intended to contradict a conclusion derived from the permeation of the wolf story by the primal scene, a conclusion which is to be recognized as the most important outcome of his sexual exploration, namely that there really is such a thing as castration. The sense of fright that accompanies the results of his musings finally forces its way out in his dream and generates its conclusion.

Fear of being eaten up by the wolves. This appeared to the dreamer not to have been motivated by the dream-content. He said: there was no need to be afraid, since the wolves looked more like foxes or dogs and they were not flying at me as if they were going to bite me, on the contrary they were quite calm and not at all terrifying. Here we recognize that the dream-work

[*Traumarbeit*] has endeavoured for a while to render painful contents harmless by transforming them into their opposite. (They are not moving, they have the finest of tails.) Until eventually this device fails to be effective and fear breaks through. It finds expression by means of the fairy-tale in which the goat-children are eaten up by the wolf-father. It is possible that this fairy-tale content even recalled the father's teasing threats when playing with the child, so that the fear of being eaten up by the wolf could just as well be an involuntary memory as a displacement-substitute.

The wish-motifs in this dream are blatantly obvious; the superficial daytime wishing that Christmas and all its presents would come (dream of impatience) is reinforced by the more deep-seated wish, permanently present during this period, for sexual satisfaction from his father, which is initially replaced by the wish to re-experience what was so absorbing on the first occasion. The psychic process then runs all the way from the fulfilment of that wish in the primal scene conjured up out of the unconscious, to rejection of the wish, which has now become unavoidable, and hence to repression.

The scope and detail of this account, imposed upon me by the endeavour to offer the reader some sort of equivalent for the evidential value of an analysis that one has seen through to its conclusion oneself, may at the same time discourage the reader from demanding the publication of analyses which extend over several years.

14. We can most easily make sense of the patient's remark if we assume that what he observed was initially coitus in the normal position, which must create the impression of a sadistic act. Only after this was the position changed, so that he had the opportunity of making other observations and forming other judgements. But there is no evidence for this assumption and it does not seem absolutely necessary to me. Even though my textual account presents it in abbreviated form, we must not lose sight of the actual situation, namely that the patient in analysis, more than 25 years old, expresses the impressions and impulses of his four-year-old self in words that he could not have used at the time. If we overlook this observation we can easily find it comical and incredible that a four-year-old should be capable of such technical judgements and erudite thoughts. This is simply another case of *postponed understanding*. At the age of 18 months the child receives a memory imprint to which he cannot react adequately, and only understands it, is only overcome by it when what has been imprinted is re-awakened at the age of four; only in analysis two decades later can he grasp in conscious intellectual activity what it was that took place inside him at that time. The analysand is then right to override these three phases of time, putting his present self in the long-forgotten situation. We follow him in doing so for, given correct self-scrutiny and interpretation, the effect must be such that one overlooks the distance between the second and third phases. We have no other means, moreover, of describing the processes of the second phase.

15. We shall find out later, when considering the matter of his anal eroticism, how he subsequently dealt with this part of the problem.

V Some Matters for Discussion

The polar bear and the whale cannot wage war, so they say, because each is confined within his own element and is unable to make contact with the other. It is equally impossible for me to hold a discussion with workers in the field of psychology or neurosis who do not recognize the premises of psychoanalysis and regard its conclusions as mere artefacts. In the last few years, however, a further form of opposition has arisen, voiced by others who, in their own opinion at least, are practitioners of analysis, have no quarrel with its techniques and results, and simply consider themselves justified in drawing different conclusions from the same material and subjecting it to other interpretations.

Theoretical contradictions are for the most part fruitless, however. As soon as we begin to move away from the material that should be our source, we run the risk of becoming intoxicated by our own assertions, and we end up putting forward views that a moment's observation would have contradicted. It seems very much more to the purpose, then, to combat divergent views by testing them against individual cases and problems.

I have argued above that it would no doubt be considered improbable that 'at the tender age of 18 months a child should be capable of perceiving such a complicated event and retaining it so accurately in the unconscious; second, that it is possible at the age of four to process the memory imprints received in this way, belatedly advancing to an understanding of what was seen; and finally, that the child should succeed by whatever method in making conscious the details of such a scene, witnessed and understood in such circumstances, in a way that is both coherent and convincing'.

This last question is purely a matter of fact. Anyone who takes the trouble to go to these kinds of depths in analysis, according to the techniques I have mapped out, will be readily convinced that it is indeed possible; those who do not do so, breaking off the analysis at some more superficial level, have renounced the right to pass judgement in this matter. But this does not settle the question of how we are to interpret what we encounter in depth analysis.

The two other reservations are based on a disparaging attitude towards impressions formed in early infancy, and a reluctance to ascribe such lasting effects to them. They prefer to seek the cause of neuroses almost exclusively in the serious conflicts of later life, and assume that the significance of childhood is simply a sham created in analysis by the neurotic's tendency to express present interests by means of involuntary memories and symbols drawn from his infant past. If we were to evaluate the significant moments of infancy in this way we would lose a great deal that goes to form the most intrinsic characteristics of analysis, as well as much, admittedly, that creates resistance to it and discourages outsiders from placing their trust in it.

Let us hold up for discussion, then, the view that scenes from early infancy such as are provided by the exhaustive analysis of neurotic individuals, of which the present case is an example, do not reproduce real events to which we may attribute some influence on the structuring of later life and on symptom formation, but are on the contrary fantasy-formations, drawing their inspiration from riper years, intended as a symbolic representation, so to speak, of real wishes and interests, and owing their emergence to a regressive tendency, a turning-away from the tasks of the present moment. If this is indeed the case, we need not bring such disconcerting expectations to bear on the inner life and the intellectual achievements of children still far from the age of discretion.

Quite apart from the wish to rationalize and simplify the difficult task, common to us all, there are various matters of fact that tend to support this view. At the very outset, moreover, one can clear up a particular misgiving that the practising analyst above all might harbour. It is true that if the interpretation of these scenes from infancy that we have put forward is the correct one, then nothing changes in the first instance in the way the analysis is carried out. If a neurotic individual does indeed have the unfortunate characteristic of turning his interest away from the present day in order to attach it to regressive fantasy substitute-formations of this kind, then there is nothing for it but to follow him along these paths and help him to bring these unconscious productions to consciousness for, leaving aside their lack of real value, they are extremely valuable to us as carriers and possessors in the present moment of the interest that we want to set free so that we can direct it towards the tasks of the present day. The analysis would have to follow exactly the same course as it would if, naively credulous, we took such fantasies for truth. The difference would be seen only at the end of the analysis, once these fantasies had been uncovered. One would then have to say to the patient: 'Good; the course taken by your neurosis has been as if, in your childhood years, you received memory imprints such as these and continued to weave stories around them. You realize, of course, that that is not possible. They were products of imaginative activity intended to divert you from the real-life tasks which confronted you. Now let us attempt to discover what these tasks were, and what connecting pathways existed between them and your fantasies.' It would be possible to implement a second phase of treatment, more closely concerned with real life, once these infantile fantasies had been dealt with.

To shorten this route, that is, to alter psychoanalytic therapy as it has been practised up to now, would be technically inadmissible. If we do not make the full extent of these fantasies conscious to the patient we cannot make available to him the interest that attaches to them. If we divert his attention from them as soon as we sense their existence and their general outlines, we are merely giving support to the work of repression that has rendered them inviolable, immune to the patient's best efforts. If we devalue them at too early a stage, perhaps by disclosing that we shall be dealing only with fantasies and that these are without any real significance, we shall never be able to enlist the patient's cooperation in leading them towards consciousness. Correctly practised, the analytic technique should remain unaltered, regardless of the value we ascribe to these scenes from infancy.

I have already mentioned that in interpreting these scenes as regressive fantasies one can appeal for support to a number of matters of fact. Above all to the fact that in therapy – in my experience to date – these scenes from infancy are not reproduced as memories but are the results of reconstruction. For many people, no doubt, this admission alone will appear to settle the dispute.

I do not wish to be misunderstood. Every analyst knows and has experienced on numerous occasions the way in which, when therapy has been successful, the patient will relate any number of spontaneous memories from childhood, and the physician will feel that he is completely innocent of the fact that they have surfaced – perhaps surfaced for the first time – since he has not suggested any content of this kind to the patient through some attempt at reconstruction. These previously unconscious memories do not even have to be true; they may be true, but their truth is often distorted and interspersed with fantasized elements in a very similar way to so-called cover-memories that have been spontaneously retained. I will say only that scenes such as we find in my patient's case, from such an early age and with such content, which then lay claim to such extraordinary significance for the history of the case, are not as a rule reproduced as memories but must be guessed at – reconstructed – from the sum total of indications, step by step and with considerable effort. This is sufficient for the purposes of my argument, whether I acknowledge that in cases of obsessive-compulsive neurosis such scenes are not conscious as memories, or whether I limit my remarks simply to the case which we are considering here.

Now I am not of the opinion that these scenes must necessarily be fantasies simply because they do not come back as memories. It seems to me that they are completely on a par with memory in that – as in the present case – they find a substitute in dreams, analysis of which regularly leads back to the same scene, reproducing every element of its content in tireless variation. To dream is, after all, to remember, even under the night-time conditions of dream-formation. It is through this recurrence in dreams that I would explain the fact that patients themselves gradually become firmly convinced of the reality of these primal scenes, with a conviction every bit as strong as that based on memory.[1]

My opponents need not regard opposition to these arguments as a lost cause, and give up the fight. It is well known that dreams can be influenced.[2] And the conviction of the analysand can be the outcome of suggestion, for which we are still seeking a role in the play of forces released in analytic treatment. A psychotherapist of the old school would suggest to his patient that he is healthy and has overcome his inhibitions, etc. etc.; the psychoanalyst, on the other hand, suggests that as a child he underwent this or that experience, which he must now recall in order to regain his health. Therein lies the difference between the two approaches.

Let us be clear that this last attempt at explanation on the part of my opponents amounts to a far more sweeping dismissal of scenes experienced in infancy than was first suggested. They were not to be realities, but fantasies. Now the demand is obviously that they should not be the patient's fantasies, but the analyst's, imposed on the analysand as a result of some personal complex or other. In response to this reproach the analyst will of course reassure himself by demonstrating how gradually the reconstruction of this fantasy – which he apparently implanted – came about, how, as it was built up, the process continued quite independently, on many counts, of any stimulus offered by the physician, how, from a certain phase of treatment onward, it appeared to be the point on which everything converged, and how, now that a synthesis has been achieved, the most diverse and remarkable results radiate out from it, how the problems and peculiarities of the patient's medical history, from the large to the very small, find their solution in this one single assumption; and he will assert that he does not see himself as possessing the astuteness necessary to concoct an event that could fulfil all these requirements at a single stroke. Even this plea, however, will have no effect on the part of the population that has not itself had the experience of analysis. Sophisticated self-deception, some will say; others: an absence of discernment; and no verdict will be reached.

We may now consider another factor that supports a hostile reading of these reconstructed scenes from infancy. It is as follows: all the processes which are brought into play in order to explain away these questionable formations as fantasies exist in reality and are to be acknowledged as significant. The averting of interest from the tasks of real life,[3] the existence of fantasies as substitute-formations for actions that have not been performed, the regressive tendency expressed through these creations – regressive in more than one sense, inasmuch as there is a simultaneous shrinking back from life and a falling back on the past – this is all to the point and is regularly confirmed by analysis. We might well suppose that this would also be sufficient to account for what are apparently involuntary memories from early infancy such as we are discussing here, and according to the economic principles of scholarship this explanation is to be preferred over the other one, which cannot manage without bringing in new and unsympathetic assumptions.

I shall permit myself at this point to draw the reader's attention to the fact that the dissenting views to be found in current psycho-analytic literature are usually based on the principle of *pars pro toto*. From a whole which has been carefully pieced together and built up one removes just one or two of the effective factors, proclaims them to be the truth and denies the importance of the other parts and of the whole in favour of these. If we examine the group for which a preference is expressed, we find that it is the one containing material already familiar from elsewhere or whatever can most readily be connected with it. Thus for Jung we find it is actuality and regression, for Adler egoistic motives. The very things that are new about psychoanalysis and are most characteristic of it are the ones that are neglected, dismissed as a mistake. In this way the revolution-ary advances of psychoanalysis, that uncomfortable notion, can most easily be repelled.

It is far from futile to emphasize that there was no need for Jung to present a single one of the factors that were invoked by the opposing point of view, to facilitate understanding of those scenes from childhood, as a new discovery. Present conflict, turning-away from reality, substitute satisfaction in fantasy, regression to material from the past, all of this has always been an integral part of my own theories, similarly structured although perhaps with minor modifications in terminology. It was not the whole of it, but only the part concerned with causality, which permeates down from reality to the formation of neuroses in a regressive direction. Alongside this I left room for a second, *progressive* [progredient] influence, which works forward from childhood impressions, showing the way to the libido that shrinks back from life, and providing an explanation for that regression to childhood that would otherwise be incomprehensible. In my view, therefore, both these factors work together in symptom-formation, but an earlier instance of their working together seems to me equally significant. I would maintain that *childhood influence already makes itself felt in the initial situation of neurosis-formation, since its intervention is crucial in helping to determine whether, and at what point, the individual fails in his attempts to master the problems of real life.*

What is at issue, then, is the significance of the infantile factor. What is needed is to find a case that can prove its significance beyond all doubt. The case that is the subject of this detailed account is one such, since its distinguishing characteristic is the way in which neurosis in later life has been preceded by neurosis in the early years of childhood. It is for this very reason that I have chosen to write about this case. If anyone were to reject it on the grounds that animal phobia does not seem important enough to be regarded as an independent neurosis, let me point out that the phobia was immediately succeeded by compulsive ritual, and by compulsive actions and thoughts that will form the subject of the next section of this essay.

Neurotic illness in the fourth or fifth year of childhood proves most importantly that the experiences of infancy are enough in themselves to produce neurosis, and that it does not require flight from a task with which life confronts the individual. We might object that even the child constantly encounters tasks that he would perhaps like to evade. This is true, but it is easy to gain an overall sense of the life of a child before he starts school, and it is possible to investigate whether it contains a 'task' responsible for causing the neurosis. However, all that we discover are involuntary impulses [*Triebregungen*], which the child finds it impossible to satisfy and which he is not yet able to master, together with the sources from which they flow.

As we might expect, the tremendous shortening of the interval between the outbreak of the neurosis and the occurrence of the childhood experiences in question massively reduces the regressive element in the causation of neurosis, and gives us a clearer glimpse of the '*pro*gressive' element, the influence exercised by earlier impressions. The present case history will, I hope, provide a clear image of this relationship. For other reasons, too, childhood neurosis will provide a decisive answer to our question as to the nature of primal scenes and those earliest childhood experiences traced in analysis.

If we start from the uncontradicted premiss that we were technically correct in formulating a primal scene of this kind, and that a comprehensive solution to all the riddles posed by the complex of symptoms produced by that childhood illness demands that all the effects radiate out from it just as all the threads of analysis lead back to it, then as far as its content is concerned it is impossible that it could be anything but the reproduction of a reality experienced by the child. For the child, just like the adult, can only produce fantasies with material that he has acquired from somewhere; and the ways in which he might acquire it are in part closed to the child (reading, for example), while the period of time available for such acquisition is short and can easily be scrutinized for sources of this kind.

In our case, the primal scene contains the image of sexual intercourse between the child's parents in a position that is particularly favourable to observation of a certain kind. Now, it would give us no proof of the reality of this scene if we encountered it in a patient whose symptoms, that is, the effects of such a scene, had emerged some time in later life. Such a patient could have acquired impressions, ideas and knowledge at a wide variety of points in that long interval of time, which are then transformed into a fantasy image, projected back into his childhood and attached to his parents. But when the effects of such a scene emerge in the child's fourth or fifth year, he must have been present to witness it at an even earlier age. In that case, however, all the disconcerting conclusions remain in place that were produced by the analysis of infantile neurosis. Unless, of course, someone wished to conclude that the patient had not only unconsciously fantasized that primal scene, but had also dreamed up the change in his character, his fear of the wolf and his religious compulsion, an excuse, however, that is contradicted by his otherwise sober manner and the tradition of straightforwardness in his family. We must stick to our guns – there is nothing else for it – either the analysis based on his childhood neurosis is a delusion from start to finish, or else the way in which I have portrayed it above is the correct one.

We have already acknowledged ambiguity in the fact that the patient's predilection for the female 'nates' [buttocks] and for coitus in the position where these are particularly in evidence apparently invites connection with his observation of his parents' intercourse, whereas a preference of this kind is a general characteristic of those archaic constitutions that are disposed to obsessive-compulsive neurosis. There is a possible explanation to hand, namely that we resolve the contradiction as over-determination. The person whom he observed in this coital position was after all his very own father, from whom he might also have inherited the same constitutional predilection. Neither his father's later illness nor the family history are against it; as I have already mentioned, an uncle on his father's side died in a condition which must be construed as the last stage of a severe compulsive disorder.

In this context let us recall that when seducing the 3¼-year-old boy, his sister uttered a strange calumny against their dear old nurse, saying that she turned everyone upside down and took hold of their genitals. It is an unavoidable notion that at a similarly tender age his sister might have witnessed the same scene as her brother did later, and that this is where she derived the suggestion of people being turned upside down in the sexual act. Such an assumption would also indicate one possible source for her own sexual impetuosity.

[It was not my original intention to enter into any further discussion here of the real value of 'primal scenes', but since in the meantime I have been obliged to treat the topic in a broader context and without any polemical intention in my *Introductory Lectures on Psychoanalysis*, it would be misleading if I failed to apply to the present case points of view that I present there as decisive. In the interests of completeness and to correct any mistakes let me therefore add the following remarks: there is indeed another possible interpretation of the primal scene that forms the basis for my patient's dream, which diverts us a good way from the verdict that we reached earlier and relieves us of a number of difficulties. Admittedly, the theoretical approach, which seeks to reduce such scenes from infancy to mere regressive symbols, will not gain anything by this modification either; in fact it seems to me that this – or indeed any other – analysis of childhood neurosis puts an end to the matter once and for all.

In my opinion, it is also possible to interpret the facts of the case as follows: we cannot forgo our assumption that the child observes coitus and in doing so acquires the conviction that castration might be more than an empty threat; the significance adhering to the positions of man and woman, in the first place for the development of his fears, and subsequently as a condition of intercourse, leaves us no choice, moreover, but to conclude that it must have been 'coitus a tergo' [from behind], 'more ferarum' [in the manner of the beasts]. Another factor is less crucial, however, and could be left aside. The child might have observed coitus between animals, rather than between his parents, and then imputed it to his parents, as if he had decided that his parents would not do it any other way.

This interpretation is supported above all by the fact that the wolves in the dream are actually sheepdogs and appear as such in my patient's drawing. Shortly before the dream, the boy had repeatedly been taken to see the herds of sheep, and there he could have seen big white dogs like this and probably watched them copulating. I would also cite in this context the number three which the dreamer produced without any obvious motivation for doing so, and would assume that he retained a memory of the sheep dogs doing so on three occasions. On the night of his dream we find, in addition to expectant excitement, the transference on to his parents of *every detail* of the recently acquired memory-image; and it is only this that made possible those powerful emotional effects. There then came a belated understanding of those impressions received perhaps a few weeks or months before, a process which every one of us may perhaps have experienced for himself. Now, the transference from the copulating dogs to his parents was not brought about by a final stage in the procedure, which was dependent on words, but by seeking out the memory of a real scene where his parents were enjoying intimacy, which he could fuse with the situation of coitus. All the details of the scene that were claimed in the analysis of the dream might have been reproduced exactly. It really was a summer afternoon, during the time when the child was suffering from malaria, the parents were both present, dressed in white, as the child awoke from sleep, but – the scene was harmless. In his eagerness to learn, the remaining details were supplied later, on the basis of what he had learned from the dogs, by the child's wish to spy on his parents while they were making love, so that now the fantasy scene unfolded with all the effects we have attributed to it, just as if it had been entirely real and had not been glued together from two components, an earlier one without any real significance and a later one which had left a deep impression.

It is immediately apparent how much this eases the effort of credulity that we are called upon to make. We need no longer assume that the parents completed their act of coitus in the presence of their child, an idea that many of us find repugnant, even if he was indeed very small at the time. The part played by postponed response is considerably reduced, since it now applies only to a few months in the child's fourth year and does not draw at all on those first dim years of childhood. There is now almost nothing that might take us aback in the child's behaviour as he effects a transference from dogs to parents and replaces fear of the father with fear of the wolf. The child is, after all, at that stage of developing his view of the world that is characterized in *Totem and Taboo* as the return of totemism. The theory that seeks to explain the primal scene of neurosis as a retrospective fantasy that takes place in later life would appear to find considerable support in this observation, despite the fact that this particular neurotic individual is at the tender age of four. Young as he is, he has succeeded in replacing an impression acquired at the age of four with a fantasized trauma occurring at the age of 18 months, a regression, however, that appears neither mysterious nor tendentious. The scene that he needed to produce had to fulfil certain conditions, which could only be found, precisely because of the circumstances of the dreamer's life, in this early time, such as the fact, for example, that his bed was in his parents' room.

Most readers will find what I can add here, drawing on the results of analysis in other cases, a decisive factor in making up their mind as to whether the interpretation I suggest is correct. It is not at all rare in the analysis of neurotic mortals to find that in very early childhood they have observed a scene – whether a real memory or a fantasy – in which the parents engage in sexual intercourse. It may perhaps be an equally frequent occurrence in individuals who do not go on to suffer from neurosis. It may perhaps form a regular part of their treasure chest of – conscious or unconscious – memories. Every time I was able to unravel such a scene through analysis, however, it demonstrated the same peculiarity that made us suspicious in the case of this particular patient, namely that it referred to 'coitus a tergo', the only position which makes an inspection of the genitals possible to the observer. We need surely doubt no longer that we are simply dealing with a fantasy that is perhaps regularly inspired by observation of the sexual intercourse of animals. Indeed, there is more: I indicated that my description of the 'primal scene' remained incomplete, since I was leaving it until later to relate the way in which the child disturbed his parents' act of intercourse. I must now add that the way in which this disturbance takes place is also the same in every case.

I can imagine that I have now made myself vulnerable to suspicions of a serious kind on the part of the reader of this case history. If I had these arguments in favour of such an interpretation of the 'primal scene' at my disposal, how could I begin to justify having first put forward a different view, one that was apparently so absurd? Or had I perhaps accumulated new evidence in the interval between writing the first draft of this case history and formulating the present additional material that obliged me to modify my original interpretation, and was yet unwilling for some reason to admit to this? Instead I shall make a different admission: it is my intention to close discussion as to the real value of the primal scene this time with a 'non liquet' [deferred judgement]. We have not yet reached the end of this case history, and in due course a moment will arise that will undermine the certainty that at present we believe we enjoy. Then there will be nothing for it but to refer the reader to those passages in my *Lectures* where I discuss the problem of primal fantasies, or primal scenes.]

Notes

1. A passage from the first edition of *Die Traumdeutung* [*The Interpretation of Dreams*] (1900) will prove at what an early stage I became concerned with this problem. On p. 126, analysing speech occurring in a dream, I wrote: *that is no longer available to us*, these words are my own; some days earlier I had explained to her 'that the earliest childhood experiences *are no longer available to us* as such, but are replaced in analysis by "transferences" and dreams'.

2. The mechanism of the dream cannot be influenced, but to some extent one can be in command of the dream-material.

3. I have good reasons for preferring to say: the averting of the *libido* from the *conflicts* of the present moment.

VI *Obsessive-compulsive Neurosis*

Now, for the third time, he was influenced in a way that decisively altered his development. At the age of 4½, when there was still no improvement in his state of irritability and anxiety, his mother decided to acquaint him with the stories of the Bible in the hope of distracting and uplifting him. She succeeded in doing so, for his introduction to religion put an end to the previous phase, but as a result the symptoms of anxiety were succeeded by symptoms of compulsive behaviour. He had previously found it difficult to fall asleep because he was afraid of having bad dreams such as he had had the night before Christmas: now, before he went to bed, he had to kiss every single holy picture in the room, recite prayers and make the sign of the cross countless times over himself and the place where he slept.

An overall view suggests that his childhood can be divided into the following epochs: first, the period of pre-history lasting up until the seduction (at age 3¼) and including the primal scene; second, the period of altered character, lasting until the anxiety dream (at age 4); third, the period of animal phobia lasting until his introduction to religion (at age 4½); and after this the period of obsessive-compulsive neurosis, lasting until after his tenth year. That there should be a smooth transition at a given moment from one phase to the next is neither in the nature of things, nor in our patient's nature: it was characteristic of him, on the contrary, to hold on to what had gone before and to allow the most diverse currents to coexist. His difficult behaviour did not disappear when his anxiety appeared but continued, slowly diminishing, into his pious period. In this last phase, however, there is no further mention of the wolf phobia. The course of his obsessive-compulsive neurosis was discontinuous; the first attack was the longest and the most intense, with others occurring at the age of eight and ten, the cause each time being visibly connected with the content of the neurosis. His mother told him the sacred story herself and also made Nanja read it aloud to him from an illustrated book. The principal emphasis of their account fell naturally on the Passion narrative. Nanja, who was very pious and superstitious, provided her own commentary, but also had to listen to the objections and doubts expressed by the young critic. If the struggles which now began to shake him eventually concluded in the victory of faith this was not least as a result of Nanja's contribution.

What he claimed to remember of his reactions when introduced to religion met at first with definite incredulity on my part. These, I maintained, could not be the thoughts of a child of 4½ or 5; he was probably attributing to his early past ideas which had grown out of the reflections of an adult of nearly 30.[1] But the patient would not hear of any such correction; I was unsuccessful in my attempts to win him over, as I had been able to do on many other occasions when we had differed in our judgements; eventually, in fact, I was obliged to believe him because of the coherence between his remembered thoughts and the symptoms he reported, as well as the way they fitted into his sexual development. I then told myself, moreover, that only a diminishing minority of adults can rise to a critique of religious doctrines such as this, a critique which I doubted this child to be capable of.

I shall now present the material which his memories supplied, and only afterwards shall I seek out the path which will lead us to understand it.

The impression that he received from narration of the sacred story, he told me, was not at first a pleasant one. He struggled to come to terms, first, with the suffering nature of the person of Christ, and then with the whole way in which his story fitted together. His dissatisfaction and criticism were directed towards God the Father. If he was omnipotent, it was his fault that people were bad and tormented other people, and then went to Hell for it. He should have made them good; he himself was responsible for everything evil and for all torments. He took exception to the commandment to offer the other cheek when someone strikes us, as he did to Christ's wish, when hanging on the cross, that the cup should pass from him, but also to the fact that a miracle did not take place to prove that he was the Son of God. In this way his critical faculties were awakened and he was rigorous and unrelenting in sniffing out the weaknesses in the sacred narrative.

Rationalistic criticism was very quickly accompanied by brooding and doubts, which may reveal that secret impulses were also at work. One of the first questions he addressed to Nanja was whether Christ also had a backside. Nanja told him that he was a God, but also a man. As a man he had everything and did everything that other men did. He found this reply most unsatisfactory but comforted himself by saying that someone's bottom was just the continuation of their legs, after all. His fear of having to demean the sacred person of God, barely calmed by this, flared up again when the question surfaced in his mind as to whether Christ also shat. He did not dare put this question to the pious Nanja, but extricated himself in a way which she could not have bettered, by telling himself that since Christ made wine out of nothing, he could also make nothing out of food and was thus able to spare himself the need to defecate.

We shall come closer to understanding such brooding thoughts if we make the connection with an aspect of his sexual development that we discussed earlier. We know that since Nanja had rejected him and he had suppressed the beginnings of genital activity as a result, his sexual life had developed in the direction of sadism and masochism. He tormented and mistreated small creatures, and fantasized about beating horses; but on the other hand he also fantasized about the heir to the throne being beaten.[2] In sadism he was able to maintain the ancient identification with his father, in masochism he had chosen that same father as his sexual object. He was thus right in the middle of a phase of pre-genital organization in which I perceive the disposition to obsessive-compulsive neurosis to lie. The gradual effect of the dream, which brought him under the influence of the primal scene, could have been to enable him to progress to the genital mode of organization, transforming his masochism towards his father into a feminine attitude towards him, into homosexuality. But the dream did not bring progress of this kind with it; it ended in fear. His relationship with his father, which should have led from the sexual objective of being punished by him to the next objective, that of being taken in sexual intercourse by his father, like a woman, was thrown back on to a more primitive level still by the protest of his narcissistic masculinity, and having been displaced on to a father-substitute was split off as fear of being gobbled up by the wolf, but was not by any means dealt with. Indeed, we can only do justice to these apparently complicated facts by maintaining our belief in the coexistence of three sexual aspirations, all focused on the father. From the time of the dream onwards he was unconsciously homosexual; during his neurosis he was at the level of cannibalism; the earlier masochistic attitude remained the dominant one. All three aspirations had passive sexual objectives; we find the same object and the same sexual impulse, but a split had occurred which caused them to evolve towards three different levels.

His knowledge of sacred history now gave him the opportunity to sublimate the dominant masochistic attitude towards his father. He became Christ, an identification that was facilitated, in particular, by the fact that they shared a birthday. This made him something great and also made him – though insufficient emphasis was put on the fact initially – a man. In his doubt as to whether Christ could have a backside we catch a glimmer of his repressed homosexual attitude, for the significance of this brooding thought can only be the question as to whether he can be used by his father as if he were a woman, as his mother was used in the primal scene. When we come to the solution of other compulsive ideas we shall find confirmation of this interpretation. The repression of his passive homosexuality corresponds to his misgivings that it is insulting to make a connection between the sacred person of Christ and outrageous ideas of this kind. We might note that he made considerable efforts to keep this new sublimation clear of additional material drawn from the sources of repression. But he did not succeed in doing so.

We do not yet understand why he now also struggled to come to terms with the passive character of Christ and his ill-treatment at his father's hands, and thus also began to deny his previous masochistic ideal, even in its sublimated form. We can assume that this second conflict was particularly favourable to the emergence of humiliating compulsive thoughts from the first conflict (between the dominant masochistic current and the repressed homosexual one), for it is only natural that in inner conflict all counter-tendencies are added together, even if they come from the most diverse sources. New material that he related will allow us to discover the motive for his struggle and for his critical attitude towards religion.

His sexual exploration had also benefited from what he had been told of sacred history. Up until then, he had had no reason to assume that only women have children. On the contrary, Nanja had led him to believe that he was his father's child and his sister their mother's, and he had particularly valued this close relationship with his father. Now he learnt that Mary was called the Mother of God. So it was women who had children, and what Nanja said was no longer tenable. Furthermore, he was confused by the stories and was no longer sure who Christ's father was. He was inclined to think it was Joseph, since he had been told that they had always lived together, but Nanja said that Joseph was only *like* his father and that his real father was God. He could make nothing of this. All he understood was, that if it was possible to talk about it at all, the relationship between father and son was nothing like as intimate as he had always imagined it to be.

The boy sensed something of the ambivalence of feeling towards the father that is enshrined in all religions, and attacked his religion because it weakened that paternal relationship. Of course his opposition soon ceased to be doubt as to the truth of the doctrine and was instead turned directly against the person of God. God had been harsh and cruel in his treatment of his son, yet he behaved no better towards human beings. He had sacrificed his son and demanded the same of Abraham. He began to be afraid of God.

If he was Christ, then his father was God. But the God that religion sought to impose on him was no real substitute for the father he had loved and of whom he did not want to be deprived. His love for his father gave him his critical sharpness. He put up a fight against God so that he could hold on to his father, and in doing so was actually defending the old father against the new one. Here he had a difficult stage in the process of detaching himself from his father to complete.

Thus it was the old love for his father, revealed in earliest days, on which he drew for the energy to combat God and for the sharpness to criticize religion. On the other hand, this hostility towards the new God was not an original act but was modelled on a hostile impulse towards his father that had come into being under the influence of the anxiety-dream, and was fundamentally only the resurgence of the same impulse. The two opposing emotional impulses that were later to rule his whole life met here in a battle of ambivalence over the issue of religion. What this struggle yielded in the form of symptoms, his blasphemous ideas, the compulsion which came over him to think 'God – crud', 'God – swine' was also for this reason a genuine compromise outcome, as we shall see from the analysis of these ideas in the context of anal eroticism.

Some other compulsive symptoms of a less typical kind lead us with equal certainty to the father, but also reveal the connection between the obsessive-compulsive neurosis and the earlier chance occurrences.

One element in the ceremonial piety that he eventually used to expiate his blasphemies was the requirement that under certain conditions he should breathe in a ritual manner. When making the sign of the cross he had to breathe in deeply each time or exhale loudly. In his language breath is the same as spirit. This, therefore, was the role of the Holy Spirit. He had either to breathe in the Holy Spirit or else to breathe out the evil spirits which he had heard and read about.[3] He also ascribed to these evil spirits the blasphemous thoughts for which he imposed such great penance on himself. He was obliged to exhale, however, whenever he saw beggars, cripples, or ugly, old and wretched people and he could not see how to connect this compulsion with the spirits. The only way he could account for it to himself was that he did it so as not to become like them.

Then, in connection with a dream, analysis brought the explanation that it was only after the age of five that he had begun to breathe out when he saw pitiful individuals, and that this was connected with his father. He had not seen his father for many long months when one day his mother said that she would take the children to the city and show them something that would make them very happy. She then took them to a sanatorium where they saw their father again; he looked ill and his son felt very sorry for him. His father, then, was the archetype of all those cripples, beggars and poor people, the sight of whom obliged him to breathe out, just as the father is normally the archetype of the grimaces seen in anxiety states and of the caricatures drawn to express contempt. We shall discover elsewhere that this pitying attitude goes back to a particular detail of the primal scene, which took effect at this late stage in the obsessive-compulsive neurosis.

The resolution not to become like them, which was the motivation for his breathing out in front of cripples, was thus the old identification with the father transformed into a negative. And yet he was also copying his father in a positive sense, for his noisy breathing was an imitation of the sounds he had heard his father make during intercourse.[4] The Holy Spirit owed its origins to this sign of erotic excitement in a man. Repression turned this breathing into an evil spirit, for which there also existed a second genealogy, that of the malaria from which he had been suffering at the time of the primal scene.

The rejection of these evil spirits corresponded to an unmistakably ascetic aspect of his character, which was also expressed in other reactions. When he heard that Christ had once driven out evil spirits into pigs, which then plunged into an abyss, he thought of the way his sister, in the earliest years of her childhood, before he could remember, had rolled down from the harbour cliff-path on to the beach. She too was one of those evil spirits and pigs; it was only a short step from this to 'God – swine'. Even his father had turned out to be dominated by sensuality in just the same way. When he was told the story of the first man, he was struck by the similarity between Adam's fate and his own. He expressed hypocritical astonishment when talking to Nanja that Adam had allowed himself to be plunged into misery by a woman, and promised Nanja that he would never get married. Around this time, as a result of his sister's seduction, his feelings of enmity towards womankind found powerful expression. They were later to trouble him often enough in his erotic life. His sister became the permanent embodiment, to him, of temptation and sin. When he had been to confession he would feel pure and free from sin. But then it would seem as if his sister was watching for an opportunity to plunge him into sin once more, and before he was aware of it he would have provoked a quarrel with his sister, which made him sinful again. In this way he was obliged to reproduce the fact of seduction over and over again. He never, incidentally, divulged his blasphemous thoughts in the confessional, even though they weighed heavily on him.

We have unexpectedly progressed to a discussion of symptoms manifested in the later years of obsessive-compulsive neurosis; let us therefore skip the very great deal that occurred in the meantime and relate how the condition came to an end. We already know that, as well as being a permanent condition, it was subject to periodic intensification, such as on one occasion, which we are unable as yet to understand, when a boy in the same street died, with whom he was able to identify. When he was ten he acquired a German tutor who quickly came to have considerable influence over him. It is most instructive to find that the whole heavy weight of piety disappeared, never to return, once he had noticed, and learnt from his teacher's didactic conversation, that this father-substitute set no store by piety and did not believe in the truth of religion. His piety fell away, along with his dependence on his father, who was now being superseded by a new, more affable father. It must be said that this did not occur without one last flaring-up of his obsessive-compulsive neurosis; he had a particularly strong memory of the compulsion to think of the Holy Trinity every time he saw three piles of dung lying together on the street. He simply never gave in to one stimulus without making a final attempt to keep hold of what no longer had any value for him. When his teacher talked him out of his cruelty towards small creatures he put a stop to his misdeeds, but not before he had had one last orgy of cutting up caterpillars. He behaved in exactly the same way in analytic treatment by developing a transitory 'negative reaction'; whenever something important had been resolved he would try to negate the effects for a while, in that there would be a worsening of symptoms that had been resolved. We know that in general children behave in a similar way in the face of prohibitions. When they have been told off, for example for making a disagreeable noise, they will repeat it once more after they have been told not to, before stopping. In doing so they make it look as if they have stopped voluntarily, thus defying the prohibition.

Under the German teacher's influence he found a new and better way to sublimate his sadism, which, as befitted his approaching puberty, had then gained the upper hand over his masochism. He developed a passion for military life, for uniforms, weapons and horses, and used this to feed his constant daydreaming. Under a man's influence he had thus got away from his passive attitudes and was initially on a fairly normal track. One after-effect of his attachment to his teacher, who left soon afterwards, was that in later life he preferred the German element (doctors, clinics, women) to the native one (representing the father), which was of great benefit for the therapeutic transference.

Another dream belongs in the period before his liberation by the teacher, which I mention here because it had been forgotten up until the moment when it surfaced in therapy. He saw himself riding a horse, pursued by a giant caterpillar. He recognized a reference here to a still earlier dream from the period before the teacher came, which we had interpreted long before. In this earlier dream he saw the devil in black robes, assuming the upright stance which had previously so terrified him in the wolf and the lion. With his outstretched finger he was pointing to a giant snail. He had quickly guessed that this devil was the demon who features in a well-known poem, and the dream itself a reworking of a widely disseminated picture showing the demon in a love-scene with a young girl. The snail, an exquisite symbol of female sexuality, stood for the woman. Guided by the demon's pointing gesture, we were quickly able to declare the meaning of the dream to be his longing for someone who could give him the final instruction he lacked in the mysteries of sexual intercourse, just as his father had first enlightened him long ago in the primal scene.

In amplification of the later dream, where the female symbol was replaced by the male one, he remembered a particular experience that had taken place a little while before. Riding on the estate one day he passed a peasant, asleep with his son lying next to him. The boy woke his father and said something to him, whereupon the father began to shout at the rider and ran after him, until he and his horse quickly moved off. This in conjunction with a second memory that on that same estate there were trees that were completely white, completely covered in caterpillar cocoons. We see that he took flight from realization of the fantasy that the son was sleeping with his father, and that he brought in the white trees to create a reference to the anxiety-dream, to the white wolves in the walnut tree. It was thus a positive eruption of fear expressed at the feminine attitude towards men, which initially he had defended himself against by means of religious sublimation; soon after that he was to defend himself against it even more effectively, by means of military sublimation.

It would be a major error, however, to assume that, once the compulsive symptoms had been eliminated, no permanent effects of the obsessive-compulsive neurosis remained. The process had led to the victory of pious belief over critical inquiry and rebellion, and was predicated upon repression of the homosexual attitude. Both factors resulted in permanent disadvantages. After this first great defeat his intellectual activity remained seriously impaired. He developed no particular eagerness to learn and demonstrated nothing of the critical acuity with which, at the tender age of five, he had subverted religious doctrine. The repression of his excessively strong homosexuality, which took place during the anxiety-dream, meant that this significant impulse was reserved for the unconscious mind, thus maintaining its original attitude towards its objective and eluding all the sublimations to which it would normally lend itself. For this reason, the patient lacked all the social interests which give content to life. Only as we succeeded through analytic therapy in releasing his homosexuality from its fetters was there a turn for the better in this state of affairs, and it was a remarkable thing to watch the way in which – without any urging on the part of the physician – each liberated element of his homosexual libido was eager to be brought to bear on life and attached to the great common concerns of humanity.

Notes

1. I also attempted repeatedly to bring the patient's story forward by at least a year, putting the seduction at 4¼ and the dream on his fifth birthday, etc. There was nothing to be gained by these intervals, after all, but the patient was not to be moved, although he was, incidentally, unable to dispel the last vestiges of my scepticism. To postpone everything by a year in this way clearly had no significance for the impression made by his story, nor for the discussions and arguments arising from it.

2. And especially about blows to the penis.

3. This symptom had developed, as we shall learn, at the age of five, when he learned to read.

4. Provided we accept the reality of the primal scene!

VII *Anal Eroticism and the Castration Complex*

I must ask the reader to remember that this history of an infantile neurosis was recovered as a by-product, so to speak, of the analysis of a patient who had fallen ill in more mature years. I was thus obliged to piece it together out of even tinier fragments than those that are normally available when any kind of synthesis is attempted. Such work, which is otherwise not difficult, finds its natural limit at the point where it becomes a question of capturing a multi-dimensional structure in the two-dimensionality of description. I must therefore content myself with offering individual limbs which the reader can join together into a living whole. The obsessive-compulsive neurosis I have described developed, as I have emphasized repeatedly, out of an anal-sadistic constitution. Up until now, however, we have only considered one of these two principle factors, sadism and its transformations. Anything concerned with anal eroticism I have deliberately left on one side in order to give a full account of it here.

Analysts have long agreed that the many involuntary impulses [*Triebregungen*] that can be summed up as anal eroticism are extraordinarily and inestimably important to the development of the individual's sexual life and to inner activity as a whole. And equally, that one of the most important expressions of eroticism derived from this source and recast in a different mould is to be found in the treatment of money, a valuable substance which, in the course of the individual's life, attracts the psychic interest which properly belongs to that product of the anal zone, faeces.[1] We have grown accustomed to tracing interest in money, where its nature is libidinal rather than rational, back to excremental pleasure, and to expect of any normal person that his relationship to money should be kept free of libidinal influences and controlled by realistic considerations.

In our patient's case this relationship was particularly badly disrupted at the time of his later illness, this being not the least important reason for his lack of independence and his inability to cope with life. Having inherited money from both his father and his uncle, he was now very rich and it was manifestly of great importance to him that people should know that he was a rich man; he could be greatly offended if he was underestimated in this regard. And yet he did not know how much he possessed, what his expenditure was, nor how much was left. It was difficult to know whether to call him a miser or a spendthrift. Sometimes he behaved one way, sometimes another, but never in a way that suggested consistent intentions. Certain striking traits of character, which I shall describe later, might lead one to conclude that he was an unrepentant swank who regarded his wealth as his greatest personal asset and who would never even begin to put feelings on a par with money. But he did not judge other people according to their wealth and there were many occasions when he actually turned out to be modest, sympathetic and ready to help. It was simply that money eluded his conscious control and held another meaning for him.

I mentioned earlier that I regarded with deep suspicion the way in which he consoled himself for the loss of his sister – who in the later years of her life had become his best friend – with the thought that now he would not need to share their parents' inheritance with her. More striking still, perhaps, was the calm way in which he could tell me this, as if he had no comprehension of the coarseness of feeling to which he was admitting. Analysis rehabilitated him to some extent by demonstrating that his pain at his sister's death had merely been displaced, but now it seemed more incomprehensible than ever that he should have thought he could find a substitute for his sister in his increased wealth.

His behaviour in another instance seemed to be a mystery even to him. After his father's death, the fortune he had left was divided between himself and his mother. It was administered by his mother, who responded to his requests for money, as he himself acknowledged, with irreproachable generosity. And yet any discussion of money matters between them would end with the most violent reproaches on his part: that she did not love him, that her only thought was to save money by keeping him short, and that she would probably prefer it if he were dead, so that she could have all the money for herself. In tears his mother would then protest her unselfish motives and he would be ashamed, assuring her quite truthfully that he really did not think of her in that way, and yet sure that the same scene would be repeated on the next occasion.

That faeces signified money to him long before he entered analysis can be seen from many chance occurrences, two of which I shall relate here. At a time when his bowels were still unconnected with his illness, he once visited a poor cousin living in a large town. As he left he reproached himself for not giving his cousin financial support, whereupon he immediately had 'perhaps the strongest urge to defecate he had ever felt in his life'. Two years later he did indeed offer to pay his cousin an allowance. And the other instance: at the age of 18, while preparing for his final examinations at school, he visited a fellow-student and came to an agreement with him which seemed advisable in the light of the fear they both felt of failing the examination.[2] They had decided to bribe the school janitor, and his share of the money they needed to find was of course the larger one. On the way home he was thinking that he would willingly pay even more if he could only pass, if only nothing would go wrong in the examination, and he did indeed have a little accident[3] before he could reach his own front door.

All this prepares us for the fact that during his later illness he suffered from extremely persistent disturbance of the bowel function, though one that fluctuated with different causes. When he entered treatment with me he had become accustomed to receiving enemas, administered by a companion; he might not experience spontaneous emptying of the bowels for months at a time, unless there was sudden stimulus from a particular quarter, following which normal bowel activity would be resumed for a few days. His principal complaint was that he felt the world to be shrouded in a veil, or that there was a veil dividing him from the world. This veil was torn open only at the moment when the content of the bowel left the bowel after an enema, whereupon he would feel healthy again, and normal.[4]

The colleague to whom I referred my patient for an assessment of his bowel condition was sufficiently perceptive to declare it to be determined by functional or even psychic factors, and to eschew medical intervention. Neither this, incidentally, nor the diet he ordered my patient to follow, were of any use. During the years in which he was in analysis he never had any spontaneous bowel movements (except under the influence of those sudden stimuli). The patient allowed himself to be persuaded that any more intensive treatment of the refractory organ would simply make the condition worse, and was content to bring about a forced evacuation of the bowels once or twice a week by means of an enema or laxative.

In discussing these disruptions to the function of the bowel I have allowed my patient's later state of illness to take up more space than I had intended in a piece of work devoted to his childhood neurosis. There were two reasons for my decision: first, the fact that the bowel symptoms had remained virtually unchanged from the period of childhood neurosis to the later one, and, second, that they were enormously significant in bringing the treatment to an end.

We know how important doubt is to the physician analysing a case of obsessive-compulsive neurosis. It is the patient's most powerful weapon, his preferred means of resistance. For years, thanks to this doubt, our patient too was able to let the efforts made in therapy bounce off him, safe behind a barricade of respectful indifference. Nothing changed, and there was no way of convincing him. Finally I recognized the significance of his bowel disorder for my intentions: it represented the touch of hysteria that is regularly found to underlie any obsessive-compulsive neurosis. I promised the patient that his bowel activity would be fully restored; my undertaking forced his disbelief into the open, so that I then had the satisfaction of watching his doubt disappear as his bowel began to 'add its voice' to the work, as if it were an hysterically affected organ, regaining its normal function, which had for so long been impaired, in the course of a few weeks.

I shall now return to the patient's childhood, to a time when faeces cannot possibly have signified money to him.

He experienced bowel disorders at a very early age, especially the most common kind, entirely normal in children, namely incontinence. We would undoubtedly be correct, however, in rejecting any kind of pathological explanation for these earliest incidents and seeing in them merely proof of his intention not to be disturbed in or held back from the pleasure accompanying the function of evacuation. He continued to be greatly amused, well into his later illness, by anal jokes and exhibitions of the kind that appeal to the natural coarseness of many sections of society.

During the era of the English governess it repeatedly came about that he and Nanja were obliged to share a bedroom with the woman they loathed. Nanja noted sympathetically that it was always on these nights that he soiled the sheets, something that he normally no longer did. He was not at all ashamed of this: it was an expression of his defiance towards the governess.

A year later (at the age of 4½), during his period of great anxiety, it so happened that he once soiled his trousers during the day. He was dreadfully ashamed, wailing as he was cleaned up that he could not go on living like this. Something had changed in the meantime, then, and by turning our attention to his lament we can track down what it was. It turned out that the words 'he could not go on living like this' were spoken in imitation of someone else. On some occasion or other[5] his mother had taken him along when she accompanied the doctor who had come to visit her to the railway station. As they walked she was lamenting her pains and bleeding and exclaimed, in those selfsame words, 'I cannot go on living like this', without imagining that the child whose hand she was holding would retain them in his memory. The lament, which he was incidentally to repeat on countless occasions in his later illness, thus signified his – identification with his mother.

Soon a missing link between the two incidents, as regards both time and content, came into his memory. Once, at the beginning of his period of anxiety, it came about that his mother, greatly concerned, issued warnings that the children were to be guarded against the dysentery that had made an appearance in the vicinity of their estate. He inquired what that might be and, when he heard that one symptom of dysentery is blood in the stools, he became very anxious and claimed to have found blood in his own stools; he was afraid of dying of dysentery, but allowed himself to be examined and persuaded that he had made a mistake and that there was no need to be afraid. We can understand that his anxiety was an attempt to carry through the identification with his mother, about whose bleeding he had heard in the conversation with the doctor. In his later attempt to identify with his mother (at the age of 4½) he had dispensed with the blood; he no longer understood what it was he was feeling, thought that he was ashamed of himself and did not know that he was seized with mortal fear; yet this is what his lament quite unambiguously reveals.

At that time his mother, suffering as she did from gynaecological complaints, was generally fearful for herself and her children, and it is perfectly probable that his anxiety was founded on identification with his mother, as well as the other motives which fuelled it.

Now, what is the significance of his identification with his mother?

Between his impudent exploitation of incontinence at the age of 3½ and his horror of it at the age of 4½ there lies the dream that inaugurated the period of anxiety, bringing a belated understanding of the scene[6] he experienced at the age of 18 months and enlightenment as to a woman's role in the sexual act. The obvious explanation is that the change in his attitude towards defecation is also connected with that great upheaval. Dysentery was clearly the name of the illness he had heard his mother complaining about, the one you could not go on living with; his understanding was that his mother's illness was not gynaecological in nature, but an illness of the bowel. Under the influence of the primal scene he inferred that the connection ran as follows: his mother's illness was due to the thing his father had done with her,[7] and his fear of finding blood in his stools, that is, of being as ill as his mother, was the rejection of his identification with his mother in that sexual scene, the same rejection that awakened him from his dream. His fear was also proof, however, that in his later processing of the primal scene he had put himself in his mother's place and envied her this relationship with his father. The organ through which he could express his identification with the female and his passive homosexual attitude towards the male was the anal zone. Dysfunction in this zone had acquired the significance of the stirrings of feminine tenderness, which it retained also during his later illness.

At this point we must air an objection, discussion of which could contribute greatly to clarification of an apparently confused state of affairs. We have had to assume that during the dreaming process he understood women to be castrated, having a wound in the place of the male member which serves the purposes of sexual intercourse, and that castration was thus the condition of female identity; under the threat of this loss he repressed the feminine attitude towards the male and awoke in fear from his homosexual raptures. How is this understanding of sexual intercourse, this acknowledgement of the vagina, to be reconciled with his choice of the bowel as a means of identification with the female? Are his bowel symptoms not founded on what is probably a more ancient conception, which entirely contradicts castration anxiety, that of the anus as the site of sexual intercourse?

It is true that this contradiction exists and that the two conceptions are inconsistent with one another. The question is merely whether they need to be consistent. We are disconcerted because we are always inclined to treat unconscious inner processes as if they were conscious ones, forgetting the profound differences between the two psychic systems.

When in excited anticipation the Christmas dream conjured up the image of his parents' sexual intercourse, once observed (or reconstructed), the old view of it no doubt occurred to him first, according to which that part of the woman's body receiving the penis was the anus. What else could he have thought when he watched this scene at the age of eighteen months?[8] But now, at the age of four, came the new event. His previous experiences, the hints he had received as to the possibility of castration, now awoke and cast doubt on his 'cloaca theory', prompting recognition of the difference between the sexes and the sexual role of the female. He then behaved as children generally do when they are given an explanation they do not want – whether of sexual matters or of anything else.

He rejected the new one – in this case, motivated by castration anxiety – and held on to the old one. He decided in favour of the bowel and against the vagina in the same way as he did later, and for similar motives, when he took his father's part against God. The new explanation was rejected, and he held fast to the old theory, which probably provided the material for his identification with the female, later appearing as the fear of a death brought on by bowel infection, and for his first religious scruples, such as whether Christ had a backside. Yet it is not as if his new insight had failed to have any effect; on the contrary, it took effect in a remarkably powerful way, providing the motivation for keeping the whole dream process in a state of repression and excluding it from later, conscious assimilation. But this was the full extent of the effect it had, for it had no influence in deciding the sexual problem. It was indeed a contradiction that, from that point onward, castration anxiety could exist alongside identification with the female by means of the bowel, but it was only a logical contradiction, which does not mean very much. Rather, the whole process is characteristic of the workings of the unconscious. Repression is a different thing from out-of-hand dismissal.

In studying the genesis of the wolf phobia we were tracing the effects of the new insight into the sexual act; now, investigating disorderly bowel activity, we find ourselves in the realm of the ancient cloaca theory. The two standpoints remain separated from each other by a stage of repression. The female attitude towards the male, dismissed through the act of repression, withdraws, so to speak, into bowel symptoms and expresses itself through the frequent episodes of diarrhoea, constipation and bowel pain of the patient's childhood years. His later sexual fantasies, constructed on the basis of correct sexual knowledge, can now be expressed regressively as bowel disorder. We cannot understand them, however, until we have uncovered the change in meaning that faeces have undergone since the patient's earliest childhood.[9]

I hinted earlier that I had kept back a part of the content of the primal scene, which I can now fill in. The child eventually interrupted his parents' intimacy by evacuating his bowels, thus providing a motive for his crying. As far as criticism of this additional information is concerned, the same holds true here as for my previous discussion of the content of this scene. The patient accepted this reconstructed concluding action and appeared to confirm it by means of 'transitory symptoms'. A further additional detail that I had suggested, namely that the father had been annoyed by the disturbance and given vent to his displeasure by shouting at the child, had to be dropped. There was no reaction to it in the material of the analysis.

The detail which I have just supplied is not, of course, all of a piece with the rest of the scene's content. Here it is not a question of something imprinted on the memory from outside, which we can expect to encounter again in any number of later indications, but rather of the child's own reaction. Not a single detail of the story would change if this manifestation had not occurred, or if it had been inserted into the sequence of events later on. There is no doubt as to how we are to understand it, however. It signifies excitement in the anal zone (in the broadest sense of the word). In other cases of a similar type the observation of sexual intercourse ended in urination; in the same circumstances an adult male would be aware of an erection. The fact that the little boy produces a stool as a sign of his sexual excitement is to be judged as characteristic of the sexual constitution that is already in place. He immediately takes up a passive attitude and shows a greater inclination towards later identification with the female than with the male.

Here he uses the contents of the bowels in the same way as any other child, in one of its first and earliest senses. Faeces are the first *gift*, the child's first loving sacrifice, a part of his own body that is relinquished, but only in favour of a beloved person.[10] Its use as an act of defiance, as in this case towards the governess at the age of 3½, is merely to give its earlier meaning as a gift a negative slant. The 'grumus merdae' left by burglars at the scene of the crime appears to have both meanings: both scorn and a regressive way of offering compensation. When a higher level has been reached, the earlier one can always be put to use in a negative, debased sense. Repression finds expression in the coexistence of antithetical impulses.[11]

At a later stage of sexual development, faeces assume the meaning of *babies*. Babies are born through the anus, after all, just like stools. The meaning of faeces as a gift readily permits this transformation. Linguistic usage refers to babies as 'gifts'; we hear more frequently of the woman 'presenting her husband with a baby', but in unconscious usage equal weight is quite rightly given to the other side of the relationship, with the woman 'receiving' the baby from her husband as a gift.

The meaning of faeces as money arises from its meaning as a gift, but branches off in another direction.

The deeper meaning behind our patient's early cover-memory of producing his first tantrum because he did not get enough Christmas presents is now revealed. What was missing was sexual satisfaction, which he had taken in an anal sense. His sexual exploration before the dream had prepared him for the fact, grasped during the dreaming process, that the sexual act solves the mystery of where babies come from. Even before the dream he did not like tiny children. Once he found a little bird, still naked, which had fallen out of the nest and, taking it for a tiny human being, had been filled with dread. Analysis demonstrated that all the tiny creatures, caterpillars and insects he had raged against had signified tiny children in his mind.[12] His own relationship with his elder sister had given him cause to think a great deal about how older children relate to younger ones; and when on one occasion Nanja told him that his mother loved him so much because he was the youngest he acquired an understandable motive for wishing that there should be no younger child to follow him. His fear of this youngest child was then re-activated under the influence of the dream that brought his parents' intercourse to his attention.

We ought therefore to add a new sexual current to those we already know about; like the others it stems from the primal scene reproduced in the dream. In his identification with the female (the mother) he is ready to give his father a child and is jealous of the mother who has already done so, and may perhaps do so again.

By way of this detour demonstrating a common point of departure in their significance as gifts, money can now attract to itself the meaning of children, and in this way take over the expression of feminine (homosexual) satisfaction. In our patient's case this process occurred once at a time when brother and sister were both staying in a German sanatorium, and he saw his father give his sister two large banknotes. In fantasy he had always harboured suspicions about his father and his sister; now his jealousy was awakened and he fell on his sister as soon as they were alone, demanding his share of the money with such violence and heaping such reproaches on her that his sister, weeping, threw the whole amount at him. It was not just the real matter of the money that had upset him, but rather the baby, the anal sexual satisfaction he desired from his father. This, then, was his source of comfort when his sister died – during their father's lifetime. The scandalous thought which occurred to him when he heard the news of her death in fact meant simply: now I am the only child and my father must love me and me alone. Yet while the thought in itself was entirely capable of becoming conscious, its homosexual background was so unbearable that it was easier to disguise it as filthy greed, for this no doubt came as a great relief.

It was the same story when, after his father's death, he reproached his mother so unjustly for wanting to cheat him out of his money, for loving money more than she loved him. His old jealous feelings that she might love a child other than himself, and the possibility that she might have hoped for another child after him, compelled him to make accusations which he himself acknowledged to be groundless.

This analysis of the meaning of faeces makes it clear that the compulsive thoughts obliging him to make a connection between God and faeces had another meaning besides the abuse he thought them to be. They were in fact a true compromise outcome in which a current of tender devotion played just as much of a part as that of hostile invective. 'God – crud' was probably an abbreviated form of an offer which sometimes comes to one's ears in unabbreviated form. 'To shit on God' or 'to give a shit for God' can also mean to give him a baby, to be presented by him with a baby. The old meaning of 'gift', negatively debased, and the meaning of 'baby' which later developed out of this are combined in the patient's compulsive phrase. The latter expresses a feminine tenderness, a readiness to renounce manliness if in return one can be loved as a woman. Precisely that impulse towards God, then, articulated so unambiguously in the delusive system devised by the paranoid president of the Senate, Schreber.

When, later, I come to describe the resolution of the patient's last symptoms, we shall see once again how his bowel disorder had placed itself at the service of the homosexual current, expressing the feminine attitude towards the father. A new meaning of faeces will now clear the ground for a discussion of the castration complex.

Given that the column of faeces stimulates the erogenous mucous membrane of the bowel, it functions as an active organ, behaving as the penis does towards the mucous membrane of the vagina and acting as a precursor of the penis, so to speak, in the cloacal phase. The surrender of faeces in favour of (out of love for) another person, for its part, becomes the model of castration and is the first case in which a part of one's own body[13] is renounced in the hope of winning favour from a beloved other. What is otherwise narcissistic love for one's own penis is thus not without some trace of anal eroticism. And so faeces, baby, penis, all come together to form a single entity, one unconscious concept – 'sit venia verbo' ['if you will excuse the expression'] – that of something small that can be separated from the body. Along these connecting pathways displacements and reinforcements of libido-charge [*Libidobesetzung*] can take place that are significant to a patient's pathology and can be uncovered in analysis.

We now know what our patient's initial attitude towards the problem of castration was. He dismissed it out of hand, maintaining that intercourse took place in the anus. When I say 'dismissed', I mean by this primarily that he refused to know anything about it, in the sense of repressing it. He did not actually pass judgement as to whether it existed or not, but effectively it did not. This attitude cannot have remained the definitive one, however, even during the years of childhood neurosis. Later on we can produce good evidence to show that he acknowledged castration as a fact. On this point, too, he behaved in that characteristic way that certainly makes both description and empathetic response so extraordinarily difficult. At first he expressed resistance, then gave in, but the one reaction did not cancel out the other. In the end two contradictory currents existed alongside one another, one of which abhorred the very idea of castration, while the other was prepared to accept it, consoling itself with femaleness as a substitute. The third current, the oldest and deepest, which had simply dismissed castration out of hand, without entertaining even the possibility of judging whether it was real or not, could no doubt also still be activated. Elsewhere[14] I have recounted an hallucination that occurred to this selfsame patient at the age of five, which in this context requires only the addition of a short commentary:

'When I was five I was playing in the garden near my nurse, using my penknife to carve the bark of one of those walnut trees[15] which also came up in my dream.[16] Suddenly I was inexpressibly terrified to discover that I had cut right through the little finger of my (right or left?) hand, so that it was only attached by the skin. I felt no pain, only great fear. I did not dare say anything to my nurse, who was only a few steps away, but sank down on to the nearest bench and just sat there, incapable of even glancing at my finger. In the end I calmed down, took a long look at my finger and, lo and behold, it wasn't damaged at all.'

We know that after he had been introduced to sacred history at the age of 4½, intense intellectual activity set in, which later turned into compulsive piety. We may therefore assume that this hallucination occurred around the time when he was making up his mind to acknowledge the reality of castration, and that it was perhaps intended to mark precisely that step. Even the patient's little correction is not without interest. If he hallucinated the same horrific experience which Tasso relates of his hero Tancred in 'Jerusalem Liberated', we are justified in suggesting that, for my young patient too, the tree represented a woman. He was thus playing the role of the father, bringing together his mother's bleeding, which he knew about, and the castration of women, the 'wound', which he now acknowledged.

The stimulus to hallucinate about cutting off a finger was provided, he told me later, by the story of one of his relatives who was born with six toes, the superfluous member being hacked off immediately with an axe. Thus women had no penis because it had been removed at birth. In this way he came to accept, at the time when he was suffering from obsessive-compulsive neurosis, what he had learned in the dream process and rejected at that time by means of repression. The ritual circumcision of Christ, and of the Jews in general, could not, moreover, have remained unknown to him at a time when he was reading and discussing the sacred story.

It was undoubtedly at this time that his father became the terrifying figure who threatens castration. The cruel God with whom he was wrestling, who allowed people to become guilty so that he could then punish them, who sacrificed his own son and the sons of men, threw the shadow of his character back on to the father – whom the boy sought to defend, on the other hand, against that same God. He has a phylogenetic schema to fulfil here and manages to do so even though his own personal experiences do not seem to square with it. The threats, or hints, of castration he had received had actually emanated from women,[17] but this did not delay the end result for long. In the end it was his father at whose hands he feared castration. On this point heredity triumphed over accidental experience; in the pre-history of the human race it was certainly the father who carried out castration as a punishment, subsequently reducing it to the practice of circumcision. The more he repressed his sensuality as the process of obsessive-compulsive neurosis went on[18] the more natural it seemed to him to endow his father, that true representative of sensual activity, with evil intentions of this kind.

The identification of his father with the castrator[19] was significant in that it was the source of an intense unconscious hostility towards him – which went as far as wishing him dead – as well as of the guilt he felt in response to this. To this extent he was, however, behaving normally, that is, like any other neurotic individual possessed by a positive Oedipal complex. What was remarkable was that in him a counter-current existed for this too, according to which his father was in fact the castrated figure, and as such demanded his sympathy.

In my analysis of the breathing rituals prompted by the sight of cripples, beggars, etc. I was able to show that this symptom could also be traced back to the father, whom he had felt sorry for when he visited him in the clinic during his illness. Analysis permitted us to trace this thread back still further. Very early on, probably even before the seduction (at the age of 3¼), there was a poor day-labourer on the estate whose job it was to carry water into the house. He was unable to speak, supposedly because his tongue had been cut out. He was probably a deaf mute. The little boy was very fond of him and pitied him with all his heart. When he died, he looked for him in the heavens.[20] This man was thus the first of the cripples for whom he felt such sympathy and, judging by the context and the point at which he was mentioned in analysis, undoubtedly a father-substitute.

In analysis other memories followed on from this of servants whom he liked; in each case he dwelt on the fact that they were in poor health or Jewish (circumcision!). The lackey who helped clean him up after his little accident at the age of 4½ was Jewish, too, as well as consumptive, and enjoyed his sympathy. All these figures can be placed in the period before he visited his father in the sanatorium, that is, before formation of the symptom, which was really intended to keep identification with the person pitied at a distance by means of exhalation. Then suddenly, in connection with a dream, the analysis turned back to the patient's very early life, giving him the opportunity to assert that he had observed the disappearance of the penis in coitus during the primal scene, pitied his father on this account and rejoiced at the reappearance of what he had thought to be lost. Another new feeling, then, inspired by this scene. Incidentally, we cannot fail to recognize the narcissistic roots of such sympathy, underlined by the word itself.[21]

Notes

1. [*Translator's note*: Throughout this chapter Freud uses the word *Kot* to denote faeces. This word can be translated into a variety of linguistic registers. It may be used coarsely, as in the verbal association of God and crud (p. 265), or more politely, as a circumlocution. Freud normally uses it in a doctorly sense, as here.]

2. The patient told me that in his mother tongue it is not possible to use the familiar German word '*Durchfall*' to designate a disturbance of the bowel. [*Translator's note: Durchfall* can mean both 'failure' and 'diarrhoea'.]

3. This expression means the same in the patient's mother tongue as it does in German. [*Translator's note*: And in English!]

4. The same effect was achieved whether someone else administered the enema, or whether he saw to it himself.

5. We cannot say for certain when this was, but it was in any case before the anxiety-dream that occurred at the age of four, and probably before his parents went away.

6. See above p. 239.

7. He was probably not mistaken in this assumption.

8. Or as long as he had no understanding of canine coitus.

9. Cf. 'Über Triebumsetzungen insbesondere der Analerotik' ['On the Transformations of Instinct [Drive]' 1917], etc.

10. It could easily be confirmed, I think, that infants only use their excrement to soil people they know and love; strangers are not considered worthy of such an honour. In *Three Essays on the Theory of Sexuality* I mention the very first use of faeces as a means of auto-erotic stimulation of the mucous membrane of the bowel; from this we progress to the fact that a defecation object is a crucial consideration for the child, who thereby expresses obedience or compliance towards that person. This relation persists in the fact that the older child, too, will only allow certain special people to put him on the pot or help him to urinate; here other purposes of satisfaction must also be taken into account.

11. It is known that the unconscious does not recognize the word 'no'; opposites coincide here. Negation is only introduced through the process of repression.

12. Likewise vermin, which frequently stand for little children in dreams and phobias.

13. This is entirely the sense in which faeces are treated by the child.

14. 'Über fausse reconaissance ("déjà raconté") während der psychoanalytischen Arbeit' ['On *fausse reconaissance ("déjà raconté")* in Psychoanalytical Work', 1914.]

15. Corrected on a later re-telling to: 'I don't think I was actually digging the knife into the tree. I am getting confused with another memory which must also have been an hallucinatory forgery; I cut into the tree with my knife and then *blood* came out of the tree.'

16. Cf. 'Märchenstoffe in Träumen' ['Fairy-tale Matter in Dreams'].

17. We know this is true of Nanja; the same thing will turn out to be true of another woman.

18. See the evidence for this on pp. 266–7.

19. Among the most excruciating and at the same time most grotesque symptoms of his later suffering was his relationship to a – tailor, from whom he had ordered an item of apparel: his respect and timidity in the face of this exalted person, his attempts to win him over with excessively large tips and his despair at the outcome of the work, whatever it might have been.

20. In this context I might mention dreams that occurred later than the anxiety-dream, but still while they were living on the first estate, which depicted the scene of coitus as an event taking place between heavenly bodies.

21. [*Translator's note*: The German word *Mitleid* (sympathy) quite explicitly means 'suffering with'.]

VIII *Supplementary Material from Earliest Childhood – Solution*

It is often the case in analysis that new material surfaces in the memory once the end is in sight, material which up until then has been kept carefully hidden. Or else an inconspicuous remark will be tossed casually into the conversation, in an indifferent tone of voice, as if it were something quite superfluous, and then something else added on another occasion which makes the physician prick up his ears, until we finally recognize that these passed-over scraps of memory hold the key to the most important of secrets, glossed over by the patient's neurosis.

At an early stage my patient had recounted a memory dating from the time when his difficult behaviour would suddenly veer over into anxiety. He was chasing a lovely big butterfly with yellow stripes, whose large wings had pointed tips – a swallow-tail, in fact. Suddenly, as the butterfly settled on a flower, he was overcome by a terrible fear of the creature and ran away screaming.

This memory recurred from time to time in the analysis and demanded some sort of explanation, which for a long time was not forthcoming. We could assume from the outset that a detail of this kind had not retained a place in his memory for its own sake, but was a cover-memory representing something more important which was somehow bound up with it. One day he said that in his language the word for a butterfly was Babuschka, or little granny; butterflies in general made him think of women and girls, while beetles and caterpillars were like boys. It must surely have been the memory of a female, then, which had been awakened in that scene of anxiety. I will not conceal the fact that at the time I suggested as a possibility that the yellow stripes of the butterfly reminded him of similar stripes on an item of clothing worn by a woman. I do so only in order to show by example how inadequate the physician's conjectures are as a general rule in solving questions that have been raised, and how wrong it is to attribute responsibility for the outcome of the analysis to the physician's fantasies and suggestions.

Many months later, in an entirely different context, the patient remarked that it was the way the butterfly's wings opened and closed once it had settled that had given him such an uncanny feeling. It had been like a woman opening her legs, and the legs then made the shape of a Roman V, which as we know was the hour at which he used to experience a darkening of his mood, both in his boyhood and in the present day.

This was a notion that would never have occurred to me and that I was the more inclined to value when I considered that the process of association it revealed was genuinely infantile in character. I have often noticed that a child's attention is drawn by movement far more often than by forms that are at rest, and he will often produce associations on the grounds of a similar kind of movement, which we adults neglect to notice or overlook altogether.

For a long time afterwards this little problem was left on one side. I will mention only the commonplace conjecture that the butterfly's pointed, protruding wing tips might have had some significance as genital symbols.

One day a memory of a kind came to the surface, hazy and diffident: very early on, even before the time of his nurse, he must have had a nursery-maid who was very fond of him. She had had the same name as his mother. He was sure he had returned her affection. A first love, then, which had vanished without trace. We agreed, however, that something must have happened then that was to be of importance later.

Then he revised his memory once more. She could not have had the same name as his mother, that was a mistake on his part, proving of course that in his memory she had merged with his mother. Her real name had come back to him by a circuitous route. He suddenly found himself thinking of a store-room on the first estate where fruit was kept after it had been picked, and of a particular sort of pear with an excellent flavour, a large pear with yellow-striped skin. In his language the word for pear was 'Gruscha', and this had also been the name of the nursery-maid.

It thus became clear that behind the cover-memory of the butterfly he had chased there lay concealed the memory of this nursery-maid. The yellow stripes were not on her dress, however, but on the pear whose name she shared. Yet where did his anxiety come from when this memory was activated? The most obvious, crass conjecture might have been that as a small child it was this nursery-maid whom he had first seen perform movements of the legs which he had fixed in his mind with the Roman symbol V, movements which allowed access to the genitals. We spared ourselves such conjectures and waited for new material to emerge.

Soon afterwards came the memory of a scene, incomplete but, as far as it went, distinct. Gruscha was kneeling on the ground, beside her a pail and a short broom made of birch twigs tied together; he was there and she was teasing him or scolding him.

We could easily supply the missing information from elsewhere. In the first months of therapy he had told me about his compulsive infatuation with a peasant girl from whom at the age of 18 he had caught the infection which led to his later illness. At the time he had been conspicuously unwilling to give the girl's name. It was an isolated instance of resistance; normally he gave unqualified obedience to the ground rules of analysis. He claimed, however, that he was so very ashamed to say the name out loud because it could only belong to a peasant; a girl of better breeding would never have been given such a name. Eventually we learned that this name was *Matrona*. It had a motherly ring to it. His shame was obviously displaced. He was not ashamed of the fact that he felt these infatuations exclusively for girls of the most lowly birth, he was ashamed only of the name. If the affair with Matrona had anything in common with the Gruscha episode, then we could locate his feelings of shame back in that earlier incident.

On another occasion he told me how very moved he was when he heard the story of Johannes Huss; his attention was caught by the bundles of twigs that were dragged to the place where he was burned at the stake. His sympathy for Huss awoke a particular suspicion in me; I have often encountered it in younger patients and have always found the same explanation to hold true. One of them had even produced a dramatic version of Huss's story; he began to write his drama on the very day the object of his secret infatuation was taken away from him. Huss is burnt to death, and, like others who fulfil the same condition, he is a hero to those who formerly suffered from enuresis. The patient himself made a connection between the bundles of twigs around Huss's funeral pyre and the nursery-maid's broom (made of birch twigs).

This material fitted together effortlessly to fill in the gaps in his memory of the scene with Gruscha. As he was watching the girl cleaning the floor he had urinated into the room; at this she had threatened him, no doubt playfully, with castration.[1] I do not know if my readers are already able to guess why I have described this episode from early infancy in such detail.[2] It establishes an important link between the primal scene and the compulsive eroticism that was later to have such a decisive effect on his fortunes, and introduces, moreover, a sexual condition which throws some light on that compulsion.

When he saw the girl crouched down cleaning the floor, on her knees with her buttocks projecting and her back horizontal, he recognized the position that his mother had assumed in the scene of coitus he had observed. In his mind she became his mother, he was overcome by sexual excitement as that image was activated,[3] and behaved in a manly fashion towards her like his father, whose actions he could then only have understood as urination. His urinating on the floor was actually an attempt at seduction, to which the girl responded with a threat of castration as if she had understood what he was doing.

The compulsion derived from the primal scene was transferred to this scene with Gruscha and its continued effect was mediated through it. The sexual condition underwent a modification, however, which testifies to the influence of the second scene; it was transferred from the woman's position to what she was doing in that position. This became evident, for example, in his experience with Matrona.

He was walking through the village attached to their (later) estate when he saw a peasant girl kneeling at the edge of the pond, washing dirty linen in the water. He fell violently and irresistibly in love with the girl on the instant, although he could not even see her face. By virtue of her posture and her activity she had taken Gruscha's place. We can now understand how feelings of shame applying to the scene with Gruscha could be linked to the name Matrona.

We can see the compulsive influence of the scene with Gruscha at work in another attack of infatuation some years earlier. For a long time he had been attracted to a young peasant girl who was in service in the household, but had not allowed himself to approach her. One day he was seized with infatuation when he came across her alone in the room. He found her crouched down, cleaning the floor with pail and broom beside her, exactly like the other girl in his childhood.

Even his definitive choice of object, so significant in his life, turned out to be dependent in its circumstantial details, which are not our concern here, on that same sexual condition, an offshoot of the compulsion that governed his sexual choice from the primal scene onwards, via the scene with Gruscha. I remarked earlier that I am well aware of the way in which my patient attempts to demean the object of his love. We can trace this back to a reaction against the pressure of his sister's superiority. I promised at the time, however, to demonstrate that this arrogant motive was not the only one determining his behaviour, but concealed purely erotic motives, which constituted a more profound determining force. His memory of the nursery-maid cleaning the floor, her position admittedly a demeaning one, brought this motivation to light. All the later objects of his love were substitutes for this one woman, whom a chance situation had made the first substitute for his mother. In retrospect we can easily recognize our patient's first response to the problem of his fear of the butterfly as a distant allusion to the primal scene (the fifth hour). The relationship between the scene with Gruscha and the threat of castration was confirmed by a particularly suggestive dream, which he was able to translate on his own. He said: 'I dreamed that *a man was tearing the wings off an asp [Espe]*'. 'Asp?'

I naturally asked, 'What do you mean by that?' – 'Well, the insect with yellow stripes on its body, the one that can sting you. It must be a reference to Gruscha, the yellow-striped pear.' – Now I was able to correct him: 'You mean a *wasp*, then [*Wespe*].' – 'Is the word wasp? I really thought it was asp.' (Like so many others, he used his unfamiliarity with German to conceal his symptomatic actions.) But an asp, that must be me, S. P. (his initials). An asp is of course a mutilated wasp. The dream tells us clearly that he is taking his revenge on Gruscha for having threatened to castrate him.

The action of the 2½-year-old boy in the scene with Gruscha is the first known effect of the primal scene, one in which he appears as a copy of his father, revealing a tendency to develop in the direction that will later merit the name 'masculine'. The seduction forces him into passivity, although we were admittedly already prepared for this by his behaviour as an onlooker during his parents' intercourse.

One aspect of the treatment history, which I must emphasize, is that in dealing with the Gruscha scene, the first experience that he could truly remember and indeed did remember without any contribution or conjecture on my part, one had the strong impression that the problem of the therapy had been solved. After this there was no more resistance; all that was needed was to gather material and piece it together. Suddenly the old trauma theory, which was after all constructed on the basis of impressions formed in the course of psychoanalytic therapy, came into its own again. Out of critical interest I made one further attempt to impose a different interpretation of his story upon my patient, one more welcome to sober common sense. I suggested that there was no reason to doubt that the scene with Gruscha had taken place, but that it meant nothing in itself; regression had caused it to seem more substantial in retrospect because of the events surrounding his choice of object, which had been diverted from his sister because of his inclination to demean and had fallen on servant-girls instead. The observation of coitus, on the other hand, might simply be a fantasy of later life, the historical kernel of which might perhaps have been the observation or experience of a harmless enema. Many readers will perhaps be of the opinion that only in making assumptions such as these had I reached a true understanding of the case; the patient looked at me uncomprehendingly and with a certain contempt as I presented this view, and never once reacted to it. I have expounded my own arguments against rationalizations of this kind above in the appropriate context.

[Not only does the Gruscha scene contain the conditions of object-choice that were to be crucial for the patient's life, however, thus guarding us against the error of over-estimating the significance of his inclination to demean women. It also enables me to justify my former refusal to trace the primal scene back to animal behaviour observed shortly before the dream, and to regard this without hesitation as the only possible solution. It surfaced spontaneously in the patient's memory without my having said or done anything. The fear of the yellow-striped butterfly, which could be traced back to it, proved that its content had been significant, or that it had subsequently become possible to invest its content with significance. We could quite confidently supply those significant elements that were no longer present to memory, by means of the accompanying associations and the conclusions suggested by them. It then transpired that his fear of the butterfly was entirely analogous to his fear of the wolf, and in both cases was a fear of castration, initially directed towards the person who had first voiced the castration threat but then transferred on to the person to whom it must adhere according to the phylogenetic model. The scene with Gruscha occurred when he was 2½; the anxiety he experienced at the sight of the yellow butterfly must have been after the anxiety-dream, however. It would be readily comprehensible if his later sense of the possibility of castration had latched on to the scene with Gruscha and generated anxiety from it; but the scene itself contains nothing offensive or improbable, only details of an entirely banal nature that there was no reason to doubt. There is nothing to encourage us to trace them back to the child's fantasy; indeed, it would hardly seem possible to do so.

The question now arises as to whether we are justified in seeing proof of his sexual excitement in the fact that the boy urinated in a standing position while the girl was kneeling on the floor, cleaning it. If so, his excitement would testify to the influence of an earlier impression, which could just as easily be the actual occurrence of the primal scene as something he watched animals do before the age of 2½. Or was the situation entirely harmless, the child emptying his bladder purely a matter of accident, and the whole scene imbued with sexuality only later on, in his memory, once he had recognized the significance of similar situations?

I do not think I am able to come to any conclusion here. I must say that I think it greatly to the credit of psychoanalysis that it can even ask questions such as these. But I cannot deny that the scene with Gruscha, the role it played in analysis and the effects it had on my patient's life can be explained most naturally and fully if we affirm the reality of the primal scene, which at other times might be seen as the product of fantasy. There is nothing fundamentally impossible in what it asserts, and the assumption that it was a reality is entirely in keeping with the stimulating influence of his observations of animals, to which the sheepdogs in the dream-image allude.

I shall turn from this unsatisfying conclusion to a question I explore in my *Introductory Lectures on Psychoanalysis.* I should very much like to know myself whether my patient's primal scene was a fantasy or a real experience, but taking other, similar cases into consideration we are obliged to conclude that it is not actually very important to reach a verdict on this matter. Scenes where parental intercourse is observed, scenes of childhood seduction and the threat of castration are undoubtedly inherited property, a phylogenetic inheritance, but they could just as well have been acquired by personal experience. The seduction of my patient by his older sister was an indisputable reality; why not the observation of his parents' coitus, too?

In the primal history of neurosis we see that the child resorts to this phylogenetic experience when his own experience is not enough. He fills out the gaps in individual truth with prehistoric truth, putting ancestral experience in the place of his own. In acknowledging this phylogenetic inheritance I am in complete agreement with Jung

(*Die Psychologie der unbewußten Prozesse* [*The Psychology of Unconscious Processes*], 1917, a work published too late to influence my own *Lectures*), but I consider it methodologically incorrect to resort to a phylogenetic explanation before one has exhausted the possibilities of ontogenesis; I do not see why we should obstinately deny the pre-history of childhood a significance that we readily concede to ancestral pre-history; I cannot overlook the fact that phylogenetic motives and products are themselves in need of the light that can be shed on them in a whole series of instances drawn from individual childhoods; and finally, it does not surprise me to find that when the same conditions remain in force they again cause the same things to come about organically in the individual as they had done in ancient times, and which they then passed down in the form of a disposition to re-acquire them over and over again.

The interval between the primal scene and the seduction (18 months – 3¼ years) is also where we must place the mute water-carrier, who was a father-substitute for my patient just as Gruscha was a mother-substitute. I do not think we are justified in referring here to an inclination to demean, even though both parents are represented by members of the servant class. The child takes no notice of social distinctions, which mean very little to him as yet, putting even quite lowly people on a level with his parents if they respond to him lovingly in the same way that his parents do. Equally, this inclination is of little significance when it comes to using animals as substitutes for his parents, for nothing could be further from the child's mind than to hold animals in low esteem. There is no thought of demeaning them when uncles and aunts are enlisted as parent-substitutes, a procedure attested by many of our patient's memories.

In the same period there are vague tidings of a phase during which he only wanted to eat sweets, so that concern was expressed for his physical well-being. He was told of an uncle who had not wanted to eat anything either and who wasted away at an early age. He also heard that he had been so seriously ill when he was three months old that they had made his shroud in readiness. They succeeded in making him so fearful that he started to eat again; later in his childhood he even took this obligation to extremes, as if to shield himself against the threat of death. His fear of dying, summoned up for his own protection, came into evidence again later, when his mother issued a warning about the danger of dysentery; later still it provoked an attack of obsessive-compulsive neurosis (p. 266). At a later stage we shall attempt to look into its origins and significance.

I would wish to claim that the eating disorder is significant as the very first instance of neurotic illness in my patient; thus the eating disorder, the wolf phobia and the compulsive piety represent the full range of infantile illnesses that predispose the individual to neurotic breakdown in the years after puberty. It will be objected that few children altogether avoid disorders such as a passing unwillingness to eat or an animal phobia. This is an argument I welcome, however. I am prepared to assert that every adult neurosis builds on childhood neurosis, but that the latter is not always powerful enough to attract attention and to be recognized as such. The objection only enhances the theoretical significance of the infantile neuroses for our understanding of those illnesses that we treat as neuroses and believe to be derived only from what affects us in later life. If our patient had not picked up compulsive piety in addition to his eating disorder and his animal phobia, his story would not be noticeably different from that of any other living soul and we would have missed out on valuable material that could keep us from making obvious mistakes.

The analysis would be unsatisfactory if it did not enable us to understand the lament in which our patient summed up his sense of suffering. He said that for him the world was shrouded in a veil, and psychoanalytic training leads us to dismiss any expectation that these words might be meaningless or accidental. The veil was only torn apart – oddly enough – in one situation, namely when, after the application of an enema, stools were passed through the anus. He would then feel well again and for a very short while would see the world clearly. Understanding the meaning of this 'veil' was as difficult as understanding his fear of the butterfly. He did not insist on its being a veil, moreover, and it became even more elusive to him, a feeling of twilight, 'ténèbres', and other such intangibles.

It was only shortly before leaving therapy that he recalled having heard that he had been born with a caul.[4] For this reason he had always considered himself to be particularly lucky, a child whom no ill could befall. This confidence only left him when he was obliged to acknowledge that his gonorrhoeal illness had done serious damage to his body. He broke down in the face of this insult to his narcissism. We might say that this was the repetition of a mechanism that had come into play once before. The wolf phobia, too, had broken out when he was forced to confront the fact that castration was indeed possible, and for him gonorrhoea was clearly on a par with castration.

The veil shrouding him from the world and shrouding the world from him was thus the caul. His lament is in fact the fulfilment of a wish-fantasy in which he is shown as having returned to the womb: a wish-fantasy, admittedly, of flight from the world. We might translate it thus: my life is so unhappy that I must go back to my mother's womb.

What is the meaning of the fact that this symbolic veil, once a real veil, is torn apart, however, at the very moment when the bowels are evacuated after a clyster [enema] and that his illness abates under these conditions? The context permits us to reply: when the birth veil is torn apart, he sees the world and is re-born. The stool is the baby, and as that baby he is born a second time to a happier life. This is the fantasy of re-birth to which Jung recently drew our attention and to which he attributed such a dominant position in the wishful fantasies of the neurotic individual.

That would be all very well, if it were a complete response. Certain details of the situation, together with the consideration that there should be a connection with the particular facts of our patient's life history, require us to take our interpretation further. The condition of re-birth is that a man administers a clyster (only later, when absolutely necessary, did he perform this function himself). This can only mean that he has identified himself with the mother, the man plays the role of his father, the clyster reproduces the act of copulation, which bears fruit in the birth of the stool-baby – that is, of himself. The fantasy of re-birth is thus intimately bound up with the condition of sexual satisfaction received from a man. Our translation now runs as follows: only when he is allowed to take the woman's place, to substitute himself for his mother in order to gain satisfaction from his father and bear a child for him, does his illness abate. Here the fantasy of re-birth is merely the mutilated, censored reproduction of his homosexual wish-fantasy.

If we look more closely, we must in fact recognize that, by setting this condition for his cure, the patient is simply reproducing the situation found in the so-called primal scene: at the time he wanted to take on his mother's attributes and in that scene he himself produced the stool-baby, as we had long ago supposed. As if spell-bound, his inner gaze is fixed on the scene that was to be decisive for his sexual life, the recurrence of which, that night of the dream, inaugurated his illness. The veil tearing is analogous to his eyes unclosing, to the window opening. The primal scene has been remodelled as the condition imposed for his cure.

We can easily take what is represented in the patient's lament, and what is represented by the exception to the condition he laments, and draw them together to form a single entity whose full meaning is then revealed. He wishes he were back in his mother's womb not simply in order to be re-born, but so as to be reached by his father during coitus, to gain satisfaction from him, to bear him a child.

To be born of his father, as he at first supposed, to gain sexual satisfaction from him, to give him a child, even if that means surrendering his manhood, and to express all this in the language of anal eroticism: with these wishes the wheel of his fixed obsession with his father comes full circle, in them his homosexuality finds its highest and most intimate expression.[5]

In my opinion this example sheds some light on the meaning and origin of fantasies of the womb and of re-birth. The former frequently stems from an attachment to the father, as in our case. There is a desire to be in the mother's womb so as to act as her substitute during coitus, to take her place with the father. As a rule the fantasy of re-birth probably constitutes a euphemism, so to speak, a toning-down of the fantasy of incestuous intercourse with the mother, an *anagogic* abbreviation of it, to borrow H. Silberer's expression. There is a desire to return to the situation in which one was in the mother's genitals; here the man identifies himself with his penis and uses it to represent his whole self. Thus it is revealed that each of the two fantasies is the counterpart of the other, expressing the wish for sexual intercourse with the mother or the father, depending on whether the individual concerned adopts a male or female attitude. We cannot discount the possibility that both fantasies, and hence both incestuous wishes, are united in our patient's lament and in the condition set for his cure.

Once again I shall attempt to re-interpret the latest results of the analysis according to the model preferred by my opponents: the patient laments his flight from the world in a typical womb-fantasy, glimpses the possibility of cure only in re-birth, as typically understood. He expresses the latter through anal symptoms appropriate to his dominant predisposition. According to the model of anal fantasies of re-birth he constructs a childhood scene that recapitulates his wishes using archaic symbols as the medium of expression. His symptoms are then interlinked in such a way that they appear to proceed from a primal scene of this kind. He was forced to embark on this whole line of retreat because he came up against a task in real life that he was too lazy to solve, or because he had every reason to mistrust his inferior attributes and thought this the best way of protecting himself against being passed over.

This would be all well and good if the unhappy man had not been only four years old at the time of the dream with which his neurosis began, the stimulus for which was his grandfather's story about the tailor and the wolf, and the interpretation of which necessitates the assumption of a primal scene of this kind. The relief that Jung's and Adler's theories might have afforded us comes to grief in the face of these petty but inviolable facts. As things are, it seems to me more likely that the fantasy of re-birth issues from the primal scene than the other way round, that the primal scene reflects the fantasy of re-birth. Perhaps we may also assume that four years after his birth the patient was just a little too young to be wishing for re-birth already. Yet I must withdraw this last argument, for my own observations prove that we have under-estimated children and are no longer able to say just what they are capable of.[6]

Notes

1. It is most remarkable that the reaction of shame is so intimately bound up with involuntary emptying of the bladder (by day or night) and not to the same extent with faecal incontinence, as one might expect. Experience leaves us in no doubt on this point. The connection regularly found between urinary incontinence and fire also gives us pause for thought. It is possible that a precipitate of the cultural history of mankind is to be found in these reactions and connections, which reach down further than any of the traces retained in myth and folklore.

2. It took place around the age of 2½, between the supposed observation of coitus and the seduction.

3. Before the dream!

4. [*Translator's note*: The German word for a 'caul', '*Glückshaube*', means literally a 'lucky bonnet'.]

5. A possible secondary sense, in which the veil represents the hymen that is torn in intercourse with the man, does not exactly coincide with the condition set for the patient's cure and has no application in his life, as virginity was without significance for him.

6. I admit that this is one of the most tricky questions in the whole of psychoanalytic theory. It did not take Adler's pronouncements or Jung's to make me look critically at the possibility that those forgotten childhood experiences – experienced at such an incredibly early stage of childhood! – which analysis claims actually took place, are in fact rooted in fantasies created in response to some later occurrence, and that anywhere in analysis where we think we find the after-effects of an infantile memory imprint of this kind we must assume that it is actually the expression of a significant constitutional moment or a disposition that has been phylogenetically pre-served. On the contrary: no cause for doubt has so preoccupied me, no other uncertainty more decisively held me back from publication. None of my opponents refers to the fact that I was the first to draw attention not only to the role of fantasy in symptom formation but also to the way in which an individual may be prompted, later in life, to 'fantasize back' to his childhood and to sexualize it retrospectively. (See *Die Traumdeutung* [*The Interpretation of Dreams*], 1st edition, p. 49, and 'Bemerkungen über einen Fall von Zwangsneurose' ['Some Remarks on a Case of Obsessive-compulsive Neurosis'].) If I nevertheless hold fast to the more problematic and less probable view and claim it as my own, I do so in the light of arguments that force themselves upon the attention of anyone investigating the case I have described here or that of any other infantile neurosis, arguments that I now present to my readers once again to enable them to make up their own minds on this matter.

IX *Recapitulations and Problems*

I do not know whether my readers will have succeeded in forming a clear picture of the genesis and development of my patient's state of illness from the report of the analysis given above. Indeed, I fear that this will not be the case. However, whereas I never normally boast of my own narrative skills, on this occasion I should like to plead mitigating circumstances. To initiate the reader into a description of such early phases and such profound strata of a patient's inner life is a problem which has never before been tackled, and it is better to solve it badly than to take to one's heels, particularly since losing heart presents certain dangers in itself. Better, then, to make a bold show of not having been put off by consciousness of one's own deficiencies.

The case itself was not a particularly auspicious one. The very thing that made it possible to gain such a wealth of information about the patient's childhood, the fact that we could study the child through the medium of the adult, was bought at the price of the most dreadful fragmentation of the analysis and a corresponding incompleteness in my account of it. Aspects of personality, a national character which is alien to our own, made it difficult to empathize with him. The contrast between the patient's charming and responsive personality, his sharp intelligence and refined way of thinking, and his complete lack of restraint at the level of the drives made it necessary to spend an excessively long time on the work of preparation and education, thus rendering any kind of overview more difficult. Though it may have posed the hardest descriptive problems, however, the patient himself cannot be held responsible for the nature of the case. In adult psychology we have happily succeeded in separating the processes of the inner life into conscious and unconscious, and describing both in clear language. As far as the child is concerned, however, this distinction almost gives way. We are often at a loss to decide what we would describe as conscious, and what unconscious. Processes that have become dominant and that, given their later behaviour, we must treat in the same way as conscious ones, were nevertheless not conscious in the child. We can easily understand why this is so: consciousness in the child has not yet developed its full range of characteristics and is not yet entirely capable of being converted into language-pictures. The way in which we are regularly guilty of confusing the phenomenon of something appearing in consciousness in the form of a perception, and something belonging to an accepted psychic system that we ought to call by some conventional name but for which we also use the term consciousness (System *Cs*), such confusion is harmless in the psychological description of an adult, but misleading in the case of a small child. To introduce the concept of the 'pre-conscious' does not help much here, for there is no reason why the child's pre-consciousness should be congruent with the adult's. We must therefore be content with having clearly recognized the obscurity which confronts us.

A case such as the one described here could obviously create an opportunity to embark on a discussion of all the results and problems of psychoanalysis. It would be an endless undertaking, and one quite without justification. We have to tell ourselves that we cannot discover everything, cannot decide everything on the basis of a single case and that we must be content to use it for what it can show us most clearly. The task of explanation in psychoanalysis is in any case narrowly circumscribed. What we need to explain are conspicuous symptom formations, by revealing how they have come about; what we are not to explain, only describe, are the psychic mechanisms and drive processes that we encounter in doing so. Formulation of new general statements on the basis of what we have learned about these last-named aspects requires numerous cases of this kind, analysed accurately and in depth. They are not easy to come by, for each individual case requires years of work. Thus progress in these areas will only take place very slowly. There is an obvious temptation, of course, to content oneself with 'scratching the psychic surface' of a number of individuals and replacing neglected effort with speculation advanced under the patronage of some philosophical school of thought or other. There are also practical necessities that can be urged in favour of such a procedure, but the necessities of scholarship cannot be satisfied by any surrogate.

I want to attempt to sketch out a synthesis, an overall view of my patient's sexual development, beginning with the earliest indications. The first thing we hear about him is of a loss of pleasure in eating that I would interpret on the basis of other experiences, but nevertheless with circumspection, as the outcome of an occurrence in the sexual sphere. I had thus to consider the first recognizable mode of sexual organization to be the so-called *cannibal* or *oral* mode of organization, in which the scene is dominated by the original dependence of sexual excitement on the drive to eat. We cannot expect to find any direct expression of this phase, but may find some indications in the appearance of disorders. The impairment of the drive to eat – which may of course have other causes as well – draws our attention to the fact that the organism has not succeeded in controlling sexual excitement. The sexual objective in this phase could only be cannibalism, eating; in our patient's case this comes to the fore as a result of regression from a higher level, in his fear of being gobbled up by the wolf. We had to translate this fear as that of being taken in coitus by the father. It is well known that at a much later stage, in girls going through puberty or slightly older, we encounter a neurosis that expresses the rejection of sexuality through anorexia; a connection may be drawn with the oral phase of sexuality. We encounter the erotic objective of the oral mode of organization once again at the height of paroxysms of love ('I love you so much I could eat you') and in affectionate contact with small children, in which the adult himself behaves in an infantile fashion. Elsewhere I have expressed the suspicion that our patient's father himself inclined to 'affectionate scolding', and when playing at wolves or dogs with the little boy had threatened in jest to gobble him up (p. 230). The patient only provided confirmation of this view through his striking behaviour in the transference. Whenever he retreated from difficulties in the therapy and sought refuge in transference, he would threaten to gobble me up, and later to subject me to every possible form of ill-treatment, all of which was merely a way of expressing his affection.

His linguistic usage has been permanently coloured in certain ways by this oral phase of sexuality: he refers to 'luscious' love-objects, describes his beloved as 'sweet'. We recall that as a child our patient only wanted sweet things to eat. When they occur in dreams sweeties and bonbons generally stand for caresses and sexual satisfaction.

It appears that there is also an anxiety that belongs in this phase (where there is a disorder, of course), which manifests itself in the form of generalized anxiety and may adhere to anything that is suggested to the child as appropriate. In our patient's case it was used to teach him to overcome his reluctance to eat, to overcompensate for it, indeed. We are led to the possible source of his eating disorder when we recall – basing ourselves on the assumption we have discussed in such detail – that his observation of coitus, which was belatedly to cast so many ripples, took place at the age of 18 months, certainly before the period at which he experienced eating difficulties. We may perhaps assume that it speeded up the processes of sexual maturity, so that it also took effect directly, if inconspicuously.

I know, of course, that we can also explain the symptoms manifested during this period, his fear of the wolf, his eating disorder, in a different, more straightforward way that takes no account of sexuality or of a pre-genital stage of sexual organization. Anyone who likes to ignore the signs of neurosis and the logical connections between phenomena will prefer this other explanation, and I shall not be able to prevent him from doing so. It is difficult to find out anything compelling about these initial stages of sexuality other than by taking the roundabout routes I have indicated.

The scene with Gruscha (at the age of 2½) shows our young patient embarking on a development that merits recognition as a normal one, except perhaps that it is somewhat premature: identification with the father, eroticism of the bladder as a substitute for virility. It too is very strongly influenced by the primal scene. Up until now we have interpreted the identification with the father as a narcissistic one, but bearing in mind the content of the primal scene we cannot deny that it already corresponds to the stage of genital organization. The male genitals have begun to play their part and will continue to do so under the influence of his sister's seduction.

We gain the impression, however, that the seduction not only encourages this development but also, to a greater extent, disrupts and diverts it. It results in a passive sexual objective that is fundamentally irreconcilable with the action of the male genitals. The first external impediment, Nanja's suggestion of castration, leads to the breakdown (at the age of 3½) of the still precarious mode of genital organization, and regression to the previous stage of anal-sadistic organization, which he might perhaps otherwise have passed through with only the same slight symptoms as those found in other children.

It is easy to recognize that the anal-sadistic mode of organization is a continuation of the oral one. The violent muscular activity towards its object by which it is characterized falls into place as an act preparatory to eating, but eating is no longer present as a sexual objective. The preparatory act becomes an objective in its own right. What is new about it in comparison with the previous stage is the fact that the receptive, passive organ has now been separated off from the oral zone, and developed in the anal zone instead. Biological parallels suggest themselves, as does the interpretation of pre-genital human modes of organization as the residue of arrangements that have been permanently retained in many classes of animal. Equally characteristic of this stage is the way in which the exploratory drive constitutes itself from its component elements.

Anal eroticism is not conspicuously in evidence. Under the influence of sadism faeces have exchanged their affectionate meaning for an aggressive one. A feeling of guilt, which indicates, moreover, that developments are taking place in areas other than the sexual sphere, plays its part in the transformation of sadism into masochism.

The seduction continues to exert an influence, in that it maintains the passivity of the sexual objective. It now transforms sadism to a great extent into its passive counterpart, masochism. It is doubtful whether we can put the boy's characteristic passivity entirely down to the seduction, for his reaction to the observation of coitus at the age of 18 months was already predominantly a passive one. The sexual excitement that he felt in observation was expressed in a bowel movement, in which we must admittedly recognize an active element. Sadism, which finds active expression in tormenting small creatures, continues to exist alongside the masochism that dominates his sexual aspirations and is expressed in his fantasies. From the time of the seduction onwards his sexual curiosity has been stirred, and is essentially directed towards two problems, namely where babies come from and whether loss of the genitals is possible; it becomes bound up with the expression of his drives. It is this that focuses his sadistic tendencies on those tiny creatures, which he sees as representing tiny children.

Our description has taken us almost up to his fourth birthday, at which point the dream causes the observation of coitus at the age of 18 months to come belatedly into effect. We can neither completely grasp nor adequately describe the processes that are now set in motion. The activation of that image, which thanks to advances in his intellectual development can now be understood, has the effect of a newly occurring event, but is also like a fresh trauma, an alien intrusion analogous to the seduction. The genital mode of organization, which had been suspended, is resumed at a stroke, but the progress made in the dream cannot be maintained. Rather, a process that can only be compared to a kind of repression causes him to reject this new knowledge and replace it with a phobia.

Thus the anal-sadistic mode of organization continues in existence, even during the animal phobia phase that now begins, but with some manifestations of anxiety mixed in. The child still pursues both sadistic and masochistic activities, while reacting fearfully against one component; the reversal of sadism into its opposite probably fares somewhat better.

We can see from the analysis of the anxiety dream that repression follows immediately after the knowledge of castration. The new knowledge is rejected because to accept it would cost the boy his penis. More careful consideration reveals something like the following: what has been repressed is the homosexual attitude in the genital sense, which had been formed under the influence of the new knowledge. This attitude remains preserved in the unconscious, however, constituted as a deeper, closed-off stratum. The driving force behind this repression appears to be the narcissistic masculinity of the genitals that comes into conflict with the passivity of the homosexual objective, a conflict for which the ground was laid long before. Repression is thus one of the outcomes of masculinity.

This might lead us into the temptation to revise one small aspect of psychoanalytic theory. It seems patently obvious, after all, that repression and the formation of neuroses proceed from the conflict between masculine and feminine aspirations, that is, from bisexuality. But such a view has its shortcomings. Of these two conflicting sexual impulses one is acceptable to the I [ichgerecht], the other offends against narcissistic interests and thus falls prey to repression. In this case, too, it is the I [Ich] who sets repression in motion in favour of one of the two sexual aspirations. In other cases, such a conflict between masculinity and femininity does not exist; there is a single sexual aspiration present, which sues for acceptance but runs counter to certain powers of the I and is therefore banished. Far more frequent than conflicts within sexuality itself are those conflicts that arise between sexuality and the moral inclinations of the I. There is an absence of moral conflict of this kind in our case. To emphasize bisexuality as the motivation for repression would be too restrictive, whereas conflict between the I and the sexual aspirations (the libido) covers all eventualities.

Against the theory of 'masculine protest' as developed by Adler, it must be objected that repression by no means always upholds masculinity against femininity; in many whole categories of cases it is masculinity that is obliged to accept repression by the I.

A more balanced evaluation of the process of repression in our particular case, incidentally, would challenge whether narcissistic masculinity is significant as the only motivating factor. The homosexual attitude that comes into being in the course of the dream is so powerful that the little boy's I fails to control it and fends it off through the process of repression. To achieve this end the I enlists the help of the narcissistic masculinity of the genitals that is in opposition to the homosexual attitude. Simply in order to avoid any misunderstanding let me state that all narcissistic impulses work out from the I and remain in the I's domain, while repression is directed towards those objects carrying a libidinal charge.

Let us now turn from the process of repression, a notion we have perhaps not succeeded in mastering entirely, to the boy's state when he awakened from the dream. If it had indeed been masculinity that had triumphed over homosexuality (femininity) during the dream process we should now find an active sexual aspiration, already explicitly masculine in character, to be the dominant one. There is no question of this, however: the essential nature of the mode of sexual organization is unchanged, the anal-sadistic phase still continues in existence and remains dominant. The triumph of masculinity can only be seen in the fact that the boy reacts fearfully to the passive sexual objectives of the dominant mode of organization (which are masochistic, but not feminine). There is no triumphant masculine sexual impulse present, but only a passive one, and an unwillingness to accept it.

I can imagine the difficulties that this sharp distinction between the active/masculine and passive/feminine will cause the reader, a distinction that is unfamiliar but essential to our purpose, and so I shall not hesitate to repeat myself. We can describe the state of affairs after the dream, then, as follows: the patient's sexual aspirations have been split, the genital mode of organization having been achieved in the unconscious and a highly intensive homosexuality constituted; above this (virtually at the level of consciousness) the earlier sadistic and predominantly masochistic sexual current continues to exist, while the I has altered its position, by and large, towards sexuality, anxiously rejecting the dominant masochistic objectives just as it reacted towards the deeper homosexual ones with the formation of a phobia. Thus the outcome of the dream was not so much the victory of a masculine current as reaction against a feminine, passive one. We would do violence to the facts if we ascribed masculine characteristics to this reaction. For the I does not have sexual aspirations, only an interest in self-protection and the preservation of its narcissism.

Let us now look closely at the phobia. It came into existence at the level of genital organization and demonstrates the relatively simple mechanism of an anxiety-hysteria. The I protects itself from something it judges to be excessively dangerous, that is, homosexual satisfaction, by developing anxiety. However, the process of repression leaves a trace that we cannot miss. The object to which the dreaded sexual objective has become attached must find representation in conscious thought by means of another. It is not fear of the *father* that comes to consciousness, but fear of the *wolf*. Once it has been formed, the phobia is not restricted to a single content. Some considerable time later the wolf is replaced by a lion. Sadistic impulses towards tiny creatures compete with a phobic response towards them, inasmuch as they represent the boy's rivals, the babies whose arrival is still possible. The genesis of the butterfly phobia is particularly interesting. It is like a repetition of the mechanism that generated the wolf phobia in the dream. A chance stimulus activates an old experience, the scene with Gruscha, whose castration threat belatedly comes into effect, whereas at the time it appeared to have left no impression.[1]

We can say that the fear that goes into the formation of these phobias is fear of castration. This statement in no way contradicts the view that the fear arises from the repression of homosexual libido. Both modes of expression refer to the same process, in which the I withdraws libido from the homosexual wish-impulse, which is converted into free-floating anxiety and then allows itself to be bound up in phobias. It is merely that the first mode of expression also indicates the motive that drives the I to act in this way.

Looking more carefully, we then find that the random choice of a single phobia does not represent the full extent of this first episode of illness (not counting the eating disorder) in our patient, but that it must be understood as a genuine case of hysteria, comprising both anxiety symptoms and conversion phenomena. An element of the homosexual impulse is retained by the organ involved, for henceforward, and in later years too, the bowel behaves like an organ that has been hysterically affected. The unconscious, repressed homosexuality withdraws into the bowel. It was this particular bit of hysteria that served us so well when it came to resolving the patient's later illness.

Now we should steel ourselves to tackle the still more complicated circumstances of the obsessive-compulsive neurosis. Let us examine the situation once again: a dominant masochistic sexual current and a repressed homosexual one, opposed to an I that is caught up in hysterical refusal; what processes could transform this state into one of obsessive-compulsive neurosis?

The transformation is not the spontaneous result of internal developments, but arises from an external, alien influence. Its visible outcome is that the boy's relationship to his father, still very much to the fore, and expressed up until then through the wolf phobia, now finds expression in compulsive piety. I cannot let this opportunity pass without pointing out that the process that our patient undergoes provides unambiguous confirmation of a claim I put forward in *Totem and Taboo* concerning the relationship of the totemic animal to the deity.[2] There I concluded that the idea of God does not develop out of the totem but arises independently from common roots to supersede it. The totem is the first father-substitute, the god a later one in which the father regains human form. We find the same thing in our patient's case. He goes through the stage of the totemic father-substitute, as represented by the wolf phobia, which is then broken off and, after a new relationship has been forged between the boy and his father, is replaced by a phase of religious piety.

The influence behind this transformation is his acquaintance with religious doctrine and sacred history, arranged by his mother. The result is exactly the one that education aspires to. The sado-masochistic mode of sexual organization draws gradually to a close, the wolf phobia quickly disappears and in the place of his frightened rejection of sexuality we find a higher form of sexual suppression. Piety becomes the dominant power in the child's life. These efforts of will are not achieved without a struggle, however: its signs are the appearance of blasphemous thoughts and its consequence the onset of a compulsive exaggeration of religious ritual.

Leaving aside these pathological phenomena, we can say that, in this case, religion has achieved everything it is employed to do in the education of the individual. It has curbed his sexual aspirations by offering sublimation and a safe anchor, and undermined his family relationships, thus preventing the isolation that threatens him by giving him access to the wider human community. The unruly, apprehensive child has become socially conscious, civilized and educable.

The principal driving force behind the religious influence was his identification with the figure of Christ, which readily suggested itself given the coincidence of his date of birth. The excessive love for his father that had made repression necessary could finally be channelled into an ideal sublimation. It was possible as Christ to love the father, now called God, with an intensity that he had striven in vain to vent on his own earthly father. The ways in which this love could be attested were clearly indicated by religion and no guilt adhered to them, whereas there was no way of separating guilt from the erotic aspirations of the individual. While the patient's deepest sexual current, already laid down as unconscious homosexuality, could still be drained off in this way, his more superficial masochistic aspirations lost very little in finding a sublimation without parallel in the passion of Christ, who had allowed himself to be mistreated and sacrificed on behalf of the divine father and to his greater glory. And so religion did its work in this boy who had gone off the rails, through the mixture of satisfaction, sublimation, diversion from sensual processes to purely spiritual ones, and the opening up of social relationships which it offers the believer.

His initial reluctance to accept religion was derived from three different sources. First, it was simply his way to ward off anything new: we have already seen a number of examples of this. Once he had taken up a given libido position he would defend it every time against the new one he was to occupy, fearful of what he would lose in giving it up and mistrusting the likelihood of finding a fully satisfactory substitute. This is an important and fundamental psychological particularity, which I put forward in *Three Essays on the Theory of Sexuality* as the capacity to become *fixed*. Referring to it as psychic 'lassitude', Jung sees it as the principal cause of all neurotic failure. I believe he is wrong to do so, for it is more far-reaching than this and has a significant part to play even in the lives of those untouched by neurosis. The fluidity or viscosity of libidinal energy charges, and of other types as well, is a particular characteristic found in many normal individuals and not even in all those of a neurotic disposition, and up until now no connection has been made between it and anything else, as if it were a prime number which cannot be divided any further. We know only one thing: the mobility of psychic charges is a property which dwindles noticeably with age. This provides us with one of the indicators for the limits of psychoanalytic influence. There are people, however, whose psychic plasticity is maintained far beyond the usual limits of age and others who lose it very early on. If these are neurotic individuals then we discover to our discomfort that in their case, under what are apparently the same conditions, it is impossible to reverse changes that can readily be controlled in others. In examining conversion in psychic processes we must therefore give consideration to the concept of an *entropy*, which is in proportional opposition to the undoing of what has already taken place.

A second target was provided by the fact that there is no single, clear relationship to God the Father underlying religious doctrine, on the contrary it is shot through with signs of the ambivalent attitude that prevailed at its inception. His own highly developed ambivalence enabled him to sniff this out and use it as a starting-point for the penetrating criticism that so astonished us in a four-year-old child. Most significant of all, however, was undoubtedly a third factor to which we may ascribe the pathological effects of his battle against religion. The current of energy pressing him towards manhood, for which religion was to provide a form of sublimation, was no longer free, as part of it had been separated off by the process of repression and thus eluded sublimation, remaining bound to its original sexual objective. On the strength of their connection the repressed part strove either to break through to the sublimated part or else to drag it down to its own level. Those first brooding thoughts circling around the person of Christ already contained the question as to whether this sublime son could also fulfil the sexual relationship to his father that the patient had retained in his unconscious. Repudiation of this endeavour resulted only in the emergence of apparently blasphemous compulsive thoughts in which physical tenderness for God continued to assert itself in a form intended to demean Him. A violent struggle [*Abwehrkampf*] to parry these compromise formations led inevitably to compulsive exaggeration of all those activities in which piety and the pure love of God found expression through the prescribed channels. The victory eventually fell to religion, but the way in which it was rooted in the drives proved incomparably stronger than the durability of what was produced by sublimation. As soon as life provided a new father-substitute whose influence was directed against religion, it was dropped and replaced by other things. We should also bear in mind the interesting complication that piety came about under the influence of women (mother and nurse) whereas masculine influence liberated him from it.

The fact that obsessive-compulsive neurosis came about at the anal-sadistic stage of sexual organization on the whole confirms the views presented elsewhere in 'Die Disposition zur Zwangsneurose' ['The Disposition to Obsessional Neurosis'] (1913). However, the pre-existence of a powerful state of hysteria makes the case more obscure in that respect. I shall conclude my survey of our patient's sexual development by highlighting the transformations it underwent in later life. In puberty the strongly sensual male current that we refer to as normal made its appearance, its sexual objective that of the genital mode of organization, and its vicissitudes fill up the time until his later episode of illness. It was directly connected with the Gruscha scene and derived from it the character of a compulsive infatuation, coming and going like an attack; it also had to struggle with the inhibitions created by the residue of the infantile neurosis. Violent breakthrough to the female meant that he finally won his full masculinity; from now on he held fast to this sexual object, but its possession brought him little joy, for a strong and now completely unconscious inclination towards the male, the sum of all the energies generated in earlier phases, was constantly drawing him away from a female object, obliging him to exaggerate his dependence on women in the interstices. His complaint in therapy was that he could not endure being with women, and all our work was directed towards the task of uncovering his unconscious relationship to the male. We could say, in a formulaic way, that the hallmark of his childhood was vacillation between the active and the passive, that of puberty the struggle for manhood and that of the period following his illness, the fight for the object of male aspirations. The cause of his illness does not come into any of the categories of 'neurotic illness' that I might refer to collectively as special cases of 'refusal' [*Versagung*][3] and so draws our attention to a gap in this series. He broke down when an organic infection of the genitals re-awakened his fear of castration, damaged his narcissism and forced him to put away any expectation that Fate had a personal preference for him. The cause of his illness was thus a narcissistic 'refusal'. His excessively strong narcissism was in complete accord with the other indications of inhibited sexual development: with the fact that his choice of hetero-sexuality, however energetic, was the focus for so few of his psychic aspirations, and also that the homosexual attitude, which is so much closer to narcissism, asserted its unconscious power over him with such tenacity. In the face of such disorders, psychoanalytic therapy obviously cannot bring about an instantaneous change of direction nor parity with normal development; it can only remove obstacles and clear the paths so that life's influences can opt for better direc-tions in which to push through the individual's development.

Let me list those peculiarities of his psyche that were uncovered in psychoanalytic therapy but on which it was not possible to throw further light nor exert any direct influence: the tenacity with which his energies became fixed, as already discussed, the extraordinary extent to which his tendency to ambivalence had been developed, and, a third feature of what we might term an archaic constitution, his ability to maintain a wide variety of violently conflicting libidinal charges, all potentially functioning alongside one another. His con-stant wavering between them, which for a long time seemed to exclude the possibility of settlement and progress, dominated the profile of his later illness, which we have touched on only briefly here. There is no doubt that this was a character trait of the unconscious, carried over into processes that had become conscious; it was only apparent, however, in the results of emotional [*affektiv*] impulses, whereas in matters of pure logic he demonstrated particular skill in detecting contradictions and inconsistencies. The impression left by his inner life was rather like that of the ancient Egyptian religion, which is inconceivable to us because it conserves all the developmental stages alongside the end-products, keeping the oldest deities and what they signified as well as the most recent, spreading them out two-dimensionally where other developing cultures create a three-dimensional image.

This concludes what I wished to say about this case. Only two of the numerous problems to which it gives rise seem to me to deserve particular emphasis. The first concerns those phylogenetically transmitted patterns that, like philosophical 'categories', enable us to accommodate our impressions of life. I should like to suggest that they are the precipitates of human cultural history. The Oedipus complex, a complete account of the child's relationship to his parents, is one example, indeed the best-known. When experiences cannot be fitted into this hereditary schema, they are reworked in the imagination, work that it would undoubtedly be profitable to examine in detail. For it is precisely these cases that are best suited to demonstrate the independent existence of the schema. We are often in a position to note how the schema takes precedence over individual experience, as for example in our case when the father becomes the castrator who threatens childhood sexuality, despite the fact that the Oedipus complex is reversed in every other respect. Another effect of this is seen when the children's nurse takes the place of the mother or the two become merged. The way in which experience contradicts the schema supplies the conflicts of infancy with a wealth of material.

The second problem is not far removed from the first, but its significance is far greater. If we consider the way in which the four-year-old child responds to the reactivated primal scene[4] – indeed, we have only to think of the far simpler reactions of the

18-month-old child to the original experience – it is difficult to dismiss the notion that some kind of knowledge that resists definition, a sort of preparation for understanding, is at work in the child.[5] What this might consist in defies the imagination; the only analogy available to us is the excellent analogy with the largely *instinctive* knowledge found in animals.

If human beings were also in possession of instinctive knowledge of this kind, it would hardly be surprising if it were directed in particular towards the processes of sexuality, although it cannot possibly be restricted to these alone. This instinctive knowledge would form the core of the unconscious, a primitive intellectual activity later dethroned by human reason when this is acquired and overlaid by it, but often, perhaps always, retaining the strength to drag higher inner processes down to its own level. Repression would be the return to this instinctive stage; in this way man would pay for his splendid new acquisition with the capacity for neurosis, while the possibility of neurosis would testify to the existence of the earlier, preliminary stage, instinctive in nature. The significance of early childhood traumas would then lie in the fact that they supply this unconscious part of the psyche with material that prevents it from being sapped by the subsequent process of development.

I know that similar thoughts have been expressed in various quarters, emphasizing the hereditary, phylogenetically acquired factor in the individual's inner life; indeed, I think we are all too ready to make room for them in our psychoanalytic evaluations. It seems to me that they are only admissible when psychoanalysis correctly observes the prescribed stages, and only starts looking for traces of what has been inherited once it has penetrated the layers of what has been acquired by the individual.[6]

(1918 [1914])

Notes

1. As I have already mentioned, the Gruscha scene was a spontaneous feat of memory on my patient's part, to which reconstruction or suggestion on the part of the doctor made no contribution; the gaps in this memory were filled in by analysis in what we can only call an impeccable manner, if we set any store by working methods in analysis. A rationalistic explanation of this phobia could only say that there is nothing unusual in the fact that a child with a predisposition to anxiety might one day suffer an attack of anxiety even on seeing a yellow-striped butterfly, probably as a result of an inherited tendency to anxiety. (Cf. Stanley Hall, 'A Synthetic Genetic Study of Fear', 1914). Ignorant of the cause, it might then look for a childhood event to which this fear might be connected, and then use the chance similarity of names and the recurrence of the stripes to construct the fantasy of an amorous adventure with the nursery-maid, still dimly remembered. If, however, in later life those secondary details of an occurrence that was harmless in itself, the floor-cleaning, the pail and the broom, show that they have the power to determine an individual's object-choice, to permanent and compulsive effect, then the butterfly phobia acquires incomprehensible significance. The facts of the case become at least as remarkable as those asserted in my interpretation, and any gain made from a rationalistic interpretation of the scene simply melts away. The Gruscha scene is thus of particular value to us, since we can use it to prepare the ground for our judgement in the matter of the primal scene, where the situation is less secure.

2. *Totem und Tabu* [*Totem and Taboo*].

3. 'Über neurotische Erkrankungstypen' ['Types of Onset of Neurosis'] (1912).

4. We may overlook the fact that this response could only be put into words two decades later, for all the effects which we attribute to this scene had already been expressed in childhood, and long before the analysis, in the form of symptoms, compulsions, etc. In this respect it is a matter of no importance whether we regard it as a primal scene or as a primal fantasy.

5. Once again I must emphasize that these reflections would be irrelevant if the dream and the neurosis had not themselves taken place in childhood.

6. [*Addition* 1923:] Here, once again, the events mentioned in this case history, in chronological order:
Born on Christmas Day.

18 months: malaria. Observes parents engaging in coitus, or intimacy between them into which he later introduced a fantasy of coitus.

Shortly before the age of 2½: scene with Gruscha.

2½: cover-memory of parents' departure with sister. This shows him alone with Nanja, thus denying the presence of Gruscha and his sister.

Before the age of 3¼: his mother complains to the doctor.

3¼: beginning of his sister's attempts to seduce him; soon after this, threat of castration by Nanja.

3½: English governess, onset of character change.

4: wolf dream, origin of phobia.

4½: influence of biblical history. Compulsive symptoms appear.

Shortly before the age of 5: hallucinates loss of finger.

5: the family leaves the first estate.

After the age of 6: visits sick father.

$\left.\begin{array}{c} 8 \\ 10 \end{array}\right\}$ Final outbreaks of obsessive-compulsive neurosis.

My account makes it easy to guess that my patient was a Russian. I discharged him, believing him to be cured, a few weeks before the unexpected outbreak of the Great War and only saw him again after the vicissitudes of war had given the Central Powers access to southern Russia. He then came back to Vienna and told me that immediately after leaving treatment he had found himself endeavouring to break free from the influence of his physician. A few months of work enabled us to deal with an element of the transference that had not yet been mastered, and since then the patient, deprived by the war of his home, his fortune and all his family relations, had felt normal and conducted himself impeccably. Perhaps the very misery he felt had contributed to the stability of his recovery by providing some satisfaction for his sense of guilt.

Some Character Types
Encountered in
Psychoanalytic Work

When the physician undertakes the psychoanalytic treatment of someone suffering from a nervous disorder, there is no sense in which his interest is engaged first and foremost by his patient's character. He is far more interested in the meaning of his symptoms, in the involuntary impulses [*Triebregungen*] they conceal and satisfy, and in the stations passed by on the mysterious road of suffering leading from those particular involuntary wishes to those particular symptoms. The techniques that he must employ, however, quickly oblige the physician to direct his thirst for knowledge towards other objects in the first instance. He observes that his investigation is threatened by resistances with which the patient counters his efforts and may attribute such resistances to his patient's character. Character now has the first claim on his interest.

The traits of character that resist the physician's endeavours are not always those which the patient acknowledges and which those around him would attribute to him. Often the patient's characteristic features reveal themselves intensified to an unimaginable degree when he appeared to possess them only in moderation; or else attitudes become apparent that he had not betrayed in other relationships in his life. The remainder of my essay will be devoted to describing some of these surprising traits of character and suggesting where we might trace them back to.

I *Exceptions*

In psychoanalytic work one is repeatedly confronted with the task of persuading the patient to renounce a pleasurable gain which is close at hand and directly achievable. He is not asked to renounce pleasure altogether; perhaps no one can be expected to do this, and even religion has to justify its demand that a man should bid farewell to earthly pleasure by promising him more commendable pleasures in incomparably greater measure in some world beyond this one. No, the patient is merely asked to renounce such satisfactions as are invariably followed by some form of damage, he is asked to do without temporarily, to learn to exchange the immediate pleasurable gain for one that is better safeguarded, even if deferred. In other words, he is to learn, under his physician's direction, to *progress from the pleasure principle to the reality principle*, progress which distinguishes the mature adult from the child. In this work of education we can hardly say that the superior understanding of the physician plays any crucial role; as a rule he is able to tell the patient nothing that his own understanding cannot tell him. But knowing something intuitively is not the same thing as being told it by someone else; the physician assumes the role of an effective other; he makes use of the influence that one human being can have over another. Or: let us remember that it is customary in psychoanalysis to implant something original and strongly rooted in the place of something derivative or modified, and let us say that in his work of education the physician uses some of the components of *love*. In this resumption of his education he is probably only repeating a process made possible in the first place by the patient's original upbringing. Next to dire necessity, love is the great educatrix and the unfinished person is induced by the love of those closest to him to respect the commandments of necessity and to spare himself the punishments meted out for transgression.

When one demands of a patient the temporary renunciation of satisfaction with regard to some pleasure, a sacrifice, a willingness to accept suffering for a time for the sake of a better end, or even just the decision to submit to some necessity standing for all necessities, one sometimes encounters individuals who have a particular motivation for struggling against this expectation. They say that they have suffered, gone without for long enough, that they have a right to be spared any further demands and will no longer submit to some unpleasant necessity, for they are *exceptions* and they intend to stay that way. In one such patient this claim had developed into a conviction that a particular providence was watching over him and would protect him from painful sacrifices of this kind. The physician's arguments have no force against inner certainties so forcefully expressed; yet initially his influence falters as well and he has no choice but to seek out the sources which feed this damaging prejudice.

Now, it is undoubtedly true that everyone would like to consider themselves an 'exception' and claim prerogatives that do not apply to other people. For this very reason, however, it is necessary for an individual to produce a special justification, one not available to everyone, if he announces himself to be a genuine exception and behaves accordingly. There may be more than one such justification; but in the cases I have investigated it was possible to prove that they had one characteristic in common, namely the *fate that had befallen them early in life*: their neurosis was connected with something they had experienced or suffered in their very earliest years, of which they knew themselves to be innocent and which in their judgement put them at an unfair disadvantage. The privileges that they assumed as a result of this injustice and the obstreperousness resulting from it had contributed in no small part to the aggravation of conflicts that later led to the outbreak of neurosis. The attitude to life outlined here was made complete in the case of one such patient when she learned that a painful organic complaint that had prevented her from realizing her life's aims was congenital in origin. As long as she considered this complaint to be something she had acquired in later life, by chance, she bore it patiently; but once it had been explained to her that it was something she had inherited she became rebellious. The young man who believed that a special providence watched over him had been the victim of a chance infection by his nurse in infancy and had consumed the whole of his later life in demands for compensation, for accident benefit, so to speak, without the slightest idea as to what his claims were based on. In his case the analysis, which reconstructed this state of affairs on the basis of faint remnants of memory [*Erinnerungsresten*] and the interpretation of symptoms, received objective confirmation through statements made by his family.

For reasons that will readily be understood I am unable to communicate any further details of these and other case histories. Neither shall I comment on the obvious analogy with the deformation of character brought about by long susceptibility to illness in childhood, nor the behaviour of whole peoples whose past is heavy with suffering. I shall not pass up the opportunity, on the other hand, to refer to that figure created by the greatest of poets, in whose character the claim to be an exception is so intimately linked to and motivated by congenital disadvantage.

In the opening monologue of Shakespeare's *Richard III*, the Duke of Gloucester, who later becomes king, says:

> But I, that am not shap'd for sportive tricks,
> Nor made to court an amorous looking-glass;
> I, that am rudely stamp'd, and want love's majesty
> To strut before a wanton ambling nymph;
> I, that am curtail'd of this fair proportion,
> Cheated of feature by dissembling nature,
> Deform'd, unfinish'd, sent before my time
> Into this breathing world scarce half made up –
> And that so lamely and unfashionable
> That dogs bark at me, as I halt by them –
> [. . .]

And therefore, since I cannot prove a lover
To entertain these fair well-spoken days,
I am determined to prove a villain,
And hate the idle pleasures of these days.[1]

On first impression we may fail to notice any connection between this programmatic speech and our chosen theme. Richard appears to be saying nothing more than: this idle age bores me, and I wish to amuse myself. However, because I am misshapen and cannot therefore sport as a lover I shall play the villain, pursue intrigues, commit murder and do whatever takes my fancy. Such frivolity of motivation would stifle any trace of sympathetic interest in the spectator if there were nothing more serious hidden behind it. But then the play would also be a psychological impossibility, for the poet must know how to create a secret background of sympathy for his hero if we are to feel admiration for his audacity and skill without experiencing an inner contradiction, and such sympathy can only be rooted in understanding, by which I mean our sense that there is something inside us that we perhaps share with him.

For this reason, I think, Richard's monologue does not say everything; he merely drops hints and leaves it up to us to follow up those hints. If we undertake this work of completion the appearance of frivolity disappears and Richard's bitterness, the detail in which he describes his misshapen form come into their own, so that we see what it is we have in common that compels us to feel sympathy even for this villain. What he is saying is: Nature has committed a grave injustice in denying me the comeliness of form that wins the love of others. Life owes me some compensation and I shall have it. I can claim to be an exception, disregarding the moral scruples which deter others. I can commit injustices because an injustice has been done to me – and now we feel that we ourselves could become like Richard, indeed, that on a small scale we already are like him. Richard is a gigantic enlargement of this single aspect which we can find in ourselves, too. We all believe that we have good reason to rail at Nature and Fate for the disadvantages meted out to us in infancy, at birth; we all demand compensation for early offences committed against our narcissism, our self-love. Why did Nature not give us Balder's golden locks or Siegfried's strength, the high brow of the genius or the aristocrat's noble profile? Why were we born in a parlour and not in a king's palace? We should succeed just as well in being handsome and refined as all those whom we envy for these qualities.

It is the poet's art, however, and an economic subtlety, that he does not make his hero express all the secrets of his motivation out loud, leaving nothing to our imagination. In this way he obliges us to supply them ourselves, providing occupation for our intellectual activity, diverting us from critical thought and holding us fast in our identification with his hero. In his place an amateur would give conscious expression to everything he wished to express and then find himself face to face with our cool intelligence in all its freedom of movement, thus making it quite impossible to deepen the illusion any further.

Let us not leave the 'exceptions' behind, however, without giving some thought to the fact that a woman's claim to privilege and liberation from so many of life's compulsions has the same basis. As we know from psychoanalytic work, women regard themselves as having been damaged in infancy, shortened by a length and reduced in value without having done anything to deserve it, and many a daughter's feelings of bitterness towards her mother are rooted in the reproach that she was brought into the world a woman and not a man.

Note

1. [*Translator's note*: All quotations from Shakespeare follow the Arden editions.]

11 *Those who Founder on Success*

Psychoanalytic work has bestowed on us the following dictum: people succumb to neurotic illness as a consequence of *refusal* [*Versagung*]. What is meant is the refusal to satisfy their libidinal desires, and something of a detour is required before we can understand this statement. For it is necessary to the development of neurosis that there should be a conflict between an individual's libidinal wishes and that part of his being that we call the I [*Ich*], which is the expression of his drive to self-preservation [*Selbsterhaltungstrieb*] and which encompasses his ideal sense of his own being. Pathogenic conflict arises only if the libido seeks to throw itself into the pursuit of paths and goals long since overcome and proscribed by the I, thus also prohibited for all future time, so that the libido only does this when it is deprived of the possibility of an ideal satisfaction, acceptable to the I [*ichgerecht*]. In this way deprivation, the refusal of a real satisfaction, becomes the first condition for the development of neurosis, even if by no means the only one.

It is all the more surprising, confusing indeed, when as a physician one discovers that on occasion individuals fall ill just at the time when a deep-seated, long-cherished wish is about to be fulfilled. It would then appear that they cannot bear their good fortune, for there is no doubt as to the causal connection between success and illness. In this way I had the opportunity to gain some insight into the fate of a woman whom I shall describe here as a perfect example of such a tragic turn of affairs.

Well-bred and of a good family, she was unable to curb her lust for life and at a very young age broke free of the parental home and took off in search of adventure; at length she made the acquaintance of an artist who was not only able to appreciate her feminine charms, but also to sense the disposition to refinement in this disgraced young woman. He took her in and found in her his faithful life's companion; she seemed only to want rehabilitation in good society in order to be entirely happy. After they had lived together for a number of years he succeeded in persuading his family to accept her and was now ready to make her his wife in the eyes of the law. At that very moment the process of refusal began to assert itself in her. She neglected the house whose rightful mistress she was about to become, believed herself to be persecuted by the relatives who hoped to take her into their family, denied her husband all social intercourse out of absurd jealousy, thwarted him in his artistic endeavours and soon succumbed to incurable psychological illness.

Observation of another patient revealed a highly respectable man, himself an academic teacher, who for many years had nurtured the understandable desire to succeed in office the master who had himself initiated him into that branch of learning. When, after the old man's retirement, his colleagues informed him that none other than he himself had been selected as successor, he started to lose heart, disparaged his own credentials, declared himself unworthy to fill the intended position and fell into a state of melancholy that excluded him from all activity for a number of years.

However different these cases may be in other respects, what they have in common is the way in which illness follows immediately after the fulfilment of a wish and destroys any enjoyment of it.

The contradiction between such evidence and the dictum that it is refusal that causes people to fall ill is not an insoluble one. It can be resolved by making a distinction between refusal *from the outside* and refusal *from within*. When in reality the object is removed that provides satisfaction for the libido, this is a refusal from the outside. It is without consequence in itself, not yet pathogenic, unless it is reinforced by a refusal from within. This must come from the I and disputes the right of the libido to other objects that it attempts to take for itself. Only then does conflict arise, together with the possibility of neurotic illness, i.e. of a substitute satisfaction achieved by making a detour around the repressed unconscious. Refusal from within thus comes into consideration in all cases, but it only becomes effective once the situation has been prepared for it by real refusal from the outside. In those exceptional cases where individuals fall ill on achieving success, refusal from within was enough in itself, only emerging, indeed, after refusal from the outside has given way to wish-fulfilment. At first sight there is something remarkable about this, but on closer consideration we recall that it is not at all unusual for the I to tolerate a wish and consider it harmless as long as it exists only as a fantasy, unlikely to be fulfilled, whereas it will be fierce in its own defence as soon as the wish appears to be close to fulfilment and threatens to become a reality. The difference between this and familiar situations of neurosis formation lies only in the fact that it is normally inner intensification of libido-charge [*Libidobesetzung*] that turns a fantasy that has been disregarded and tolerated into a dreaded opponent, whereas in these particular cases the signal for the outbreak of conflict is given by a real external transformation.

Analytic work readily demonstrates that it is the *power of conscience* that forbids the individual to enjoy the benefits of this long hoped-for turn for the better in the circumstances of his life. It is a difficult task, however, to ascertain the nature and origin of these inclinations to judge and punish, which often surprise us with their existence where we had not expected to find them. I shall discuss what we know of them or suspect to be true by drawing not on cases which I have observed as a physician – for reasons that will be familiar – but on figures created by the great poets out of their rich understanding of the human soul.

One character who caves in once she has achieved the success that she has fought for with energetic singleness of purpose is Shakespeare's Lady Macbeth. There has previously been no hesitation in her, no sign of inner struggle, no aspiration to anything except overcoming the scruples of her husband, who is ambitious and yet inclined to mildness. She is prepared to sacrifice even her womanliness to her murderous intentions, without considering what a crucial role that womanliness must play once it comes to defending the position achieved by criminal means, the goal of her ambition.

(Act I, Scene 5):

> Come, you Spirits
> That tend on mortal thoughts, unsex me here,
> [. . .] Come to my woman's breasts,
> And take my milk for gall, you murth'ring ministers.

(Act I, Scene 7):

> I have given suck, and know
> How tender 'tis to love the babe that milks me:
> I would, while it was smiling in my face,
> Have pluck'd my nipple from his boneless gums,
> And dash'd the brains out, had I so sworn
> As you have done to this.

A single stirring of resistance seizes her before the deed is performed (Act II, Scene 2):

> Had he not resembled
> My father as he slept, I had done't.

Now that the murder of Duncan has made her queen, there is a
fleeting intimation of something like disappointment, surfeit. We do
not know where it has come from. (Act III, Scene 2):

> Nought's had, all's spent,
> Where our desire is got without content:
> 'Tis safer to be that which we destroy,
> Than by destruction dwell in doubtful joy.

And yet she endures. In the banquet scene which follows she alone
keeps her head, covering up her husband's confusion, finding a pretext
for dismissing the guests. And then she disappears from sight. When
we see her again (in Act V, Scene 1), it is as a sleepwalker, obsessed by
the impressions of that night of murder. She is talking her husband

into his courage as she did then: 'Fie, my lord, fie! a soldier, and afeard? What need we fear who knows it, when none can call our power to accompt?' She hears the knocking at the door that terrified her husband after the deed. At the same time, however, she endeavours to 'undo what cannot be undone'. She washes the hands that are stained with blood, which smell of blood, and is conscious of the futility of her endeavours. The woman who apparently felt no remorse has apparently been prostrated by remorse. At her death, Macbeth, who has meanwhile become as unyielding as she showed herself to be in the beginning, can find only a brief epilogue for her:
(Act V, Scene 5):

> She should have died hereafter:
> There would have been a time for such a word –

And now we ask ourselves what it was that broke this character who appeared to have been forged in the hardest of metals. Was it merely the loss of illusion, the other face that we see once the deed has been done; must we conclude, looking back, that in Lady Macbeth, too, an inner life [*Seelenleben*] originally soft and of womanly mildness had worked itself up to a concentration and extremity of tension that simply could not be sustained, or can we look for some sign that would supply a more profound motivation for her collapse and bring it closer to us in human terms?

I believe it is impossible to judge. Shakespeare's *Macbeth* is an occasional play written for the accession of King James, formerly king of Scotland. The material was already in existence and had been treated simultaneously by other writers, whose work Shakespeare had probably drawn on, as he generally did. It offered remarkable parallels with the present situation. The 'virgin queen' Elizabeth, of whom it was said that she would never have been able to bear a child, who had once described herself with an exclamation of pain, on hearing the news of James's birth, as a 'barren branch',[1] had been obliged by that very childlessness to name as her successor the Scottish king. He, however, was the son of that Mary whose execution she had ordered, albeit unwillingly, and who, despite the way in which political considerations had clouded the affair, was still a blood relation and could have been described as the recipient of her hospitality.

The accession of James I was like a demonstration of the curse of barrenness and the blessings of continuing generation. And the development we see in Shakespeare's Macbeth hinges on that very opposition. The fateful sisters have promised Macbeth that he will become king, but to Banquo they promise that his sons will inherit the crown. Macbeth rebels against this pronouncement of Fate, for he is not content with the satisfaction of his own ambition, but wants to found a dynasty, he does not want to have committed murder only in order to benefit others. We overlook this point if we see Shakespeare's play simply as a tragedy of ambition. Since Macbeth himself cannot live for ever, it is clear that there is only one way in which he can refute that part of the prophecy which goes against him, namely by having children himself, children who can then succeed him. He appears to expect this, moreover, of his powerful wife:
(Act I, Scene 7):

> Bring forth men-children only!
> For thy undaunted mettle should compose
> Nothing but males.

And it is equally clear that, if he is disappointed in this expectation, he must submit to Fate, or else his actions lose their objective and purpose and are transformed into the blind rage of a man whose doom is sealed, but who will first destroy everything within his grasp. We see that Macbeth undergoes this development, and at the height of the tragedy we find that devastating exclamation, whose ambiguity has so often been recognized, which perhaps contains the key to his transformation:
(Act IV, Scene 3):

> He has no children.

Of course this means: only because he is childless himself was he able to murder my children; but there could be more to it; above all, it might reveal the most profound motive that not only forces Macbeth so far beyond the bounds of his own nature but also touches the only weak place in the character of his hard-hearted wife. If we stand on the summit marked by these words of Macduff's and look around us, however, we see that the whole play is strewn with references to the father–children relationship. Gracious Duncan's death is little other than patricide; in Banquo's case Macbeth kills the father while the son escapes; with Macduff he kills the children because the father has fled. The fateful sisters conjure up for him the vision of a bloody child with a crown on its head; the armed head that appears before this is surely Macbeth himself. In the background, however, there rises up the sombre figure of the avenger Macduff, who is himself an exception to the rules of generation, since he was not born from his mother's body but cut out of it.

It would, then, be entirely in accordance with poetic justice, which is founded on the principle of talion law, if Macbeth's childlessness and his lady's infertility were the punishment for their crimes against the sacredness of generation, if Macbeth were unable to become a father because he had robbed a father of his children and children of their father, and if Lady Macbeth had in this way been unsexed as she had implored the 'murth'ring ministers'. I believe that Lady Macbeth's illness and the transformation of her depravity into remorse would then be entirely understandable as a reaction to her childlessness, which convinces her of her impotence in the face of the laws of nature and at the same time reminds her that she has been deprived by her own fault of the better part of the profit from her crime.

In Holinshed's *Chronicles* (1577), from which Shakespeare drew the material for *Macbeth*, Lady Macbeth is mentioned only once, as an ambitious woman who goads her husband into murder so that she herself may become queen. We are told nothing of the fate that awaits her nor of any development in her character. On the other hand it appears that the motivation for Macbeth's transformation into a bloody brute was very much along the lines we have just suggested. For in Holinshed *ten years* elapse between the murder of Duncan, which makes Macbeth king, and his later misdeeds, ten years in which he proves himself to be a strict but just ruler. Only after this interval does the change in him occur, influenced by the tormenting fear that the prophecy made to Banquo might be fulfilled just as that of his own destiny had been. It is only now that he has Banquo killed and then finds himself swept along from one crime to the next, as he is in Shakespeare. Holinshed does not say explicitly that it is his childlessness that forces him along this path either, but there is time and space enough for this to be the obvious motivation. This is not the case in Shakespeare. The events of the tragedy flash past us with breathtaking speed, so that it is possible to calculate, from the evidence of characters in the play, that it is something like *one week* in duration.[2] This acceleration deprives our attempts to reconstruct the motivation for the dramatic change in the characters of Macbeth and Lady Macbeth of all foundation. There is no time for the repeated dashing of their hopes for children to wear down the woman and drive the man into a defiant frenzy, and the contradiction remains that, while so many subtle connections within the play and between the play and the occasion of its writing all appear to coincide in the motif of childlessness, the temporal economy of the tragedy explicitly rejects any development of character proceeding from motives other than the most internal.

In my opinion it is impossible to guess, however, what these motives might be that in so short a time turn a timid man of ambition into an uninhibited brute and a steely instigator of crime into a sick woman crushed by the weight of her remorse. I think we must abandon the possibility of penetrating the triple layer of obscurity into which the poor state of preservation of the text, the unknown intentions of the poet and the mysterious meaning of the saga have settled. Neither am I prepared to accept the objection that such investigations are pointless in the face of the magnificent effect which the tragedy has on the spectator. It is true that the poet can overwhelm us by his art during the performance and paralyse thought, but he cannot prevent us from attempting subsequently to understand that effect from the point of view of its psychological mechanism. Nor does it seem appropriate to observe that the poet is free to condense the natural time taken by the sequence of events at whim, if by sacrificing vulgar probability he can achieve an intensification of the dramatic effect. For such a sacrifice may be justified when it disturbs only our sense of what is probable,[3] but not when it dissolves causal connections, and it would hardly be detrimental to the dramatic effect if the passage of time were left vague, instead of being explicitly restricted by remarks in the text to a few days.

I am so reluctant to abandon a problem such as that posed by *Macbeth* on grounds of insolubility that I shall venture to introduce an observation that may show us a new way out. In a recent study of Shakespeare Ludwig Jekels believes that he has identified an element of the poet's technique that might also be relevant to *Macbeth*. In his view, Shakespeare often divides a character into two people, each of whom appears totally incomprehensible until put back together again as a single unit. This could be the case with Macbeth and Lady Macbeth, too; if so it would of course be pointless to attempt to see her as a separate personality and seek a motive for her transformation without taking into account the figure of Macbeth, who completes her. I shall not pursue this trail any further, but shall merely refer the reader to an aspect which appears conspicuously to support this interpretation, namely that the seeds of fear which burst open in Macbeth on the night of the murder mature not in him but in Lady Macbeth.[4] It is he who suffers hallucinations about the dagger before the deed is done, but it is she who later falls prey to mental breakdown; he who after the murder hears voices crying in the house: 'Sleep no more! [. . .] Glamis hath murther'd Sleep, and therefore Cawdor/Shall sleep no more',[5] but we hear nothing to the effect that King Macbeth can no longer sleep, whereas we see the queen getting up out of her sleep and betraying her guilt in sleepwalking; it is he who stands there helplessly with bloody hands lamenting that all great Neptune's ocean will not wash the blood clean from his hand; at the time she comforts him: 'A little water clears us of this deed', but later it is she who washes her hands for a quarter of an hour at a time but cannot remove the stains left by the blood. 'All the perfumes of Arabia will not sweeten this little hand' (Act V, Scene 1). And so the thing that he fears in his agony of conscience is fulfilled in her; she embodies remorse after the deed, he defiance, together they exhaust the possibilities of reaction to crime, like two disunited parts of a single psychic entity and perhaps two attempts to portray a single likeness.

If we have been unable to answer the question as to why, in Lady Macbeth's case, her health breaks down in the aftermath of success, perhaps we have a better prospect of doing so with regard to the creation of another great dramatist who enjoys engaging with the task of psychological explanation with unrelenting strictness.

Rebekka Gamvik, a midwife's daughter, has been brought up as a free-thinker by her adoptive father Dr West, taught to despise the way in which a morality based on religious faith seeks to fetter our desires. After the doctor's death she arranges accommodation for herself on Rosmersholm, the ancestral seat of an ancient family whose members do not know how to laugh and who have sacrificed joy to the rigid fulfilment of duty. On Rosmersholm there live the pastor Johannes Rosmer and his sickly, childless wife Beate. Seized with a 'wild uncontrollable craving' for the love of this aristocrat, Rebekka decides to do away with his wife, who is standing in her way, and to this end uses her 'courageous, free-born will' which no considerations can inhibit.[6] She arranges for a medical textbook to fall into her hands which claims that procreation is the sole purpose of marriage, so that the poor woman loses her faith in the rightfulness of her marriage; she allows her to suspect that Rosmer, whose reading and thinking she shares, is about to cast off his old faith and join the party of enlightenment; and after she has shaken the wife's faith in her husband's moral reliability she gives her to understand that she, Rebekka, will soon be leaving the house in order to conceal the consequences of an illegal association with Rosmer. Her criminal plan is successful. The poor woman, who is already considered melancholic and of unsound mind, throws herself off the bridge into the millstream, convinced of her own lack of worth and not wishing to stand in the way of her beloved husband's happiness.

Rebekka and Rosmer have now lived alone on Rosmersholm for years in a relationship that he chooses to regard as a purely spiritual, ideal friendship. However, as the first shadows of malicious rumour fall on their relationship at the same time as Rosmer begins to feel tormenting doubts as to his wife's motives in seeking death, he asks

Rebekka to become his second wife in order to confront the sad past with a new living reality (Act II). After a brief moment of jubilation at his proposal she declares in the very next breath that it is impossible, and that if he presses her she will 'go the way that Beate went'. Rosmer cannot understand her refusal; but it is all the more incomprehensible to us, since we know more about Rebekka's actions and intentions. We can be in no doubt, however, that she means the no that she has given him.

How could it have come about that this adventuress with her courageous, free-born will, who has recklessly fought her way through to the realization of her desires, will not reach out and pluck the fruit of success now that it has been offered? She provides the explanation herself in Act IV: 'That is the terrible thing: now that I am being freely offered all the happiness in the world – I have become a woman whose own past bars the way to happiness.' She has become another woman in the meantime, then, her conscience has been awakened, she has acquired a consciousness of guilt that denies her any pleasure.

And what is it that has awakened her conscience? Let us listen to what she says and then ask ourselves if we can entirely believe her. 'It is the way that the Rosmers look at things – or at least the way you look at things – that has infected my will . . . And made it sick. Subjugated me to laws that previously had no force for me. Living together with you – do you know, it has ennobled my mind.' We must assume that this influence has only made itself felt since she has been able to live alone with Rosmer: '– in quietude – in solitude – when you told me your thoughts without keeping anything back – every single mood as soft and as delicate as they were to you –, that was when the great transformation started to happen.'

Shortly before this she had been lamenting the other side of this transformation: 'Because Rosmersholm has taken away my strength, because it has paralysed my courageous will. And ruined it! The time is past when I could dare anything and everything. I have lost the energy to act, Rosmer.'

Rebekka offers this explanation after she has freely confessed her criminal actions to Rosmer and Kroll, the brother of the woman she has removed. With masterly subtlety Ibsen establishes by the use of tiny details that this woman Rebekka does not lie but is also never entirely honest. Just as – despite her freedom from prejudice – she takes a year off her age, so her confession to the two men is incomplete and has to be supplemented on a number of essential points as a result of Kroll's insistent questioning. We too are free to assume that the explanation for her renunciation reveals one thing only in order to conceal another.

We have no reason, certainly, to mistrust the statement that the air on Rosmersholm and Rosmer's company have had both an ennobling and – a paralysing effect on her. She is expressing what she knows and feels. But that need not have been all that was taking place inside her; nor should she necessarily have been able to account to herself for everything. Rosmer's influence might just have been masking another influence, and one remarkable feature of the play points in this direction.

Even after her confession, in the final exchange that brings the play to its close, Rosmer asks her once again to be his wife. He forgives her for the evil she did out of love for him. And now she does not reply, as she should, that no forgiveness can take away the feelings of guilt caused by her malicious deception of poor Beate, but burdens herself with a different reproach, which sounds strange to us coming from a free-thinker and cannot be thought to merit the importance which Rebekka attributes to it: 'Alas, my friend – never mention it again! It is an impossibility! – For you must know, Rosmer, that I have a past.' She is indicating, of course, that she has had sexual relations with another man, and we note that these relations, which occurred at a time when she was free and not responsible to anyone, appear to her to constitute a greater barrier to union with Rosmer than her truly criminal behaviour towards his wife.

Rosmer declines to hear a word about this past. We can guess at it, although everything that points towards it in the play remains subterranean, so to speak, and has to be inferred from veiled references. References that are woven so artfully into the play that it is admittedly impossible to misunderstand them.

Between the first occasion when Rebekka refuses Rosmer and her confession, something happens that is of decisive significance for the turn taken by events. Kroll, the headmaster, pays her a visit, intending to humiliate her by telling her he knows that she is illegitimate, the daughter of that Dr West who adopted her after her mother's death. His intuition has been sharpened by hatred, but he does not think he is telling her anything new. 'Indeed, I thought you knew all about it. Otherwise it would have been remarkably odd to have allowed yourself to be adopted by Dr West.' 'And then he takes you in – immediately after your mother's death. He treats you harshly. And yet you stay with him. You know that he will not leave you a penny. And indeed, all you got was a case of books. And yet you endure living with him. Take care of him right to the end.' 'What you did for him I take to be a daughter's natural instinct. Everything else about you I take to be the natural result of your parentage.'

But Kroll was in error. Rekekka knew nothing of the fact that she was supposed to be Dr West's daughter. When Kroll started up with his obscure allusions to her past, she was assuming that he meant something else. Once she has grasped what he is getting at she is able to maintain her composure a little longer because she is able to believe that her enemy is basing his calculations on the age she gave him on a previous visit, which was wrong. Once Kroll has refuted her objection with the triumphant statement: 'That may be so. But the calculation can still be right, because a year before he was given the post, West was up there briefly on a visit', then, with the announcement of this new piece of information, she loses all control. 'It isn't true.' – She paces the room, wringing her hands: 'It is impossible. You just want me to believe that. It just simply cannot be true. Cannot be true! Simply cannot!' She is in such a terrible emotional state that Kroll is unable to bring her back to what he has told her.

Kroll: 'But my dear – for heaven's sake, why are you in such a passion? I am really quite frightened. What am I to believe and think – !'
Rebekka: 'Nothing. You are to believe nothing and think nothing.'
Kroll: 'Then you really ought to explain why you are taking this matter – this possibility – so much to heart.'
Rebekka: (recovering her composure): 'It is quite simple, Mr. Kroll. I have no wish to be thought of as illegitimate.'

Rebekka's baffling behaviour will admit of only one solution. The information that Dr West could be her father is the heaviest blow she could receive, for she was not only this man's adopted daughter, but also his mistress. When Kroll begins to speak, she thinks he is alluding to this relationship, which she would probably have admitted to, invoking her right to freedom of action. That was far from Kroll's thoughts, however; he knew nothing of the liaison with Dr West, just as she knew nothing of his paternity. She *cannot* be thinking of anything other than this liaison when she finally turns Rosmer down on the pretext that she has a past, which makes her unworthy to be his wife. Probably, had Rosmer wanted to know, she would only have told him half of her secret and kept the harder part of it to herself.

But now, at least, we understand that this past seems to her the more serious obstacle to their marriage, the more serious – crime.

Having discovered that she has been her own father's mistress she submits to the overpowering sense of guilt that now erupts. She makes the confession to Rosmer and Kroll that brands her as a murderess, renounces for good the happiness which she had fought to gain through crime and makes ready to leave. But the true motivation for her sense of guilt, which causes her to founder on her own success, remains a mystery. We have seen that it is something quite other than the atmosphere of Rosmersholm and Rosmer's civilizing influence.

Anyone who has followed the argument thus far will not miss the opportunity to raise an objection that could then justify many a doubt. It is that Rebekka's first rejection of Rosmer takes place before Kroll's second visit, and thus before his revelation of her illegitimate birth, at a time, then, when she does not know that she is guilty of incest – if we have understood the poet aright. And yet her rejection is energetic and serious in intent. The sense of guilt that causes her to renounce what she has gained through her deeds thus takes effect even before she knows anything of her capital crime, and if we can admit this much then perhaps we should eliminate incest altogether as a possible source of her sense of guilt.

Up until now we have treated Rebekka West as if she were a living person and not a creation of the poet Ibsen's imagination, directed as it is by critical understanding of the highest sort. Let us attempt to hold firm to that same point of view in dealing with this objection. It is a fair objection: an element of conscience had already been awakened in Rebekka before she knew anything of the matter of incest. There is nothing to prevent us from attributing responsibility for this transformation to the influence that Rebekka herself acknowledges and accuses. This does not redeem us, however, from the necessity of acknowledging the second motive. Rebekka's response to what Kroll tells her, and her confession immediately afterwards in reaction to it, leave us in no doubt that only now is the more powerful, the decisive motive for her renunciation taking effect. We are dealing here precisely with a case of multiple motivation, in which a deeper motive emerges from behind the more superficial one. The laws of poetic economy decreed that the case should be presented in this way, for the deeper motive ought not to be noisily dissected but should remain hidden, not subject to easy detection by audience or reader, for otherwise it would have given rise to profound resistance, caused by feelings of painful embarrassment which might undermine the effect of the play.

We are justified in our demand, however, that the motive put forward as an excuse should in some sense be internally consistent with the one it conceals, should evidently be derived from it in a modified form. And if we can have confidence in the poet's abilities, believing that this conscious poetic combination proceeds logically from unconscious premises, we can also attempt to show that he has fulfilled that demand. Rebekka's consciousness of her guilt springs from the reproach of incest even before Kroll makes her consciously aware of it with his analytical sharpness. If we reconstruct the past hinted at by the poet, expanding those hints into narrative, we should say that she cannot have been oblivious to the intimate relationship between her mother and Dr West. It must have made a powerful impression on her when she succeeded her mother in this man's affections, and she was dominated by the Oedipus complex even if she did not know that this commonly held fantasy had become a reality in her case. When she arrived in Rosmersholm the inner force of that first experience drove her actively to bring about the same situation which on the first occasion had come about without any active contribution from her, namely to do away with the wife and mother in order to take her place with the husband and father. With convincing vividness she describes how she was forced against her will to take one step after another to eliminate Beate:

'But do you really think I went about my business with cool detachment? I was not then what I am today as I stand here before you and tell my story. And then I think that human beings must have two kinds of will. I wanted Beate out of the way! Somehow. And yet I never thought it would come to that. With every step forward that I was tempted to take it was as if something inside me cried: No more! Not a single step further! – And yet I could not stop. I had to go just the tiniest bit further. And a tiny bit further still. And then a bit – always a little bit further. – And that's how it happened. That's how such things come about.'

She is not glossing over anything here, but giving a true account. Everything that happened to her on Rosmersholm, her passion for Rosmer and her hostility towards his wife, was already a consequence of the Oedipus complex, a compulsive re-creation of her relationship with her mother and Dr West.

And for that reason the sense of guilt that first makes her reject Rosmer's proposal is fundamentally no different from the much greater sense of guilt that forces her to confess once Kroll has made his disclosure. However, just as under Dr West's influence she had become a free-thinker, despising religious morality, so her new love for Rosmer transforms her into a woman of conscience and nobility. This much of the processes taking place inside her she is able to understand, and for this reason she is justified in describing Rosmer's influence as the motivation for the change that she has undergone, the only one accessible to conscious thought.

Any physician working in the field of psychoanalysis knows how frequently, how regularly the girl who enters a household as servant, companion, governess, consciously or unconsciously weaves a daydream, the content of which, drawn from the Oedipus complex, tells her that the woman of the house will somehow cease to exist and the master will take her to wife instead. *Rosmersholm* is the greatest work of art in the genre that deals with this everyday fantasy of girlhood. The added detail that the heroine's daydream has been preceded by the corresponding reality in her earlier life is what makes the tale tragic.[7]

After a lengthy sojourn with the poets we can now return to the experiences of medicine. Only to establish in a few words, however, that the two are in complete agreement. Psychoanalytic work teaches us that the forces of conscience that cause an individual to fall ill on the brink of success and not through refusal, as is normally the case, are intimately bound up with the Oedipus complex, with our relationship to mother and father; indeed, this may be true of our consciousness of guilt altogether.

Notes

1. Cf. *Macbeth* (Act III, Scene 1) [Freud erroneously places the scene in Act II]:

> Upon my head they plac'd a fruitless crown
> And put a barren sceptre in my gripe,
> Thence to be wrench'd with an unlineal hand,
> No son of mine succeeding.

2. Darmstetter [*Macbeth*] (1881, LXXV).

3. Such as Richard III wooing Lady Anne by the bier of the king he himself has murdered.

4. Cf. Darmstetter, *loc. cit.*

5. [*Translator's note*: Freud uses the name 'Macbeth' throughout, where Shakespeare's text has 'Glamis' and 'Cawdor'.]

6. [*Translator's note*: Quotations from Ibsen's *Rosmersholm* are translated directly from Freud's German text, as this differs somewhat from the available English translation.]

7. The presence of the theme of incest in *Rosmersholm* has already been demonstrated by the same means as are employed here in O. Rank's extremely wide-ranging work *Das Inzest-Motiv in Dichtung und Sage* [*The Motif of Incest in Poetry and Saga*], 1912.

III *Criminals who Act Out of a Consciousness of Guilt*

In telling me about their youth, particularly the years preceding puberty, highly respectable people have told me later in life how they once committed illegal actions: theft, fraud and even arson. I tended to pass over such confessions, informing my patients that the weakness of moral inhibitions at this stage of life is well known, and made no attempt to integrate them into any more meaningful context. Eventually, however, I was provoked into a more thorough study of such cases by certain lurid instances, ones that lent themselves more readily to analysis, in which such misdemeanours were committed by patients who at the time were in treatment with me and where the individuals concerned were well past the first flush of youth. My analytic work then led to the surprising conclusion that such deeds were committed above all because they were forbidden and because carrying them out brought with it some kind of inner relief for the perpetrator. Suffering as he did from an oppressive consciousness of guilt, the origin of which was unknown, the pressure on him, once he had committed a crime, was reduced. At least it was now possible to locate his consciousness of guilt somewhere.

However paradoxical it might sound, I must assert that the consciousness of guilt was there before the misdemeanour, and that the former did not proceed from the latter, but rather the misdemeanour proceeded from the consciousness of guilt: We should be entirely justified in describing such individuals as committing crimes out of a consciousness of guilt. We had of course been able to demonstrate the pre-existence of the sense of guilt from a whole series of other remarks and effects.

To establish the existence of a curiosity is not the end of the

346

matter as far as research is concerned. Two further questions remain to be answered, first, where this obscure sense of guilt before the deed comes from and, second, whether it is likely that causation of this kind has any larger part to play in human crime.

The pursuit of an answer to the first question promised to provide us with information as to the source of human feelings of guilt in general. The results of analytic work regularly lead us to the conclusion that this obscure sense of guilt is derived from the Oedipus complex and is a reaction to those two great criminal intentions, killing the father and engaging in sexual intercourse with the mother. By comparison, the crimes committed in order to pin down the individual's sense of guilt certainly afforded some relief for those thus tormented. It is important to remind ourselves that patricide and mother-incest are the two great human crimes, the only ones that primitive societies persecute and abhor; also how close other investigations have led us to the assumption that humanity has acquired its conscience, which now gives the impression of being an inherited spiritual force, by way of the *Oedipus complex*.

Our answer to the second question goes well beyond psychoanalytic work. In the case of children one can readily observe that they are 'bad' in order to provoke a punishment of some kind, and that after they have been punished they calm down and are quite happy. Later analytic investigation frequently brings us back on to the trail of the sense of guilt that made these children look for punishment. Among adult offenders we must of course disregard all those who commit crimes without any sense of guilt, those who have not developed moral inhibitions of any kind as well as those who believe that their actions are justified by their struggle against society. But for the majority of other criminals, those for whom the criminal statutes were actually made, the establishment of such a motivation for crime might well be worthy of consideration; it could cast light on many an obscurity in the psychology of the criminal and provide a new psychological basis for punishment.

A friend has drawn my attention to the fact that 'the criminal who acts out of a sense of guilt' was already familiar to Nietzsche. We catch a faint glimmer of the pre-existence of the sense of guilt and the use of action to rationalize it in Zarathustra's speeches entitled 'Of the Pale Criminal'. We must leave it to future investigations to decide how many criminals are to be numbered among these 'pale criminals' of Nietzsche's.

(1916)

"Freud ultimately did more for our understanding
of art than any other writer since Aristotle."
—Lionel Trilling

The Joke and Its Relation to the Unconscious
Translated by Joyce Crick
Introduction by John Carey

In a rich collection of puns, witticisms, one-liners, and anecdotes, Freud answers the question "why do we laugh?" *The Joke and Its Relation to the Unconscious* explains how jokes provide immense pleasure by releasing us from our inhibitions and allowing us to express sexual, aggressive, playful, or cynical instincts that would otherwise remain hidden.

ISBN 978-0-14-243744-5

The Psychology of Love
Translated by Shaun Whiteside
Introduction by Jeri Johnson

This volume brings together Freud's illuminating discussions of the ways in which sexuality is always psychosexuality—that there is no sexuality without fantasy, conscious or unconscious. In these papers Freud develops his now famous theories about childhood and the transgressive nature of human desire.

ISBN 978-0-14-243746-9

The Psychopathology of Everyday Life
Translated by Anthea Bell
Introduction by Paul Keegan

Starting with the story of how he once forgot the name of an Italian painter—and how a young acquaintance mangled a quotation from Virgil through fears that his girlfriend might be pregnant—this volume brings together a treasure trove of muddled memories, inadvertent action, and verbal tangles. Freud's dazzling interpretations provide the perfect introduction to psychoanalytic thinking in action.

ISBN 978-0-14-243743-8

The Schreber Case
Translated by Andrew Webber
Introduction by Colin McCabe

In 1903, Judge Daniel Schreber, a highly intelligent and cultured man, produced a vivid account of his nervous illness dominated by the desire to become a woman, terrifying delusions about his doctor, and a belief in his own special relationship with God. Eight years later, Freud's penetrating insight uncovered the impulses and feelings Schreber had about his father, which underlay his extravagant symptoms.

ISBN 978-0-14-243742-1

Studies in Hysteria
With Joseph Breuer
Translated by Nicola Luckhurst
Introduction by Rachel Bowlby
Hysteria—the tormenting of the body by the troubled mind—is among the most pervasive of human disorders; yet, at the same time, it is the most elusive. Freud's recognition that hysteria stemmed from traumas in the patient's past transformed the way we think about sexuality. *Studies in Hysteria* is one of the founding texts of psychoanalysis, revolutionizing our understanding of love, desire, and the human psyche. As full of compassionate human interest as of scientific insight, these case histories are also remarkable, revelatory works of literature.

ISBN 978-0-14-243749-0

The Uncanny
Translated by David McClintock
Introduction by Hugh Haughton
Freud was fascinated by the mysteries of creativity and the imagination. His insights into the roots of artistic expression in the triangular "family romances" (of father, mother, and infant) that so dominate our early lives reveal the artistry of Freud's own writing. Freud's first exercise in psycho-biography, his celebrated study of Leonardo, brilliantly uses a single memory to reveal the childhood conflicts behind Leonardo's remarkable achievements and his striking eccentricity.

ISBN 978-0-14-243747-6

"The Wolfman" and Other Cases
Translated by Louise Adey Huish
Introduction by Gillian Beer
When a disturbed young Russian man came to Freud for treatment, the analysis of his childhood neuroses—most notably a dream about wolves outside his bedroom window—eventually revealed a deep-seated trauma. It took more than four years to treat him, and the "Wolfman" became one of Freud's most famous cases. This volume also contains other case histories, all of which show us Freud at work, in his own words.

ISBN 978-0-14-243745-2

Printed in the United States
by Baker & Taylor Publisher Services